Locomotives of the
GNRI

LOCOMOTIVES of the GNRI

Dedicated to Paddy Mallon of Dundalk who has contributed so much over the years to our knowledge of GNR(I) locomotives and to the restoration of 'Slieve Gullion' and 'Merlin'.

Norman Johnston has been a lifelong student of GNR locomotive history and is the grandson of a GNR Station Master. He has written several books including *The Fintona Horse Tram, The GNR in County Tyrone, The Norman Impact on the Medieval World* and *Peace, War and Neutrality 1939-45*. He is a retired school teacher and currently a publisher.

6 5 4 3 2 1

© Norman Johnston
Newtownards 1999

Designed by Colourpoint Books, Newtownards
Printed by W & G Baird, Antrim

ISBN 1 898392 48 X

Colourpoint Books
Unit D5, Ards Business Centre
Jubilee Road
NEWTOWNARDS
County Down
Northern Ireland
BT23 4YH
Tel: (02891) 820505
Fax: (02891) 821900
E-mail: info@colourpoint.co.uk
Web-site: www.colourpoint.co.uk

Copyright of photographs

Whilst all photographs have been credited, where the photographer is known, it has not been possible, in every case, to trace the copyright owners. Colourpoint Books will be happy to pay copyright fees in retrospect, to any photographer we have been unable to contact.

Photographs from the Welch Collection, of the Ulster Museum, are reproduced with the kind permission of the **Trustees of The National Museums and Galleries of Northern Ireland**.

Photographs from the collections of Real Photographs Ltd, the Locomotive Publishing Company, and Locomotive and General Railway Photographers, are reproduced with the kind permission of the **National Railway Museum, York**.

End paper photograph by Neil Sprinks (see page 141)

LOCOMOTIVES
of the
GNRI

NORMAN JOHNSTON

Colourpoint

U class 4-4-0 No 197 *Lough Neagh* in sky blue livery at Dundalk on 27 May 1949. *Photo Duffners.*

Contents

Route Map

(For clarity, not all stations are shown on this map.)

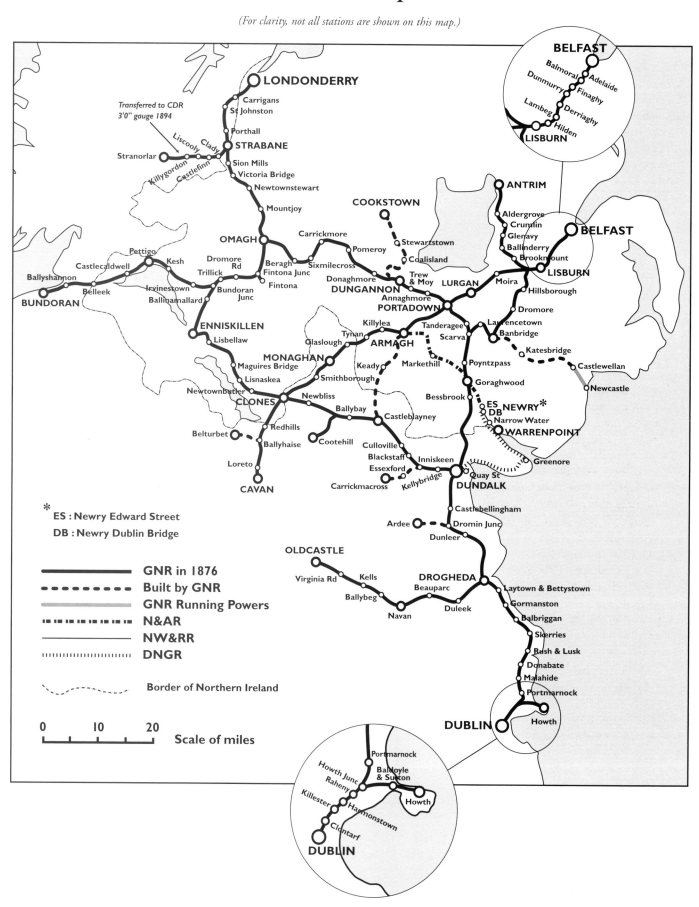

BELFAST
Balmoral
Adelaide
Dunmurry
Finaghy
Derriaghy
Lambeg
Hilden
LISBURN

LONDONDERRY
Carrigans
St Johnston
Porthall
STRABANE
Sion Mills
Victoria Bridge
Newtownstewart
Mountjoy

Transferred to CDR 3'0" gauge 1894
Liscooly
Clady
Stranorlar
Killygordon
Castlefinn

COOKSTOWN
Stewartstown
Coalisland
Carrickmore
Pomeroy
OMAGH
Beragh
Sixmilecross
Fintona Junc
Donaghmore
Fintona
DUNGANNON
Trew & Moy
Annaghmore
LURGAN
Moira

ANTRIM
Aldergrove
Crumlin
Glenavy
Ballinderry
Brookmount
BELFAST
LISBURN
Hillsborough
Dromore

Pettigo
Kesh
Castlecaldwell
Dromore Rd
Trillick
Ballyshannon
Belleek
Irvinestown
Bundoran Junc
Ballinamallard
BUNDORAN
ENNISKILLEN
Lisbellaw

PORTADOWN
Killylea
Tynan
Tanderagee
Scarva
Laurencetown
Banbridge
Glaslough
ARMAGH
Katesbridge
MONAGHAN
Maguires Bridge
Keady
Markethill
Poyntzpass
Castlewellan
Lisnaskea
Goraghwood
Newcastle
Newtownbutler
Smithborough
Bessbrook
CLONES
Newbliss
ES **NEWRY** *
Ballybay
DB
Redhills
Ballyhaise
Castleblayney
Narrow Water
Belturbet
Cootehill
Culloville
WARRENPOINT
Blackstaff
Inniskeen
Loreto
Essexford
Greenore
Kellybridge
Quay St
CAVAN
Carrickmacross
DUNDALK

* **ES : Newry Edward Street**
DB : Newry Dublin Bridge

Castlebellingham
Ardee
Dromin Junc
Dunleer

OLDCASTLE
DROGHEDA
Laytown & Bettystown
Virginia Rd
Kells
Beauparc
Gormanston
Ballybeg
Balbriggan
Navan
Duleek
Skerries
Bush & Lusk
Donabate
Malahide
Portmarnock
DUBLIN
Howth

——— **GNR in 1876**
- - - **Built by GNR**
——— **GNR Running Powers**
-·-·- **N&AR**
——— **NW&RR**
·········· **DNGR**

∿∿∿ **Border of Northern Ireland**

0   10   20   **Scale of miles**

Portmarnock
Howth Junc
Baldoyle & Sutton
Raheny
Killester
Harmonstown
Howth
Clontarf
DUBLIN

6

Preface and Acknowledgements

A book on the locomotives of the GNR has been long overdue in Irish railway publishing, but has not previously been attempted, as writing it is no easy task. Of all the companies in Ireland, the GNR has by far the most complicated locomotive history, though one of the best documented. Hitherto, the main published knowledge on the subject has been found in various articles over the years in the *Journal of the Irish Railway Record Society* and *Five Foot Three* (the annual magazine of the Railway Preservation Society of Ireland). Books which have included chapters on the subject are Kevin Murray's *The Great Northern Railway of Ireland*, the late Dr E M Patterson's *The Great Northern Railway of Ireland* and the late O S Nock's *Irish Steam Since 1916*. More recently, Peter Rowledge covered the subject in tabular form in his *Irish Steam Locomotive Register*.

The genesis of this particular book goes back many years. My childhood memories of the GNR as my local railway were a vital ingredient. Later, a spell in Musgrave Park Hospital, Belfast, in 1957, adjacent to the GNR main line, gave me the opportunity to study GNR locomotives at close quarters and I was fascinated. The discovery of Dr Patterson's book in the mid-1960s allowed me to learn something of the early history of these locomotives and I was particularly intrigued by the very different appearance the PP and Q classes had before 1914. Shortly after, I made the acquaintance of Des FitzGerald of Armagh, who shared my fascination with the GNR and had set himself the challenging task of finding a photograph of every GNR locomotive that ever ran.

Des FitzGerald's picture collection forms the illustrative core of this book and I am heavily indebted to him for making it available to me. Charles Friel is another marvellously helpful collector, who has contributed so much to this and other Colourpoint books. I am very greatful for being given free access to his collection and for his guidance on many of the more technical aspects of this book. Charles also made his library available to me and loaned me many of the personal notebooks of L J Watson, Chief Draughtsman at Dundalk from 1892 to 1933.

Others who have contributed to the book with advice and information, include Joe Cassells, Irwin Pryce, Bill Scott and Derek Young. Derek provided additional help by making his slide collection available to me.

I also wish to acknowledge my indebtness to the diligent research into GNR locomotives carried out by the late R N Clements, up to his death in 1994. Mr Clements spent years studying the minutes and records of the GNR and its constituent companies and the results of his labours are now in the archives of the Irish Railway Record Society. R N Clements and I corresponded regularly on the subject of GNR locomotives some twenty years ago, and the information gleaned from his notes is the basis of much that is written in this book. I am most grateful to the IRRS in Dublin for giving me ready access to this material and in particular to Brendan Pender's patience and assistance in accommodating my exploration of it. In a real sense, R N Clements is as much an author of this book as I am.

More recently, I made the acquaintance of Paddy Mallon of Dundalk, who had a lifetime's service at Dundalk Works and whose knowledge of the technical aspects of GNR locomotives is second to none. Paddy has given me access to much original GNR material, including diagram books, locomotive lists going back to 1889, and correspondence from the files of the late H E Wilson, the last Locomotive Engineer of the GNR. Paddy has personal experience going back to the 1920s and I feel honoured to be able to dedicate the book to him.

In addition to Paddy Mallon's collection, I am indebted to Elizabeth Oxborrow-Cowan of the Manchester Museum of Science and Industry for access to the Beyer Peacock files and to Ed Bartholomew of the National Railway Museum, York, for access to the Sharp Stewart and Dübs files. Brian Boyle of Belfast gave me access to original material relating to the division of the GNR in 1958. All of these sources have helped make this book possible and, as a retired history teacher, I hope I have been as true to them as possible. In GNR locomotive history there are a lot of uncertainties and, as R N Clements used to insist in our correspondence many years ago, the words 'possibly' and 'probably' must be taken very seriously!

As always, my grateful thanks to those who undertook the formidable task of proof-reading this 85,000 word book. These who kept me on the straight and narrow in this way were Michael and Aileen Pollard of Omagh, John and Charles Friel of Belfast and my wife Sheila.

Introduction

With a route mileage of over 550 miles, the Great Northern Railway (Ireland) was the second largest railway in Ireland. It connected Ireland's two largest cities and other quite large centres of population so, in terms of mileage and geographical spread, it was a significant railway. However, its locomotive fleet of just over 200 meant that it did not count as a major railway by the standards of the larger English and Scottish companies. In fleet size, it was in the same league as companies like the North Staffordshire Railway (192 locomotives in 1923), the Hull and Barnsley Railway (149) and the Furness Railway (138). However, these lines served limited geographical areas, unlike the GNR(I), so a more apt comparison could be made with the smaller Scottish railways, the Great North of Scotland (115) and the Highland Railway (173).

Nevertheless, the locomotives of the GNR had a very strong appeal to railway enthusiasts. In Ireland this had much to do with the fact that the GNR was familiar to enthusiasts in both parts of Ireland, whereas the LMS (NCC) was little known south of Belfast, or the GSR north of Dublin. For British enthusiasts, the appeal had a lot to do with the fact that, in the 1950s, the GNR was the one railway that could recapture the atmosphere of the pre-grouping railways before 1923. When it was broken up in 1958, it had enjoyed over 82 years of independent existence and over two-thirds of its locomotives were pre-1923.

This atmosphere was reinforced by the strong sense of *espirit de corps*, and pride in the company, evident among GNR staff. This *espirit de corps* is illustrated by an incident in the early days of the Northern Ireland troubles, around 1973, when a former GNR employee, by then with Northern Ireland Railways, was shot. When news of this reached former GNR staff, south of the border, who had been working for CIE for the previous fifteen years, it was in these words: "I hear one of *our* men has been shot."

Today, in the preservation era, many enthusiasts have had their interest in GNR locomotives rekindled by travelling behind or photographing the two GNR mainline 4-4-0s in action – No 85 *Merlin* and No 171 *Slieve Gullion* – operated by the Railway Preservation Society of Ireland. These locomotives are the only active 4-4-0s in the British Isles and *Merlin* is the only active mainline compound.

The Great Northern Railway (Ireland) was created in 1876, by the amalgamation of four earlier operating companies, namely the Dublin and Drogheda Railway, the Dublin and Belfast Junction Railway, the Irish North Western Railway and the Ulster Railway. These companies themselves were responsible for operating a number of smaller companies, most of which the GNR continued to operate. In the years following the amalgamation, the GNR absorbed some of these other railways and also acquired three further operating companies which brought additional locomotives into the fleet – the Newry and Armagh Railway (1879), the Belfast Central Railway (1885) and the Newry, Warrenpoint and Rostrevor Railway (1886). The GNR also built additional branches.

Whilst this process of amalgamation and absorption was by no means unusual, it was more common for it to happen in the 1840s than the 1870s. The relatively late date of the formation of the GNR meant that the constituent companies all had time to develop substantial locomotive fleets in their own right and, in the case of some, their own distinctive 'house style'. Because a knowledge of these companies is essential to understanding the diversity of locomotives owned by the GNR in its early days, the first four chapters of this book deal with the locomotives of the constituent companies up to 1876. Whilst this occasionally involves describing locomotives which were scrapped before 1876, I hope my readers will forgive this indulgence. Their inclusion seems justified on the grounds of completeness.

The well-known aesthetic characteristics of GNR locomotives did not begin to develop until the arrival of James Park, from Doncaster, to take charge of the new locomotive works at Dundalk in 1880. It was to be 1885 before he introduced the 4-4-0 type, which was to be the standard wheel arrangement for GNR passenger locomotives right up to the demise of the company in 1958. Despite its small size, the GNR produced a succession of memorable locomotive designs which put to shame many larger companies. The company led the way in many fields, including electric lighting for carriages and, as early as the 1930s, the GNR was a major pioneer in diesel traction. In 1950, it became the first railway in the British Isles to operate a fleet of diesel multiple unit trains. Although the history of GNR steam locomotives is the major theme of this book, I have devoted a short chapter to GNR diesel traction.

The information on locomotives in this book is more detailed than that hitherto published in other books. In recent years more accurate delivery dates, for Sharp Stewart locomotives in particular, have come to light. This has allowed me to revise some previously published dates. For example, two Dublin and Drogheda locomotives, previously thought to have been delivered in 1863-4, were both definitely December 1863. I have also discovered that some previously published calculations of tractive effort were inaccurate and all have been recalculated using the formula on page 13.

There is one point I would like to clear up before moving to the locomotives themselves. Readers will have noticed that I have referred above to the GNR and occasionally to the GNR(I). Strictly speaking, and certainly up to 1923, the Irish GNR was known as the GNR(I) to distinguish it from the Kings Cross and Doncaster-based Great Northern Railway. However, GNR(I) engines were always lettered simply 'G N R' and, in Ireland itself, it was always 'GNR' in everyday usage. Therefore, throughout the text of this book, I will refer to the Irish company simply as the GNR and will only add 'Ireland' where its lack might lead to confusion. I hope that enthusiasts of the English GNR will forgive this liberty and will, in fact, be intrigued by the similarity between their GNR and ours.

GNR(I) Locomotive Classification

The GNR(I) had its own peculiar locomotive classification system and the purpose of this section is simply to explain how this evolved.

Before 1876, the pre-amalgamation companies probably identified their engines by number and maker. This continued into the early days of the GNR, as the locomotives were still serviced at the existing workshops in Derry, Belfast, Dundalk and Dublin. Things changed, however, when the new Dundalk Works opened in 1881. When James Park arrived from Doncaster to take charge of the new works, at the end of 1880, he found himself in charge of around fifty locomotive types. With so many types, some system was needed to identify what part fitted which engine. A new alphabetical classification system was initiated by Park, who used upper case letters to identify cylinders, crank axles and boilers. Thus his own goods design, introduced in 1882, had an A class crank axle, an AB class cylinder block and an AB class boiler. (The cylinder block and boiler were common with those on earlier goods engines utilising the B class crank axle.) In another example, the ex-Dublin & Drogheda Railway 2-2-2s had N class cranks, M class cylinders and G class boilers.

Gradually, the letters identifying crank axles evolved into a system that identified the locomotive class, though this was not until the late 1890s. Crank axles were complicated structures, the axle on inside cylinder engines requiring cranks for two cylinders, and additional cranks and eccentrics for the valve gear. The crucial dimension which affected crank axles was the stroke of the cylinders. Thus, an engine with a 20" stroke required a crank axle with a 10" throw, and a 22" stroke needed an 11" throw on the main crank. However, the design of the crank axle was also affected by whether the engine had inside or outside cylinders. Early outside cylinder engines usually had the valve gear inside. Therefore the driving axle had cranks for the valve gear only, as the pistons acted on the outside of the wheel. A double-framed engine had *four* bearings for each axle (two on an inside-framed engine) and thus its own design of axle. The design also differed for each manufacturer. In the 1870s, the 17"x 24" cylindered 0-6-0s manufactured by Dübs, Sharp Stewart and Beyer Peacock, all had different designs of crank axle.

In the system evolved by Park after 1881, crank axles were grouped according to stroke, as follows:

| A-F | – 24" stroke | L | – 21" stroke |
| G-K | – 22" stroke | M-N | – 20" stroke |

Oddly, in contrast to this systematic order, classes O-X were an assortment of different sized cranks in no particular order. These were mostly on older or non-standard locomotives, many of them outside cylinder or double-framed types. Presumably, Park expected these to disappear fairly quickly so that he would need only classes A-N. Using Park's system, the GNR locomotive fleet in 1881 can be classified as follows (The initials in brackets are those of the originating company – see chapters 1-5):

A – 24" Beyer Peacock – 0-6-0 No 5 (ex-D&DR) and Park's new standard 0-6-0 which appeared in 1882.

B – 24" Sharp Stewart and Neilson – 0-6-0 Nos 6, 26, 27, 34, 62, 63, 65-67 (GNR), 0-4-2 No 35 and 0-6-0 No 36 (ex-D&BJR), Neilson 0-4-2 Nos 57, 58, 70, 71 (ex-INWR).

C – 24" Ulster Railway – 0-6-0 Nos 137, 138 (ex-UR), 103, 114-116, 142, 143 (GNR Northern Division). *[GNR ND was the former UR section up to 1885]*

D – 24" Beyer Peacock – 0-6-0 Nos 40, 41 (ex-D&BJR).

E – 24" Dübs/INWR – 0-6-0 Nos 44, 77, 78; 0-4-2 No 76 (ex-INWR).

F – 24" Beyer Peacock, double-framed – 0-4-2 Nos 133-136 (ex-UR).

G – 22" Beyer Peacock and Fairbairn – 2-4-0 Nos 3, 24, 25, 42, 59, 80 (GNR), 12 (ex-D&DR), 2-2-2 Nos 122, 124, 125 (ex-UR), 0-4-2 Nos 10, 11, 20 (ex-D&DR), 0-6-0 No 21 (ex-D&DR).

H – 22" Beyer Peacock and UR, double-framed – 2-4-0 Nos 101, 120, 121, 123, 126-129 (ex-UR).

J – 22" Beyer Peacock – 2-4-0 Nos 37-39 (ex-D&BJR), 84-87 (GNR). *[When the double-framed 2-4-0s were scrapped, these became the H class.]*

K – 22" Sharp Stewart and UR – 0-4-2 Nos 102, 104 (GNR ND), 105-107, 130-132, 139-141 (ex-UR).

L – 21" Dübs/INWR – 2-4-0 Nos 72-75 (ex-INWR).

M – 20" UR double-framed, from 1860s – 2-2-2 Nos 109, 111 (ex-UR), 2-4-0 Nos 108, 110, 112, 113 (ex-UR).

N – 20" Beyer Peacock – 2-2-2 Nos 13-16 (ex-D&DR), 55, 56 (ex-INWR), 2-4-0 No 53 (ex-INWR).

O – 22" Longridge – 2-4-0 No 54, 2-2-2 No 60 (both ex-INWR).

P – 20" Sharp Stewart, double-framed, from the 1840s – 0-4-2 Nos 1, 2 (ex-D&DR) and probably 2-4-0 No 30 (ex-D&BJR).

Q – 20" Sharp Stewart, double-framed, from the 1860s – 2-2-2 Nos 22, 23 (ex-D&DR).

R – 18" Sharp Stewart, double-framed, from the 1840s – 2-4-0 No 9 (ex-D&DR), 2-2-2WT Nos 28, 29 (ex-D&BJR).

S – 22" Sharp Stewart – 0-4-2 Nos 31-33 (ex-D&BJR), 51, 52 (ex-INWR).

T – 18" Grendon – 2-2-2 Nos 7 (ex-D&DR), 43 (ex-INWR), 0-4-2 No 45 (ex-INWR).

U – 20" Sharp Stewart, double-framed, from 1850s – 2-2-2 Nos 17, 18 (ex-D&DR), 46-48 (ex-INWR), 2-4-0 Nos 117-119 (ex-UR).

V – 17" Manning Wardle – 0-6-0ST Nos 61, 64 (ex-INWR).

W – 20" Jones, outside cylinder – 2-4-0 Nos 68, 69 (ex-INWR).

X – 22" Vulcan – 0-4-2 Nos 81, 82 (ex-N&AR).

Notes: To avoid confusion, ex-UR locomotives listed on the previous page are identified by their post 1885 numbers (when 100 was added to them). From the amalgamation in 1876 to 1885 the Northern Division retained the former UR numbers unchanged and these duplicated those of Southern Division locomotives, as 1-43.

Several locomotives did not appear in the classification but, as they were one-off examples, they may simply have been identified by engine number. Alternatively, they may have shared crank axles with other classes, These engines were:

- *Grendon 2-4-0 No 4 (ex-D&DR), possibly 'N'*
- *Neilson 2-2-2ST No 8 (ex-D&DR), possibly 'R'*
- *Fairbairn 2-4-0 No 19 (ex-D&DR), possibly 'S'*
- *Grendon 0-6-0 Nos 49, 50 (ex-INWR), possibly 'A'*
- *Stephenson 0-6-0 No 83 (ex-N&AR), possibly 'A'*
- *Sharp 2-4-0T No 85A (ex-N&AR), possibly' W'*

As old locomotives were scrapped, some letters became available for re-use. Thus, O was reused for the small 2-4-0Ts acquired from the NW&RR and BCR in 1885-6, P for the BCR 4-4-0T and T for the small 4-4-0Ts introduced in 1885. (These later came to be known by their boiler classification, BT, which stood for 'bogie T' rather than 'B tank'). Class J was used for the 4-2-2s and 4-4-0s also introduced in 1885, the singles being known as JS. Eventually the earlier J class 2-4-0s were reclassified H to avoid confusion. Throughout the early chapters of this book, I will refer to the pre-amalgamation engines by their GNR classification. I have slightly modified them to distinguish variations within the class. For instance, the N class had two wheel sizes, which I have distinguished as N5'6" and N6'0", though this sub-division was not used by the GNR.

The system was then modified in the 1890s. Enlarged A class goods engines became AL and, since the new P class 4-4-0s had two different sizes of driving wheel, these were distinguished as P6'6" and P5'6". Even this had limitations, since nearly all new locomotives had either 24" Beyer Peacock cranks (P) or 26" Neilson cranks (Q). As this would have led to many types having the same classification, a series of suffix and prefix letters was introduced. These were **G** (goods or 0-6-0 version) as in PG, QG, SG, etc; **T** (tank engine version) as in JT, QGT, RT, etc; **L** (enlarged) as in AL, QL,

LQG, etc; and **N** (Nasmyth Wilson-built engines of 1911) as in NQG and NLQG.

Other modifications were added in later years. George Glover, who took charge of the locomotives after 1912, ceased to identify engines by their cranks. Instead, each new family of locomotives had its own class letter to identify related classes. Thus, S, T, U and V were added in sequence. New versions of each class had a figure added in small type, as in SG, SG2, SG3. After 1919, as older locomotives were superheated, a small 's' suffix was added, as in PGs, Qs, LQGs, etc. From 1929, the two sizes of boiler carried by the superheated PPs class were distinguished as PPs4'3" and PPs4'6". Finally, in 1948, the simple expansion version of the three cylinder V class 4-4-0 Compounds was identified as the VS class.

Power classification

Confusion is sometimes created by the red, cast iron, power classification letters added to the cab sides of 0-6-0 locomotives after 1908. These identified the *haulage capacity* of locomotives rather than their class. Until 1920 they worked as follows:

A – Classes A, AL and B (17" cylinders)

B – Classes PG, QG and NQG (18½" cylinders)

C – Classes LQG, NLQG, SG and SG2 (4'9" boilers or 19" cylinders)

D – Classes C, D and E (17" cylinders with 5'0" wheels)

The introduction of the large SG3 goods engines in 1920 required a new power class, so the old D became E. Superheating led to further adjustments, so the power classes eventually became as follows:

A – Classes A, AL and B

B – Classes PGs, QGs and UG (no letter carried on the latter)

C – Classes NQGs ('Rebuilt C'), SG and SG2

D – Classes LQGs, LQGNs ('Rebuilt D'), SG3 ('Big D')

E – Classes C, D and E

Since A-E were both power classifications and engine classifications, there was scope for some confusion here.

Technical Matters

As it is now almost thirty years since the end of steam traction on Irish railways, I am aware that some of my readers may be unfamiliar with some of the measurements and terminology used in this book. This section is for them and can be ignored by 'dyed in the wool' steam enthusiasts over the age of forty!

Measurements

Firstly, all measurements are given in imperial units rather than metric. These are the units used in the steam age and will not translate readily into metric.

Measurements of **weight** are in imperial tons and hundredweight (cwt), in the case of large objects, like locomotives and tenders. Smaller weights are usually in pounds (lbs).

> One ton = 20 cwt = 2,240 pounds
>
> One imperial ton = 1,016,047 kilos = 1.016047 metric tonnes
>
> One pound = 0.45359237 kilos

Measurements of **distance** are generally in miles or, for locomotive dimensions, in feet and inches, or just inches.

> One mile = 1.60934 kilometres.
>
> One foot = 12 inches = 304.8mm.
>
> One inch = 25.3999 mm

Feet and inches are usually indicated in this manner: 5'6" (for five feet, six inches).

Area measurement is usually in square feet (sq ft) for the heating surface of boilers and grate area of fireboxes.

> One square foot = 144 square inches = 929.028 square centimetres

Builders and dates

Most GNR steam engines were built by outside manufacturers, like Beyer Peacock and Neilson Reid. Locomotives were identified by a **works number** on a brass or cast iron plate mounted on the locomotive frame or cab. Not all manufacturers used works numbers but, where known, they are listed in the appendices. The dates of locomotives, eg 7/1903, indicate the month of *delivery* to the GNR. Withdrawal dates are the date the engine was taken out of service. They were not necessarily *scrapped* on these dates. In the appendices, the scrap date is given only when it differs markedly from the withdrawal date. The GNR also built locomotives at its Dundalk Works, though, at first, major components, like boilers, were bought in from outside. Engines built at Dundalk also carried works numbers.

Locomotive Types

Steam engines are categorised according to their wheel arrangement and purpose. On a **tender engine**, the coal and water are carried in a truck (usually six-wheel) behind the engine, called the **tender**. The wheel arrangement is described using the **Whyte system**, but the wheels on the tender are not counted as part of the engine. Wheels are divided into **leading**, **driving** and **trailing** wheels, starting at the chimney end of the locomotive. Thus a 4-4-0 has four leading wheels, four driving wheels and no trailing wheels. An 0-4-2 has no leading wheels, four driving wheels and two trailing wheels, etc. In Victorian times, before the Whyte system was introduced, locomotives were described by words: single (2-2-2), bogie single (4-2-2), front-coupled (0-4-2), hind coupled (2-4-0), bogie hind coupled (4-4-0) and six coupled (0-6-0).

Tank locomotives carry their water and coal on the frames of the engine and have no tender. They are generally used for shorter journeys. Tank engine wheel arrangements are identified by the addition of a letter T, eg 0-6-0T or 4-4-2T. A plain **T** indicates a **side tank** engine with the water carried in tanks on either side of the boiler, resting on the frames. **ST** indicates a **saddle tank**, in which a single curved tank was placed over the boiler. **WT** is a **well tank**, an arrangement common on very early tank engines, where a small quantity of water was carried low down in a tank between the frames. Though not relevant to the GNR, there were also **pannier tanks** (**PT**) and **back tanks** (**BT**). On a tank engine, all the wheels are counted in the wheel arrangement.

Frames and wheels

Locomotive frames consist of two long, parallel, vertical plates, spaced almost five feet apart, running the length of the locomotive. These are braced at intervals by cross beams and all major components are bolted to the frames. In the twentieth century, frames were usually **inside** (ie with the wheels outside the frames) and made of steel plate. However, on many early locomotives there were **outside frames** and some had **double frames**, with the wheels between the frames, in which case each wheel had two bearings. A lot of early Victorian engines had wooden outside frames with the timber sheathed by two thin iron plates. These were called **sandwich frames** and can be identified in photographs by the seemingly large number of rivets on the frames. Most double-framed engines had outside sandwich frames and inside plate frames. Tenders normally had outside frames.

The wheelbase measurements quoted in this book are the distance between each axle, starting at the front end. Length, where quoted, is usually the length of the main frame, excluding the buffers, which are about another two feet. **Weight** is the weight of the engine **in working order**, ie with the boiler filled with water to the correct level. Similarly, the weight of a tender includes the coal and water. A locomotive in a museum, without water in the tender or boiler, will sit higher on its springs than if it was in working order. Wheel diameters, where quoted, refer to the driving wheels (dw) unless otherwise stated. The driving wheels on goods engines were usually 4'6" to 5'3" diameter, on ordinary passenger engines 5'6" to 6'0" and on express locomotives 6'3" to 7'0".

Cylinders and motion

Most GNR locomotives had two inside cylinders, with the cylinder block bolted between the frames just ahead of the leading axle (or above the bogie in the case of 4-4-0s and 4-4-2Ts). This provided an extremely strong and rigid structure. Cylinder dimensions are always quoted in inches, with the diameter followed by the stroke (eg 18"x 24"). In a six-wheeled locomotive the crank axle was normally the central axle and, in the case of a 4-4-0 or 4-4-2T, the leading coupled axle. The **connecting rods** were tapered, the **small end** being connected to the pistons and the **big end** to the crank axle.

The admission of steam to the cylinders was controlled by **slide valves** (and in later designs, **piston valves**). These were activated by **valve gear**, which was connected to **eccentrics** on the **crank axle**. (An eccentric is a crank whose centre is offset from that of the axle. Thus, while the axle simply rotates, the offset crank executes a different, or 'eccentric', motion.) The valve gear also enabled the driver to reverse the locomotive. Unlike a car, a steam engine can travel equally fast in forward or reverse. However, it was not normal to reverse a tender engine at speed. The most common type of valve gear on GNR locomotives was **Stephenson link motion**, which required two eccentrics for each set of gear. The crank axle was, therefore, rather crowded between the frames, requiring space for two cranks and four eccentrics, the eccentrics sitting between the cranks. This was tight enough on an Irish 5'3" gauge engine, but must have been even worse on the British 4'8½" gauge!

Some early locomotive designs used outside cylinders with inside gear (see chapter 3). This had the advantage of making the crank axle less crowded, and therefore stronger. However, the disadvantage was that six wheeled engines with outside cylinders tended to develop a swaying or 'hunting' motion, since the coupling rod cranks were set at 180° to each other, acting on the extremities of the axle. Except for slow shunting engines, outside cylinders were best suited to engines with eight or more wheels, and preferably ten or more (eg 2-8-0s, 4-6-0s and 4-6-2s). Three cylinder engines had two outside cylinders and one inside, whilst four cylinder engines had two outside and two inside. Three and four cylinders give a smoother motion as the thrust on the axle is more balanced and there is less hammer blow. The GNR built only five designs of engine with outside cylinders. These

were: the two classes of railmotor, built in 1905-06 with Walschaerts gear; 0-6-0T No 31 of 1927, the Works shunter, which also had Walshaerts gear; the V class 3 cyl compound 4-4-0s of 1932, which had three sets of Stephenson gear between the frames; and the VS class 4-4-0s of 1948, which had two sets of Walshaerts gear outside and one inside. Since Walshaerts gear required only one eccentric, the VS crank axle was relatively strong, with only one crank and one eccentric between the frames.

Boilers

Locomotive boilers have three main elements. At the front is the **smokebox**, which collects the hot gases as they pass through the boiler and expels them through the chimney. This process is aided by the force of the exhausted steam, as it leaves the cylinders through the **blast pipe**, which is situated in the bottom of the smokebox, directly in line with the chimney. When the engine is not in motion, steam is not being exhausted and there is no natural draught. However, the top of the blast pipe has a perforated ring around the outside, called the **blower**. The driver uses the blower to direct a jet of unused steam up the chimney, thus maintaining the draught.

Secondly, there is the **boiler barrel** itself which is the cylindrical section between the edge of the smokebox and the start of the firebox. This is, basically, a water-filled cylinder, the lower two-thirds of which contains a honeycomb of boiler tubes which link the firebox to the smokebox. Water circulates around the outside of the tubes and hot gases from the fire pass through the tubes. On top of the boiler is a **dome**, or other collecting device, to collect the steam from the boiling water and pass it to the cylinders. The boiler is never totally filled with water, but the water level must be above the level of the firebox crown (explained opposite). The crucial boiler statistics to quote are: the maximum **boiler pressure** (bp) expressed in pounds per square inch (eg 175 lbs); the diameter and length of barrel of the boiler in feet and inches (eg 4'6"x 11'3"); the number and diameter of the tubes (eg 172 x 2") and the heating surface. The external diameter of a boiler is greater than the quoted figure because boilers have to be lagged to prevent heat loss. Early lagging was by timber slats held on by barrel type hoops. Later there were plates covering the lagging and eventually engines were lagged using asbestos under the plates.

From about 1910 onwards, many locomotives were **superheated**. This meant raising the temperature of the steam by fitting around twenty **large tubes** (about 5¼" in diameter) along the boiler barrel, through which the steam from the dome was passed, in narrow pipes called **superheater elements**, from the smokebox end, almost up to the firebox, four times (twice in each direction). This extra heating raised the temperature of the steam well above that of the boiler, to about 315°C, and made it **dry steam**. Boilers without superheaters are said to be **saturated** (ie they have **wet steam**). Superheated steam expands more in the cylinders and provides greater power.

The firebox is the most complex part of the boiler. It is like a cube within a cube, in that there is an **inner firebox** and an **outer firebox**. The space in between is filled with water and, at the top and front, is directly connected to the boiler barrel. The firebox is the hottest part of the boiler. It usually has flat, or almost flat, sides and the inner firebox is braced against the outer by **firebox stays**. Most GNR boilers were round-topped and staying a flat surface to a round shell is difficult. For this reason, many railways moved over to the **Belpaire firebox**, in which the boiler is flat sided at the firebox end. This made staying easier. The top surface of a firebox is the **crown** and at the bottom is the **foundation ring** which surrounds the **grate**. The width of the foundation ring determines the minimum gap between the inner and outer fireboxes, usually 2½" to 4½".

In quoting firebox dimensions, this book will give the length, followed by the width, of the outer firebox (eg 4'4"x 4'6"), the **grate area** (eg 13.95 sq ft) and the heating surface. The **heating surface** (hs) is the area of water in direct contact with heat and is made up of two components – the boiler tubes and the firebox (eg 879.3 + 94.1 = 973.4 sq ft). Superheated engines have a third component, which is the surface area of the superheater elements. Boiler heating surface is fairly easy to calculate, provided you know the length, number and size of the tubes (bearing in mind that the tubes are usually about 4½" longer than the boiler barrel, since the rear tubeplate is on the **inner** firebox). Firebox and superheater heating surfaces are more difficult to calculate, due to the complex shapes of the firebox and superheater elements.

Tractive effort

In essence, this is an entirely meaningless figure and is only of value for making comparisons between the power of one steam engine and that of another. Although quoted in pounds (lbs), tractive effort is a multiplication of inches and pounds. To calculate **tractive effort** you need to know the driving wheel diameter, the cylinder dimensions and the boiler pressure. In late Victorian times, locomotive power was compared using a calculation called **tractive force**. This ignored boiler pressure and the formula for tractive force was:

$$\frac{D^2 \times S}{W}$$

[D = cylinder diameter in inches, S = stroke of the cylinders in inches, W = driving wheel diameter in inches]

This gave the tractive force per pound of boiler pressure. Thus an engine with 6'0" wheels and 16"x 22" cyls had a tractive force of 78.22 per lb of boiler pressure.

Tractive Effort is the same figure multiplied by the boiler pressure in pounds. Since boiler pressure varies throughout a journey, and is rarely at its maximum, the standard for calculating tractive effort is 85% bp. The formula is thus:

$$\frac{D^2 \times S \times P \times 85}{W \times 100}$$

For the example given above, if the boiler pressure was 130 lbs, tractive effort would be 8,643 lbs. For a three cylinder engine, the above formula needs to be multiplied by 150% and for a four cylinder engine, doubled.

I hope this short technical section will help explain some of the basics that are needed to fully follow the content of this book.

Chapter 1
The Dublin and Drogheda Railway

The Dublin and Drogheda Railway was the most southerly component of the GNR and its locomotives became the core of the GNR fleet in 1876, retaining their D&DR numbers into GNR days. For this reason, we begin our study of GNR locomotives with the D&DR, although, in strictly chronological terms, the Ulster Railway began to operate earlier.

The D&DR was incorporated in August 1836 and, like most Irish railways, was built to a gauge of 5'3". Progress at construction was slow and the line did not open until 26 May 1844. Even then, it was to be two more years before the Dublin terminus at Amiens Street (now Connolly Station) was completed, and April 1855 before the Boyne viaduct was built at Drogheda, linking the D&DR to the Dublin and Belfast Junction Railway (D&BJR). Only two other lines were built by the D&DR. These were the Howth branch, opened on 30 July 1846, and a long branch from Drogheda to Oldcastle, opened in stages – to Navan on 15 February 1850, to Kells on 11 June 1853 and to Oldcastle on 17 May 1863. At the amalgamation, the D&DR had a route mileage of just under 75 miles. The main line and the Howth branch are still open and the Drogheda-Navan section still carries goods traffic.

The locomotives of the Dublin and Drogheda Railway fall into two main groups. Its first generation consisted of seventeen locomotives built between 1843 and 1847 when the mainline and Howth branch were opened. These were small and primitive and were already obsolete by the late 1850s. With few new lines being built, the engine fleet did not expand significantly and the only way larger locomotives could be obtained was by scrapping and replacing the older ones. Ten of the original fleet had already gone by 1863 and only four survived long enough to be taken over by the GNR.

The second generation consisted of fifteen locomotives, mostly replacements, built between 1854 and 1863. After 1863, only two further locomotives were built, so that, by 1876, the D&DR had a somewhat older fleet than the other component companies of the GNR.

D&DR locomotives were numbered in the order of their delivery and, in the early days, carried names as well as numbers. These were a curious mixture of names inspired by British royalty (*Prince, Victoria, Alice,* etc) and Irish themes (*St Patrick, Hibernia,* etc). Naming was probably abandoned after 1849. At one time it was thought that some engines of the 1850s had names like *Collen Bawn* and *Brian Boroimhe*. This was based exclusively on the recollections of an old man called J F McEwan, still alive in the early 1900s. However, it is now established that the names he attributed to engines were the names of ships owned by the Drogheda Steam Ship Co.

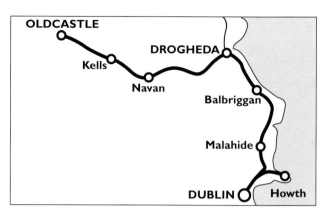

Naming was resumed in the 1870s by William Curry, Locomotive Engineer 1863-80 (of both the D&DR and early GNR). The later names were probably painted on and were mostly names of planets (*Saturn, Venus,* etc) or on the theme of classical mythology (*Achilles, Diana,* etc). Only a few appear in GNR lists after 1876, and oral evidence of old men, interviewed in the 1940s about the others, is conflicting. Therefore, it is far from certain what name was applied to particular engines, especially since no photographs exist of any D&DR engine bearing a name. In any case, most of the names were short-lived, only a few being perpetuated by the GNR. Names, whether original or later, are mentioned in the text and listed at the end of the chapter.

The first generation 1843-47

The Dublin and Drogheda bought its first locomotives from Sharp Brothers of Manchester. These engines were developments of the early Sharp 2-2-2 and 0-4-2 designs built by the same firm for the Ulster Railway in 1841-42 (See page 39). Nos 1 *Nor Creina*, 6 *Dublin*, 7 *Princess* and 11 *Prince* were 0-4-2s with 5'0" driving wheels, 15"x 20" cylinders and 3'6"x 9'6" boilers. No 1 had 98 2" boiler tubes and a 4-wheel tender of 850 gallons capacity, whilst the other three had 111 boiler tubes and 1000 gallon 6-wheel tenders. Although Dr E M Patterson (in *The Great Northern Railway of Ireland,* 1962) quotes them as weighing 23 tons, this probably only applied to Nos 1 and 6, after they were heavily rebuilt in 1861 and 1866 respectively.

Seven 2-2-2s were ordered, in three batches. The first to be delivered, No 2 *St Patrick*, had 5'0" driving wheels (unusually small for a 2-2-2) and 15"x 18" cylinders. Its other dimensions were: leading and trailing wheels 3'6", boiler 3'6"x 9'0" with 98 tubes, weight 16 tons, tender 1000 gallons. Nos 3-5 were ordered early in 1844 and were similar to No 2, except for 5'6" driving wheels, 14"x 18" cylinders and 111 tubes. They were named *Fag an Bealagh, Albert* and *Victoria* respectively. In May three more, Nos 8-10 (*Alice,*

Fig 1: Diagram of John G Bodmer's balanced motion with two pistons working in opposite directions in each cylinder.

The Engineer

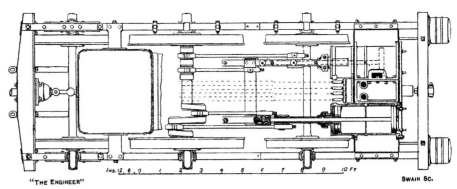

"THE ENGINEER"   SWAIN SC.

Alfred and *Queen*) were ordered.

No 10 of this batch was unique. This locomotive was experimentally fitted with 'Bodmer's expansion'. J G Bodmer built some engines himself in Manchester between 1834 and 1845, but others were built by Sharp Brothers. His system used cylinders twice the normal length with two pistons to each cylinder (Fig 11). The rear piston rods were connected to the cranks in the usual manner but the front piston rods were connected to crossheads, coupled rearwards, by rods, to arms rocking on a fixed cross shaft. The arms were attached to connecting rods, attached to cranks fixed at 180° in relation to the cranks driven by the rear pistons. A further curious feature of the arrangement was that the rear piston rods were hollow, so as to allow the front piston rods to pass through them. It is usually assumed that this required outside cylinders but, as the diagram illustrates such an arrangement with an inside cylindered 2-2-2, I am not totally convinced that D&DR *Queen* had outside cylinders. No 10 was not a success and was rebuilt as a 2-4-0, with conventional inside cylinder motion in 1848.

Nos 3 and 4 were converted to 2-2-2WTs to operate the Howth branch, probably in 1846. Nos 1, 6 were rebuilt in 1861 and 1866 respectively, with 5'2½" driving wheels and 14½"x 20" cylinders, and also received new boilers. No 9 got a new boiler in 1868 and was converted to a 2-4-0. Nos 2, 4, 8, 10 and 11 had short lives and were replaced in 1856-63.

Another locomotive was acquired in 1844, becoming No 12 *Firefly*. This was built by the Butterley Iron Company of

Ripley (which dated back to 1790 and mostly built industrial locomotives). *Firefly* probably dated from 1841 and was used by Jeffs in building the Dublin and Drogheda Railway. He then sold it to the Dublin and Drogheda. It is likely that *Firefly* was a double framed 2-2-2 with horizontal outside cylinders, as two locomotives of this type, *Ariel* and *Hercules*, were built for the Midland Counties Railway in 1839 and Butterley probably used the same design. Whatever its origin, No 12 was highly unsatisfactory. It had no driving wheel flanges and frequently derailed. Payment was deferred for several years. It saw little service and was sold in 1853, probably to a contractor.

The first Locomotive Superintendent of the D&DR was Sylvester Lees who was in charge from the opening of the line in 1844. In September 1848, he left to take up a similar post at Bury Works, on the East Lancashire Railway. It is known that he remained there some time after the ELR merged with the Lancashire and Yorkshire Railway in August 1859. Lees would no doubt have influenced the decision to purchase Grendon locomotives in 1845.

The Drogheda firm of Thomas Grendon and Son had just commenced building locomotives and it was natural that the local railway should be among its first customers. Three inside cylinder singles (2-2-2) were acquired in 1845 (see Fig 3) – Nos 13 *MacNeill*, 14 (unnamed) and 15 *Hibernia*. They

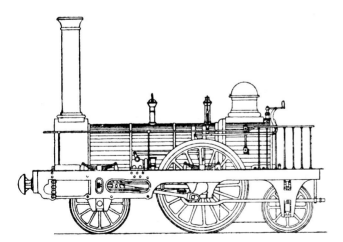

Fig 2: Midland Counties Railway Butterley 2-2-2 *Ariel*. This was almost certainly the design of D&DR No 12 *Firefly*. *Ariel* had 13"x 18" cylinders and, assuming 5'6' DW, this drawing indicates that it had 3'6" LW, 3'0" TW and a wheelbase of 6'3"+ 5'3".

Fig 3: The probable appearance of a Grendon 2-2-2. Five locomotives of this type (Nos 13-17) were built for the D&DR in 1845-47. They had 5'6' driving wheels and 14"x 18" cylinders. No 16 was built as a well tank.

R N Clements, courtesy IRRS

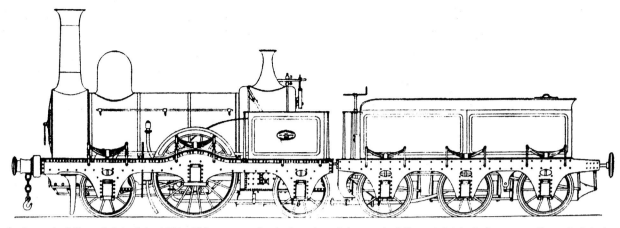

Fig 4: A standard Sharp 2-2-2 of the 1850s. This was a modernised version of the standard Sharp 2-2-2 built for many railways in Britain and Ireland in the period 1846-49. D&DR Nos 12 and 18 were of this type and identical locomotives were built for the D&BJR, the Dundalk and Enniskillen Railway (D&ER) and the Ulster Railway. The type became the original GNR U class.

J H Houston, IRRS collection

had 5'6" driving wheels, 14"x 18" cylinders and 1200 gallon tenders. Two more were acquired in 1847, No 16 (unnamed) appearing as a well tank and No 17 *Drogheda* as a tender engine.

Apart from No 17, none had a long life compared to the similar engines built for the Dundalk and Enniskillen Railway. Nos 13-16 had all gone by 1861. No 17 was obviously the best of the five and, in 1873, was rebuilt with a new boiler of 797 sq ft heating surface and 13"x 18" cylinders. It lasted well into GNR days, finally facing the cutters torch in 1891.

The second generation 1854-63

Sylvester Lees was succeeded by Patrick Connor in December 1849. Connor had been Lee's assistant and held the post until December 1860. He turned to a variety of manufacturers for whatever few locomotives he required. Presumably the choice of manufacturer was decided by tendering. In those days there was little appreciation of the desirability of standardisation. Two Sharp singles (Fig 4) were delivered in 1854 (Nos 12 and 18). These had 5'6" driving wheels and 15"x 20" cylinders and were basically a development of the standard Sharp single of the late 1840s. These were rebuilt in 1870-71 and, as members of the GNR U class, lasted until 1886. In their latter days they were mainly on the Oldcastle branch.

The Manchester firm of William Fairbairn and Sons had started as an iron foundry in 1816 and commenced locomotive manufacturing in 1839. It built over sixty locomotives for Irish railways before Fairbairn sold the locomotive side of his business to Sharp Stewart in 1863. In 1855, this firm delivered No 19, a 2-4-0 goods locomotive, to the Dublin and Drogheda Railway. Little is known about this engine apart from the fact that it had 5'0" driving wheels and was inside framed. It was probably similar to locomotives built in 1853-54 for the Waterford and Limerick Railway and, if so, probably had 16"x 21" cylinders. It was rebuilt in 1869 with a

new Grendon boiler and then, or later, named *Pluto*. As rebuilt, it weighed 26 tons 7 cwt and had 16"x 22" cylinders. It was scrapped in 1887.

In 1856, Grendons were favoured with another order, this time for a 2-4-0 passenger engine, No 4. This engine was similar to a batch built for the neighbouring Midland Great Western Railway (MGWR) and had inside frames, 5'6" driving wheels and 15"x 20" cylinders. It was rebuilt in 1875 with 16"x 22" cylinders, a new boiler which had a heating surface of 954 sq ft and then weighed 28½ tons. It was named *Drogheda* on rebuilding, retaining this name until at least 1885. It was scrapped in 1888.

The next locomotives were ordered from Beyer Peacock, which had been set up in 1854, Charles Beyer having previously been manager of Sharp Brothers. The firm survived until the 1960s and was to have long associations with the Great Northern Railway, which became a faithful customer. The Belfast and County Down Railway, in 1857, was the first Irish railway to buy Beyer engines. Two standard Beyer types were built for the Dublin and Drogheda in 1858 and 1859. Nos 11, 20 (1858) were 0-4-2 goods engines with 5'0" driving wheels and 16"x 22" cylinders. Nos 14, 15 (1859) were 2-2-2 express engines with 6'0" driving wheels and 15"x 20" cylinders. As the numbers indicate, three were replacements

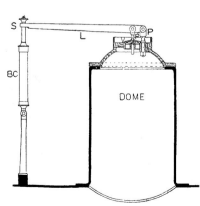

Fig 5: A spring balance safety valve. This type of valve was almost universal from the 1840s to the 1860s. The lever (L) has a fixed point (P) and extends to S, where its upward movement is resisted by the spring in the balance casing (BC), which can be adjusted to the required pressure. The steam acts upon the valve (V) forcing it against the lever at the point P.

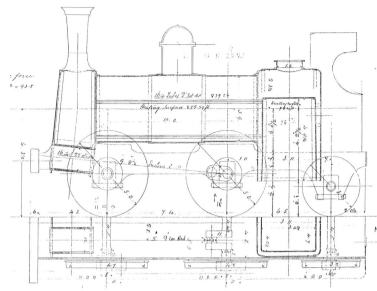

Fig 6 (left): This fairly detailed drawing of the Beyer Peacock 0-4-2 design dates from the early 1880s and was among a batch of very old drawings unearthed at Dundalk when the GNR was being broken up. The cylinders are inclined at 1 in 11 to clear the leading coupled axle and the smokebox front similarly angled. Originally the dome was on the firebox, as in the photograph of the 2-2-2 below. The drawing has been modified by the GNR to show the addition of a cab and the repositioning of the dome on the boiler barrel during rebuilding in 1879-84. Four 0-4-2 goods engines were built to this design in 1858-63.

Courtesy P Mallon

Fig 7 (below): The Beyer drawing of the 2-2-2 design shows that the two designs had a lot of components in common. They had the same boiler, firebox and trailing wheels. The boiler was 3'9"x 10'0" and the firebox 3'11" long. These 2-2-2 locomotives were the favoured type for the Limited Mail trains in the early 1880s.

Courtesy P Mallon

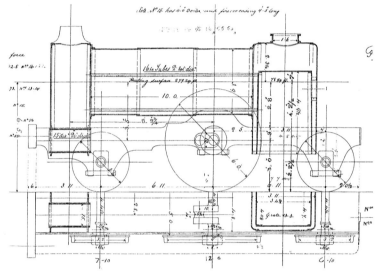

Below: Unfortunately, no pictures have come to light of any of the first generation of Dublin and Drogheda locomotives. The earliest is this 1858 Beyer Peacock photograph of one of the four inside framed 2-2-2 engines delivered in 1859-61 (Nos 13-16). These had 6'0" driving wheels and 15"x 20" cylinders and were later the GNR N class. Note the open splasher, the dome and spring balance safety valves mounted on the firebox and the small spectacle plate, features that would also have been evident on the 0-4-2s. This engine is either No 14 or No 15.

Real Photographs 88000

Right: This photograph at Dundalk in 1902 shows No 11, one of the 1858 pair of Beyer 0-4-2s. This engine had been rebuilt at Dublin in 1879, with a new boiler to the original design. The cab is merely an addition to the existing side sheets. Note how the locomotive has engine brakes as well as tender brakes, a modification probably added in 1897. No 11 was scrapped in January 1903, a few months after this picture was taken.

H Fayle, courtesy IRRS

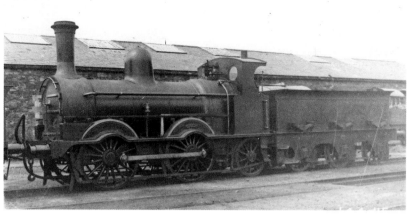

Below: Neilson 2-2-2ST No 8 of 1862. This locomotive was built for the Howth branch and had both side and saddle tanks.

LPC 2565

for earlier engines. The drawings show that the two designs had a lot of components in common, particularly the boilers and fireboxes. None of these locomotives carried names when built, but most were named in the 1870s (see page 21).

In Febuary 1861, William Dundas replaced Patrick Connor as Locomotive Superintendent but he only stayed until August 1863. Dundas continued the policy of buying Beyer products, adding two more of the 6'0" singles – Nos 13 (1860) and 16 (1861) – and two more of the 0-4-2s – Nos 10 (1862) and 21 (1863). These probably had their domes on the boilers, as in Fig 6. Like most early Beyer Peacock engines, these two classes gave sterling service and were all rebuilt, some twice, the 2-2-2s lasting until 1896-1901 and the goods engines until 1903-15. Readers will be interested in the fact that 0-4-2 No 20, as GNR No 9, was the locomotive struck by the runaway train at Armagh in 1889. Although thrown off the track by the impact, it survived and, when withdrawn in 1915, was the last surviving Dublin and Drogheda locomotive. The Beyer 2-2-2s (as the GNR N class) were the first GNR express type. Indeed, No 16 was specially renewed in 1880 for the inauguration of the accelerated Limited Mail. This train was used to carry the English mails forward from Dublin to Belfast, after they had arrived by ship. It was limited to first and second class carriages.

Two other classes were introduced by Dundas. Neilson 2-2-2ST No 8 of 1862 was a one-off and cost £1547. It was built for the Howth branch, sharing this duty with old Sharp

2-2-2WT No 3 of 1844. It had 5'0" driving wheels, 12"x 18" cylinders, a small 3'4¼" diameter boiler of 730 sq ft heating surface, and weighed 21 tons 16 cwt. As can be seen from the photograph opposite, it had both side and saddle tanks and an all over roof, but no side sheets to the cab. In later years, side sheets were fitted but the rear protection was removed. Twin spring balance safety valves were fitted to the dome. No 8 was scrapped some time between 1885 and 1887.

Two more double-framed Sharp 2-2-2s, Nos 2 and 22, came in December 1863. These were the last of the traditional Sharp 2-2-2s to be built for Ireland and had the usual 5'6" driving wheels and 15"x 20" cylinders. They were also the last brand new 2-2-2s to be built for any of the constituent GNR companies. For some reason, No 22 was soon fitted with 6'0" driving wheels, probably after breaking a crank axle in 1865. Apart from this, neither was rebuilt. In 1877, No 2 was renumbered 23 by the GNR as part of a minor tidy up of numbers. No 22 was scrapped in 1888 and No 23 in 1894.

The Curry years 1863-75

In August 1863 William Curry was appointed Locomotive Superintendent of the Dublin and Drogheda Railway. Curry was a native of Carlisle and came to the D&DR from the Great Southern and Western Railway (GS&WR) at Inchicore on the other side of Dublin. At the beginning of 1864, there were twenty-two locomotives in stock, half of them built in the previous six years, so the fleet was in reasonable shape. Only two new engines were to be added in the remaining twelve years of the Dublin and Drogheda. William Curry concentrated on rebuilding the earlier locomotives at his Dublin Works, which were on the site of the present Connolly shed. It is possible that he re-equipped the Dublin Works, because virtually no rebuilding had been carried out by his predecessors, other than 0-4-2 No 1 in 1861. In contrast, the years 1866-75 saw nine engines rebuilt. Three engines were rebuilt before 1870 – 0-4-2 No 6 (1866), 2-2-2 No 9 as a 2-4-0 (1868) and 2-4-0 No 19

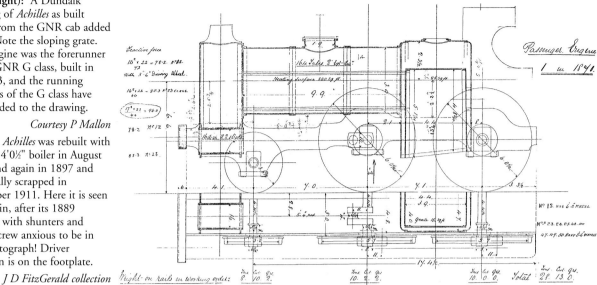

Fig 8 (right): A Dundalk drawing of *Achilles* as built (apart from the GNR cab added later). Note the sloping grate. This engine was the forerunner of the GNR G class, built in 1875-83, and the running numbers of the G class have been added to the drawing.

Courtesy P Mallon

Below: *Achilles* was rebuilt with a GNR 4'0½" boiler in August 1889 and again in 1897 and was finally scrapped in December 1911. Here it is seen at Dublin, after its 1889 rebuild, with shunters and engine crew anxious to be in the photograph! Driver Shannon is on the footplate.

J D FitzGerald collection

(1869). The two Sharp singles of 1854 were reboilered in 1870 (No 18) and 1871 (No 12).

There was no need for any new designs until 1871 when old Nos 5 (2-2-2) and 7 (0-4-2) were scrapped. Curry ordered two engines from Beyer Peacock which were to have a significant influence on early GNR locomotive design. Firstly, in November 1871, came No 12, a standard Beyer Peacock 2-4-0 which was to be the forerunner of the GNR G class 2-4-0s. It had main dimensions as follows: driving wheels 6'0½", cylinders 16"x 22", boiler 3'9"x 9'9", heating surface 945 sq ft, grate area 15 sq ft, tractive effort 7,978 lbs (assuming 120 lbs boiler pressure) and weight 28 tons 13 cwt. This engine was named *Achilles* shortly after delivery and had a slightly sloping grate, as can be seen from the diagram. The G class engines built from 1875 onwards were to the same design, but with 5'6" wheels. In a minor tidy up of numbers,

Grendon 2-2-2 No 17 now became No 7 and Sharp 2-2-2 No 12 (rebuilt that same month) became No 17, alongside sister No 18.

The second new engine was an 0-6-0 goods locomotive, No 5, which came in September 1872, and was shortly afterwards named *Hercules*. It was the first 0-6-0 on the D&DR, though 0-4-2 No 21 was rebuilt to this wheel arrangement in 1873. *Hercules* was built alongside the two new D&BJR 0-6-0s at Manchester, though to a different design. The main dimensions of *Hercules* were as follows: driving wheels 5'0", cylinders 17"x 24", boiler 3'9"x 10'3", heating surface 988 sq ft, grate area 15 sq ft, tractive effort 12,773lbs (assuming 130 lbs boiler pressure) and weight 29 tons 9 cwt. The boiler was identical to that of *Achilles* save for the six inches of extra length. *Hercules* was the forerunner of what became the standard GNR goods design up to 1891 (ie

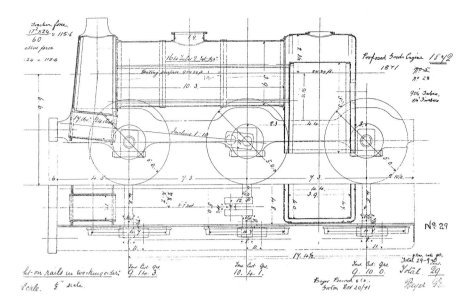

Fig 9 (left): The only new 0-6-0 built for the D&DR was No 5 *Hercules* in 1872. It had such typical 1870s features as a raised firebox and a sloping smokebox front. This design became the basis for the GNR A and B classes of standard goods engines until 1891, which had 4'7" wheels. No 5 was rebuilt with a standard A class boiler in 1889 and renumbered 29. It was placed on the duplicate list in 1895 and scrapped in July 1911.

Courtesy P Mallon

Left: No photograph of *Hercules* has come to light. This photograph was once thought to be No 5, but is, in fact, an official photograph of a locomotive to the same design built by Beyer Peacock in 1874 for the South African Railways.

C P Friel collection

Above: The D&DR acquired a second 0-6-0 in 1873 by altering Beyer 0-4-2 No 21 of 1863 to an 0-6-0, though it retained 16"x 22" cylinders. Note the modified running plate, as compared to the earlier picture of 0-4-2 No 11 (page 18). It was again rebuilt in 1887, this time with a 3'11" GNR boiler (as seen here), though it seems strange that a new boiler fitted at this late date should have a raised firebox. Perhaps it was a new barrel on a reconditioned firebox. The engine has a typical D&DR square edged cab roof. This view was taken some time after 1894, when it had become No 21A. Curiously, No 21 had been renumbered 32 in 1889, but it reverted to 21A (rather than becoming 32A) on the duplicate list in 1894! The engine was scrapped in 1908.

J D FitzGerald collection

GNR Classes A and B) and, indeed, was rebuilt with a standard A class boiler in 1889. Its wheel base was 7'3"+ 7'3", and it had the same 'chassis' as the standard engines. It differed from the later engines only in details, chiefly the larger wheel diameter (standard engines were 4'7"). *Hercules* and *Achilles* lasted until 1911.

Around 1870, the D&DR resumed the policy of naming engines. Since the names were mostly removed again after a few years, there is patchy evidence on this subject. However, the two remaining Sharp 0-4-2s, Nos 1 and 6 became *Nestor* and probably *Samson*; 2-4-0 No 9 became *Saturn*; the last surviving Grendon 2-2-2, No 7, became *Venus* (though possibly not until rebuilding in 1873). The 1854 Sharps, Nos 17 and 18, became *Apollo* and, probably, *Diana*. Fairbairn 2-4-0 No 19 became *Pluto*. Grendon 2-4-0 No 4 was *Drogheda*. The newer engines received names for the first time. Of the Beyer Peacock singles, No 13 was *Ulysses*, No 15 *Aurora* and another was *Jupiter*. The Beyer goods engines are thought to have been 10 *Mercury*, 11 *Ajax* and 20 *Vulcan*. It is not known whether 0-6-0 No 21 was named. The Sharp 2-2-2s of 1863, Nos 2 and 22, were possibly *Mars* and *Neptune*. There is no evidence that the Neilson 2-2-2ST was named. It is highly unlikely that the name *Uranus* would have been passed over when the other seven planets were used, so this may have been the name of the fourth Beyer single.

In conclusion, I should mention that, in 1874, Curry commenced modernising his Beyer 'express' 2-2-2s. This involved closing in the open splashers, fitting new boilers (to the original design, but with the dome on the centre ring) and fitting cabs. The first to be dealt with was No 14, which received a new boiler in March 1874. The others followed in early GNR days. Old Grendon 2-4-0, No 4 *Drogheda*, was reboilered in March 1875, in the first month of the new Northern Railway (see Chapter 5). All in all, thirty-four locomotives were built for the Dublin and Drogheda Railway. At the amalgamation there were twenty-two locomotives in the fleet, comprising nine 2-2-2s, two 2-2-2Ts, four 2-4-0s, five 0-4-2s and two 0-6-0s. On average the D&DR fleet was somewhat old by 1875, with only two engines under ten years old. This accounts for the comparatively early disappearance of most D&DR types, but as against that, the fact that William Curry became the first Locomotive Superintendent of the new GNR, meant that the D&DR had a direct influence on early GNR locomotive design.

Above: Ex-D&DR N class 2-2-2 No 13 around 1895. This locomotive started life in 1860 as one of the four Beyer 2-2-2s illustrated on page 17. It was rebuilt with a new boiler and a square-roofed cab in March 1876. This was later replaced with the Stirling style cab seen here, possibly in 1892 when it received 15½" cylinders. It was scrapped in 1896. Note the brake blocks fitted to the driving and trailing wheels on rebuilding and the large sand box on the splasher. These engines were the principal GNR express type until 1885.

LPC 5114

Dublin and Drogheda Railway – first generation locomotives

No	Name	Date	Works No	Type	DW	Cyls	Rebuilt	GNR Class	Remarks	Withdrawn
1	*Nor Creina*	11/1843	SB 239	0-4-2	5'0"	15"x 20"	10/1861	P	later *Nestor*	8/1892
2	*St Patrick*	11/1843	SB 235	2-2-2	5'0"	15"x 18"	–	–	–	1863-64
3	*Fag-an-Bealach*	5/1844	SB 254	2-2-2	5'6"	14"x 18"	1846 (2-2-2WT)	–	–	1875
4	*Albert*	5/1844	SB 255	2-2-2	5'6"	14"x 18"	1846 (2-2-2WT)	–	–	1856
5	*Victoria*	5/1844	SB 256	2-2-2	5'6"	14"x 18"	–	–	–	1871
6	*Dublin*	6/1844	SB 258	0-4-2	5'0"	15"x 20"	7/1866	P	later *Samson*?	10/1892
7	*Princess*	6/1844	SB 259	0-4-2	5'0"	15"x 20"	–	–	–	1871
8	*Alice*	11/1844	SB 272	2-2-2	5'6"	14"x 18"	–	–	–	1862
9	*Alfred*	11/1844	SB 273	2-2-2	5'6"	14"x 18"	4/1868 (2-4-0)	U?	later *Saturn*	1885
10	*Queen*	12/1844	SB 277	2-2-2	5'6"	14"x 18"	12/1848 (2-4-0)	–	Bodmer's expansion	1862
11	*Prince*	12/1844	SB 278	0-4-2	5'0"	15"x 20"	–	–	–	1857
12	*Firefly*	4/1844	Butterley	2-2-2	?	?	–	–	built c1841	1853
13	*MacNeill*	1/1845	Grendon	2-2-2	5'6"	14"x 18"	–	–	–	1860
14	–	5/1845	Grendon	2-2-2	5'6"	14"x 18"	–	–	–	1859
15	*Hibernia*	5/1845	Grendon	2-2-2	5'6"	14"x 18"	–	–	–	1859
16	–	5/1847	Grendon	2-2-2WT	5'6"	14"x 18"	–	–	–	1861
17	*Drogheda*	5/1847	Grendon	2-2-2	5'6"	14"x 18"	3/1873	T	Ren 7 *Venus* (1871)	1891

(**Heavy type** indicates locomotives which passed to the GNR)

Dublin and Drogheda Railway – locomotives built 1854-72

No	Name (1870)	Date	Works No	Type	DW	Cyls	Rebuilt (DDR)	Class (GN)	Rebuilt (GNR)	Withdrawn
2	*Mars?*	12/1863	SS 1473	2-2-2	5'6"	15"x 20"	1865 (6'0"dw)	Q	–	9/1894
4	*Drogheda*	1856	Grendon	2-4-0	5'6"	15"x 20"	3/1875	?	–	1888
5	*Hercules*	9/1872	BP 1161	0-6-0	5'0"	17"x 24"	–	A	3/1889	7/1911
8	–	9/1862	Neilson 855	2-2-2ST	5'0"	12"x 18"	–	?	–	1885-87
10	*Mercury?*	5/1862	BP 257	0-4-2	5'0"	16"x 22"	–	G	7/1884	7/1905
11	*Ajax?*	1/1858	BP 75	0-4-2	5'0"	16"x 22"	–	G	1879, 1897	1/1903
12	*Apollo*	1854	SS 809	2-2-2	5'6"	15"x 20"	11/1871 (ren 17)	U	–	1886
12	*Achilles*	11/1871	BP 1042	2-4-0	6'0½"	16"x 22"	–	G	8/1889, 1897	12/1911
13	*Ulysses*	10/1860	BP 185	2-2-2	6'0"	15"x 20"	–	N	3/1876, 8/1892	5/1896
14	?	1/1859	BP 105	2-2-2	6'0"	15"x 20"	3/1874	N	1/1885	5/1896
15	*Aurora*	1/1859	BP 106	2-2-2	6'0"	15"x 20"	–	N	1880	2/1901
16	?	2/1861	BP 195	2-2-2	6'0"	15"x 20"	–	N	1877, 11/1887	11/1898
18	*Diana*	1854	SS 810	2-2-2	5'6"	15"x 20"	9/1870	U	–	1886
19	*Pluto*	1855	Fairbairn	2-4-0	5'0"	?	10/1869	?	–	1887
20	*Vulcan*	2/1858	BP 76	0-4-2	5'0"	16"x 22"	–	G	1880, 4/1900	6/1915
21	–	12/1863	BP 430	0-4-2	5'0"	16"x 22"	1873 (0-6-0)	G	2/1887	6/1908
22	*Neptune?*	12/1863	SS 1484	2-2-2	5'6"	15"x 20"	–	Q	–	1888

Chapter 2
The Dublin and Belfast Junction Railway

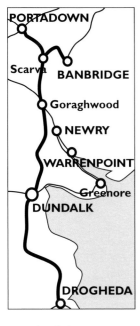

The Dublin and Belfast Junction Railway was the smallest of the four constituents of the GNR, with 62 route miles and only 22 locomotives in its fleet. The purpose of the company, as suggested by its title, was to complete the Belfast-Dublin route by linking the D&DR at Drogheda with the Ulster Railway at Portadown. The D&BJR was incorporated on 21 July 1846 and the Drogheda to Dundalk section was opened on 15 Febuary 1849. In Drogheda the line terminated at Newfoundwell on the northern bank of the Boyne river. Until 1855, passengers from the D&DR had to make their own way over the river.

On 31 July 1850 a further 10½ miles, to a temporary terminus at Wellington Inn, was opened. Construction from the Portadown end reached Mullaghglass, near Newry, on 6 January 1852 and was completed through to Wellington Inn on 10 June 1852. However, there was not yet a through connection to Dublin, as the River Boyne in Drogheda still had to be bridged. The river had quite steep banks and, since Drogheda was a port, had to be crossed at a height of over 100 feet. The construction of this viaduct took until 5 April 1855.

Originally the Drogheda to Navan line was to have been built by the D&BJR but, as it commenced on the southern side of the river, the delay in building the huge viaduct across the River Boyne led to the transfer of this route (opened 1850) to the Dublin and Drogheda Railway. The D&BJR had only one branch line, which opened on 25 March 1859. This ran from Scarva, on the main line, to Banbridge, a sizable town some 6¾ miles to the east. This was built by a nominally separate company, the impressively named Banbridge, Newry, Dublin and Belfast Junction Railway. Apart from the Banbridge branch, the entire route of the D&BJR is still open and forms part of the Belfast-Dublin main line jointly operated by NIR and Iarnrod Éireann.

The locomotive history of the D&BJR was also the most straight forward of the four constituent companies. Unlike the D&DR, the D&BJR locomotives never carried names. A total of twenty-two locomotives were built, all to the standard designs of Sharp Stewart and Beyer Peacock. Two were scrapped in 1873 and a third by the short-lived Northern

Railway in 1875 (see Chapter 5), leaving nineteen to transfer to the GNR.

In an initial rush of enthusiasm, the D&BJR Directors placed an order with Sharp Brothers, in December 1845, for no fewer than sixteen of their standard 5'6" 2-2-2 locomotives, and a month later for six 0-4-2 goods locomotives. For the latter, 4'10" driving wheels were specified. This unusual diameter was recommended by the contractor, Sir John MacNeill, who had ordered engines from Bury with this diameter of driving wheel. Sharps were not happy, pointing out that their standard sizes were 4'6" and 5'6". Within six months the Directors faced up to the over ambitious nature of their order and reduced it to twelve engines (eight 2-2-2s and four 0-4-2s). The slow pace of construction of the line meant that even these were not required for some time and it was to be June 1848 before the first pair were delivered. In February 1848 the company had tried to cancel eight of the remaining ten and the exasperation of Sharp Brothers was barely disguised. They wrote:

We really cannot consent to cancel the remainder of your order. In May 1846, we cancelled 10 engines out of 22, we cannot now cancel the remaining eight, but we are quite willing to suspend delivery ...

In the event, delivery of the twelve engines was stretched out until 1854!

From the opening in February 1849 until June 1852, the line was operated by the main contractor, William Dargan, using the D&BJR's locomotives and his own. Dargan also operated two other local railways at this time – The Dundalk and Enniskillen (Chapter 3) and the Newry, Warrenpoint and Rostrevor (Chapter 6).

The first four locomotives, Nos 1-4, delivered in 1848, were standard Sharp 2-2-2s, a well-known type used also on the Ulster Railway. They had 5'6" driving wheels, 15"x 20" cylinders and were double framed (Fig 10). However, I would say that coupled engines, rather than light singles, would have been better suited to the D&BJR's line, since there were long banks between Dundalk and Newry in the region of 1:100 to 1:120. This problem did not become evident until after 1852, when this steep stretch was opened. The remaining four singles (Nos 5-8) were delivered in December 1852. These were again to Sharp's standard design but it seems unlikely that they were built with the 90 lb boilers of the 1848 engines and it is more likely that they were to the modernised design built for the D&DR and D&ER from 1854 onwards with 120 lbs boilers (Fig 4, page 16). We cannot be sure; they may even have been an intermediate version.

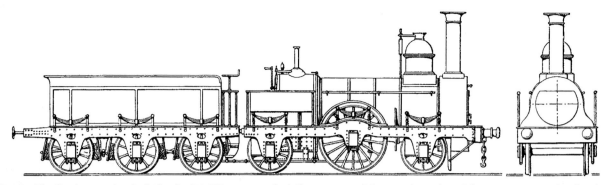

Fig 10: The first locomotives built for the D&BJR were standard Sharp 2-2-2s of the type shown here. These engines were fitted with smokebox wingplates. Nos 1-4 were built to this design in 1848 but Nos 5-8 of 1852 may have been to the modified design with 120 lb boilers introduced by Sharp from 1852. Certainly No 13, built in 1854 was to the new design. *Author's collection*

After the Dargan contract ended, the company resumed control of locomotives. From November 1852, R Ogilvie was in charge. He resigned in April 1853, discouraged by the lack of equipment. His replacement, Thomas Harden, had worked as Dargan's agent during the 1849-52 haulage contract and was familiar with the line.

The four 0-4-2s had still to be delivered, but in the event these were built to two designs and neither had MacNeill's 4'10" driving wheels! The first to come, in October 1853, was No 9, a fairly powerful machine, with 4'6" driving wheels, 16"x 24" cylinders and a boiler 4'0"x 11'0", giving a heating surface of 1178 sq ft and a weight of 26 tons, 7 cwt. It was identical to the UR engines built in 1857-61 (see Fig 27, page 40).

By now the D&BJR was frantic for new engines and the next three were urgently demanded from Sharp Stewart, a complete reversal of the position in 1848! Nos 10-12 came in April 1854, but were classed as 'luggage engines' and were smaller machines than No 9. They had main dimensions as follows: driving wheels 5'0", cylinders 16"x 22", boiler 3'10"x 10'2", heating surface 988 sq ft and weight 24 tons, with a tractive effort of 9,574 lbs, compared to the 11,605 lbs of No 9. These lighter 0-4-2s were eventually to be the first GNR S class, and they completed the Sharp Stewart order originally placed in 1846!

By 1854, the steep banks between Dundalk and Newry were taking their toll on the earlier 2-2-2 locomotives. Boiler tubes, cylinders and even driving wheels were in need of replacement. At this stage there were no proper workshops and little equipment for heavy overhauls. Harden bought new maintenance equipment, like a lathe, and new Works buildings were constructed in the mid-1850s. These were situated on the site of the later GNR Works and were demolished in 1880.

Some new engines were added to stock in the next few years. Surprisingly, in May 1854 another Sharp 2-2-2 (No 13) arrived. This one was definitely of the same type as the

"THE ENGINEER"   SWAIN SC

Fig 11: Sharp built six 0-4-2 goods locomotives for the D&BJR, both to standard Sharp designs. Nos 9 and 14 were the heavier (Fig 27, page 40) but Nos 10-12 and 15 were built to Sharp's lighter design, seen above. These had 5'0" driving wheels and 16"x 22" cylinders and were described as 'luggage engines'. Similar locomotives were built for the D&ER in 1858. The UR locomotives of 1866 (page 43) were a development of this design. *The Engineer*

D&DR and D&ER machines (GNR U class) and had been constructed alongside the latter. In May 1857, No 14, another heavy 0-4-2 was delivered and, in September, No 15, another of the 'luggage engines'.

For the opening of the Scarva-Banbridge branch, tank engines were required. Initially, Harden entered into negotiations with Grendons of Drogheda for these, but Grendons were unwilling to accept a penalty of £10 per day for late delivery. Grendons offered the loan of a tank engine they had in stock, in the event of late delivery. However, the order went to Sharp Stewart, who delivered two light 2-2-2WTs (Nos 16 and 17) in October 1858, later becoming the GNR R class. They had 5'0" driving wheels, 12"x 18" cylinders, a heating surface of 670 sq ft and weighed 23 tons 7 cwt.

Seventeen engines sufficed for D&BJR needs until 1866, though I suspect that, with no coupled passenger engines, there must have been a lot of double-heading between Dundalk and Goraghwood, from which the N&AR provided a connection into Newry town after 1854. The Belfast and Ballymena Railway, which had a similar gradient to the D&BJR, moved over to 2-4-0s and 0-6-0s in the 1850s.

Above: Until 1858, the D&BJR relied entirely on Sharp Stewart designs but, in 1866, Beyer Peacock designed and built two magnificent 2-4-0 express engines for the Limited Mails between Drogheda and Portadown. No 18 (seen here), and sister No 19, had 6'0" driving wheels and 16"x 22" cylinders, with 4'0"x 10'7" boilers. These engines were of quite modern appearance for 1866, with flush topped fireboxes and a centrally placed dome. However, they were cabless and had open splashers. Note the sandbox placed below the running plate. A third member of the class (No 20) was added in 1868, the trio becoming GNR Nos 37-39 and, in 1898, Nos 44-46. They were withdrawn in 1911-20.

F Moore library

Left: This view shows No 20 running as GNR No 46 in the early 1900s. No 46 was rebuilt in 1885 and scrapped in 1911. This view is shortly after 1900 and shows the attractive GNR green livery of that period with the company crest on the splasher. Note the main changes since 1866 – solid splashers, cab, Ramsbottom valves, and GNR chimney. As rebuilt, these engines were identical to the H class.

H Fayle, courtesy IRRS

Whatever might be said about the suitability of D&BJR locomotives, there was at least a degree of standardisation, compared to the neighbouring D&DR or D&ER.

In March 1866, the D&BJR entered a rather different league when it took delivery of its first engines from Beyer Peacock. These were 2-4-0 express locomotives, designed by Beyer Peacock, and intended to haul the Limited Mail trains. Nos 18 and 19 had 6'0" driving wheels, 16"x 22" cylinders, boilers 4'0"x 10'7", a heating surface of 1068 sq ft and a tractive effort of 7,978 lbs. They weighed 32 tons 10 cwt. As built, they had a dome on the middle ring of the boiler, open splashers and only a spectacle plate to protect the crew.

Compared to the contemporary UR and D&DR 2-4-0s, they were quite large machines, with a 4'4" long firebox and a good steaming capacity. They were also rather modern-looking with flush-topped fireboxes. A third one (No 20) was

added in July 1868. The design was so successful that it was perpetuated, in slightly modernised form, by the GNR in 1880-81 with Nos 84-87 (the H class). Shortly afterwards, the D&BJR engines (by then GNR Nos 37-39) were rebuilt to conform.

There was surprisingly little rebuilding of the earlier Sharp engines, a reflection of the poorly equipped D&BJR workshops. 2-2-2 No 5 got a new boiler in 1870, but the engine only lasted until 1879 as its frames were poor. In December 1872, No 1 received a more drastic rebuild, emerging as a 2-4-0 with thirteen more years of useful life. This engine also got a new boiler. Two of the 0-4-2s were also rebuilt with new Sharp Stewart boilers, these being Nos 12 (1873) and 11 (1874). More rebuilding followed in GNR days and eventually all the 0-4-2s except No 15 were rebuilt.

The best known, and longest lived, of the D&BJR engines

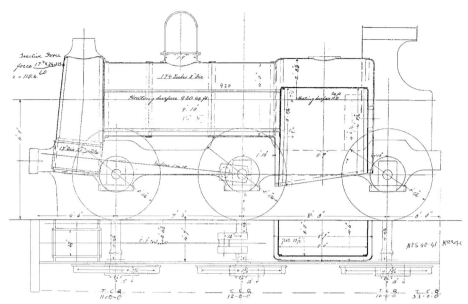

Fig 12 (left): The last locomotives built for the D&BJR were 0-6-0 Nos 21 and 22, built in 1872 by Beyer Peacock. Despite the fact that Beyers were building an 0-6-0 with 17"x 24" cylinders for the D&DR, the D&BJR pair were to a different design. Nos 21 and 22 were a modification of the 1867 Beyer design for the Great Southern and Western Railway (the famous '101' class). Nos 21 and 22 had the unusual wheel diameter of 5'1½", with a long rear wheelbase to accommodate a 5'7" firebox. They became GNR Nos 40 and 41 in 1876.

Courtesy P Mallon

Fig 13 (below): D Class 0-6-0 No 41, as rebuilt in 1888 with a 3'11½"x 10'3" A class boiler. Oddly, No 40 was rebuilt in 1889 with a longer 11'0" boiler of the same diameter. The firebox on both was only 4'4" long, 1'3" shorter than the original design.

Courtesy P Mallon

were Nos 21 and 22, the two 0-6-0s built by Beyer Peacock in July 1872, which lasted until 1937 and 1934 respectively and were later known as the GNR D class. As mentioned in the previous chapter, they were built alongside D&DR No 5 *Hercules*, but to a different design. They had 5'1½" driving wheels, 17"x 24" cylinders, and a 4'0" x 9'10" boiler, with a large 5'7" firebox that had a sloping grate. This made for a free-streaming engine with 1030 sq ft heating surface and a 19.6 sq ft grate. The wheelbase was 7'3"+ 8'3" compared to the 7'3"+ 7'3" of *Hercules*.

The genesis of the design goes back to locomotives built by Beyer Peacock in 1867 for the Great Southern and Western Railway. These were the first of the famous '101 class' of the GS&WR, of which two examples (Nos 184 and 186) survive in preservation. This became Ireland's most numerous steam locomotive class. No fewer than 119 were built for the GS&WR, mostly at Inchicore Works, Dublin, though these did not have a sloping grate.

The last Locomotive Engineer of the Dublin and Belfast Junction Railway was Thomas Armitage, who replaced Harden in 1872. He left in 1875, when the Northern Railway was formed, to take up the same post on the Waterford and Limerick Railway.

By the mid-1870s, the D&BJR had rather a mixed bag of locomotives, the worst being the eight remaining Sharp singles, which were very well-worn. Indeed, Nos 7 & 8 were scrapped in 1873, effectively meaning that the new 0-6-0s had replaced them. No 6 was scrapped in 1875 without being allocated a Northern Railway number. The others did not last long into GNR days; Nos 2 and 4 were scrapped in 1876; No 3 went in 1877 and the last two, Nos 5 and 13, in 1879. As the smallest of the pre-amalgamation companies, the D&BJR had the smallest locomotive fleet, but it did contribute one notable design – the H class 2-4-0.

Left: Nos 40 and 41 became the GNR D class. Rebuilding in 1888-89, and again in 1913-15, removed any resemblance they originally bore to the GS&WR '101' class. Here, No 40 is seen at Knockmore Junction with a train from Antrim, probably just after its 1913 rebuild, when it received an AL class boiler. In this form it survived until 1937, the last D&BJR engine in service.
Maj Gen Sir Cecil Smith

Dublin and Belfast Junction Railway locomotives

No	Date	Works No	Type	DW	Cyls	Rebuilt	GNR No	Class	Remarks	Withdrawn
1	6/1848	SB 529	2-2-2	5'6"	15"x 20"	12/1872 (2-4-0)	30	?	-	1885
2	6/1848	SB 530	2-2-2	5'6"	15"x 20"	-	(23)	-	-	1876
3	9/1848	SB 534	2-2-2	5'6"	15"x 20"	-	24	-	-	1877
4	9/1848	SB 535	2-2-2	5'6"	15"x 20"	-	25	-	-	1879
5	12/1852	SS 707	2-2-2	5'6"	15"x 20"	1870	26	-	-	1879
6	12/1852	SS 708	2-2-2	5'6"	15"x 20"	-	-	-	-	1875
7	12/1852	SS 709	2-2-2	5'6"	15"x 20"	-	-	-	-	1873
8	12/1852	SS 711	2-2-2	5'6"	15"x 20"	-	-	-	-	1873
9	10/1853	SS 738	0-4-2	4'6"	16"x 24"	6/1876	35	B	ren 35A (6/1895)	5/1900
10	3/1854	SS 774	0-4-2	5'0"	16"x 22"	1877, 1889, 1898	31	S	ren 31A (1889)	6/1903
11	3/1854	SS 775	0-4-2	5'0"	16"x 22"	7/1874	32	S	-	1885-87
12	3/1854	SS 776	0-4-2	5'0"	16"x 22"	1873	33	S	-	6/1890
13	12/1852	SS 707	2-2-2	5'6"	15"x 20"	1870	27	-	-	1879
14	5/1857	SS 992	0-4-2	4'6"	16"x 24"	1879	36	B	-	5/1893
15	8/1857	SS 1006	0-4-2	5'0"	16"x 22"	-	34	S	-	1880
16	10/1858	SS 1081	2-2-2WT	5'0"	12"x 18"	-	28	R	-	1885-87
17	10/1858	SS 1082	2-2-2WT	5'0"	12"x 18"	-	29	R	ren 29A (1889)	1889
18	3/1866	BP 632	2-4-0	6'0"	16"x 22"	6/1888	37	H	ren 44 (1898), 44A (6/1911)	9/1914
19	3/1866	BP 633	2-4-0	6'0"	16"x 22"	12/1886	38	H	ren 45 (1898), 45A (6/1911), 201 (6/1915)	1920
20	7/1868	BP 835	2-4-0	6'0"	16"x 22"	12/1885	39	H	ren 46 *(1898), 46A (3/1910)	1911
21	7/1872	BP 1159	0-6-0	5'1½"	17"x 24"	6/1889, 1/1913	40	D	ren 40A (1913), 40 (1914)	1937
22	7/1872	BP 1160	0-6-0	5'1½"	17"x 24"	10/1888, 9/1915	41	D	ren 41A (1913), 41 (1914)	1934

* It is possible that this locomotive was briefly No 48 in 1898 before becoming No 46

The H class had J class cranks and H class cylinders.

Chapter 3
The Irish North Western Railway

The INWR, with 194 miles of route, was the largest constituent of the GNR measured by mileage but, in financial terms, the most impoverished. More by circumstances than design, it ended up operating a long main line of 121½ miles and five branches. The history of the company can be briefly outlined as follows.

It began life as the Dundalk and Enniskillen Railway, incorporated on 21 July 1845. From the beginning, it was closely associated with the D&BJR. It was incorporated on the same day and opened its Dundalk-Castleblaney section on 15 February 1849, the same day as the D&BJR opened from Drogheda to Dundalk. Both lines were also operated by the contractor William Dargan though, in the case of the D&ER, this arrangement lasted only to the end of 1850. The line was gradually extended towards Enniskillen, Ballybay being reached on 17 July 1854, Newbliss on 14 August 1855, Lisnaskea on 7 July 1858, Lisbellaw on 16 August and Enniskillen on 15 February 1859. This brought the D&ER into contact with the Londonderry and Enniskillen Railway which had reached the town five years earlier, having been opened in stages between April 1847 and August 1854. From 1 January 1860, the D&ER leased the L&ER, but, with one exception, the twelve L&ER locomotives were not taken into D&ER stock until 1862.

Although this acquisition was an ambitious step, the D&ER pressed on with other projects. A branch to Cootehill was opened on 18 October 1860 and, on 1 April 1862, the 15 mile line from Clones to Cavan opened. This was under

the auspices of the Clones and Cavan Extension Railway which, though worked by the D&ER, was partly financed by the UR, D&DR and D&BJR. With these extensions to its empire, the D&ER, by Act of Parliament on 7 July 1862, assumed the more appropriate title 'Irish North Western Railway'. The INWR had planned to build a branch to Belturbet, Co Cavan, but lack of money forced postponement of this plan. Another acquisition came in 1863, when the INWR undertook to operate the Finn Valley Railway from Strabane to Stranorlar, opened on 1 September. This line was destined to later become part of the narrow gauge County Donegal Railways. Finally, on 13 June 1866, the Enniskillen, Bundoran and Sligo Railway's 35½ mile branch to Bundoran was opened, again worked by the INWR. This brought the INWR up to its final mileage of 194 miles owned or operated. Sadly, today not a single mile of this once extensive system survives, the last fragment being the Barrack Street branch, Dundalk, which closed on 31 December 1995.

The INWR locomotive fleet was also the most diverse of any of the four constituents of the GNR and was acquired in a more piecemeal fashion than the others. By 1876, the fleet (37 engines at its maximum) included many obsolete and under-powered machines which, on other lines, would have been replaced much earlier. It included locomotives built by ten different manufacturers as well as three engines built by the INWR themselves at their Dundalk (Barrack Street) works. Maintenance of such a diverse and ageing fleet must have been a major headache. With little money to spend on engines and rolling stock, only four locomotives were ever replaced. The INWR had a succession of locomotive superintendents after the Dargan contract ended. These were:

R Bell	October 1850
John Blue	September 1852
R Needham	October 1852
Frederick Pemberton	December 1858
Thomas Haigh	February 1870
Charles Clifford	March 1871

The most significant of these was Charles Clifford, who remained for further 36 years on the GNR, becoming Locomotive Engineer from 1895 to 1912. He was responsible for some of the most graceful locomotive designs produced by the GNR, including the famous S class 4-4-0s, of which No 171 *Slieve Gullion* is a preserved example. INWR locomotives carried numbers only and a total of forty were bought or acquired. When the company joined the Northern Railway on 1 January 1876, it passed 34 locomotives on to the new concern, all of which entered GNR stock a few months later.

Dundalk and Enniskillen locomotives

To operate the D&ER, four locomotives were ordered from Thomas Grendon and Sons of Drogheda. Two, delivered in June 1848, were standard Grendon singles and were similar to Dublin and Drogheda Nos 13-17 (see Fig 3, page 15). They had 5'6" driving wheels and 14"x 18" cylinders. Both were used by Dargan as part of his haulage contract. The other two were 0-4-2 goods locomotives, delivered in April and July 1849, after the Dargan contract had commenced. These were the first goods engines to be built by Grendon and were seriously under-powered, because Grendon's idea of how to design a goods locomotive was simply to alter the wheel arrangement of a standard single! They thus had only 14"x 18" cylinders and small boilers. The driving wheels had the unusual diameter of 4'4". Dargan probably numbered these Grendon engines 5-8, to avoid confusion with D&BJR Nos 1-4.

When the Dargan contract ended in October 1850, both Grendon singles passed to the D&ER, becoming D&ER Nos 1 and 2. No 2 was withdrawn in 1874, but No 1 was rebuilt by the GNR in 1877 and lasted until 1886-87. Only one of the 0-4-2s was returned, becoming D&ER No 3. We do not know which of the pair this was. Dargan retained the other, as it was probably an ideal contractor's engine. No 3 was rebuilt in 1875 and lasted until 1885. It was probably used for little more than shunting.

After resuming control from Dargan, the D&ER added a new standard Sharp single (No 4) to its fleet in December 1852. Two more (Nos 5 and 6) followed in May 1854, in time for the extension to Ballybay. These were somewhat more powerful machines than the Grendon singles and were identical to the engine illustrated in Fig 4 (page 16). These engines were scrapped in 1883-85 as members of the GNR U class.

The next four locomotives were for goods traffic. Two Grendon 0-6-0s were delivered in October 1855 (No 7) and April 1856 (No 8). These were the earliest six-coupled locomotives to operate on any of the GNR constituents and were of the 'long boiler' type. This meant that the heating surface was increased by lengthening the boiler barrel from the usual 10-11 feet to 13-14 feet. To accommodate this extra length, the firebox was placed behind the rear coupled axle. For this reason, the rear axle was moved closer to the centre axle than was normal, giving long-boiler engines an unbalanced appearance and a long rear overhang. Similar engines were built for the MGWR. These locomotives had main dimensions as follows: driving wheels 5'0", cylinders 16"x 24", heating surface 1090 square feet and weight 26 tons. No 7 lasted until about 1889, but No 8, as GNR No 50, was rebuilt in 1879 with a GNR boiler and 16½" cylinders. Renumbered 59 (and later 59A), it survived until November 1903, the last Grendon locomotive to remain in traffic anywhere (Fig 15).

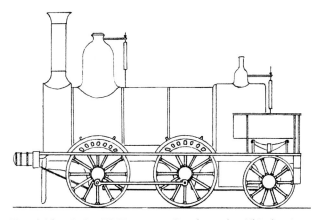

Fig 14 (above): D&ER No 3 was a Grendon 0-4-2. This drawing is probably conjectural but shows the main characteristics of these Grendon engines. No 3 was rebuilt at Dundalk in 1875. It became GNR No 45 and was withdrawn in 1885.

Courtesy IRRS

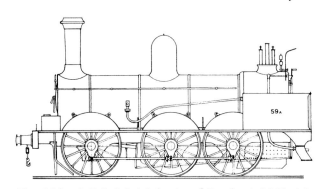

Fig 15 (above): P O Cuimin's drawing of Grendon 0-6-0 No 8 (as GNR No 59A) was, probably, based on the photograph below. Notice the fore-shortened nature of the wheel arrangement and the overhang of the firebox at the rear. Based on the drawing, the boiler barrel was 13 feet long and the wheelbase 6'10"+ 5'4". No 59A was the last Grendon engine to operate.

Courtesy IRRS

Below: Despite the poor quality of this photograph, its inclusion is justified as actual photos of 'long boiler' type locomotives are rare. No 59A was scrapped in December 1903. This picture shows that it remained cabless until the end.

J D FitzGerald collection

In April 1858, Sharp Stewart delivered two 0-4-2s, Nos 9 and 10. With 5'0" wheels and 16"x 22" cylinders, these were less powerful than the Grendon 0-6-0s. They were identical to D&BJR Nos 10-12 (Fig 11, page 24). Since both railways operated from Dundalk and had identical 0-4-2s numbered 10, there must have been some potential for confusion!

Top: This picture, at the old Belfast running shed, succeeds in capturing something of the atmosphere of the very early days of the GNR. It was found at the back of Adelaide Shed, Belfast when it was closed in 1966. It shows No 56 (ex-INWR 14), one of the three 5'6" 2-2-2s built by Beyer Peacock for the D&ER in 1859-61. This photograph, dates from before 1883, when the engine was rebuilt with a new boiler and a Stirling cab. It can be seen in its final condition below, after reverting to its original number in 1895.   *C P Friel collection*

Again, the 1885 clear-out of old INWR locomotives saw the demise of No 10, which had not run for several years, but No 9 had been rebuilt in 1880 and survived until 1895.

In March 1859, the D&ER took delivery of its first Beyer Peacock locomotive, 2-2-2 No 11. This was the first of three such engines, the other pair – Nos 13 and 14 – being delivered in August 1861. Unlike the Sharp engines, they had inside frames but had the usual 5'6" driving wheels and 15"x 20" cylinders. These were to be the only Beyer Peacock engines purchased by the company, but were a good investment. They became the GNR N class, in company with D&DR Nos 13-16, which were identical, save for 6'0" wheels. No 11 had a particularly interesting history. It was altered to a 2-4-0 in 1875 and, as GNR No 53, was rebuilt again in 1883. Finally, in 1889, it was completely renewed with a flush-topped boiler and 16"x 22" cylinders to become virtually a standard G class locomotive, in which form (as No 22 from 1895) it lasted until 1914 (Fig 16).

Above: The same engine, as N class 2-2-2 No 14, ex-Works at Dundalk in May 1897. It was scrapped in 1907. Sister No 13 was the last GNR single, when scrapped in 1910.
L J Watson

The other two remained as singles but were rebuilt twice, on the second occasion receiving 16" cylinders. After running for twenty years as GNR Nos 55 and 56, they reverted to their original D&ER numbers in 1895 and survived until 1907 (No 14) and 1910 (No 13). No 13 had the distinction of being not only the last GNR 'single', but the last tender 'single' in Ireland (GSR 2-2-2WT No 483 lasted until 1936).

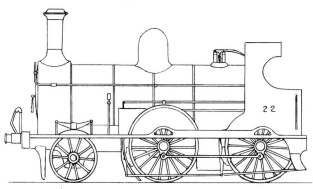

Fig 16 (above): No 22 started life as D&ER No 11, the first of the Beyer 2-2-2s illustrated opposite. It was altered to a 2-4-0 in 1875 and, in 1889, was completely renewed with 16"x 22" cylinders and a new boiler, to become virtually a standard G class locomotive. It had been successively GNR Nos 53 (1876), 54 (1892), 22 (1895) and 22A (1908) and was withdrawn in 1914.
Courtesy IRRS

Above: Four Neilson 0-4-2s were delivered in 1861 (15 & 16) and 1863 (28 & 29). This is a builder's photograph of one of the first pair, probably No 15. Note the rather crude sanding equipment between the driving wheels. Unusually for such an early design, the firebox is flush with the boiler. These engines became GNR Nos 57, 58, 70 and 71 and were rebuilt in 1881-83.

J D FitzGerald collection

Right and top right: In 1895, Nos 70, 71, 57 and 58, were renumbered 100-103 respectively. Here, No 102 is seen ex-Works at Dundalk on 14 September 1897. Note than the tender has not been repainted. This is probably the same locomotive as seen in the Works photo above.
L J Watson

Engine No 12 was a second-hand Longridge 2-4-0, purchased from the Londonderry and Enniskillen Railway in 1860 after the D&ER had taken a lease on the L&ER. As its history belongs more properly to the L&ER section, I will deal with it more fully in a moment.

In 1861, the D&ER ordered two 0-4-2 goods locomotives from the Glasgow firm of Neilson (later Neilson Reid). These engines were Nos 15 and 16 and had 5'3" driving wheels, 16"x 24" cylinders, a heating surface of 979 sq feet, and weighed 26 tons. They proved excellent engines and two more were ordered in 1863, after the L&ER engines had been absorbed. These were Nos 28 and 29, all four being rebuilt in the early 1880s and lasting over forty years. A further twelve engines to this basic design were built for the MGWR in 1863-64 but do not form part of this book. After some years as GNR Nos 57, 58, 70 and 71, the entire class was renumbered 100-103 in 1895. Meanwhile the remaining eleven locomotives of the L&ER had been taken into D&ER stock in 1862 and we must now describe them.

The Londonderry and Enniskillen Railway

The L&ER was leased by the D&ER from 1st January 1860 and, apart from No 2 (purchased by the D&ER), its locomotives were taken into stock in 1862, around the time that the D&ER became the Irish North Western Railway. The L&ER operated a 59½ mile main line between the two towns of its name and also the famous Fintona branch, ⅔ mile long, worked by horse traction. London financial interests lay behind both the L&ER and its neighbour, the Londonderry and Coleraine Railway, and some directors sat on both boards. The L&ER was incorporated in July 1845 and the line was opened in stages: to Strabane (19 April 1847), Newtownstewart (9 May 1852), Omagh (13 September 1852), Fintona (15 June 1853), Dromore Road (16 January 1854) and Enniskillem (19 August 1854).

The locomotives of the L&ER were quite different from anything else on the GNR and fell into two main types – long boiler tender engines and light 2-2-0WTs. The first locomotives were ordered from the firm of R B Longridge, based at Bedlington, Northumberland. Michael Longridge had been a partner in Robert Stephenson's Darlington Works, founded in 1823, but also had his own Bedlington Iron Works which supplied parts to Stephenson. In 1837, he began manufacturing locomotives himself, building mainly Stephenson long-boiler locomotives under patent license, but went out of business in 1852.

Six engines were ordered in 1845, three for the L&ER and three for the L&CR. They were all of the Stephenson 'long boiler' type, with flangeless driving wheels, 15"x 24" cylinders and a boiler centre line only 5'6" above the rails. However, no doubt for the sake of variety, each order consisted of three different locomotives! One was a 2-4-0 'goods' engine with 4'11" driving wheels, inside cylinders and a 3'7"x 13'1" boiler. Another was a 2-2-2 'passenger' engine with 6'1" driving wheels, outside cylinders and a 3'8"x 12'7½" boiler. Finally, one was a 2-4-0 'luggage' engine with 5'6" driving wheels, outside cylinders and a 3'8"x 13'7" boiler. These were almost certainly L&ER Nos 1-3 respectively. Compared to other contemporary locomotives,

these engines were quite powerful, with 90 lbs boilers and respective tractive efforts of 7,002 lbs (No 1), 5,659 lbs (No 2) and 6,259 lbs (No 3).

Whilst the L&ER was able to accept delivery of its three, the L&CR was much slower in construction and the first engine arrived five years before the line was completed! Although delivery was accepted, the other two were cancelled. The engine in question was of the 2-4-0 'goods' type and, after sitting at Derry for two years, the L&CR loaned it to the L&ER in 1848 with the understanding that, when their line opened, it would be returned. For a time, therefore, the L&ER operated *four* Longridge engines and when the time came to return the loaned engine in 1852, they gave the L&CR the 'luggage' engine, leaving the L&ER with two 'goods' engines, numbered 1 and 3, and one 'passenger' engine, numbered 2.

The Longridge engines were about the best of the L&ER's varied collection and had long, though complicated, careers. The 'single', No 2, was substantially rebuilt in 1854 as a 2-4-0 goods engine with inside cylinders and 4'9" driving wheels. It was the engine sold to the D&ER around 1860, becoming their No 12. It became GNR No 54, was rebuilt in 1878 with a GNR boiler and 15"x 22" cylinders, and withdrawn in 1890.

One of the 'goods' 2-4-0s, No 1, received 4'7" driving wheels, either in 1850 or in 1857. It was given a larger firebox to burn coal in 1856 and became INWR No 17. It got a new firebox in 1874, possibly at this time also getting a shorter boiler, with the firebox between the rear axles. It became GNR No 59 and was scrapped in 1879.

Its sister, No 3, became INWR No 18 and was also substantially rebuilt, ending up as a 2-2-2 with 5'6" driving wheels, 15"x 22" cylinders and a shorter boiler, with the firebox between the rear axles. It is not known for certain if all these alterations were at the same time, as work was done in 1869 (probably), 1871 and by the GNR in 1877, by which time it was No 60. Nos 54 and 60 were both listed as O class crank by the GNR. No 60 was scrapped in 1892.

The other type of locomotive that was characteristic of both the L&ER and the L&CR was the light 2-2-0WT, introduced because of the low level of passenger traffic on these lines. These were probably ordered on the recommendation of Robert Dods, Locomotive Superintendent of the L&ER from October 1848 to March 1854 (and of the L&CR from October 1852).

The first example of this type of engine on the L&ER was built by W Bridges Adams of Bow Works, London, who had a special interest in light railways. Adams believed in building engines no larger than the load required and using a high boiler pressure (120 lbs at a time when 90 lbs was normal) to reduce the size and weight of the boiler and firebox. His locomotive for the L&ER was No 4, delivered in June 1850. It had 5'0" driving wheels, 9"x 15" outside cylinders and weighed only 10 tons. It was semi-permanently coupled to a four-wheeled coach, which was a brake composite, with one passenger compartment, and a van which may have served as second class. This engine had a tractive effort of only 2,065

Fig 17: The Longridge locomotives were to Stephenson's designs. Although this example of a Stephenson long boiler locomotive was built for an English railway, it gives some idea of what L&ER No 2 might have looked like.

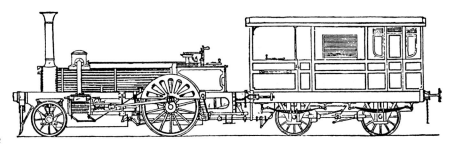

Fig 18: L&ER 2-2-0WT No 4, built by W Bridges Adams in 1850. As well as the brake van with one first class compartment, it probably hauled a four-wheeled third class coach. Note the outside steam pipe emerging directly from the dome, the wooden lagging on the boiler and the entirely exposed footplate. This locomotive became INWR No 19 and was scrapped in 1873.

Author's collection

lbs and was later to be contemptuously described by the railway writer E L Ahrons, as a 'steam perambulator'. It was loaned to the L&CR for trials and they later ordered six similar engines from Sharp Brothers (see Fig 34, page 55). No 4 became INWR No 19 and was scrapped in 1873.

Four similar locomotives, of a slightly enlarged type, were ordered to Adams patent from Longridge but, as Longridge went out of business at that time, they were constructed by Kitson, Thompson and Hewitson of Leeds (later Kitson and Co) in 1852. The intention was to use two on each Derry-based line, but they all came to the L&ER, as the L&CR was not open at the time of delivery. They were L&ER Nos 5-8 and were slightly larger than No 4, with 5'0½" driving wheels, 10"x 16" outside cylinders and 2,698 lbs tractive effort. Like No 4, they "couldn't pull you out of bed", as engine drivers in Ireland would say of a weak engine! They were known as the 'Gemini' class, but there is no evidence that they operated in pairs. All got new 5'2" wheels in 1855-56 and No 7 was converted to burn coal in 1858.

They became INWR Nos 20-23 after 1862. No 22 was withdrawn in 1871, but drove machinery at Dundalk Works for two years before being scrapped in 1873. Of the others, No 23 was scrapped in 1875 and the other two nominally became GNR Nos 62 and 63 in 1876. However, they were withdrawn within a year and probably never carried their new numbers. It is thought that these were the small engines that were used to power machinery in the cresote plant at Dundalk Works, until about 1882.

The third and final class of 2-2-0WTs were Nos 11 and 12, ordered from Adams, but built by Robert Stephenson and Co of Newcastle on Tyne, and delivered in September 1852. They probably ran initially on the L&CR, and came to the L&ER a few months later, which would account for them being numbered after 2-2-2 Nos 9 and 10, which arrived in October. Nos 11 and 12 had 5'2" driving wheels, 11"x 18" cylinders and a tractive effort of 3,583 lbs. They weighed 14 tons, as against 11 tons for the Kitson engines, and 10 tons for No 4. They became INWR Nos 24 and 25 and later GNR Nos 66 and 67. No 66 ended its days on the Cootehill branch and No 67 on the Finn Valley line. Both were scrapped in 1879.

All of these 2-2-0WTs were so light that they were prone to derailments. On 9 October 1857, one was thrown off the line near Derry, due to a collision with a wandering cow. In this incident the fireman was killed.

Four other locomotives remain to be briefly described. A very unwise purchase in October 1852, was a pair of second-

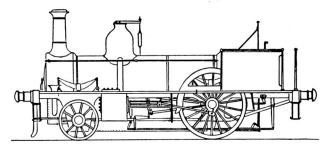

Fig 19: L&ER Nos 11 and 12 were Stephenson 2-2-0WTs of 1852. This design also had outside steam pipes, but does have a spectacle plate. The valve gear is clearly visible. Despite the drawing, the wheels did have flanges!

Courtesy IRRS

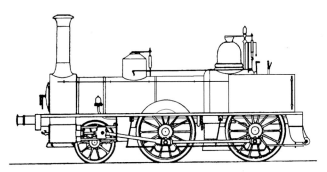

Fig 20: L&ER Nos 13 and 14 were 2-4-0 goods locomotives built by John Jones of Liverpool in 1855. This drawing is based on a Jones tank engine built for a South American Railway. Note that the cylinders were horizontal in contrast to the contemporary 'Crewe type' of the LNWR. *Author's collection*

hand ex-UR 2-2-2 locomotives, *Ajax* and *Achilles*, built in 1841. These were originally broad gauge engines (see Chapter 4, page 39). In 1849 the UR had sold them to the Belfast engineering firm of Coates and Young for £575 each. Here they were 'refurbished' and sold to the L&ER for £1013-10-0 each, a good rate of profit. However, they turned out to be in very poor shape and it is doubtful if they did any useful work. In 1857 the L&ER sold them for scrap at £75 each (a loss of £1952 in total for the L&ER). Since Nos 9 and 10 were never part of the INWR fleet, they are not listed in the table on page 37.

The final pair of engines turned out to be a better investment and lasted about 40 years. These were Nos 13 and 14, which were 2-4-0s with 4'7" driving wheels and horizontal 15"x 20" outside cylinders. They were built by John Jones of Liverpool, in 1855. Jones built a total of about fifty locomotives, but these were the only ones built for Ireland.

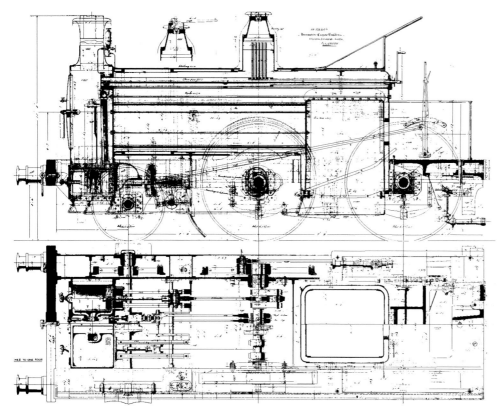

Fig 21 (left): This Dübs drawing of 2-4-0 Nos 32 and 33 of 1866 is interesting in showing that these were double-framed engines. However, the outside frames were shallow and carried bearings only for the leading wheels, the driving wheels having inside bearings. Dübs based the design on a batch of six locomotives built that same year for the North British Railway in Scotland – the '341' class.

Nos 32 and 33 had 6'0" driving wheels and 15" x 21" cylinders and became GNR Nos 74 and 75 of the L class. They were rebuilt in 1884-85, renumbered 124 and 125 in 1895, placed on the duplicate list in 1902 and withdrawn in 1906 and 1904 respectively.
National Railway Museum, York

Fig 22 (below): The external appearance of Nos 32 and 33, based on the Dübs drawing.
Courtesy IRRS

Known as the 'long backs', they became INWR Nos 26 and 27, later GNR Nos 68 and 69 (W class crank). They were reboiled in 1876 and 1879 and scrapped in 1894 and 1896 respectively, the last L&ER engines in service.

The motive power of the Fintona branch was in a category of its own in more ways than one. This line was worked by horse traction from 1854 until its closure in 1957, using an adapted railway carriage until 1883 and, after that, a specially constructed tram car. Early on, the custom of calling the horse 'Dick' developed. The motive power of this branch has sometimes been described as a one horse power hay-burner, of 0-(2-2)-0 'wheel arrangement'!

All in all, the L&ER possessed fourteen locomotives, which were built by no fewer than six manufacturers and, in the case of four of these manufacturers, were the only examples of their products on the GNR. The L&ER had their own workshops at Londonderry, which continued in use after the INWR takeover, but the heavy work was concentrated at Dundalk.

Irish North Western Railway locomotives

We now turn to locomotives acquired or built after the D&ER was renamed the INWR. After the construction of the second pair of Neilson 0-4-2s (Nos 28 and 29), no further engines were acquired until the opening of the Bundoran branch in 1866. Two Manning Wardle 0-6-0 saddle tanks had been used by Brassey and Field, the contractors of this line, and these were sold to the INWR in 1866, becoming Nos 30 and 31 These were among the earliest engines built by Manning Wardle, with Works numbers 4 (1859) and 18

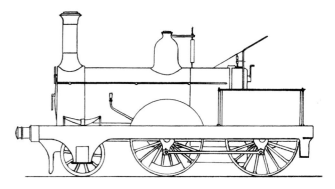

(1860). They carried the names *Rutland* and *Malvern* and had been used on the construction of the Worcester and Malvern Railway, before being regauged and shipped to Ireland in 1864. Unusually for Manning Wardle engines, they had inside cylinders (11"x 17"). They had 3'3" wheels, a heating surface of 392 sq feet and weighed 16½ tons. It would appear that, probably in late 1874, they were renumbered 19 and 22, as they became GNR Nos 61 and 64 in 1876 (V class crank). They were renumbered 91 and 92 in 1885, by which time they were confined to shunting at Dundalk and were scrapped in 1891.

Also in 1866, two 2-4-0 passenger engines were built by Dübs and Co, another well-known Glasgow firm. They were based on S W Johnson's design for the North British Railway and had 6'0" driving wheels, 15"x 21" cylinders, a 4'0"x 10'0" boiler and weighed 28 tons. They were numbered 32 and 33 in the INWR list, but possibly not until later, as they were initially paid for by the contractor Brassey. The 21" stroke was unusual, as most engines at this time were 20", 22" or 24". They were reputedly unpopular engines with crews as they

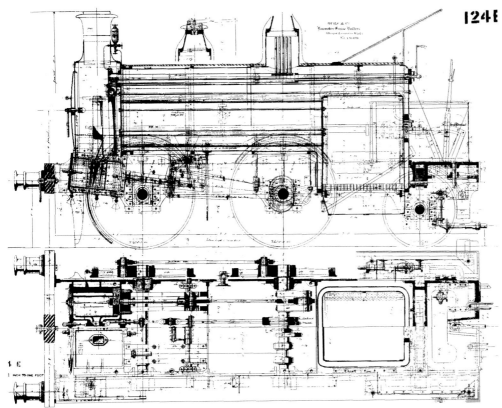

124E

Fig 23 (left): Another Dübs engine was 0-4-2 No 34 of 1867, which had 5'3" driving wheels and 16"x 24" cylinders. Apart from the ashpan, the boiler and firebox were identical to the 2-4-0s. This engine became GNR No 76. It was rebuilt in 1888 (with an A class crank and a K class boiler) and renumbered 44. In typical GNR fashion it was renumbered again in 1898 (to 78) and, after two spells on the duplicate list, was withdrawn in January 1909.
National Railway Museum, York

Fig 24 (below): In 1871-72 Dübs built two 0-6-0 goods locomotives for the INWR, Nos 35 and 36. A third was built at Dundalk in 1876, emerging as GNR No 44. (It would have been INWR 2.) This drawing shows the original appearance of these engines.
Courtesy IRRS

were bad steamers and the firebox was shallow. In the 1880s, as GNR Nos 74 and 75 of the L class, they were rebuilt with new boilers and 16" cylinders.

The following year, Dübs and Co supplied a goods 0-4-2, No 34, the engine again initially belonging to Brassey. No 34 had 5'3" driving wheels and 16"x 24" cylinders. It had the same design of boiler as the 2-4-0s and weighed 30 tons, making it a little heavier than the Neilson 0-4-2s. It later became GNR No 76 (E class crank) and was rebuilt in 1888 with standard parts, including an A class crank axle and a K class 10'3" boiler.

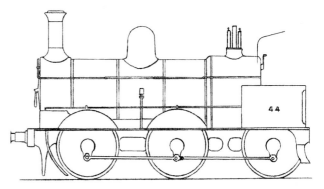

Dübs remained the preferred buyer for the next two engines as well. Nos 35 and 36, built in 1871-72, were 0-6-0 goods engines, based on Wheatley's standard goods engines for the NBR. They had 5'0" driving wheels, 17"x 24" cylinders, 4'0"x 10'1" boilers and 5'5" fireboxes, giving the rather large grate area of 16.5 sq feet. To accommodate the longer than usual firebox between the rear axles, the locomotives had a wheelbase of 7'2"+ 7'9". The heating surface was 1109 sq ft and they weighed 35 tons 11 cwt. These locomotives became GNR Nos 77 and 78 of the E class.

In March 1871, Charles Clifford became Locomotive Superintendent of the Irish North Western. He was keen to build locomotives at the company's Barrack Street works in Dundalk and, early in 1873, he

Above: This rather faded photograph, taken around 1910, is of the second of the Dübs 0-6-0s built for the INWR in 1871-72. These became GNR Nos 77 and 78 in 1876 and were the E class. They were renumbered 38 and 39 in 1898. No 39 was rebuilt as shown in 1892. It was renumbered 194 in 1913 and further rebuilt in 1915, lasting until 1948.
P Mallon collection

built a new 2-4-0 there. This engine were basically to the design of the 1866 Dübs engines, so it probably had the same type of frames. It had 5'6" wheels, 15"x 21" cylinders and weighed 30 tons. It was to have been No 5, but probably entered service as No 37. However, probably in late 1874, it was renumbered 31. As GNR No 73, it received new 16"x 21" cylinders in 1882 and was scrapped in 1892.

In July 1874, a second 2-4-0 was built at Dundalk. Numbered 22 at first, it was renumbered 30 later in the year and was slightly larger than No 31. It had 6'0" driving wheels, 16"x 21" cylinders, inside frames throughout and weighed 31 tons. It had narrow splashers which necessitated coupling rod splashers. This engine became GNR No 72 in 1876, all four 2-4-0s with 21" cranks being L class.

No 72 (No 43 from 1895) was given 16½"x 22" cylinders in 1898 and received a new flush-topped boiler in 1901. It

went on the duplicate list in 1911, but survived into the Glover era to become No 202 in 1914, and lasted until 1921, by which time it was shedded at Newry.

As explained in Chapter 5, a new 0-6-0, similar to Nos 35 and 36, was under construction at Dundalk when the INWR joined the Northern Railway on 1 Jan 1876. Work on this engine was halted for a time, but it emerged as GNR No 44 a few months later. It would have been INWR No 2. In 1888 it exchanged numbers with the Dübs 0-4-2, to become 76, so that the three E class locomotives were neatly 76-78. No 76 differed from the other pair in having a square-roofed cab in its early days, but eventually it received the standard 'Stirling' pattern. These three engines lasted until 1948 and were not only the longest lasting INWR engines, but the last pre-amalgamation engines on the GNR, though ex-UR No 138 also survived until 1948.

Above: This is the third member of the E class, completed early in 1876 as GNR No 44. In 1898, all three E class 0-6-0s had been renumbered 37-39. Unlike Nos 38 and 39 on the previous page, No 37 had a square cornered cab. In this view at Clones, we see No 37 as rebuilt in 1903. It is carrying the power classification letter 'D', fitted around 1908, but changed to 'E' in 1920.

J D FitzGerald collection

Irish North Western Railway locomotives

No	Date	Works No	Type	DW	Cyls	GNR No	GNR Class	Rebuilt	Remarks	Withdrawn
1	6/1848	Grendon	2-2-2	5'6"	14"x 18"	43	T	1877		1886-87
2	6/1848	Grendon	2-2-2	5'6"	14"x 18"	-	-	-		4/1874
(2)	1876	INR	0-6-0	5'0"	17"x 24"	44	E	11/1903	ren 76 (1888), 37 (1898) 37A (3/1913), 37 (10/1913)	6/1948
3	4/1849	Grendon	0-4-2	4'4"	14"x 18"	45	T	1875		1885?
4	12/1852	SS 706	2-2-2	5'6"	15"x 20"	46	U	-		1880-83
5	5/1854	SS 785	2-2-2	5'6"	15"x 20"	47	U	-		1880-83
6	5/1854	SS 786	2-2-2	5'6"	15"x 20"	48	U	3/1877		1885
7	10/1855	Grendon	0-6-0	5'0"	16"x 24"	49	?	1880	ren 49A? (1886)	3/1889?
8	4/1856	Grendon	0-6-0	5'0"	16"x 24"	50	?	1879	ren 59 (1885), 59A (1894)	12/1903
9	4/1858	SS 1052	0-4-2	5'0"	16"x 22"	51	S	1880	ren 51A (1892)	10/1895
10	4/1858	SS 1053	0-4-2	5'0"	16"x 22"	52	S	-		early 1885
11	3/1859	BP 107	2-2-2	5'6"	15"x 20"	53	N	1875 (2-4-0), 1883, 5/1889 (G)	ren 54 (1892), 22 (1895) ren 22A (10/1908)	1914
12	1846	Longridge	2-4-0	4'9"	15"x 24"	54	O	1878 (15"x 22")	Ex-L&ER No 2 (1860)	4/1890
13	8/1861	BP 223	2-2-2	5'6"	15"x 20"	55	N	1878, 2/1890	ren 13 (1895), 13A (1/1902)	1910
14	8/1861	BP 224	2-2-2	5'6"	15"x 20"	56	N	1883, 5/1892	ren 14 (1895), 14A (1902)	6/1907
15	10/1861	N 692	0-4-2	5'3"	16"x 24"	57	B	1882	ren 102 (1895), 102A (1901)	3/1907
16	10/1861	N 693	0-4-2	5'3"	16"x 24"	58	B	1883	ren 103 (1895), 103A (1901)	6/1902
17	11/1846	Longridge	2-4-0	4'7"	15"x 24"	59	O	1850? 1857? 1874	Ex-L&ER No 1 (1862) ren 79 (1877)	1879
18	1/1846	Longridge	2-4-0	4'11"	15"x 24"	60	O	1871? (2-2-2), 1877 (15"x 22")	Ex-L&ER No 3 (1862) ren 60A (1889)	3/1892
19	6/1850	Adams 8	2-2-0WT	5'0"	9"x 15" (O)	-	-	-	Ex-L&ER No 4 (1862)	1873
20	1/1852	KTH 288?	2-2-0WT	5'0½"	10"x 16" (O)	(62)	-	-	Ex-L&ER No 5 (1862)	1876
21	1/1852	KTH 289?	2-2-0WT	5'0½"	10"x 16" (O)	(63)	-	-	Ex-L&ER No 6 (1862)	1877
22	3/1852	KTH 290?	2-2-0WT	5'0½"	10"x 16" (O)	-	-	-	Ex-L&ER No 7 (1862)	6/1871
22	7/1874	INW	2-4-0	6'0"	16"x 21"	72	L	1898, 1/1901	ren 30 (1874), 43 (1895), 43A (6/1911), 202 (10/1914)	1921
23	3/1852	KTH 291?	2-2-0WT	5'0½"	10"x 16" (O)	-		-	Ex-L&ER No 8 (1862)	late 1875
24	9/1852	RS 818	2-2-0WT	5'2"	11"x 18" (O)	66	-	-	Ex-L&ER No 11 (1862)	1879
25	9/1852	RS 819	2-2-0WT	5'2"	11"x 18" (O)	67	-	-	Ex-L&ER No 12 (1862)	1879
26	9/1855	Jones	2-4-0	4'7"	15"x 20" (O)	68	W	1876	Ex-L&ER No 13 (1862) ren 68A (1892)	8/1894
27	10/1855	Jones	2-4-0	4'7"	15"x 20" (O)	69	W	1876	Ex-L&ER No 14 (1862) ren 69A (1892)	7/1896
28	6/1863	N 950	0-4-2	5'3"	16"x 24"	70	B	1881	ren 100 (1895), 100A (1900)	2/1901
29	6/1863	N 951	0-4-2	5'3"	16"x 24"	71	B	1883	ren 101 (1895), 101A (1900)	3/1904
30	1860?	MW 18?	0-6-0ST	3'3"	11"x 17"	64	V	-	Ex Brassey (4/1866), ren INW 22 (1874), ren 64A (1883), 92 (1885)	10/1891
31	1859?	MW 4?	0-6-0ST	3'3"	11"x 17"	61	V	-	Ex Brassey (4/1866), ren INW 19 (1874), ren 61A (1883), 91 (1885), 91A (1892)	early 1891?
32	11/1866	Dübs 122	2-4-0	6'0"	15"x 21"	74	L	1878, 1885	ren 124 (1895), 124A (1902)	3/1906
33	11/1866	Dübs 123	2-4-0	6'0"	15"x 21"	75	L	1873?, 1884	ren 125 (1895), 125A (1902)	6/1904
34	1867	Dübs 124	0-4-2	5'3"	16"x 24"	76	E	1888 (A crank)	ren 44 (1888), 78 (1898), 78A (1899), 78 (9/1906), 78A (3/1908)	1/1909
35	4/1871	Dübs 462	0-6-0	5'0"	17"x 24"	77	E	6/1894, 8/1915	ren 38 (1898), 38A (6/1911) ren 193 (10/1913)	6/1948
36	11/1872	Dübs 595	0-6-0	5'0"	17"x 24"	78	E	10/1892, 12/1915	ren 39 (1898), 39A (6/1911) ren 194 (10/1913)	6/1948
37	1873	INW	2-4-0	5'6"	15"x 21"	73	L	1882	ren INW 31 (1874), 73A (1892)	8/1892

Chapter 4
The Ulster Railway

The Ulster Railway was the second railway to open in Ireland and the oldest constituent of the GNR. It was incorporated on 19 May 1836 with powers to build a 36¼ mile line between Belfast and the cathedral city of Armagh. The first stretch opened was from Belfast (Great Victoria Street) to Lisburn on 12 August 1839. The line was subsequently extended to Lurgan (18 November 1841) and Portadown (12 September 1842). After this, the company was in no hurry to complete the line to Armagh and required a new Act of Parliament to complete the scheme. The Portadown-Armagh line opened on 1 March 1848.

By then a new complication had entered the situation. The Belfast-Portadown line was broad gauge, with the trains running on rails 6'2" apart. By 1844, when a number of new railways were under construction, opinion among engineers on railways in Britain (apart from Brunel on the Great Western) had moved away from broad gauges. Following a Board of Trade report on the situation in Ireland, Parliament decreed in 1846 that the gauge in Ireland would be 5'3". Whilst this only applied to new lines (like the extension to Armagh), the Ulster Railway did not want the inconvenience of two gauges and converted the Belfast-Portadown line to the new gauge in 1847-48.

Following the opening of the Belfast-Armagh line, the Ulster Railway subsequently extended to Monaghan on 25 May 1858 and to Clones on 2 March 1863. This provided a connection with the Irish North Western Railway which had reached Clones in 1858. The UR was also a financial backer of the Portadown, Dungannon and Omagh Railway, which it worked from the outset. This line opened to Dungannon on 5 April 1858 and to Omagh on 2 September 1861, making another connection with the INWR. The Ulster Railway also worked the Banbridge, Lisburn and Belfast Railway which opened a 15 mile line from Knockmore Junction to Banbridge on 13 July 1863. The final extension to the Ulster Railway empire came with the opening of the Dublin and Antrim Junction Railway's line from Knockmore Junction to Antrim on 13 November 1871. This was also operated by the UR and brought the route mileage worked by the UR up to 140 miles by the amalgamation. Today, 44 miles remain open.

Over a period of 37 years, the Ulster Railway owned 61 locomotives, 14 of which were built at the UR workshops in Belfast. The UR had the best equipped workshops of the constituent companies and was the most ambitious in the work it undertook. In 1876, it contributed 37 locomotives to the initial GNR fleet.

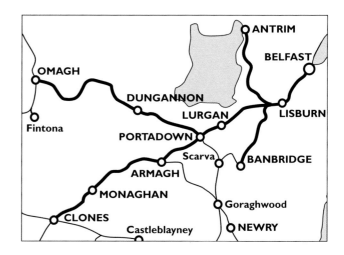

Broad gauge locomotives

The Ulster Railway was the only Irish line to use a broad gauge and owned nine 6'2" gauge locomotives, all of which carried names rather than numbers, as listed opposite. All were built by Sharp Roberts of Manchester, which had been founded in 1827, and had commenced locomotive manufacturing in 1833. The first two UR engines (Works Nos 48 and 49) were among the first locomotives to be built by this company. Like most early locomotives, the UR broad gauge engines had outside sandwich frames and inside cylinders.

The first three locomotives, *Express*, *Fury* and *Spitfire*, built in 1839, were the first 2-2-2s to be built for Ireland.

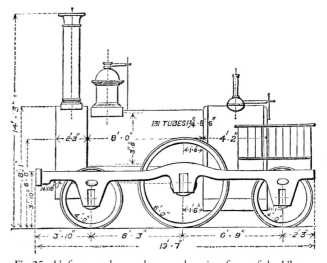

Fig 25: Unfortunately, no photographs exist of any of the Ulster Railway's broad gauge engines, but the first three 2-2-2 locomotives were very similar to GWR No 7 *Lion*, a broad gauge engine, built by Sharp Roberts in 1837. The main difference between *Lion* and the UR locomotives was that UR locomotives had a 6'0"+ 5'6" wheelbase. *Author's collection*

Name	Date	Works No	Type	DW	Cyls	Number (1848)	Wdn
Express	6/1839	48	2-2-2	6'0"	13"x 18"	1	1859
Fury	7/1839	49	2-2-2	6'0"	13"x 18"	2	1859
Spitfire	9/1839	57	2-2-2	6'0"	14"x 18"	-	To BNCR 1847
Etna	6/1841	130	2-2-2	5'6"	14"x 18"	3	1859
Firefly	6/1841	133	2-2-2	5'6"	14"x 18"	4	1859
Achilles	11/1841	155	2-2-2	5'6"	14"x 18"	-	sold 1849
Ajax	11/1841	156	2-2-2	5'6"	14"x 18"	-	sold 1849
Samson	9/1842	206	0-4-2	5'0"	14"x 20"	5	1872
Hercules	9/1842	207	0-4-2	5'0"	14"x 20"	6	1873

They had 6'0" driving wheels, 4'0" leading and trailing wheels, a 3'6"x 8'0" boiler working at 55 lbs pressure and a weight of 14 tons 11 cwt. *Express* and *Fury* had 13"x 18" cylinders and a tractive effort of 1,975 lbs, whilst *Spitfire* had 14"x 18" cylinders and a tractive effort of 2,290 lbs. They would have been capable of hauling a 50 ton train at 25 mph.

Four more 2-2-2s were built in 1841. *Etna*, *Firefly*, *Achilles*, and *Ajax*, were broadly similar to the 1839 batch but, significantly, the wheel diameter was reduced to 5'6", probably to improve traction, the new size becoming the standard for most future Irish singles. The boiler pressure was raised to 60 lbs. The first Dublin and Drogheda singles, described on pages 14-15, were similar in dimensions.

Samson and *Hercules*, built in 1842, were the first 0-4-2s in Ireland, though not the first four-coupled. That honour went to a contractor's locomotive, an 0-4-0 originally built in 1841, by Murdock and Aitken of Glasgow, for the 4'6" gauge Slamannan Railway in Scotland. This engine was used by the contractor Jeffs on the Dublin and Drogheda contract in 1841-44. The UR 0-4-2s had 5'0" driving wheels, 14"x 20" cylinders, a 3'8"x 8'0" boiler, working at 55 lbs, giving a tractive effort of 3,054 lbs. They weighed 14 tons 15 cwt.

All nine broad gauge engines were small and were already obsolete by the late 1840s, as train sizes increased. Six of them were regauged in 1847-48 to run on the 5'3" gauge. At some stage, probably at the time of regauging, they received new wider fireboxes. The original narrow boxes were designed for the 4'8½" gauge in Britain. None of them survived into GNR days. The 2-2-2s were already out of use by 1856 and were scrapped in 1859. The 0-4-2s lasted longer but, by 1867-68 were fit only for shunting or ballast work. They were scrapped in 1872-73.

As noted in Chapter 3, *Achilles* and *Ajax* were purchased by the Belfast firm of Coates and Young who eventually regauged them and, in 1852, sold them to the Londonderry and Enniskillen Railway, where they were numbered 9 and 10.

Spitfire had a more colourful later history. Perhaps as early as 1842, it was rebuilt as a 2-2-2WT with 11"x 18" cylinders and, after regauging in 1847, was passed to the Belfast and Ballymena Railway in October 1847, as a stop-gap until the B&BR's own engines were delivered. The UR did well out of

this deal, a few months later receiving a new Sharp 2-2-2, called *Hawk*, in exchange for *Spitfire* and £300! At some point the two locomotives exchanged nameplates, so the old *Spitfire* became B&BR *Hawk*. In 1854, it was extensively rebuilt as a 2-4-0T with 5'6" wheels and a new boiler. In this form it remained in B&BR stock until 1863, when it was sold to Thomas Firth. It is known that this engine was then owned by two contractors in turn and was eventually scrapped after lying at Broadstone, in Dublin, from 1870 to 1873.

The early standard gauge locomotives

Prior to 1857, and from at least 1846, a Mr Firth (probably Thomas) was Locomotive Superintendent of the Ulster Railway. When the UR planned to build its Armagh extension to the 5'3" gauge, new locomotives were required. Six new 2-2-2s were built in 1846-47 by Sharp Brothers. Sharp was no longer in partnership with Roberts after 1843 and the firm was known as Sharp Brothers from 1843-52, after which it became Sharp Stewart. The move from Manchester to Glasgow did not come until 1888.

These singles were of a type already described in the chapter on the Dublin and Belfast Junction Railway. The principal dimensions were: driving wheels 5'6", cylinders 15"x 20", boiler 3'8"x 10'0", pressure 80 lbs, and tractive effort 4.636 lbs, making them more than twice as powerful as the earlier singles. They initially carried names only. These (in the order of their later numbers) were *Cyclops*, *Lucifer*, *Pluto*, *Jupiter*, *Cerberus* and *Vulcan*. As explained above, in December 1847 one of the B&BR batch came to the UR, as a replacement for the original *Spitfire*. This engine had been B&BR *Hawk* and became UR *Spitfire*, though the minutes do not refer to it by name before 1856. All these singles, except *Cyclops*, were renewed in 1864-69 and survived into GNR days. Meanwhile, around 1848, UR engines were given numbers, the new singles becoming Nos 7-13. This implies that the numbers 1-6 were allocated to the converted broad gauge engines. However, since the UR minutes of this period always refer to these by name only, it is likely that the numbers were never carried

In 1853, two new goods locomotives, Nos 14 and 15, were built by Sharp Stewart. They had double frames and

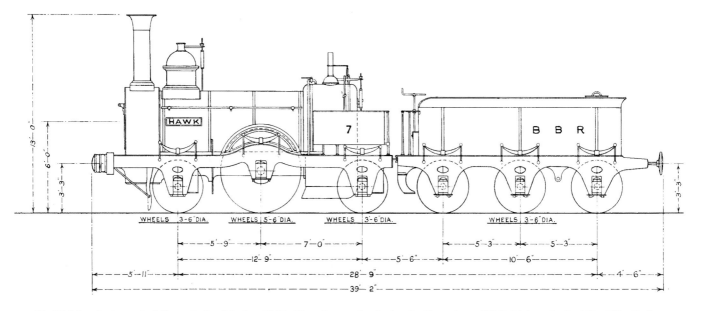

Fig 26 (above): A standard Sharp single of the late 1840s. These locomotives had main dimensions of 5'6" driving wheels, 15" x 20" cylinders and 80 lbs boiler pressure. Six (Nos 7-12) were built new for the UR in 1846-47. This drawing shows No 7 *Hawk* of the Belfast and Ballymena Railway, before it was transferred to the UR, where it became No 13 *Spitfire*.

J H Houston, courtesy P Mallon

were quite powerful, with 4'6" wheels, 16"x 24" cylinders and 4'0"x 11'0" boilers. They remained unnamed until the 1860s, when they became *Callan* and *Neagh* respectively. They lasted until 1875.

In December 1856, a fifth goods engine, No 16 (later *Bann*) was delivered. It was an inside framed Sharp 0-4-2 with a boiler pressure of 120 lbs and a tractive effort of 11,605 lbs. It was otherwise similar in dimensions to Nos 14 and 15. Two more of this type were added later (see Fig 27, below). No 16 was also identical to D&BJR 0-4-2 Nos 9 and 14.

In anticipation of the opening of the Portadown and Dungannon Railway and the extension to Monaghan, three more passenger locomotives were added to stock in 1857-58. Nos 17-19 (named *Shamrock*, *Rose* and *Thistle* in the 1860s) were a slightly modernised version of the standard Sharp

2-2-2, with improved boilers, pressed to 120 lbs, and a tractive effort of 6,955 lbs (see Fig 4, page 16, for their original appearance). No 17 was delivered in June 1857, whilst Nos 18 and 19 were dispatched by ship in November. However, No 19 was lost overboard and was not replaced until June 1858. This is why Nos 18 and 19, despite having adjacent Works numbers, were delivered seven months apart. Presumably, there is still a Sharp single at the bottom of the Irish Sea!

The John Eaton era

On 27 April 1857 John Eaton became Locomotive Superintendent of the Ulster Railway. He was still in post when the GNR was formed in 1876, and was allowed to remain in sole charge of the locomotives, of what then

Fig 27 (left): No 4 *Owenreagh* was the third of three Sharp Stewart 0-4-2 goods locomotives built in 1856-61. It had 4'6" driving wheels, 16"x 24" cylinders and 120 lbs boiler pressure. The other two were Nos 16 (1856) and 3 (1860). Two were also built for the D&BJR in 1853-57 and three of an 0-6-0 version for the Belfast and Ballymena Railway in 1857-61. Note the dome on the front ring of the boiler, the total absence of cab and the tall cover on the Salter safety valve on the firebox. This Sharp drawing shows interesting detail of the valve gear and lever reverse.

National Railway Museum, York

became the Northern Division, right up to his retirement in 1885. Under his regime it is known that the locomotives were painted in a brick red livery, but nothing is known about earlier UR liveries. Eaton also resumed the policy of naming locomotives. All new locomotives, from 1859, were named as built or shortly after delivery, and earlier unnamed engines received names by 1866. Eaton came from that breed of Victorian engineers who firmly believed that steam locomotives should not have cabs and that enginemen who wanted them were 'soft'. Up to 1885, UR drivers had no weather protection apart from a spectacle plate.

Up to Eaton's time, all UR locomotives had been Sharp products, but, in 1859, two other manufacturers undercut Sharp's price. Eaton wanted a pair of 2-2-2s with 5'6" driving wheels and 15"x 20" cylinders. Beyer Peacock offered them at £2200 each and Fairbairns £2280 each (Sharp's price had been £2425). Although the tenders were for a *pair* of engines, Eaton persuaded the firms to each sell him *one* at the quoted price! Surprisingly they both agreed. However, the engines were so satisfactory that, in January 1861, both firms received follow-up orders for two more.

The Beyer Peacock engines were Nos 1 *Lagan* (1859), 22 *Iveagh* and 23 *Tyrone* (1861). For many years, there was doubt as to whether these were inside or outside-framed, but I can now say with certainty that they had inside frames and were identical to INWR Nos 11, 13 and 14 (see page 30).

The Fairbairn engines were Nos 2 *Blackwater* (1859), 24 *Breffney* and 25 *Clanaboy* (1862) They had inside main frames, but also shallow outside frames with bearings only for the leading and trailing wheels. This arrangement of frames was first used *Jenny Lind*, an engine built in 1847 for the Midland Railway in England. The Fairbairn engines had slightly larger boilers than the Beyer ones, the heating surface being 1019 sq ft, compared to 925.4 sq ft.

The completion of the line to Omagh in 1861, and rising traffic generally, led to a further expansion of the fleet. Two more Sharp 0-4-2s (Nos 3 *Erne* and 4 *Owenreagh*), similar to No 16, were built in 1860-61, followed by the additional Beyers and Fairbairns mentioned above. Eaton, for the first time, began to have an imput into engine design himself. In January 1861, he ordered two Sharp double-framed 2-2-2s (Nos 20 *Ulidia* and 21 *Dalraida*) to his own specification. These were delivered in July and had a wheelbase of 6'10"+ 6'8", compared to the usual 5'11"+ 6'10". These 'big Sharps' also had 4'0" diameter boilers, instead of the usual 3'9". By 1862, the UR fleet had increased to twenty-five.

In common with many other Irish railways around this time, the UR felt the need for more powerful passenger locomotives, and the next class built were double-framed

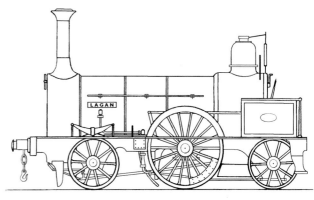

Fig 28 (above): Beyer Peacock 2-2-2 No 1 *Lagan*, built in 1859. Note how the lever for the spring balance valve emerges from the dome casing. Two more, Nos 22 and 23 were added in 1861, but had the dome on the boiler. Despite being inside-framed, Nos 1 and 23 were later rebuilt as double-framed 2-4-0s.

B Craig

Above: 2-2-2 No 125 *Clanaboy* was one of three engines (Nos 2, 24 and 25) built for the Ulster Railway by William Fairbairn in 1859-62. These engines were unusual in that they had inside bearings for the driving wheels and outside for the carrying wheels. No 125 was rebuilt in 1879 with a more modern boiler and, in the 1880s, received a GNR cab. In this view *Clanaboy* is seen at Lisburn in the mid 1890s, having just arrived from Belfast. It was scrapped in 1898. *L&GRP 24022*

2-4-0s with 6'1" driving wheels and 16"x 22" cylinders. Nos 26-29 (*Ulster, Munster, Leinster* and *Connaught*, respectively) were built by Beyer Peacock in 1863 to Eaton's own design. They must have been much more adequate on the Carrickmore banks of the Omagh line than the 20" singles used hitherto. These engines had 4'0"x 10'5" boilers, pressed to 120 lbs, with a heating surface of 979 sq ft, and a tractive effort of 7,872 lbs. The frames were plate (rather than sandwich) and the engines weighed 31 tons 12 cwt. The dome was placed on the front ring of the boiler, probably in an attempt to keep the steam passages as short as possible.

These engines were rebuilt several times in GNR days and lasted almost to the First World War. Their success led Eaton to rebuild Sharp 2-2-2 Nos 17-19 as 2-4-0s, in 1863-65, by altering the frames to accommodate new driving wheels. Exact rebuilding dates are uncertain, but are thought to have been 1/1865 (17), 8/1863 (18) and 6/1864 (19).

Surprisingly, when Eaton began to renew the 1846-47

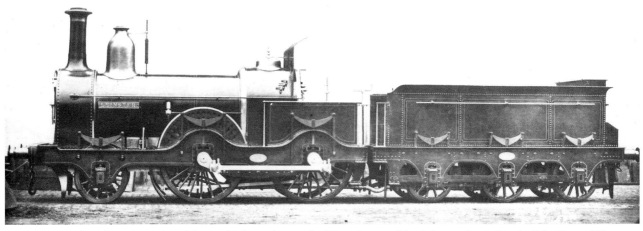

Top: UR Nos 26-29 (Beyer Peacock 1863) were the first 2-4-0s on the UR and some of the design work was done by John Eaton, UR Locomotive Superintendent from 1857 to 1885. No 28 *Leinster* was one of this batch and had 6'1" driving wheels and 16" x 22" cylinders. Note the bent weather board which offered the only protection on the footplate. The Beyer tender is of interest, as it shows a tool box at the rear. This was common on UR engines and was an Eaton design feature which first appeared in 1859. *Real Photographs 88005*

Centre: Double-framed 2-4-0 No 129 *Connaught* leaving Balmoral about 1895 in the Down direction with a train of six-wheelers. These are all standard GNR types, except the third vehicle. The sidings in the foreground led into Balmoral goods yard. *L&GRP 21270*

Bottom: UR Nos 17-19 were built by Sharp Stewart in 1857-58 as 2-2-2s and originally looked like Fig 4 on page 16. Examples ran on all four constituents of the GNR. No 17 *Shamrock* was converted to a 2-4-0, probably in January 1865, and reboilered in 1871 to the condition seen here. This early 1880s photograph is the only known picture of a locomotive in GNR Northern Division brick red livery. Note the letters 'GNR' on the footplate side sheet, rather than the tender, reflecting UR practice. UR engines carried the engine number only on the front buffer beam and the rear of the tender. *P Mallon collection*

Sharp 2-2-2s, in 1864, the first renewals (Nos 9 and 11) were turned out as 2-2-2s. This was probably for reasons of economy, as they retained their original frames and motion but received new boilers and fireboxes. They are sometimes regarded as new engines, but were probably really rebuilds, as they were renewed again in 1882 and 1884. Unfortunately no photographs or drawings of them have survived.

Expansion after 1865

In 1865, the Ulster Railway was very short of goods engines, probably due to an upsurge in goods traffic at that time. There were seven in stock, but old Nos 5 and 6 (of 1842) were fit only for shunting and Nos 14 and 15 (of 1853) were probably in poor shape. Eaton designed a double-framed 0-4-2 locomotive and ordered four from Beyer Peacock in June. Inagine his horror, when he wrote to Beyer Peacock in October to inquire about progress, and received the reply that work on them had not yet commenced!

Eaton did a quick trawl of all the locomotive manufacturers to see if any of them had suitable locomotives available. Sharp Stewart came to his rescue. Waiting at Liverpool docks, at that very moment, was a consignment of three 0-4-2 locomotives destined for the 5'3" gauge Sao Paulo Railway in Brazil! This was part of an order for six, the others having been dispatched on 3 October. If Eaton wanted them,

they could be diverted to Belfast for £2435 each (including tenders). Eaton jumped at the opportunity!

These locomotives arrived at the start of 1866, dismantled and packed in crates, presumably wheels in one crate, frames in another, etc. Work on their assembly began on 17 January. They became UR Nos 30-32 and were soon named *Nore, Ovoca* and *Foyle* respectively. With inside frames, 5'0" driving wheels and 16"x 22" cylinders, they were ideal for mixed traffic – light mixed and goods trains and short haul passenger. They came with four-wheel tenders and colonial style awnings over the footplate, but the latter were never fitted. Six more, to similar dimensions, were added in the 1870s, all becoming the GNR K class.

The four Beyer Peacock goods engines finally arrived in August 1866. These became Nos 33-36 (*Shannon, Liffey, Carntual* and *Donard* respectively), later the GNR F class. Eaton seemed to favour double-frames and had already used them on his 2-4-0 design. The F class were quite powerful engines and had 5'0" driving wheels, 17"x 24" cylinders and 4'0"x 10'10" boilers. They weighed 32 tons and, assuming 120 lbs boiler pressure, had a tractive effort 11,792 lbs. These engines were probably the last new double-framed 0-4-2s to be built for service in the British Isles.

In 1865 the facilities at Belfast were greatly improved when new workshops were opened. From this point on,

Left: Nos 30-32 were small inside-framed Sharp 0-4-2s. which came to the UR by diverting an order intended for Brazil. Originally No 131 would have looked more like the engine in Fig 11 (page 24), with a dome on the front ring and no cab. No 131 was rebuilt in 1882, to the condition seen here.
In this view, *Ovoca* (as GNR No 131) is waiting to depart from Belfast with a local passenger train in the mid 1890s. The driver is polishing the hand rail and the fireman is probably returning from connecting the communication wire to the first coach. No 131 has a good head of steam. It was rebuilt again in 1897, when it received a standard A class boiler, and was scrapped in 1909.
L&GRP 21271

Right: 0-4-2 Nos 33-36 were sturdy Beyer Peacock double-framed goods locomotives, which became the GNR F class. This Beyer Peacock builder's photo of No 33 *Shannon* shows much interesting detail of the UR livery, suggesting that the frames, smokebox and footplate side sheets were painted a darker colour than the boiler, firebox and splashers. Note the try cocks on the side of the firebox. These were used to ascertain the level of water in the boiler, in the days before gauge glasses. Note also the rather cumbersome rodding to operate the sander. Both the dome and firebox have safety valves and the running plate curves up to clear the coupling rod cranks.
F Moore Picture Library

Fig 29 (top): In 1867-69, Eaton renewed four of the 1846-47 Sharp 2-2-2 locomotives at his Belfast workshops as 2-4-0s with new frames, 15"x 20" cylinders and new boilers with raised fireboxes. Nos 8 *Lucifer* and 12 *Vulcan* were renewed in 1867 and Nos 10 *Jupiter* and 13 *Spitfire* in 1869. This is No 8 *Lucifer*.

Courtesy IRRS

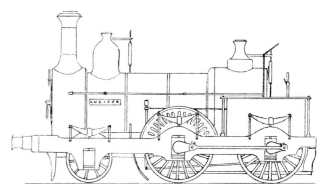

Fig 30 (below): The Ramsbottom safety valve originated on the LNWR in the 1860s. Each cylindrical outlet (CO) has a valve (V) at the top. The top of the spring pulls down against the bolt (B) and can be adjusted by the nut (N) at the lower end. The bottom of the spring is connected by a stirrup-link (SL) to the centre of the lever (F) so that steam pressure has to act against the force of the spring in order for the valves to lift. The lever is pivoted to a valve at one end and the other end is within the driver's reach. By moving the lever up (for the nearest) or down (for the furthest) he can relieve a sticking valve.

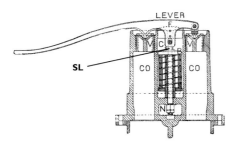

Centre: No 10 *Jupiter* is seen here as GNR No 110, following further rebuilding in 1885, when it received a GNR boiler and cab, Ramsbottom safety valves and 16"x 20" cylinders. It lasted until 1904. These engines became GNR Class M. Note the strange upturn at the front of the running plate to accommodate the buffer beam and the absence of any vacuum brake equipment. *L&GRP 24136*

Eaton was able to undertake substantial rebuilding work and even to construct new locomotives. Eaton concentrated future construction on three standard types.

The Beyer double-framed 2-4-0s of 1863 had given early problems with broken crank axles. When Eaton complained, Beyer claimed that this was a common problem with double-framed engines with coupled wheels. I would tend to be sceptical of this explanation, as the replacement axles lasted for over 300,000 miles! Despite the problem, Eaton made the double-framed 2-4-0 his standard passenger class, though no brand new engines of this type were built.

In 1867, he renewed old Sharp singles Nos 8 and 12 as 2-4-0s, followed by Nos 10 and 13 in 1869. Although they received new frames, and new boilers by Dübs, they retained 15"x 20" cylinders, suggesting that the expensive 'engine' parts of the old locomotives were reused. The only unrebuilt engine among the 1846-47 Sharp singles, No 7 *Cyclops*, was scrapped in 1870. Sharp 2-4-0 Nos 17-19 were further rebuilt in 1871-75 with new boilers, similar to the originals, and 16"x 20" cylinders (see page 42, lower). The GNR designated these 2-4-0s with 20" cylinders, the M class and the more powerful 16"x 22" cylindered engines (like Nos 26-29) the H class.

In 1874, No 23 *Tyrone*, one of the 1861 Beyer singles, was renewed. Oddly, this inside-framed 2-2-2 was renewed as a double-framed 2-4-0, though, in this instance, with 16"x

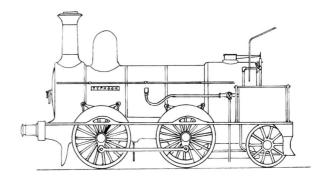

Fig 31 (above): Following the success of the Sharp 0-4-2s of 1866, four more were built, to a slightly modified design, in 1871-74, at the UR works in Belfast and a further two by Sharp Stewart in 1876. No 5 *Typhoon* was built at Belfast in 1874. It had a dome on the front ring of the boiler and spring balance valves on the firebox.

Courtesy IRRS

22" cylinders. By the formation of the GNR in 1876, the UR passenger fleet consisted of twelve 2-4-0s and nine 2-2-2s. However, a second Beyer 2-2-2, No 1 *Lagan* (built in 1859), was in process of renewal as a 2-4-0 at this point.

The second type, on which Eaton standardised, was the light, inside-framed 0-4-2 mixed traffic design, developed from the Sharp engines of 1865. The UR continued to build 0-4-2s much longer than any other Irish railway, apart from

the Waterford, Dungarvin and Lismore Railway. Four more of this type were built at Belfast. They were Nos 7 *Cyclone* (1871), 6 *Tornado* (1872), 5 *Typhoon* and 39 *Tempest* (both 1874). They were dimensionally similar to Nos 30-32 of 1866, but differed in some details. Two more, Nos 40 *Sirocco* and 41 *Simoom*, were ordered from Sharp Stewart and were delivered in May 1876, just after the amalgamation.

The third standard type was an 0-6-0 goods design. The first two of these, Nos 37 *Stromboli* and 38 *Vulcano*, were built at Belfast in 1872-73. As the GNR C class, were destined to be the last former Ulster Railway locomotives to remain in service. No 37 lasted until 1939 and No 38 until 1948. They had inside frames, 5'0" driving wheels and 17"x 24" cylinders. In 1875, Eaton had begun the construction of more of this class, but with 4'7" driving wheels. The first of these was completed after the amalgamation and will be described at the next chapter.

At the formation of the GNR in 1876, the Ulster Railway had a fleet of 37 locomotives, the largest among the GNR constituent companies. The UR fleet consisted entirely of tender engines, comprising nine 2-2-2s, twelve 2-4-0s, fourteen 0-4-2s and two 0-6-0s.

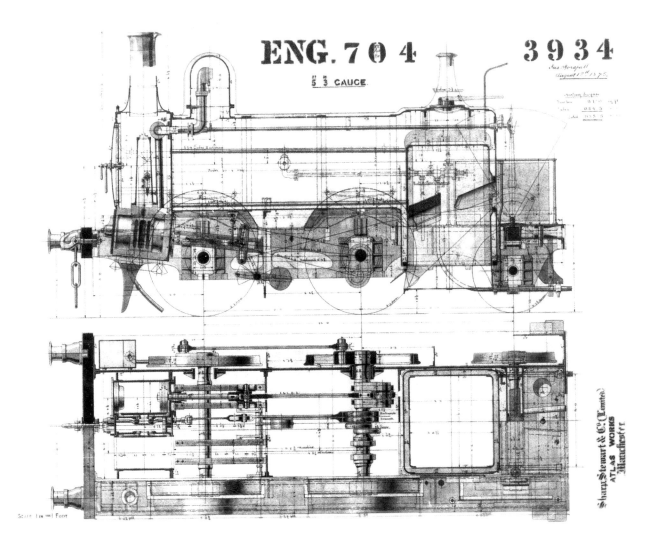

ENG. 7 0 4   3 9 3 4

5' 3" GAUGE.

Sharp, Stewart & Co (Limited)
ATLAS WORKS
Manchester

Scale 1in = 1 Foot

Fig 32 (top): This is a Sharp Stewart drawing of one the two 0-4-2s they built for the UR in 1876. The four built at Belfast in 1871-74 were probably similar. Note the raised firebox, the absence of a cab, the cased Naylor safety valves on the firebox and the forward position of the dome. However, the smokebox is not raked back, as would have been the case with the 1866 engines. These engines had 5'0" driving wheels and 16"x 22" cylinders and became the GNR K class.

National Railway Museum, York

Bottom: No 6 *Tornado* of 1872 was one of the Belfast-built examples of the K class. It is seen here as GNR No 106, following its rebuilding in 1889. It now has a cab, a GNR standard A class boiler and the dome in the more conventional centre position. Note the traversing jack sitting just ahead of the cab. This allowed a derailed engine to be raised and then inched over onto the track again. *Tornado* was renumbered 106A in 1906 and scrapped the following year. The other five were withdrawn in 1906-11. The photograph was taken at the old Belfast running shed, probably around 1905.   *H Fayle, courtesy IRRS*

Ulster Railway, and GNR Northern Division, 5'3" gauge locomotives

No	Name	Date	Works No	Type	DW	Cyls	Rebuilt or renewed (UR)	GNR Class	Rebuilt or renewed (GNR)	Wdn
1	*Lagan*	7/1859	BP 151	2-2-2	5'6"	15"x 20"	–	H	8/1876 (2-4-0), 10/1897 (boiler)	11/1913
2	*Blackwater*	10/1859	Fairbairn	2-2-2	5'6"	15"x 20"	–	–	–	1881
2	*Blackwater*	1881	GNR	0-4-2	4'6"	16"x 22"	–	K	–	3/1901
3	*Erne*	3/1860	SS 1156	0-4-2	4'6"	16"x 24"	–	B	–	1877
3	*Etna*	12/1877	GNR	0-6-0	4'6½"	17"x 24"	–	C	4/1895	1925
4	*Owenreagh*	7/1861	SS 1274	0-4-2	4'6"	16"x 24"	–	B	–	1879
4	*Owenreagh*	1880	GNR	0-4-2	4'6"	16"x 22"	–	K	–	5/1899
5	*Typhoon*	mid 1874	UR	0-4-2	5'0"	16"x 22"	–	K	3/1893	10/1911
6	*Tornado*	5/1872	UR	0-4-2	5'0"	16"x 22"	–	K	10/1889	8/1906
7	*Cyclops*	5/1846	SB 343	2-2-2	5'6"	15"x 20"	–	–	–	early 1870
7	*Cyclone*	early 1871	UR	0-4-2	5'0"	16"x 22"	–	K	8/1888	5/1908
8	*Lucifer*	11/1846	SB 366	2-2-2	5'6"	15"x 20"	1867 (2-4-0)	M	1876 (16"), 1886 (H)	2/1906
9	*Pluto*	5/1846	SB 344	2-2-2	5'6"	15"x 20"	6/1864	M	–	1882
9	*Pluto*	1882	GNR	0-4-2	4'6"	16"x 22"	–	K	–	3/1907
10	*Jupiter*	11/1846	SB 367	2-2-2	5'6"	15"x 20"	1869 (2-4-0)	M	1885 (16"x 20")	7/1905
11	*Cerberus*	2/1847	SB 392	2-2-2	5'6"	15"x 20"	7/1864	M	1884 (*North Star*, 16"x 22")	6/1901
12	*Vulcan*	2/1847	SB 394	2-2-2	5'6"	15"x 20"	1867 (2-4-0)	M	1885 (H)	8/1905
13	*Spitfire*	12/1847	SB 509	2-2-2	5'6"	15"x 20"	11/1869 (2-4-0)	M	1876 (16"x 20")	1888
14	*Callan*	9/1853	SS 741	0-4-2	4'6"	16"x 24"	–	–	–	1875
14	*Vesuvius*	4/1876	GNR	0-6-0	4'6½"	17"x 24"	–	C	3/1894	1924
15	*Neagh*	9/1853	SS 742	0-4-2	4'6"	16"x 24"	1869	–	–	1875
15	*Hecla*	6/1876	GNR	0-6-0	4'6½"	17"x 24"	–	C	6/1896	1924
16	*Bann*	12/1856	SS 975	0-4-2	4'6"	16"x 24"	–	B	–	1877
16	*Teneriffe*	6/1878	GNR	0-6-0	4'6½"	17"x 24"	–	C	4/1895	1925
17	*Shamrock*	6/1857	SS 989	2-2-2	5'6"	15"x 20"	1/1865? (2-4-0), 1871	U	–	1886-87
18	*Rose*	11/1857	SS 1007	2-2-2	5'6"	15"x 20"	8/1863 (2-4-0), 1873	U	–	1887
19	*Thistle*	6/1858?	SS 1008	2-2-2	5'6"	15"x 20"	6/1864 (2-4-0), 1875	U	–	1886-87
20	*Ulidia*	7/1861	SS 1275	2-2-2	5'6"	15"x 20"	–	H	6/1879 (2-4-0)	1/1906
21	*Dalriada*	7/1861	SS 1276	2-2-2	5'6"	15"x 20"	–	H	6/1877 (2-4-0), 2/1901 (boiler)	10/1914
22	*Iveagh*	8/1861	BP 225	2-2-2	5'6"	15"x 20"	–	N	1879 (G)	2/1900
23	*Tyrone*	6/1861	BP 226	2-2-2	5'6"	15"x 20"	1874 (2-4-0)	H	1885	7/1903
24	*Breffney*	early 1862	Fairbairn	2-2-2	5'6"	15"x 20"	–	?	1878 (G)	1895
25	*Clanaboy*	early 1862	Fairbairn	2-2-2	5'6"	15"x 20"	–	?	1879 (G)	12/1897
26	*Ulster*	11/1863	BP 367	2-4-0	6'1"	16"x 22"	–	H	1881, 5/1897	9/1909
27	*Munster*	12/1863	BP 369	2-4-0	6'1"	16"x 22"	–	H	1881, 2/1899	3/1911
28	*Leinster*	11/1863	BP 368	2-4-0	6'1"	16"x 22"	–	H	1883, 5/1898	1914
29	*Connaught*	12/1863	BP 370	2-4-0	6'1"	16"x 22"	–	H	1883, 6/1899	3/1912
30	*Nore*	1/1866	SS 1649	0-4-2	5'0"	16"x 22"	–	K	1/1880	1894
31	*Ovoca*	1/1866	SS 1651	0-4-2	5'0"	16"x 22"	–	K	1882, 2/1897	8/1909
32	*Foyle*	1/1866	SS 1652	0-4-2	5'0"	16"x 22"	–	K	12/1879	4/1904
33	*Shannon*	8/1866	BP 634	0-4-2	5'0"	17"x 24"	–	F	1882, 10/1901	1913
34	*Liffey*	8/1866	BP 635	0-4-2	5'0"	17"x 24"	–	F	12/1890	10/1911
35	*Carntual*	8/1866	BP 636	0-4-2	5'0"	17"x 24"	–	F	6/1890	10/1909
36	*Donard*	8/1866	BP 637	0-4-2	5'0"	17"x 24"	–	F	4/1883, 2/1902	11/1912
37	*Stromboli*	1872	UR	0-6-0	5'0"	17"x 24"	–	C	1885, 7/1912	9/1939
38	*Vulcano*	1873	UR	0-6-0	5'0"	17"x 24"	–	C	1885, 2/1913	6/1948
39	*Tempest*	mid 1874	UR	0-4-2	5'0"	16"x 22"	–	K	6/1893	3/1908
40	*Sirocco*	5/1876	SS 2560	0-4-2	5'0"	16"x 22"	–	K	10/1895	12/1907
41	*Simoom*	5/1876	SS 2561	0-4-2	5'0"	16"x 22"	–	K	10/1893	8/1906
42	*Torrent*	7/1879	BP 1870	0-6-0	4'6½"	17"x 24"	–	C	11/1899	1925
43	*Avalanche*	8/1879	BP 1871	0-6-0	4'6½"	17"x 24"	–	C	10/1898	1925

Chapter 5
The Birth of the GNR(I)

At the start of the 1870s, Belfast was the fastest growing urban centre in Ireland and, with a population of 175,000, had already become Ireland's second largest city. It was, therefore, quite ridiculous that the Dublin to Belfast route was the only main line railway in Ireland that was not controlled by one company. The Dublin-Cork (GS&WR) and Dublin-Galway (MGWR) lines had been built as single entities from the start, and the Belfast-Londonderry line (B&NCR) had been unified since 1861. Yet, to get from Dublin to Belfast or Dublin to Londonderry involved two, or even three, changes of train en route. The need to amalgamate the various companies in the area had been evident for many years but was now becoming pressing. It was this pressure that led to the creation of the Great Northern Railway Company (Ireland) in 1876.

The Northern Railway 1875-76

The first step towards the creation of the new company came on 1 March 1875. On that date the Dublin and Drogheda Railway and the Dublin and Belfast Junction Railway merged to form a new entity called the Northern Railway Company (Ireland). This short-lived railway was to be the core of the eventual GNR(I).

Here we are chiefly concerned with the locomotive side of things and the Northern Railway started out with twenty-two locomotives from the D&DR and twenty from the D&BJR. The twenty-two D&DR engines retained their D&DR numbers as 1-22, but the D&BJR locos were renumbered 23-41. One D&BJR engine, Sharp Stewart 2-2-2 No 6 of 1853, was not included in the renumbering scheme. Most likely, its future was in some doubt and it was scrapped later that year. One interesting point is that the opportunity was taken to renumber the D&BJR engines in a logical order – Sharp 2-2-2s first (Nos 23-27), the two 2-2-2WTs (28 and 29), then the 2-4-0 rebuild (No 30), the light 0-4-2s (31-34), the heavy 0-4-2s (35 and 36), the Beyer Peacock 2-4-0s (37-39) and finally, the Beyer 0-6-0s (40 and 41).

Part of the amalgamation terms were that all senior officers and directors would remain in post if they so wished. This led to the NR having two Locomotive Superintendents, but Thomas Armitage (D&BJR) left later in the year to take up a similar post on the Waterford and Limerick Railway. William Curry of the D&DR remained and was to play a major role over the next five years.

The Northern Railway started life with two workshops, but the Dundalk works of the D&BJR did little more than routine heavy overhauls. The Dublin works of the former D&DR was in process of reboilering the second generation of D&DR passenger engines (see Chapter 1) and No 4, the solitary Grendon 2-4-0, was completed in March 1875.

Retaining 16"x 20" cylinders, it got a new boiler of 954 sq ft heating surface and weighed 28½ tons. Later in the year, No 3, a 2-2-2WT dating from 1844, was scrapped, the only NR engine not to enter GNR stock.

The first new locomotives to be built were ordered from Beyer Peacock in April 1875 and delivered in November. These were 2-4-0 Nos 3 and 42, which were members of what was to be, eventually, the GNR G class. They were pure Beyer Peacock in design and were a 5'7" driving wheel version of ex-D&DR 2-4-0 No 12 *Achilles*, built in 1871. They thus reflected Curry's influence. The new engines had 16"x 22" cylinders, a raised firebox to the boiler, and were a fairly conservative design. At the end of 1875 there were 42 engines in stock.

The second stage in the amalgamation took place when the INWR joined the NR on 1 January 1876. At this date the INWR had thirty-four locomotives in stock, numbered 1-36 with Nos 2 and 23 blank. In due course, the INWR locomotives were renumbered, but not in the systematic manner of the ex-D&BJR engines. Instead, forty-two was added to the existing numbers, 1 becoming 43 and 36 becoming 78, etc. This left Nos 44 and 65 blank. Since the INWR Locomotive Superintendent, Charles Clifford, was allowed to remain at Barrack Street, Dundalk in charge of the engines of the former Irish North, the likely explanation is that the details of the renumbering were left to him. Meanwhile, in March 1876, 2-2-2 No 13 *Ulysses*, freshly rebuilt with a new boiler, was outshopped from the NR Dublin Works.

As described in Chapter 3, a new E class 0-6-0 was under construction at Barrack Street works, Dundalk at the end of 1875. Work on this was suspended for a while and the engine was eventually completed as No 44, probably in the early part of 1876. This was the last engine to be built to INWR design and, like its Dübs sisters, it lasted until 1948.

The third and final stage in the amalgamation came on 1 April 1876, when the Ulster Railway joined with the Northern Railway to form the Great Northern Railway Company (Ireland). This was the crucial corner-stone of the whole operation as it was hard to persuade the financially strong UR to link itself to the weaker INWR and D&BJR. Some idea of the financial position of each company can be gauged from the fact that, if we regard D&DR shares as worth 100, the D&BJR came in at 77.5, the INWR at 50 and the UR at 124.5. This meant that £1,000 worth of INWR shares were now worth £500 of GNR stock and the same value of UR shares £1,245. By this time, the combined Board of Directors had swollen from 16 to 29. It was to be ten years before 'natural wastage' reduced this to a more manageable twelve.

The old UR now became the 'Northern Division' of the GNR and the politics of amalgamation were such that the 'Northern Division' retained considerable autonomy, particularly in locomotive matters. In something reminiscent of the old LNWR, with its division between Crewe (N Division) and Wolverton (S Division), the GNR (ND) retained its Belfast works and for the first nine years was allowed to continue building new locomotives to its own designs. John Eaton, the ex-UR Locomotive Superintendent, was senior to both Curry and Clifford, having been in post for nineteen years. Although other aspects of the UR were absorbed into the GNR, Eaton continued to behave as if his locomotive department was not really part of the GNR. He did not renumber his engines (which logically should have become Nos 79-115) and they retained their own separate number series until 1885. He also retained the brick red UR livery, his only concession being that the cabs were now lettered 'GNR' instead of 'UR'. The contribution of the Northern Division to GNR locomotive history follows shortly.

The GNR locomotive fleet in 1876

It is appropriate at this stage to look at the locomotive situation of the GNR as at 1 April 1876. The GNR started out with 113 locomotives, ie 76 inherited from the NR and 37 from the UR. These figures exclude the E class 0-6-0 under construction at Dundalk and the two C class 0-6-0s nearing completion at Belfast, none of which had entered traffic, but do include UR 2-2-2 No 1 *Lagan* which was being renewed at Belfast.

There was a wide assortment of types and a bewildering range of classes. From the aspect of maintenance it must have been a nightmare, especially with work divided between five workshops and little prospect of reducing the variety of types for many years to come. It is difficult to estimate the number of classes. Some were represented on more than one line and others, which had started life as the same class, now differed due to rebuilding. At a best estimate there were 48 different classes, based on certain assumptions I am making about the similarity of some types. Of these, 17 had only one representative, 16 had only two, 5 had three representatives and 6 had four. Only 4 classes had more than four examples. These were:

(i) Seven standard Sharp 2-2-2s of the 1850s (GNR U class) – Nos 17, 18 (D&DR), 26, 27 (D&BJR) and 46-48 (INWR).

(ii) Six light Sharp 0-4-2s (16"x 22" cylinders) of the same vintage (GNR S class) – Nos 31-34 (D&BJR), 51 and 52 (INWR).

(iii) Five heavy Sharp 0-4-2s with 16"x 24" cylinders (GNR B class) – Nos 35, 36 (D&BJR), 3, 4 and 16 (UR numbers).

(iv) Seven Sharp and UR light 0-4-2s with 16"x 22" cylinders (GNR K class) – UR Nos 5-7, 30-32 and 39. Two more of this class were on order.

Thirty of the 113 engines were singles (2-2-2), though there were also some single-wheeler tanks. Thirty-one were rear-coupled (2-4-0), two of these with outside cylinders. A further thirty-three were front-coupled (0-4-2), the most numerous wheel arrangement on the GNR at this stage. Only ten were six-coupled (0-6-0) though, as noted, three more were nearing completion in Belfast and Dundalk. Finally, there were nine tank locomotives

One very obvious point emerging from these statistics is the scarcity of tank engines. The UR never had any, the D&BJR had only two 2-2-2WTs, and the D&DR one 2-2-2ST. The INWR had more tank engines than the other constituents – four 2-2-0WTs and two 0-6-0STs – though, even here, the 2-2-0WTs were about to be withdrawn. None of the companies had built a tank engine since 1862 and the GNR did not build any until 1885.

There was also a notable shortage of what in the 1870s would have been counted as 'modern' engines, ie inside framed 2-4-0 tender engines with 16"x 22" (or 21") cylinders and 0-6-0s with 17"x 24" cylinders. There were ten of the former – Nos 3, 42 (NR), 12 (D&DR), 37-39 (D&BJR) and 72-75 (INWR) – and only seven 'modern' 0-6-0s – Nos 5 (D&DR), 40, 41 (D&BJR), 77, 78 (INWR) and 37 and 38 (UR numbers).

The Northern Division 1876-1885

The proud tradition of independence that characterised the Ulster Railway continued into GNR days, since Eaton was allowed to remain in charge of the GNR Northern Division locomotives until his retirement in 1885. Northern Division locomotives also remained cabless until Dundalk took control in 1885.

Therefore, the absorption of the UR into the GNR had little immediate impact on locomotive policy. Effectively Curry and Clifford were only concerned with the Southern and Irish North Divisions. Eaton was actually allowed to continue building new locomotives to his own design, at least until 1882, and also pursued an independent policy of renewals and rebuilding. Even after he had retired, there was difficulty persuading the Belfast workforce to move to Dundalk and the Northern Division retained its workshops at Belfast for a few more years.

Eaton continued the policy of building the three standard types described in Chapter 4 – ie inside-framed light 0-4-2s and heavy 0-6-0s and double-framed 2-4-0s. In May 1876, the last of the six Eaton 0-4-2s were delivered from Sharp Stewart. These were Nos 40 *Sirocco* and 41 *Simoom* which, like the first four, were named after winds. Counting the three Sharp engines of 1866, there were now nine of this type, all later GNR K class.

The first two Eaton 4'7" 0-6-0s were nearing completion in the Belfast Works at the time of the amalgamation. These were Nos 14 *Vesuvius* and 15 *Hecla*, which were turned out in April and June 1876, respectively. The main dimensions were: driving wheels 4'6½" (later 4'7" with thicker tyres), 17"x 24" cylinders, wheelbase 7'2"+ 7'10", and boilers 4'0⅜"x 10'11½".

Above: Unfortunately, no photos exist of the C class 0-6-0s in their original condition before rebuilding in 1894-99. In this view, No 148 *Teneriffe*, is on an Up goods train at Dundalk station in the late 1890s. This engine was built as Northern Division No 16 in 1878, became 116 in 1885 and was renumbered 148 in 1889. It was rebuilt as seen here in 1895 and scrapped in 1925.   *LPC 4023*

The boiler pressure was 135 lbs and the tractive effort 14,604 lbs. The boilers were telescopic, the other two rings being 4'1¼" and 4'2⅛" in diameter. Apart from the last two, this class was named after volcanoes.

Four more locomotives were added in 1877-79. These were Nos 3 *Etna* (12/1877), 16 *Teneriffe* (6/1878), 42 *Torrent* (7/1879) and 43 *Avalanche* (8/1879). The last two were built by Beyer Peacock and the others at Belfast. In theory, Nos 14 and 15 were renewals of double-framed Sharp 0-4-2s of 1853 and Nos 3 and 16 of Sharp 0-4-2s of 1857-60. In reality, little more than the wheels and some parts of the motion are likely to have been reused, and the C class were always regarded as new engines.

The design was really a 4'7" version of UR Nos 37 and 38 (1872-73) and all eight were regarded as the C class by the GNR. Three interesting features of these engines should be noted. Firstly, the 7'10" between the driving and rear axles allowed the engines to accommodate a large firebox and Nos 42 and 43 were eventually fitted with AL class boilers in 1898-99. Secondly, the tenders attached to the engines were of an unusual design, because on the outside rear of them there was a hinged box to accommodate fire irons and other tools. This is evident in rear or side views, as can be seen. Tenders with tool boxes were also attached to the K class 0-4-2s. Thirdly, the C class engines were easily distinguished

from the Southern Division 0-6-0s and later examples, by their curved running plates, those on all other GNR 0-6-0s being straight.

Eaton also continued to renew 'singles' as double-framed 2-4-0s. Three more were renewed in 1876-79 – Nos 1 *Lagan* (8/1876), 20 *Ulidia* (6/1879) and 21 *Dalriada* (6/1877). In 1885, M class 2-4-0 No 12 *Vulcan* (of 1867) was rebuilt at Belfast with 16"x 22" cylinders, bringing it into line with the engines listed above, and No 8 *Lucifer* of this type was similarly treated at Dundalk in 1886. This was one of the first ex-UR locomotives to get a GNR cab.

Some 'singles' were rebuilt with 16"x 22" cylinders, retaining their existing frames – Nos 22 *Iveagh* (1879), 24

Above: Another view of No 148, this time at Dundalk Works after rebuilding. As built, these engines were cabless and had raised fireboxes. Northern Division locomotives had narrow splashers and a wide curved running plate. Note the rear toolbox.

L J Watson

Top right: H class 2-4-0 No 121 *Dalriada* at Dublin about 1895. This locomotive was originally a Sharp single, built in 1861 for the Ulster Railway. It was renewed as a 2-4-0 at the Northern Division's Belfast Works in 1877, receiving 16"x 22" cylinders and a new boiler with the dome on the first ring. This was probably the last engine so treated – sister No 120, rebuilt in 1879, had the dome on the centre ring. *Dalriada* was rebuilt again in 1901(see page 85). *C P Friel collection*

Fig 33 (below): Three new 0-4-2s were built at Belfast in 1880-82. These were nominally rebuilds of earlier engines of three different classes. This drawing shows their original cabless appearance. They were GNR K class.

Courtesy IRRS

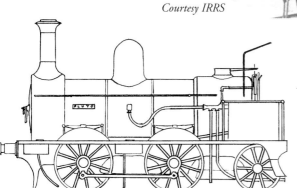

Breffney (1878) and 25 *Clanaboy* (1879). They remained as 2-2-2s.

The last new class introduced by the Northern Division comprised three more of the inside-framed 0-4-2s favoured by Eaton. The new engines (also regarded as K class) were Nos 4 *Owenreagh* (1880), 2 *Blackwater* (1881) and 9 *Pluto* (1882). All perpetuated the identities of earlier 0-4-2 and 2-2-2 locomotives, but I suspect that this was to keep the accountants happy! It is likely that Eaton was told he could not built *new* engines any longer, but he could *rebuild* existing ones. Only No 4 is likely to have passed on much material to its replacement, being already a 4'6" 0-4-2. The

other two were double-framed singles so, other than the tenders, there wasn't much to re-use. However, it is likely that the new engines used driving and trailing wheels from the 0-4-2s broken up in 1877.

This class had 4'6" driving wheels, 16"x 22" cylinders, 3'11"x 10'1" boilers, working at 140 lbs pressure, and a tractive effort of 12,411 lbs. Their wheelbase was 7'2"+ 6'6". They survived only until 1898-1907 and were not rebuilt. Only two photographs exist and these show them to have straight frames, shallow splashers, and the old-fashioned raised fireboxes.

As a final swan song to the Eaton era, old double-framed 2-2-2 No 11 *Cerberus* of 1864 was renewed in 1884. This engine had a long history going back to 1847 when it had started life as one of the early standard Sharp singles. It had already been rebuilt in 1864, retaining 15"x 20" cylinders, but modernised with a 120 lbs boiler. It was now renewed again with 16"x 22" cylinders and replacement frames, as No 11 *North Star* (111 after 1885). We are fortunate to have a photo of No 111 in its new metamorphosis after 1884, because this shows something very interesting – that it has Fairbairn style frames, ie double frames but no outside bearings on the driving wheels, the leading and trailing wheels having outside bearings.

Left: K4'6" class 0-4-2 No 102 *Blackwater* at Belfast shed about 1898. These three hybrid 0-4-2s had short lives, the last going in 1907. Unlike other Northern Division coupled types, they had straight running plates. In the background are JS class 4-2-2 No 89 *Albert* and K5'0" class 0-4-2 No 105 *Typhoon*.

L&GRP 9155

Right: This is a lucky sighting of 2-2-2 No 111 *North Star* at Belfast, a detail from a larger photograph (see page 86). This engine had a long career, as explained in the text. Its renewal in 1884 was the last major job carried out at the old Belfast Workshops before all repairs were transferred to Dundalk. When scrapped in 1901 it was the last ex-UR single in service.

C P Friel collection

Since *North Star* lasted only seventeen years in its new guise, I suspect that the frames were second-hand and came from Fairbairn 2-2-2 No 2, broken up in 1881 in place of one the new K class 0-4-2s! – a typical example of 'waste nothing'. Essentially, 2-2-2 No 11 and the rebuilt Nos 24 and 25 were now the same type.

In June 1885, John Eaton at last took retirement and the wind of change was about to blow over the Nothern Division of the GNR.

The Southern Division 1876-80

The first new locomotives ordered by the Southern Division arrived in 1877. There was a pressing need for more modern goods engines and many old engines needed urgent replacement, most notably the notorious INWR 2-2-0WTs and the last remaining D&BJR Sharp 2-2-2s. Clifford was given responsibility for the new 0-6-0 goods engines and the design was drawn up in co-operation with Sharp Stewart.

However, it is clear from looking at the drawings that the design was based on Beyer's 0-6-0 of 1872 for the Dublin and Drogheda Railway, No 5 *Hercules*. It shared the same wheel base and had a similar chassis, though the boiler was 3'10" diameter as against 3'9".

The new engines were delivered in February 1877 and had 4'7¼" driving wheels, 16"x 24" cylinders and (probably) boilers of 130lbs pressure. The details, like the shape of the chimney and the design of the crank axle, showed Sharp Stewart influence. These engines would later be the GNR B class and,

Above: G class 2-4-0 No 25, as built. This was one of four delivered by Beyer Peacock in December 1877. The design was based on ex-D&DR 2-4-0 No 12 of 1871, but had 5'6" driving wheels in place of the latter's 6'0" wheels. These were small engines with 16"x 22" cylinders and 3'9" diameter boilers. Note the louvred splashers and the absence of vacuum brake equipment. The small sandbox is below the running plate ahead of the leading driver.

F Moore's Railway Photographs

Right: B class 0-6-0 No 65 of 1877, one of the first batch of four of this nine strong class of Sharp Stewart engines. It is seen here at Dundalk on 22 September 1897 about a year before being rebuilt with a more modern boiler. This design was based on ex-D&DR No 5 of 1872.

L J Watson

Below: This view of No 50 of the G class, shows minor alterations between 1877 and 1896 when this picture was taken. The splasher is now solid and the sandbox is above the running plate. Note the traversing jack on the front of the running plate. Counting the Northern Railway examples, eight of this class were built. However, ex-D&DR No 12 was regarded as the same class and ex-INWR 2-4-0 No 53 (22 after 1895) was rebuilt to G class in 1889, so the class was eventually ten strong. No 50 was originally No 59.

L J Watson

with one exception, this batch lasted until 1930. The 16" cylinders were a surprise. Perhaps Clifford thought that 4'7¼" wheels matched to 16" cylinders would give as much power as the 5'0" wheels of *Hercules* matched to 17" cylinders. The respective tractive efforts were 12,288 lbs (B class) and 12,773 lbs (*Hercules*). Whatever the reason, it came to be viewed as a mistake and in 1887 they were upgraded to 17" (apart from No 6, done in 1893).

The new engines were 25 *Meath*, 62 *Tyrone*, 63 *Donegal*, and 65 *Derry* but, before the year was out, No 25 was renumbered 6. This was to vacate the number 25 for a new passenger 2-4-0, of which more in a moment. The GNR occasionally carried out odd renumberings of its engines, and most made sense if examined closely. In this case, there were two Q class Sharp singles numbered 2 and 22, so No 2 became 23 (this number was vacant). There were two old Sharp P class 0-4-2s numbered 1 and 6, so No 6 became 2! Thus No 25 could take the number 6.

In December 1877 Beyer Peacock delivered four more G class passenger 2-4-0s (Nos 24, 25, 59 and 80), identical to the 1875 pair. It has always seemed strange to me that the third one was No 59. This number had hitherto been occupied by a Longridge 2-4-0, which was apparently renumbered 79 in 1877. As the Longridge engine was scrapped in 1879, renumbering it in 1877 doesn't make a lot of sense. In any case, we have just seen examples of Curry trying to bring engines of the same class together in the list. It would have made more sense for the third new 2-4-0 to have become 79 and left the old engine as 59 until it was scrapped.

The Beyer 2-4-0s and Sharp 0-6-0s had very different styles of chimney. On the Beyer 2-4-0s the chimney narrowed towards the top, whilst the Sharp 0-6-0s had chimneys which *widened* towards the top. Both classes had steam sanding equipment fitted, as was the practice, to the front pair of driving wheels only.

It is appropriate at this point to say something about early GNR policy on naming locomotives. All Northern Division engines continued to carry names, as had been UR policy. On the Southern Division, only a small number of ex-D&DR locomotives carried names and these were retained until the engines concerned were either rebuilt or scrapped. For new construction, Curry adopted the rather curious practice of naming the *goods engines*, but not the passenger ones! The goods engines were named after Irish counties, initially those in GNR territory but eventually, as the fleet expanded, the names selected came from anywhere in Ireland.

More B class locomotives

Three more B class 0-6-0s were built by Sharp Stewart in September 1879 – Nos 27 *Dublin*, 66 *Monaghan*, and 67 *Fermanagh* – but with 17"x 24" cylinders and 140 lb boilers, raising the tractive effort to 14,939 lbs. No 66 of this batch (as GNR 149) lasted until 1938, ending its days on the Belfast dock lines, the others going in 1930. Like the earlier B class engines, they had cabs, raised fireboxes and tenders with outside springs placed above the running plate. Two more –

Top: B class 0-6-0 No 66 *Monaghan*, photographed in ex-Works condition at Dundalk in August 1897. No 66 was one of the 1879 batch of this class. It was rebuilt in 1899 and scrapped in 1938. L J Watson was the Chief Draughtsman at Dundalk from 1892 to 1933 and was a keen amateur photographer.

L J Watson

Centre: H class 2-4-0 No 86 of 1880. Four of this class were built in 1880-81, essentially to the same design as ex-D&BJR Nos 37-39. They had 6'1½" driving wheels and 16"x 22" cylinders. No 86 was destined to be the locomotive whose failure on the Armagh-Newry line in 1889, led to Ireland's worst railway disaster. It was rebuilt in 1900 and scrapped in 1932.

F Moore's Railway Photographs

Bottom: N class 2-2-2 No 15, as renewed in 1880 at the former D&DR Dublin Works. Some details, such as the louvred splashers, reflected the recently built 2-4-0 locomotives. Note the surprising lack of a sander. This locomotive was withdrawn in 1901.

J D FitzGerald collection

Nos 26 *Armagh* and 34 *Louth* – followed in 1880 and were withdrawn in 1931 and 1932, respectively. Incidentally these were the last Sharp Stewart locomotives to be built for the GNR and the last new engines to have the front of the smokebox angled back 10° from the vertical to match the angle of the cylinders. This entire class of nine engines was rebuilt between 1896 and 1900 with 4'2" diameter flush-topped boilers, similar to those later used on the A Class, with which they shared a common wheel-base and cylinders. However, they still differed from the A Class in having the older style of square cab, with a distinct angle between the roof and the side

sheets. By 1938, No 149 was the last GNR engine to retain this feature.

In July 1880, 2-4-0s Nos 86 and 87 came from Beyer Peacock. These differed from the 1875-77 2-4-0s in having larger 4'0" x 10'7" boilers and 6'1½" driving wheels and were, in fact, an up-dated version of Nos 37-39, the ex-D&BJR engines of 1866-68. Indeed, the earlier engines were to be rebuilt between 1885 and 1888 to bring them into line. They had the traditional Beyer Peacock louvred splashers of the 1870s and were the first new GNR engines to have the firebox flush with the boiler, though Nos 37-39 had this feature as early as 1866. No 86 of this pair was to achieve notoriety a few years later, in 1889, when its failure on the steep Armagh-Newry line was the primary cause of the Armagh disaster. These engines were intended for faster mainline trains, in contrast to the smaller G class but, with only 6'1½" driving wheels, one hesitates to describe them as 'express' engines. Two more of this type, Nos 84 and 85, were added in November 1881. These engines had a J class crank but, following the introduction of the J class 4-4-0s in 1885, they were eventually reclassified as the H class.

Of course, up to 1881 both the Dublin and Dundalk Works continued to rebuild the earlier engines. It would be tedious in the extreme to describe these in detail, so the interested reader should refer to the appendices at the end of this book. A few general observations are worth making, however. Single wheelers were seeing something of a revival in the 1870s and 1880s, because the invention of steam sanding had solved some of their adhesion problems. Although the GNR built no new singles until 1885, they did rebuild Nos 13-16, the ex-D&DR 6'0" N class engines. The last to be dealt with, No 15 in 1880, was given a particularly thorough rebuild, including a longer 4'5" firebox, requiring new (or possibly just lengthened) frames. For this reason it was regarded as 'new' and its cab was fitted with a plate reading 'Great Northern Railway Works Dublin, 1880'. Although they had 5'6" wheels, ex-INWR 2-2-2 Nos 55 and 56 were also regarded as N class and were also rebuilt around this time. In 1879, 0-4-2 No 36 was rebuilt as an 0-6-0, probably making it similar to the newer B class engines.

The Newry and Armagh Railway

Before turning to the development of GNR locomotive policy under Park, we must digress for a moment to look at the locomotives of the Newry and Armagh Railway, a small and impecunious concern which was absorbed by the GNR on 30 June 1879.

The Newry and Armagh Railway had started out in July 1845 with an ambitious plan to build a 72 mile line from Newry to Enniskillen, via Armagh. By 1 March 1854, it had taken nine years to reach Goraghwood on the D&BJR, a distance of 3½ miles! Originally, it was called the Newry and Enniskillen Railway but, in 1857, it changed its destination to the more realistic target of Armagh and changed its name accordingly. It finally reached Armagh, 21 miles from Newry, on 25 August 1864. The N&AR owned a total of nine locomotives, six of which were passed to the GNR, five of them becoming GNR Nos 81-85.

For the opening to Goraghwood in 1854, two locomotives were acquired. These initially carried names only and were not numbered until some time after 1859. The name of the first is not recorded but it may have been called *Enniskillen*. It was one of the six 2-2-0WTs built by Sharp Brothers for the L&CR in 1853 (Fig 34). It was sent directly from Manchester to the Dublin Trade Exhibition in April 1853 and, from there, went to the L&CR in October. Before it commenced work at Coleraine, it was sold to the N&AR, arriving at the end of 1853. It was used on opening day, 1 March 1854.

A more unsuitable engine for the steeply graded Newry-Goraghwood line could not be imagined! It had 5'3" driving wheels, 11"x 18" cylinders and a 3'2"x 9'6" boiler. It later became No 3 and in 1866 was altered to a 2-2-2WT, then or at some other time, receiving 10" cylinders. It was sold in 1874 for £450 and did not come into GNR stock.

The second engine, *Newry*, was an 0-4-0T built by the Scottish firm Hawthorns of Leith, at an unknown date and

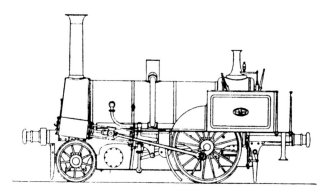

Fig 34 (above): N&AR 2-2-0WT No 3 as built by Sharp Brothers in 1853. It was built for the Londonderry and Coleraine Railway but sold to the N&AR before entering service.
The Locomotive

Fig 35 (below): N&AR 0-4-2T No 2 was built by Hawthorn of Leith as an 0-4-0T and was acquired in 1854. This sketch shows its general outline. *The Locomotive*

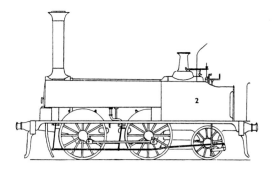

purchased from Moore, the contractor of the Newry-Goraghwood section, in February 1854. It later became No 2 and was still an 0-4-0T in 1872. It was extensively repaired in 1877-8, with new cylinders and boiler tubes, and this may have been when it was altered to an 0-4-2T.

Certainly, when it entered GNR stock in 1879, it was an 0-4-2T with 4'6" driving wheels, 13"x 18" cylinders and a boiler 3'5"x 8'7" (Fig 35). It does not appear to have carried a GNR number. Dundalk made diagrams of all the N&AR locomotives in September 1879 (reproduced here) and that for No 2 is the only one not to show a GNR number. A letter of April 1884, relating to its sale, refers to it as 'N&AR No 2'. Whilst some have suggested that it was No 86, I feel that, if this were so, the two new 2-4-0s of 1880 would not have been numbered 86 and 87, since the 0-4-2T was not withdrawn until 1884.

A third locomotive was added to stock in 1859 and was No 1. The minutes describe it as "a new and powerful engine." It was built by Fairbairns and nothing else was known about it until recently. However, before Mr Clements died, he found a document relating to Fairbairn, to the effect that, in Dec 1858, they were paid £2100 on behalf of the N&AR for an engine with 5'2" driving wheels, 14"x 20" cylinders and either leading or trailing wheels 4'0" (the writing was faint and could have been LW *or* TW). These dimension were similar to those of the double-framed 2-4-0 supplied to the L&CR in 1859. In 1864, No 1 was sold to Watson, contractor on the Goraghwood-Armagh section.

When the Goraghwood-Newry section was completed in 1864, more locomotives were required. Two Stephenson long boiler 0-6-0s, dating from 1859-60, were purchased second-hand from the contractors, Watson and Overend, becoming Nos 1 and 4. They had 4'7½" driving wheels, 16"x 24" cylinders, 3'6½'x 12'6½" boilers and weighed 25½ tons. They became GNR Nos 83 and 84. No 84 was scrapped in 1881 but No 83 lasted to 1886 (Fig 36). Kit O'Connor remembered one of them getting as far as Dublin around 1881. It promptly derailed in Amiens Street yard and was bundled back to Newry as quickly as possible!

No 5 was an outside cylinder 2-4-0T, also acquired in 1864. The origins of this engine are unclear. It seems to have come to the N&AR via Sharp Stewart, but was not necessarily built by them. It had 5'0" driving wheels, 15"x 22" cylinders and weighed 32 tons 1 cwt. The sketch (Fig 37) is based on its known dimensions. It appears to be of the type known as 'Standard Indian 2-4-0' which was built by at least ten firms. When John Jones of Liverpool went out of business in 1863, one of his last orders was for some of this type and it is possible that his uncompleted stock was taken over by Sharps. Certainly the sketch bears a close resemblence to the drawing of the Jones engine on page 33 (Fig 20). Whatever its origins, No 5 became GNR No 85 and, as 85A, ended its days around 1895 shunting in Dublin, where it was unofficially known as 'The Buck', possibly a reference to a surging motion or, perhaps, it was difficult to control.

Nos 6 and 7 were Vulcan 0-4-2s, originally built in 1864 as saddle tank engines, but rebuilt when they were found to be too heavy for the line. They were built to N&AR order and became GNR Nos 81 and 82, designated the X class. They had 5'0½" driving wheels, 16"x 22" outside cylinders, telescopic boilers 4'0⅞"x 10'10½" and as tender engines weighed 27½ tons. No 81 was withdrawn in 1887. No 82 was rebuilt with a new boiler in 1880-81 and lasted until 1896.

The last N&AR locomotive to arrive was a brand new 0-4-2, built by Sharp Stewart in 1878. Its N&AR number is not known but probably was No 3. It was similar to the UR K class, with 5'0" driving wheels and 16"x 22" cylinders (see page 46). The N&AR could only afford to pay £545 of the £2365 bill for this engine, so it was still owned by Sharp Stewart in 1879. For this reason, it did not enter GNR skock and was sold to the Belfast Central Railway in 1880. It will re-enter our story in Chapter 6.

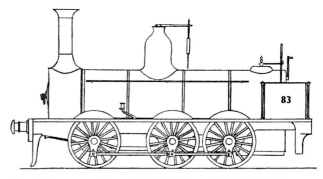

Fig 36: Newry and Armagh 0-6-0 No 1 as GNR No 83. This engine was built by R Stephenson and Co in 1859.

The Locomotive

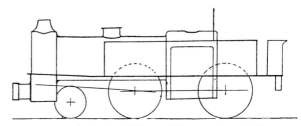

Fig 37: A rough sketch of 'The Buck' – N&AR 2-4-0T No 5 – based on its known dimensions. This was possibly a John Jones engine and became GNR No 85. It was scrapped in 1894.

The Locomotive

Fig 38: N&AR Nos 6 and 7 were powerful outside cylinder Vulcan 0-4-2s (originally 0-4-2ST). This is a representation of No 7 which became GNR No 82. It was rebuilt in 1880-81 and scrapped in 1896.

Adapted from a drawing in *The Locomotive*

Chapter 6
Doncasterising the GNR(I)
J C Park 1880-1895

It was a logical step that the newly formed GNR(I) should build new workshops. In May 1879, the Directors had decided to construct a new Carriage and Wagon Works at Dundalk, but were actually planning to build the Locomotive Works at Dublin, where the present running shed was nearing completion. The decision to site the Locomotive Works at Dundalk was not finally made until October 1879. The new Works were intended to replace the existing four workshops. The Londonderry shops of the old L&ER had already closed in 1876. Dundalk was a much more central location than Dublin and easily accessible to the former INWR.

The site chosen was south of the present Dundalk station and west of the main line. It included the area occupied by the old D&BJR shops, which were demolished during the construction. Construction commenced late in 1879 and took almost two years. The Works were finally occupied in October 1881, after which the older workshops in Dublin and Dundalk (Barrack Street) closed. Eaton, however, remained in control of the Belfast shops for a further four years, so Dundalk Works at first serviced only Southern and Irish North Western Division locomotives.

Whilst the facilities were excellent for the time, it was unfortunate that the 314'x 39' locomotive erecting shop was positioned with its gable facing the main line, so that entry to the shop had to be by a traverser, through a series of doors along the length of the building. The locomotives sat side by side in the shops rather than in parallel lines. This meant that the 39'0" width of the building dictated the maximum length of locomotives which could be accommodated.

Whilst 39'0" was adequate for the small locomotives of the 1880s (typically 22 feet without tender and 36 feet with), it was short-sighted in the long run. As locomotives became larger, tenders had to be removed before any locomotive entered shops, which was very unusual elsewhere. Even without tenders, nothing larger than a 4-4-0 could be accommodated, precluding a 4-6-0 or twelve wheel tank engine design. Even the ten-wheel Glover 4-4-2 tanks of 1914-30 were so tight in the erecting shop, that their rear buffers had to be temporarily removed to get them in.

J C Park

To manage the new Works, the GNR Directors decided, on 12 October 1880, to advertise outside for a new

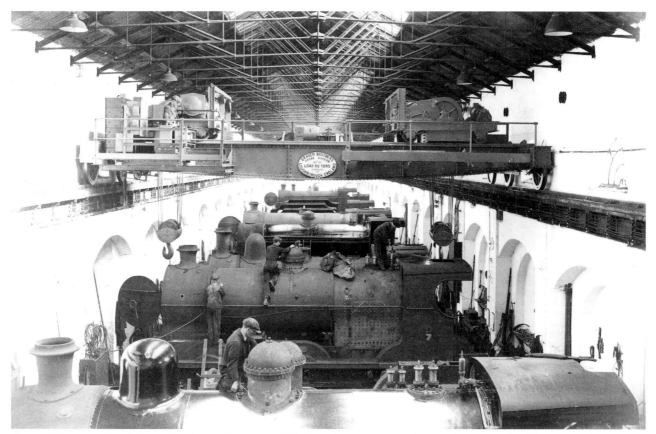

Above: The narrow Dundalk erecting shop in September 1945. Seven locomotives and three tenders occupy the different bays. In the centre foreground is SG3 class 0-6-0 No 7 of 1920.
Courtesy Duffners

Top: An interesting view of the Dundalk Works traverser in use, in August 1897, with the doors into the erecting shop visible on the right. The later Glover 4-4-2Ts had a wheelbase longer than the traverser and to allow them to use it, the rear radial truck had to be temporarily jacked up.

L J Watson

Centre: A close up, taken on the same occasion, shows B class 0-6-0 No 62 in course of rebuilding. A new boiler is being steam tested. The building on the left is boiler shop.

L J Watson

Mechanical Engineer who would have the necessary experience and be senior to William Curry (then Locomotive Superintendent).

By coincidence, the successful applicant was James C Park of the English GNR. He was appointed on 30 November 1880 and probably took up post on 1 January 1881. Park had been District Locomotive Superintendent at Peterborough and was junior to the famous Patrick Stirling. His arrival at Dundalk in 1881 was to mark the beginning of Doncaster influence at Dundalk for some years to come. Curry, meanwhile, seems to have accepted the appointment of Park with good grace. He moved to Dundalk as Park's assistant and Clifford went to Dublin as District Locomotive Superintendent. Eaton remained at Belfast, effectively in a similar post. Amongst the innovations made by Park was the introduction of the alphabetical classification of boilers, cylinders and crank axles, explained at the start of this book. This was introduced in 1881 or early 1882 and led to the locomotive classification system well known to GNR enthusiasts.

The duplicate list

Park also introduced the concept of the duplicate list, which was first used in November 1881, when new 2-4-0 No 85 used the number of an ex-N&AR 2-4-0T, which became 85A. The duplicate list had several functions and was widely used by railways in Britain. Firstly, it allowed new locomotives to be built in numerical blocks, without waiting for old engines to be scrapped. Thus, the new 2-4-0s of 1880-81 were 84-87 even though old No 85 was not scrapped until 1894. Without this system, the new engines would have had scattered numbers. Secondly, engines on the 'duplicate list' were often regarded as 'written off' in terms of capital value and depreciation. The main list was the 'capital list' but duplicate engines might continue in service for several years. Thirdly, it was a useful device for fooling the Directors and Accountants into thinking that there were fewer locomotives than there really were! For many years the GNR had no locomotive

numbered higher than 150, but there were usually up to 15 duplicates as well. Accountants regarded large numbers of locomotives as wasteful, but the Operating Department saw things differently!

Doncaster influence

The Doncaster influence made itself felt in a number of ways. Firstly, Park adopted the English GNR green livery for the locomotive fleet – the same shade of green, the same lining and style of lettering. There was a similar copying of Doncaster style in the carriage fleet. Park introduced new standard designs for six-wheeled stock to replace the diverse collection of four and six-wheelers inherited in 1876. The pattern of panelling used in these was a straight copy of current Doncaster practice and was used by the GNRI right down to 1935, when the flush-panelled era began. The varnished finish to carriages and the lining details reflected Doncaster standards.

In his first two years, Park was too busy getting the new

Dundalk Works up and running to devote much attention to locomotive design. When his first new engines appeared in 1882, the Doncaster influence was evident in much of the detailing. In particular, the design of the smokebox and its fittings and especially the chimney was a copy of Stirling's and certain other details, such as the combined splasher and sandbox showed Doncaster influence. The GNRI rounded cab roof resembled the Stirling cab but, unlike the Doncaster design, had a shallow cut out in the side sheets. On the other hand, Park fitted his locomotive boilers with domes, whereas Stirling engines were domeless and had the regulator in the smokebox.

Park also introduced a new design of tender. Hitherto, GNR tenders had used an old fashioned design with a narrow tank and outside springs placed above the running plate (see page 187). Park's designs were a faithful copy of the Stirling tender, with the springs out of sight and hidden inside of the frames. This allowed a wider water tank and, initially, 1550 gallon (11'6" wheelbase) and 1700 gallon (12'0" wheelbase) tenders were produced. Taller tanks eventually produced 2000, 2400 and 2500 gallon versions. This basic design was standard for GNRI tenders until 1909 but was unpopular with the fitters because of the difficulty in accessing the springs. However, the similarities to Doncaster practice were, on the whole, superficial and more to do with the *appearance* of the engine. No Stirling influence has been traced in the mechanical design of Park's GNRI engines. We will now move on to look at Park's locomotive designs, class by class.

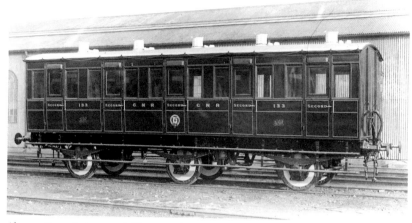

Above: Second class coach No 133, showing the Doncaster style of panelling and livery, introduced for Park's new standard range of six-wheelers in 1882. This vehicle was constructed in 1888.
Courtesy Duffners

Below: The first A class 0-6-0 was No 79 *Cavan*, delivered in April 1882. Note the Stirling inspired 2000 gallon tender and the rounded cab with short roof. This was the standard GNR cab until 1913. The attractive Beyer Peacock builder's plate was attached to the centre splasher on both sides. No 79 (as 69 after 1937) was sold to the SL&NCR in 1940 and scrapped in 1949.
L J Watson

A class 0-6-0 1882-1891

Until Eaton's retirement, Park was restricted to supplying locomotives only for the Southern and Irish North Western Divisions, so only six new locomotives were built before 1885 and even these were modifications of existing designs rather than completely new ones.

The first was a new version of the standard GNR goods locomotives constructed since 1877. The first four were Nos 79, 83 (1882), 61 and 64 (1883), built by Beyer Peacock. These engines had a flush topped boiler 3'11⅝"x 10'3" with 164 2" tubes, giving a heating surface of 989 sq feet at 130lb (later 140lb) pressure. They retained the 17"x 24" cylinders of the B class, but thicker tyres made the wheels 4'7¼".

The class was subsequently expanded to a total of fifteen, as follows: Nos 80-82 (BP, 1886), 28, 145, 146 (BP, 1888), 60 (Dundalk, 1890), 31, 149, 150 (BP, 1890) and 33 (Dundalk, 1891). As described above, these were the first engines to show Doncaster influence in their detailing, though their mechanical design was probably done by Beyer Peacock. The locomotives carried names of Irish counties, except for the two built at Dundalk, which were Nos 60 *Dundalk* and 33 *Belfast*.

The A class was rebuilt in 1905-18 but was never superheated. Two (Nos 31 and 149) were sold to the SL&NCR in 1928 and 1931. A further seven of the class were withdrawn in 1935-37 and No 69 (79 until 1937) was sold to the SL&NCR in 1940. The other five remained in traffic throughout the war years. No 68 (originally 82) went in 1948, No 28 in 1956 and the last three survived long enough to enter CIE stock in 1958. Of these, Nos 33 and 60 (the two built at Dundalk) went the following year, leaving No 150 to survive until 1961.

Above: A class 0-6-0 No 61 *Sligo* was one of the 1883 pair. It is coupled to one of the older tenders with outside springs. Probably its newer Stirling tender had been transferred to one of the 2-4-0s built in the 1875-81 period. It was common practice on the GNR for newer tenders to be given to passenger engines. No 61 was rebuilt in 1905 and scrapped in 1935. *H Foyle, courtesy IRRS*

Left: Park's first passenger locomotives were a pair of 2-4-0s built in 1883, Nos 46 and 47. No 46 was renumbered 48 in 1898 and is seen here inside Dundalk running shed after rebuilding in 1903. These engines were a modified version of the G class 5'6" 2-4-0s built in 1875-77, and were the last 2-4-0s to be built for the GNR. The Stirling features mirrored those on the contemporary A class 0-6-0s. Note the side chains on the old outside sprung tender to which it is attached. From this angle the G class were very diminutive locomotives, but the Doncaster lined green livery is clearly in evidence.

J D FitzGerald collection

Modified G class 2-4-0 1883

In 1883 James Park designed his first passenger engines. These were a slightly modified version of the G class 2-4-0s built in 1875-77. Nos 46 and 47 had solid splashers combined with sandboxes, rounded cabs and Doncaster pattern chimneys. Mechanically, they were similar to the earlier version and were the last new GNR engines to be built with raised fireboxes. No 46 was renumbered 48 in 1898 (to allow the 1866 H class 2-4-0s to become Nos 44-46).

The two engines were rebuilt in 1903 with 4'0½" flush-topped boilers and 16½"x 22" cylinders. They were scheduled to be scrapped in 1914, but were reprieved due to the war and renovated in 1915. Final withdrawal came in 1921. Although these were the last 2-4-0s to be built, H class 2-4-0s Nos 84-87 of 1880-81 outlasted them by eleven years.

1885 – In control at last

The year 1885 was to be something of a watershed in GNR locomotive history. In that year eleven locomotives were built and Park introduced three new designs in one year. It was also the year that John Eaton retired from the Northern Division (he had been suffering from ill health since 1883) and Park was able to assume direct control of the whole GNR fleet. Curry was sent to Belfast to replace Eaton. The Northern Division's 43 locomotives were renumbered 101-143 in the GNR fleet and the brick red livery was phased out. Park was

Above: JS 4-2-2 No 88 *Victoria*. This view shows the well-proportioned lines of these engines. Note the unusual rectangular Beyer Peacock builder's plate. The engine is coupled to a 1700 gallon tender of 1884. The device on the cab roof was a fitting which enabled passengers, in an emergency situation, to alert the driver by blowing the whistle. The wire used can be seen suspended along the tender.

L J Watson

now able to give the locomotives a uniform 'look'. As engines went through shops they were given Stirling cabs and 'Doncaster green' livery. However, although heavy work was concentrated at Dundalk, the Belfast Works remained open for a few more years. This would seem to have had something to do with resistance from the Northern Division workforce in Belfast to any move to Dundalk. Even as late as 1889, a GNR locomotive list divides the fleet into Northern Division and others, implying that the Northern Division still had repair facilities.

From 1885, Park embarked on a systematic programme of modernisation and replacement of older locomotives. Each year up to 1890, three engines were built by Beyer Peacock, alternating between batches of A class 0-6-0s and J class 4-4-0s. In addition, two of the new T class 4-4-0Ts were built each year at Dundalk and large numbers of standard six-wheeled carriages were emerging from Dundalk Works.

JS class 4-2-2 1885

Given Park's connection with the English GNR, it was not at all surprising that his first express locomotive design should be a bogie single. Stirling's famous eight foot singles were already legend and 39 were in service when Park produced his own design for the GNRI. Unlike the Doncaster 'eight footers', the GNRI JS class were inside cylinder machines and, as such, were the first of a new breed of bogie single. Examples soon followed on the Caledonian Railway (No 123, 1886), the Midland Railway (1887) and the North Eastern Railway (1888). However, in contrast to these relatively powerful machines, the GNRI singles had only 16"x 22" cylinders, as against the more normal 18"x 26". They used the J class crank axle of the earlier 6'1" 2-4-0s (Nos 84-87). 'JS' presumably stood for 'J Single'.

Left: This view of *Victoria* was taken at Dundalk running shed around 1902 and shows the reversing lever on the driver's side. Visible behind is a T class 4-4-0T in original condition, with a straight-sided smokebox.

H Fayle, courtesy IRRS

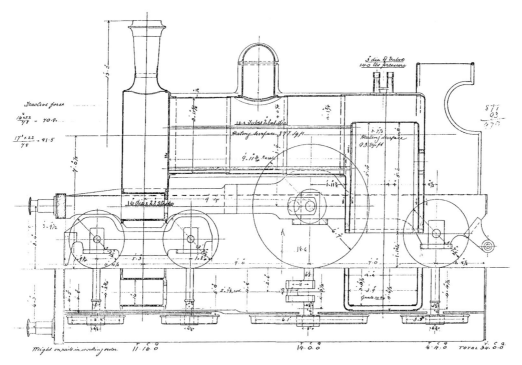

Fig 39 (left): The JS 4-2-2 design of 1885, with 6'7" driving wheels and 16"x 22" cylinders. The boiler was 3'11¾₆" x 9'11¾" with 164 2" tubes giving a heating surface of 877 sq ft. With 140 lbs boiler pressure, the tractive effort was 8,484 lbs. Note the bend in the frames between the bogie and the driving wheels.

Courtesy P Mallon

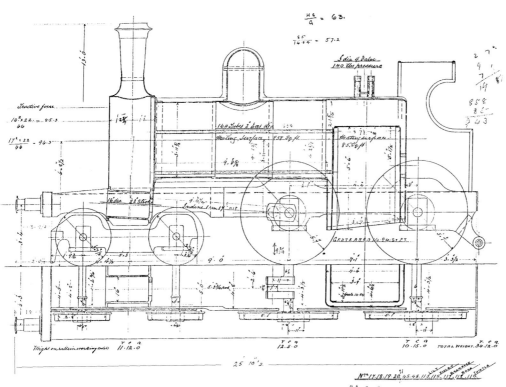

Fig 40 (left): The J class 4-4-0 design of 1885. Driving wheels 5'7", cylinders 16"x 22", tractive effort 10,003 lbs. Although the 4-4-0s and 4-2-2s used the same bogie and the same tube arrangement, there were many differences. In the J class the boiler barrel was three inches shorter and pitched four inches lower. The cylinders were inclined at 1 in 17 and the grate was sloped.

Courtesy P Mallon

The Park bogie singles were beautifully proportioned machines and were delivered by Beyer Peacock in Febuary 1885, numbered 88 and 89. They were the first bogie engines on the GNR and the first to have 6'7" driving wheels, thereafter standard for GNR express engines. They were also the only bogie singles to run in Ireland. Unusually for GNR Southern Division passenger engines, they were named, the nameplates (*Victoria* and *Albert*) being attached to the splashers in the position normally occupied by the Beyer Peacock builder's plate. The main dimensions can be gleaned from the drawing above.

Victoria and *Albert* were put into service on the 'Limited Mail' trains, which consisted of only five six-wheelers leaving Dublin – the mail van, a second, a first, a brake van and a through composite for Londonderry. The Down 'Mail' left Dublin at 8.15 am and reached Belfast in 3 hours 5 minutes at 11.20 am. Speed averaged just over 39 mph for 112½ miles, when stops are excluded. The Up 'Mail' left Belfast at 3.15 pm and reached Dublin at 6.15 pm, exactly 3 hours later. The two engines were able to alternate on this service. As train weights increased in the 1890s, the 'Limited Mails' eventually needed coupled locomotives and, in 1896, the singles were relegated to suburban trains on the Howth branch. They were withdrawn in 1904, when even this traffic became too much for them. They were replaced by two P class 4-4-0s which assumed the same names and numbers and probably utilised the tenders, bogies and cab fittings from the singles.

J class 4-4-0 1885-89

Close on the heels of the bogie singles came the first GNRI 4-4-0 design. These were not the first 4-4-0s in Ireland, the GS&WR having introduced the type in 1877 with their '2' class. However, the GNR were the second Irish company to introduce the type, followed closely by the W&LR.

The J class had main dimensions of 5'7" driving wheels, 16"x 22" cylinders and 140 lbs boiler pressure. They had a tractive effort of 10,003 lbs. The first four (17, 18, 117 *Shamrock* and 118 *Rose*) arrived from Beyer Peacock in March 1885, followed by Nos 45 and 48 in April. These two were renumbered 15 and 16 in 1898. Two more batches followed in 1887 (Nos 19, 20 and 119 *Thistle*) and 1889 (Nos 21, 115

Lily and 116 *Violet*). As was customary at this time, only those intended for the Northern Division (Nos 115-119) were named. However, No 15 later became *Pansy* and flower-inspired names were planned for the others (Nos 16-21) but never applied. They were to have been *Iris, Marigold, Hollyhock, Foxglove, Sunflower* and *Columbine*, respectively.

Although they had much in common with the JS class, they had different frames and their boilers, though of the same diameter, were 3" shorter and pitched 4" lower, giving them quite a squat appearance. They were initially used on the Portadown-Londonderry line and between Dundalk and Omagh on the Irish North. Later, they worked on lightly trafficked lines like the Antrim branch. The J class used the same crank axle as the 4-2-2s and 2-4-0 Nos 84-87. To avoid confusion, the J class 2-4-0s were reclassified 'H' in Clifford's time. Up to then, H class engines had been ex-UR double-framed 2-4-0s.

These twelve engines were the most numerous GNR 4-4-0 class until 1904, but are almost forgotten today because all were scrapped in the early 1920s. Whilst adequate for the short six-wheeled trains of the 1880s, they had nothing in

Above: J class 4-4-0 No 117 *Shamrock* in original condition, with 1550 gallon tender, around 1900. Note the feedwater pipe on the side of the boiler. This was the first GNR class of 4-4-0 and makes interesting comparison with the earlier *Shamrock* which it replaced, seen on page 42.

Inspector A Johnston,

Left: Early lineside shots in Ireland are rare. J class 4-4-0 No 16 makes a spirited exodus from Londonderry early in the 20th century with a train of six-wheelers, the leading vehicle of which appears to be a mail van. The low pitch of the boiler on early GNR engines must have made access to the inside motion very difficult.

L&GRP 21717

reserve and had no more power than the 2-4-0s of the 1860s which they superseded. Between 1902 and 1907 the entire class was rebuilt with 175 lb, 4'4" boilers and, around the same time, received 17"x 22" cylinders, increasing the tractive effort to 14,115 lbs. However, they rapidly became obsolete after 1912 as heavier bogie stock reached the rural branches where they were employed.

The Belfast Central Railway

Before looking at the third new design of 1885, we must digress for a moment to look at the Belfast Central Railway, which was purchased by the GNR in September 1885. This short railway was incorporated in July 1865, with ambitious plans to connect the three railways which served Belfast (the UR, BCDR and BNCR) and construct a central station for the city. The BCR ran into serious financial problems and was not opened until 1875 and, even then, only in part. The planned central station was never built.

When the GNR took over the BCR in 1885, a passenger service was operating between Queens Bridge station (near the BCDR terminal) and a junction with the GNR at Donegall Road. This soon ceased and the GNR used the line primarily to give it access to the docks and for inter-change goods traffic between the GNR, the BNCR and the BCDR. The line closed with the cessation of rail freight in 1965.

Ironically the dream of a single terminus for Belfast only came to pass in recent years after the modern NIR opened Belfast Central station (and reopened the Belfast Central Railway) in 1976. It was later connected to the former LMS (NCC) line at York Road in 1994, with the new cross harbour bridge named after the contractor William Dargan. The BCR locomotives inherited in 1885 were as follows:

Nos 1 and 2 were Black Hawthorn 0-6-0STs, with 3'6" wheels and 14"x 20" cylinders, built in 1868 and 1874. No 1 was a contractor's engine, purchased from Kelly and McFarlane when the Maysfield-York Road line was completed in 1875. This pair became GNR Nos 93 and 94 and were respectively scrapped in 1892 and (probably)1894.

No 3 was a Beyer Peacock 2-4-0T, delivered in May 1878. It had 5'0" driving wheels, 14"x 20" cylinders, weighed 20 tons 9 cwt and had a 3'6¹⁄₁₆"x 8'10" boiler, with 604 sq ft of heating surface. This became GNR O class No 95 and lasted until 1898.

No 4 was a Beyer Peacock 4-4-0T built in 1880. It was really a bogie version of No 3, built to slightly larger dimensions, with 15"x 20" cylinders and a 4'0¼"x 9'9" boiler. It became GNR P class (later BP class) No 96. This engine had a long life. It was given 16" cylinders in 1887 and was rebuilt with a new 165 lb boiler in 1904, in which year it became the pilot engine at Dundalk passenger station. It was a familiar sight there, until withdrawal in 1950. It became No 96A in 1906 and 195 in 1915. It was the last absorbed engine to remain in traffic. It is sometimes claimed that No 96 was named 'Windsor' for a time, but this is due to confusion with a BT class locomotive, which was renumbered 96 in 1906 and was photographed carrying this name.

No 5 was the ex-Newry and Armagh Sharp Stewart 0-4-2 of 1878, which was described in Chapter 5 and was sold to the BCR in 1880. The GNR seemed determined not to own this engine! Having refused to purchase it in 1879, when they took over the N&AR, they did not take it into stock in 1885 either. Instead, it was sold in 1886 to the BNCR, where it became No 50 (subsequently No 9) and lasted until 1907.

The ex-BCR engines were Nos 93-96. In 1885, the GNR had renumbered the two ex-INWR Manning Wardle 0-6-0STs to 91 and 92 and seem to have decided to allocate subsequent numbers, in this series, to tank locomotives. The 0-6-0STs had formerly been 61 and 64, but numbers in that series were now allocated to 0-6-0 tender engines.

T (later BT) class 4-4-0T 1885-93

When the T class 4-4-0Ts were designed in 1884, the GNR had only six tank locomotives. These were Neilson 2-2-2ST No 8 of 1862 (D&DR), Sharp 2-2-2WT Nos 28 and 29 of 1858 (D&BJR), Sharp 2-4-0T No 85A of 1864 (N&AR) and Manning Wardle 0-6-0ST Nos 91 and 92 of 1859-60 (INWR). With some developing suburban traffic,

Left: Belfast Central Railway 2-4-0T No 3 at Donegall Road station in May 1880 with one of the BCR's 45'0" tri-composite six-wheelers. These became the longest six-wheelers in the GNR. No 3 was built by Beyer Peacock in 1878 and became GNR O Class No 95. It appears again in the background of the top photo on page 86. No 95 was scrapped in 1898.
D FitzGerald collection

Opposite top: Belfast Central 4-4-0T No 4, running as GNR No 96. It became GNR P class (BP for 'bogie P' after 1892). It was rebuilt as shown in 1887 and again in 1904. Note the lack of valance on the running plate and the similarity in the cab roof design between Nos 3 and 4.
L&GRP 9156

Below: A later view of the ex-BCR 4-4-0T, on 5 August 1936 at Dundalk. It was rebuilt as shown in 1904, after which it became the Dundalk pilot. After 1915 it ran as 165 and was scrapped in 1950, the last non-standard engine in service. Note the short wheelbase bogie and the built-up bunker.

R G Jarvis

and several short branch lines to operate, Park saw the need for a small general purpose tank locomotive. His design may have been influenced by the BCR 4-4-0T of 1880, described above.

With hindsight, Park would have been wiser to have built a heavier 4-4-0T, similar to the Beyer designed No 96, which had 5'0" driving wheels and 15"x 20" cylinders. His own design was much smaller, with 4'7" driving wheels and only 14"x 18" cylinders. In general proportions, the T class were remarkably similar to the contemporary LB&SCR 'Terrier' 0-6-0Ts. The Brighton engines, built in 1872-80, had 4'0" driving wheels, 13"x 20" cylinders, 3'6"x 7'10" boilers and a boiler pressure of 140 lbs. The similarity is particularly striking when the comparison is made between a 'Terrier' and GNR No 1, which was rebuilt in 1921 as an 0-6-0T.

The first three members of the T class were Nos 97-99 delivered by Beyer Peacock in October 1885. No 97 was later named *Lisburn* and, for a time, No 99 (as 96 after 1906) was *Windsor*. The remaining ten were built at Dundalk and No 100, completed in June 1887, was the first locomotive to be built at the new Works. This engine was soon renumbered

1 and the others followed in sequence – Nos 2 (December 1887), 3, 4 (1888), 5, 6 (1889), 7 (1891), 8 (1892), 91 and 92 (1893). From No 2 onwards, the engines were built with 15"x 18" cylinders.

These engines were used on Belfast-Lisburn and Dublin-Howth suburban traffic and also on some of the shorter branches like the Ardee branch. From 1909, they appeared on the new Armagh-Castleblaney line. Nos 1-6, 97 and 99 were rebuilt with 150 lb boilers between 1906 and 1914, but this did not really alter their appearance. In 1910, No 98 (98A since 1905) ceased work, but was not broken up until after 1922. In 1914, the boiler pressure on Nos 1-6 was raised to 160 lbs so that they could work Belfast-Lisburn push-pull trains.

The basic problem with the BT class 4-4-0Ts was that they were much too small for their purpose. Like the J class, they were adequate when built, but had nothing in reserve when heavier bogie coaching stock was introduced. By the end of the First World War, there were no longer any trains light enough to justify their retention. The entire class was withdrawn in 1920-21 except for No 1 which, in April 1920,

Top: The first three BT class 4-4-0Ts, Nos 97-99, were delivered by Beyer Peacock in October 1885 and were the first new tank engines built for the GNR. Note the simple wrap-over cab. No 99 became 99A in 1905 and then 96 in 1906. It was named *Windsor* for a time and was scrapped in 1921.

LPC 2539

Fig 41 (centre): Diagram of the BT class 4-4-0T of 1885. The bogie wheels were only 2'7" in diameter (3'1½" on the J class). The cylinders were inclined at 1 in 16.

Courtesy P Mallon

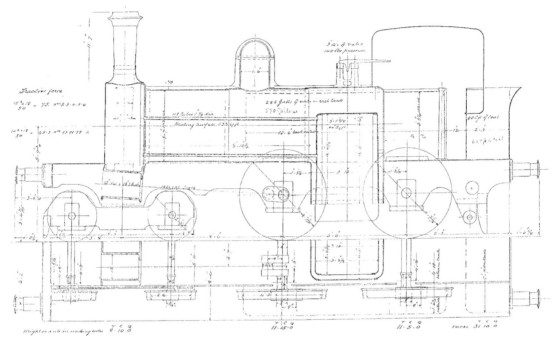

Opposite bottom: A later view, of No 91, built at Dundalk in August 1893. The first four enginesof this class had 14" cylinders and the others 15". Whilst the early examples had straight-sided smoke-boxes, later engines, like No 91, had them curved. Note the steam sanding equipment fitted to this engine. It must have looked delightful in its lined green livery.

L J Watson

Right: BT 0-6-0T No 119 at Londonderry in July 1932. The similarity to the LB&SCR 'Terrier' 0-6-0T is very striking. No 119 started life in 1887 as No 100 and became No 1 in 1888. It was the first locomotive built at Dundalk Works and survived as a shunter at Londonderry until 1935.

J A G H Coltas

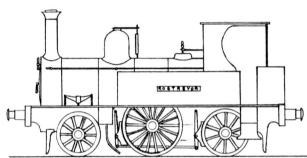

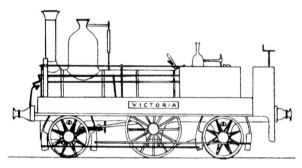

Fig 42 (above left): 2-2-2T *Rostrevor*, in its earlier days, probably resembled *Victoria*, but was rebuilt in 1883 to the condition seen here. It became GNR No 100 and was withdrawn in August 1896.

Courtesy IRRS

Fig 43 (above right): 2-2-2WT *Victoria* – based on the photograph on the left. Note the brakes on the leading and trailing wheels.

Courtesy IRRS

Left: *Victoria*, probably photographed at Dundalk in 1886, before it was broken up. It looks every inch an 1850 engine. Note the crude horizontally hinged smokebox door. The steam chest is visible between the front wheels.

J D FitzGerald collection

was rebuilt as an 0-6-0T and, the following year, renumbered 119. As No 119, it was shunter at Londonderry until 1935. However, No 5 remained at Dundalk as a stationary boiler until 1931 and another (possibly No 2) at Belfast.

The Newry, Warrenpoint and Rostrevor Railway

The last operating company absorbed by the GNR was the NW&RR, which was taken over in July 1886. This short line had been incorporated in July 1846 and opened from Newry to Warrenpoint on 28 May 1849. It never reached Rostrevor, though a separate company built a horse tramway to the town in 1877. The only other construction undertaken was a connecting line to the N&AR station in Newry in

1861. This was built by a non-operating company, called the Town of Newry Connecting Railway.

The NW&RR started off with three Bury 2-2-2 tender engines built in 1848-49. These proved grossly over-powered for the traffic on the line and, when the contractor William Dargan took a five year lease to operate the route in 1850, he replaced them with his own engines. Dargan later sold the Bury engines to the Waterford and Limerick Railway. When the NW&RR resumed control of their line in 1855 they purchased the three Dargan engines then in use.

Nos 1 and 2 were Grendon 2-2-2WTs with 5'0" driving wheels and 11"x 16" cylinders. They were built for Dargan, probably in 1851. No 1 was rebuilt in 1883, at which date,

Left: L J Watson, who joined the GNR in 1879 and was Chief Draughtsman at Dundalk from 1892 to 1933. He had a major input into the design of GNR locomotives under Park, Clifford and Glover.

Right: *Warrenpoint*, a Beyer Peacock 2-4-0T built in 1882, became GNR O class No 90 and was withdrawn in 1898.

Real Photographs 88012

probably, it was named *Rostrevor*. It entered GNR stock in 1886, as No 100, and was scrapped in 1892. It briefly became 100A in 1887, when BT class 4-4-0T No 100 was built, but reverted to 100 when the new tank became No 1. A C W Lowe (usually unreliable on NW&RR matters) is the only evidence for No 2 being called *Mourne*. No 2 was not taken into GNR stock but, probably, lasted until 1886.

Victoria, probably No 3, was a smaller Grendon 2-2-2WT with 4'0" driving wheels, 9"x 15" cylinders and a tiny boiler of 351 sq ft heating surface. It was built in 1850 and displayed at an exhibition in Dublin that July. It was withdrawn by 1885, but still existed when the GNR took over the line. Fortunately, L J Watson ordered it to be photographed before it was broken up.

A fourth Grendon tank engine, *Drogheda*, was purchased in 1866. Its wheel arrangement is not known but it was very likely a 2-2-2WT, similar to *Victoria*. It was probably not new in 1866 and may have been the Grendon engine offered to the D&BJR in 1858 (see page 24). It had 4'0" driving wheels

and 9"x 13" cylinders and probably was No 4, though referred to in the minutes only by name. Of *Victoria* and *Drogheda*, one was withdrawn in 1882 and one in 1885. One (probably *Drogheda*) was sold to a contractor in 1885 and *Victoria* definitely was at Newry in 1886.

The newest engine in the NW&RR fleet was *Warrenpoint*, a Beyer Peacock 2-4-0T built in 1882. It was probably No 5 and became GNR O class No 90. It was essentially the same design as No 95, the ex-BCR 2-4-0T. Its dimensions were: driving wheels 5'0", cylinders 14"x 20", boiler 3'6¾"x 8'10", firebox 3'7"x 4'1", HS 602 sq ft and weight 28 tons 11½ cwt. As GNR No 90 it survived until 1898.

The Armagh disaster 1889

Ireland's most serious railway accident occurred on 12 June 1889 on the Armagh to Newry line. The train involved was a Methodist Sunday School excursion setting out for Warrenpoint which, as explained above, was now part of the

Left: The locomotive on the regular 10.35 am Armagh to Newry train was ex-D&DR 0-4-2 No 9. This engine was following the excursion and was flung from the track when struck by the runaway. Nos 9 and 11 were regular performers on this line and No 9 is seen here somewhere between Goraghwood and Markethill on a later occasion with 6 six-wheelers. Ironically, it would have been a better choice for the excursion than No 86. No 9 was built in 1858 and had been No 20 until 1887. It became 9A in 1911 and eventually 201 in 1914, before being scrapped the following year.

J D FitzGerald collection

GNR system. The locomotive supplied by Dundalk was H class 2-4-0 No 86. A 0-6-0 should have been sent for this heavy train of 14 six-wheelers which had to negotiate gradients of 1:82 and 1:75 for the first 3½ miles. No 86 failed on this bank and came to a standstill 3 miles out of Armagh.

The driver decided to split the train and take the first four coaches on to Hamiltonsbawn, the next station. He should have waited for the arrival of the lightly loaded 10.35 regular, due to leave Armagh 20 minutes after him and hauled by 0-4-2 No 9. This train could have banked him for the last half mile.

The carriages had non-automatic vacuum brakes so, when the train was split, the rear 10 carriages were protected only by the hand brake on the guard's van. As No 86 started forward with the front portion, the engine rolled back slightly and the jolt started the rear portion rolling back.

The guard's brake was unable to control the runaway, which rapidly gained speed, with 600 parents and children locked inside. Meanwhile, No 9 with the 10.35 had left Armagh, signalling being of the time interval system. The crew spotted the runaway and acted quickly enough to throw their engine into reverse gear and slow to 5 mph. By this time, the excursion coaches were doing 40 mph downhill. At the last moment the fireman jumped clear but driver Murphy stayed on the tender. The impact flung No 9 off the line onto its side but the tender stayed on the rails. The last three carriages of the excursion disintegrated completely, killing virtually everyone inside.

The carriages of the 10.35 split into two portions and now began to run away, but the guard, and Murphy on the tender, managed to bring each portion to a halt. However, Murphy was injured in the initial impact and died seven months later.

In all, 88 people were killed and an estimated 400 injured. Nineteen of the dead were under 15 years of age. This figure would have been higher, but many of the parents who died in the last three carriages, hurled their children from the train just before the impact. The accident had a major impact on all railways in the British Isles and led to the Board of Trade insisting on the fitting of automatic vacuum brakes to all passenger trains, and the introduction of absolute block working, in place of the time interval system, for starting trains. This meant that a train could not depart until the preceding train had definitely cleared the section ahead.

The rebuilding programme

When the GNR was formed in 1876, there had been 113 locomotives in the initial fleet. The locomotive stock had increased gradually to 128 at the end of 1879 (including six ex-N&AR), 144 at the end of 1885 (including four ex-BCR) and 149 at the end of 1889 (including two ex-NW&RR). It should be remembered that although 54 new locomotives had been built since the amalgamation, 95 pre-amalgamation or absorbed engines were still in service in 1889.

Rebuilding of these earlier locomotives occupied much time at the Dundalk workshops. Among the engines rebuilt in the 1880s were N6'0" 2-2-2 Nos 14 and 16; 2-4-0 Nos 12, 42 and 53 (G class), 37-39 (H class), 73-75 (L class), 110 and 112 (M class – double framed), 123 *Tyrone* (H class – double-framed); P class 4-4-0T No 96; 0-4-2 Nos 10 (G class), 31 (S class, with 24" cylinders to class B), 57, 58, 70 and 71 (B class), 76 (E class, as No 44), 82 (X class, ex-N&AR), 106 and 107 (K5'0"); 0-6-0 Nos 5 (A class, as No 29), 21 (G class 0-6-0), 40 and 41 (D class); 137 and 138 (C class).

The first bogie carriages

In the past, writers have linked the enlarged designs introduced in 1892-93 to the introduction of the automatic vacuum brake in the years after 1889. It is more likely that the new designs were due to the introduction of heavier coaching stock at this time. This was a result of the addition of lavatories to trains after 1889. The first lavatory equipped carriage on the GNR was a 38'6" bogie composite, the first of a pair built in 1889-90 (Nos 382, 383) for the Limited Mail trains and the first bogie carriages on the GNR.

Lavatories were initially only for first class compartments, but second class received them gradually after 1890. The change over to bogie stock was slow and six-wheelers continued to be built in quantity up to 1897. The only bogie stock built by Park, other than Nos 382 and 383, were composites Nos 397 and 398, mail van No 7 (all 1892), Royal saloon No 400 (1893), tricompo No 404 (1895) and the first catering vehicles – Nos 338 (breakfast car, 1895) and 401 (clerestory diner, 1895). These vehicles appeared on the principal expresses between Belfast and Dublin.

Left: P6'6" class 4-4-0 No 83 *Narsissus*, as running around 1900. This engine was built in 1892 and was one of the first GNR 6'7" 4-4-0s. No 83 was rebuilt in 1913 with a 4'6" boiler and superheated in 1931.

LPC 5621

Below: P6'6" 4-4-0 No 72 of 1895 with an Up train at Balmoral, shortly after 1900. A rather motley collection of carriages is in tow, the leading vehicle being a brand new K1 100 seat bogie third. Behind is a standard R3 lavatory composite and some older six-wheelers. There also appear to be some horse boxes, so this may be a special for the Dublin horse show. Alternately, the horses may have come from the nearby Balmoral show.

L&GRP 21267

P6'6" class 4-4-0 1892-1895

These four engines were the first GNR express 4-4-0 locomotives and were a big improvement on the earlier 6'0" 2-4-0s used up to this time. They had 6'7" driving wheels, 17"x 24" cylinders, 4'1"x 10'3" boilers, at 140 lbs boiler pressure and 4'11" fireboxes. These were the first GNR locomotives to have all steel boilers and, as with all passenger tender engines up to 1899, they were built by Beyer Peacock. In 1892, Beyer Peacock were building their own design of Worsdell Von Borries compounds for the BNCR and BCDR and suggested to the GNR that the P class be built as two cylinder compounds. The GNR wisely declined and was not to have a compound until 1932.

The coupled wheelbase was 8'0" and the bogie centre line was 9'6" ahead of the leading drivers. The standard 5'3" wheelbase bogie, with 3'1½" wheels, was used. Nos 82 and 83 (*Daisy* and *Narcissus* after 1896) were delivered in February 1892. There was obviously an initial intention to allocate numbers in the 80-89 series to express locomotives. The H class 2-4-0s and the JS bogie singles already occupied 84-89. A class 0-6-0 Nos 82 and 83 had to be renumbered 68 and 69 to make way for the new engines.

Above: P5'6" 4-4-0 No 53 of 1892 at Dundalk around the turn of the century. Note the 1700 gallon Stirling tender, numbered LL, and the wire to the cab roof which allowed passengers to blow the whistle in an emergency. No 53 was scrapped in 1950.

L J Watson

Right: P5'6" 4-4-0 No 54 was the example built in 1895 with a slightly larger 4'2" boiler. In this August 1897 view at Dundalk, No 54 is scarcely two years old and has a 2000 gallon tender attached. Judging by the boiler diameter, the chimney is nearly four feet long.

L J Watson

This policy was not continued with the second pair, which came in March 1895. They were Nos 72 and 73 (later *Daffodil* and *Primrose*). They differed from the first pair in having 150 lbs, 4'2" diameter boilers, raising the tractive effort from the original 10,448 lbs to 11,194 lbs and weight from 39 tons 6 cwt to 40 tons 16 cwt.

These engines had long lives due to the financial stringencies of the 1930s. Instead of being scrapped at the age of 40, as had been the norm up to 1930, they were superheated in 1931-32 and lasted another 26 years. In their latter days, they were a familiar sight on the 'Irish North'.

P5'6" class 4-4-0 1892-1895

Contemporary with the P6'6" class came a 5'7" version, initially built for service on Belfast-Dublin mainline trains, other than the Limited Mails. Nos 51-53 arrived in the autumn of 1892 and were identical to the 6'7" engines, apart from smaller driving wheels, 38 tons 15 cwt weight and 12,320 lbs tractive effort. No 54, built in February 1895, embodied the improvements made to Nos 72 and 73 with a 4'2" boilers and 13,199 lbs tractive effort.

Additions to the P5'6" class were made by Clifford in

1905-06 and these will be dealt with in Chapter 7. Nos 51 and 52 were named *Hyacinth* and *Snowdrop* after 1896. Nos 53 and 54 were to have been *Carnation* and *Pink* but the names were never applied. Nos 51-54 were later rebuilt with 175 lbs 4'6" boilers and then superheated in the 1920s.

AL class 0-6-0 1893-1896

In December 1893, Park introduced the AL class. It is sometimes assumed that these engines were A class 0-6-0s but with larger boilers. This is not, in fact, the case. Although they retained the 17"x 24" cylinders of the A class, the AL class had a new chassis with a wheelbase of 7'6"+ 7'6", compared to 7'3"+ 7'3" on the A class. The 4'2" boiler and firebox were identical to those used on the 1895 P class engines. The AL class was 2½ tons heavier than the A class and 5½" longer. The boiler was pitched 2" higher than on the A class and, unlike the A class, the centre driving wheel springs were below footplate level. Since these locomotives carried the power classification letter 'A' on the cabside, they were often confused with the A class proper, only three of which survived until 1957.

Left: AL class 0-6-0 No 35 *Clare* around 1900. This Beyer Peacock example was built in 1894 and was beautifully finished for a goods locomotive. However, judging by the amount of slack visible in the coal on the 1700 gallon tender, the crew of this engine will have their work cut out for them.

Maj Gen Sir Cecil Smith

Below: A Works photo of No 29 *Enniskillen*, one of the Dundalk built examples. This was the 14th locomotive built at Dundalk. No 29 was completed in 1895 and rebuilt in 1918. Note the company initials in scroll carried on the centre splasher. This was used when the splasher was too small for a crest.

R Welch, courtesy Ulster Museum

Left: Rebuilding of the G class commenced in 1887 and the first six were completed by 1899. No 23 was rebuilt in 1893. It was one of only two locomotives built for the short-lived Northern Railway in 1875 and originally looked like the engine on page 52, The new boilers were 4'0½" dia and flush-topped. No 23 joined the duplicate list in 1908 and was withdrawn in 1911. This view is between 1900 and 1908. Note the small narrow tender (probably 1500 gallons).

LPC 5472

Fig 44 (opposite): Dundalk drawing for a proposed 4-4-0T design in 1894. It would have had 5'7" driving wheels and 16"x 22" cylinders but was never approved. Note James Park's signature.

P Mallon collection

The class was constructed as follows: Beyer Peacock built Nos 36 (1893), 59, 151-153 (1894), 57 (1895) and 58 (1896). The names on the Beyer Peacock built series continued the counties theme and are listed on page 200. Nos 151-153 were very soon renumbered 141, 140 and 35 respectively (probably because the Directors objected to having more than 150 locomotives!). Dundalk Works built Nos 32 (1894), 29, 55 (1895) and 56 (1896). The Dundalk-built members were named after principal GNR stations, so these engines were *Drogheda*, *Enniskillen*, *Portadown* and *Omagh*, respectively.

The AL class was rebuilt with 4'6" boilers in 1914-19 (see Chapter 8). The class remained intact until 1957, when Nos 36, 140 and 141 were withdrawn.

Rebuilding work

In the early 1890s, Dundalk continued the work of modernising and improving the locomotive fleet. All rebuilt engines received flush-topped fireboxes and, where possible, standard components were fitted, even if the engine was elderly.

The last new work was done on the N class singles, No 13 receiving 15½" cylinders and Nos 55 and 56 larger 16" cylinders. Two more G class 2-4-0s were reboilered (Nos 23 and 25) and three H class 2-4-0s were given new cranks (Nos 83, 85 and 87, the last two also receiving 17" cylinders). Standard A class boilers were fitted to K class 0-4-2 Nos 105, 139-141 and F class 0-4-2 Nos 134 and 135 (lengthened to 11'0" on the F class). C class 0-6-0 Nos 103, 144, and 148 and E class 0-6-0 Nos 77 and 78 were rebuilt.

Park's last design

In 1894, James Park had begun the design of a new suburban tank to supersede the rather under-powered BT class 4-4-0Ts. There was a particular need for more powerful tanks on the Howth branch. Park drew up two alternative designs in September 1894, both of which are reproduced here from original Dundalk drawings signed by Park himself, and also by L J Watson, the chief draughtsman. Both involved locomotives with 5'7" driving wheels and 16"x 22" cylinders, and were essentially tank versions of the J class 4-4-0. One was a 4-4-0T design with the standard passenger bogie and 7'1" coupled wheelbase. However, the 4-4-0 wheel arrangement was not ideal for a suburban tank as the rear driving wheels would lead when the engine was running in reverse. In the end, Park opted for the 2-4-2 radial tank design shown. This had a shorter front end, but allowed for a larger cab (8'0" as opposed to 6'3") and a radial truck would lead in both directions of running.

Although Doncaster had favoured the 0-4-4T design, radial tanks had been highly successful on several major English railways, particularly the LNWR, L&YR and the GER. On a 2-4-2T, the wheelbase was fixed but the leading and trailing wheels, on the radial trucks, had several inches of side play to enable the engine to negotiate curves. The Dundalk drawing is marked "Approved for 2 engines". Unfortunately Park died in post in August 1895, just before the first engine was completed at Dundalk. This class will therefore be dealt with in Chapter 7.

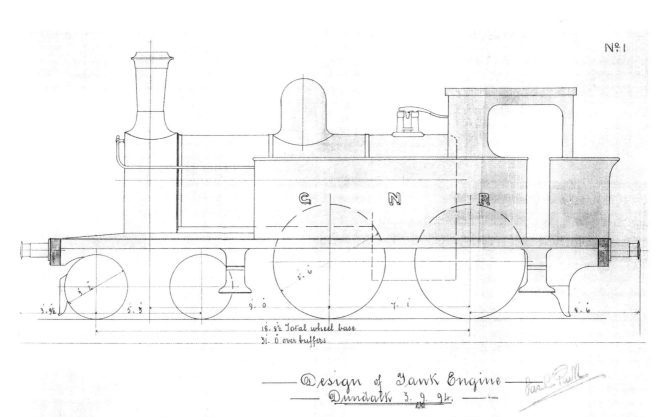

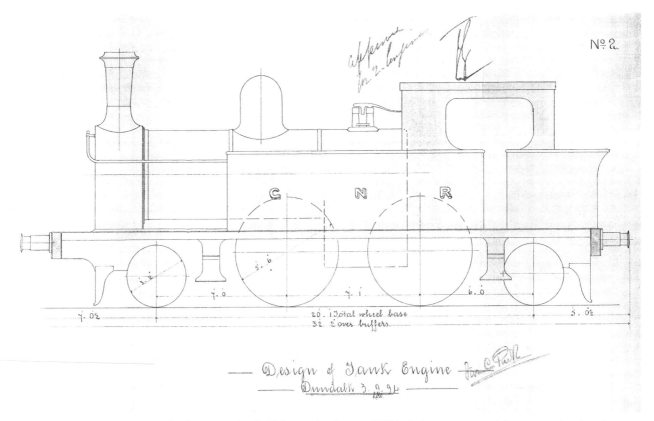

No 2.

C N R

Design of Tank Engine for C Park
Dundalk 3. 9. 94

Fig 45 (above): Dundalk drawing for the proposed 2-4-2T design, dated 3. 9. 94. This design was approved for construction (see above the safety valves) and Nos 93 and 94 resulted in 1895-96. The design was inspired by the successful LNWR Webb 5'6" 2-4-2Ts of 1890.

P Mallon collection

Above: Belfast shed about 1896. On view, from left to right, are 2-4-0 No 114 *Lagan*, AL 0-6-0 No 141 *Westmeath*, a B class 0-6-0, an ex-UR F class 0-4-2, A 0-6-0 No 146 *Wicklow* and JS 4-2-2 No 89 *Albert*. The presence of the latter suggests an early afternoon scene.

L&GRP 88160

Chapter 7
Knowing your Ps & Qs
Charles Clifford 1895-1912

The death of James Park, in August 1895, was mentioned at the end of Chapter six. Curry (District Locomotive Superintendent at Belfast) had already retired in April 1892 and Charles Clifford was the obvious internal candidate to succeed Park. Clifford had originally served his apprenticeship on the Dublin and Wicklow Railway before joining the INWR in 1861. In 1871 he became INWR Locomotive Superintendent and continued to manage Barrack Street Works for the GNR until the new Dundalk Works opened in 1881. After that, he spent eleven years in Dublin as District Locomotive Superintendent, before moving to Belfast to succeed Curry in 1892.

Clifford, therefore, had an enormous amount of experience under his belt by 1895 and could see the short-comings of the locomotive fleet from the Operating Department's point of view, as well as the engineering side.

If any criticism was to be made of Park in his years at Dundalk, it was that, for all their aesthetic qualities, his engines were under-powered. There had been no significant increase in the size of goods engines since the early 1870s. Even the AL class still had 17"x 24" cylinders. Of the passenger engines, only the eight most recently built engines had cylinders larger than 16"x 22" and as for the tiny BT 4-4-0Ts, their usefulness was limited to hauling a handful of six-wheelers.

In contrast, the Clifford era was to be a period when size became really important. In particular, the Dundalk express 4-4-0 designs got larger with almost every batch, culminating in the famous S class design of 1913. Likewise, goods engines increased rapidly in size so that, by 1906, large engines with 18½"x 26" cylinders were in production. By 1910, GNR locomotives were in the same league as those of the GS&WR, Ireland's 'premier line'.

The reasons for these increases in size are not hard to find. The period from 1895 to the First World War saw a steady growth in traffic for the railways, as the Irish economy prospered. Farmers were doing well and disposable incomes were rising. Goods traffic grew steadily and passenger numbers were increasing. Trains got longer and suburban traffic, stimulated by the development of electric trams, was on the rise. This coincided with new developments in express train carriage design. On-train catering greatly added to train weights. The GNR introduced dining cars on its main trains in 1895-96 and added them to other express trains in 1900 and 1905. At first, these were non-corridor; passengers wishing to dine had to sit in the dining car for the whole journey. In 1900, Clifford built the first GNR corridor train, though this and later corridor trains were really semi-corridor, as third class had to wait until 1913 before being offered corridor stock. Early on, Clifford also decided to move over to the construction of bogie coaching stock only. Apart from some brake vans, the last six-wheelers were built in 1896.

The locomotive fleet in 1895

It is appropriate to pause at this point and evaluate the locomotive fleet as it stood in August 1895, when Clifford took over. In 1895, there were 152 locomotives, compared to 113 in 1876 (though two more AL class 0-6-0s were under construction at Dundalk). The fleet was made up as follows (1876 figures in brackets): nine 2-2-2 (30); thirty-one 2-4-0 (31); two 4-2-2 (nil); twenty 4-4-0 (nil); twenty-six 0-4-2 (33); forty-seven 0-6-0 (10); two 2-4-0T (nil); fourteen 4-4-0T (nil); one 0-4-2ST (nil). The 48 classes of locomotive in 1876 had been reduced to 37 by 1895 and would be reduced still further over the next few years.

JT class 2-4-2T 1895-1902

The first of the JT class was completed in August 1895, the month that James Park died. Although this was really a Park design, I am dealing with the class in this chapter for convenience. The first two engines were Nos 93 (August 1895) and 94 (Febuary 1896) which at first were unnamed but soon became *Sutton* and *Howth*. These two engines had iron boilers 4'0½"x 9'9" with 4'4" fireboxes. The main dimensions were 5'7" driving wheels, 16"x 22" cylinders, 140 lbs boiler pressure and 10,003 lbs tractive effort. Oddly, these two engines were given square-roofed cabs. Although classified JT, the boilers used were G class rather than J class and, with the absence of a bogie, they would have been more accurately classified 'GT'.

A second pair, Nos 90 *Aster* and 95 *Crocus*, emerged from Dundalk Works in 1898. These replaced the two O class 2-4-0Ts of the same numbers. Clifford improved the design by fitting 160 lbs steel boilers and 16½"x 22" cylinders, which

Top: JT class 2-4-2T No 93 of 1895, prior to being named *Sutton*. Note the square-roofed cab which was replaced when the engine was rebuilt in 1917. No 93 is now preserved at Cultra, Co Down.
L&GRP 24157

Centre: JT 2-4-2T No 13 *Tulip* of 1902. This engine was renumbered 91 in 1920 and rebuilt in 1925. It was destined to be the last survivor, in traffic, of this small class and was withdrawn by CIE in 1963.
J D FitzGerald collection

Bottom: PP 4-4-0 No 70 *Precursor* as built in 1896. Note the burnished coupling rod and reversing lever. The first six engines had a large sandbox ahead of the leading splasher.
LPC 3214

increased the tractive effort to 12,158 lbs. This pair also received round-topped cabs and were named from the outset.

In 1902, a third and final pair were built, Nos 13 *Tulip* and 14 *Viola*. These had 17"x 22" cylinders and larger 4'2" diameter boilers, pressed to 175 lbs. These were the modifications then being applied to the J class 4-4-0s, as they were rebuilt. These final JT class 2-4-2Ts carried 1000 gallons of water and 2 tons of coal and their tractive effort was 14,116 lbs. Nos 90 and 95 were upgraded to 17" cylinders around this time. In March 1920, Nos 13 and 14 exchanged numbers with BT 4-4-0T Nos 91 and 92, which allowed the whole class to become neatly 90-95.

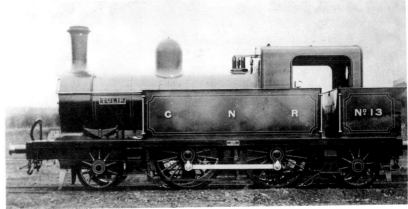

Between 1917 and 1925 the entire class was rebuilt with new 4'2" boilers and 16½"x 22" cylinders, giving a tractive effort of 12,504 lbs at 175 lbs boiler pressure. They dominated the Dublin suburban workings until the early 1920s, after which they found employment on short branch lines. In 1933, the GNR took over the operation of the Dundalk, Newry and Greenore Railway and the JT class 2-4-2Ts were ideal for this route. The closure of the DNGR in 1951 rendered most of them surplus to requirements and all, except No 91, were withdrawn in 1955-57. No 91 was retained to work the Belturbet branch and it was shedded at Clones until passenger services on the branch ended in 1957. No 91 passed to CIE and did further (mainly shunting) work, until the end of CIE steam in 1963. One member of the class has survived. This is No 93, the first of the class which, on withdrawal in 1955, was donated to the Belfast Transport Museum. It is now in the Ulster Folk and Transport Museum, Cultra, Co Down.

PP class 4-4-0 1896-98

Clifford's first express passenger design was the PP class, introduced in April 1896. Six were built by Beyer Peacock in 1896-98 but the class was later expanded to seventeen, by further construction in 1906-11. We will deal with the later engines further on. It is interesting that the original drawings for the PP class refer to it as the 'Precursor' class, named after the first engine, No 70 *Precursor*.

Clifford based his new design on the P class but with an 8'3" coupled wheelbase, instead of 8'0". The cylinders were

Left: An interesting view of *Precursor* passing Balmoral in the Down direction. The train consists entirely of standard six-wheelers apart from the leading vehicle, a K1 bogie third.

L&GRP 21269

Below: Neilson Reid works photo of Q class 4-4-0 No 133 *Apollo*, built in September 1899. This angle shows the rather shallow frames at the front end. Note the gracefully curved bogie splasher.

Real Photographs 14837

18"x 24", instead of 17"x 24", and the firebox was 6" longer at 5'5". The boiler was 4'2"x 10'2", with a heating surface of 1,128 sq ft and 150 lbs pressure. The grate was 18.3 sq ft. Tractive effort was 12,550 lbs. These engines had coil springs on the driving axles, hench the nickname 'Wee Bouncers'.

The first three to be constructed were Nos 70 *Precursor*, 71 *Bundoran* and 74 *Rostrevor*. With these three, the policy of naming passenger engines was resumed and names were planned for the earlier J and P class engines. However, not all were applied. The PPs were an immediate success and displaced the bogie singles from the Limited Mail trains. With them appeared the first of the standard B1 2500 gallon tenders with inside springs, the first three being probably a modified version of the earlier 2400 gallon tender. The B1 tender remained standard until 1909. In March 1898, a slightly enlarged version of the PP class appeared, consisting of Nos 75 *Jupiter*, 76 *Hercules* and 77 *Achilles*. These names had at one time been applied to former D&DR locomotives. The new engines had an extra half-inch in cylinder diameter and had 4'3" boilers, pressed to 160 lbs. Tractive effort was increased to 14,140 lbs.

The PP class was one of the most outstanding designs to emerge from Dundalk. It is often said that Dundalk never produced a bad steaming engine and the PP class, especially in their final superheated form, were excellent engines for secondary lines and capable of anything from light regular trains to heavy excursions. The entire class remained intact until 1957 and No 74 of the first batch was, actually, the last of the whole class in traffic, surviving at Newry shed until 1963.

Q class 4-4-0 1899-1904

Clifford considerably upped the stakes with his next 4-4-0 design. The PP class was very clearly a stop-gap, because the Q class represented a quantum leap in GNR locomotive design. The new design had 6'7" driving wheels like the earlier engines, but 18½"x 26" cylinders and a 175 lbs boiler measuring 4'6"x 11'0" with a 5'10" firebox (5" longer than the PPs). This gave a grate area of 19.9 sq ft and a heating surface of 1,362 sq ft. Weight was 46 tons 3 cwt and tractive effort 16,755 lbs. The bogie was of a new design with a 5'9" wheelbase compared to the earlier 5'3" and a graceful curved splasher. The coupled wheelbase was 8'8", the leading coupled wheels being 10'3" behind of the bogie centre line. The boiler centre line was 7'6" above rail level and the boiler had 240 1¾" tubes (later reduced to 236).

For the first time, the GNR had an express engine which could vie with the best in Ireland and Britain. The only obvious weakness was that the 1" frames were too shallow in height so that, in later years, cracked frames were common.

(Continued on page 80)

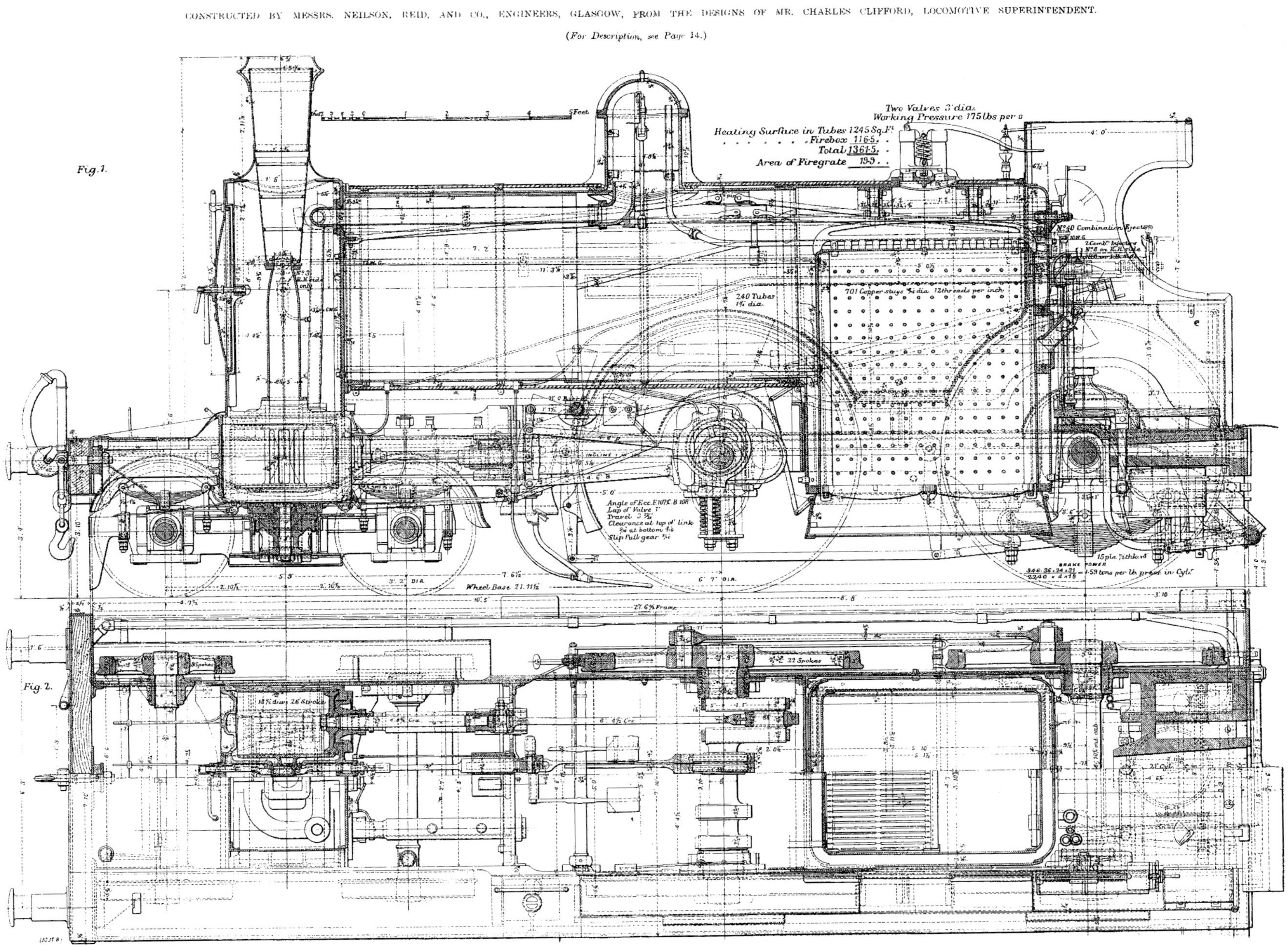

CONSTRUCTED BY MESSRS. NEILSON, REID, AND CO., ENGINEERS, GLASGOW, FROM THE DESIGNS OF MR. CHARLES CLIFFORD, LOCOMOTIVE SUPERINTENDENT.

(For Description, see Page 14.)

Fig 46: Detailed diagram of a Q class 4-4-0 locomotive, as reproduced in *Engineering* July 6, 1900.

P Mallon collection

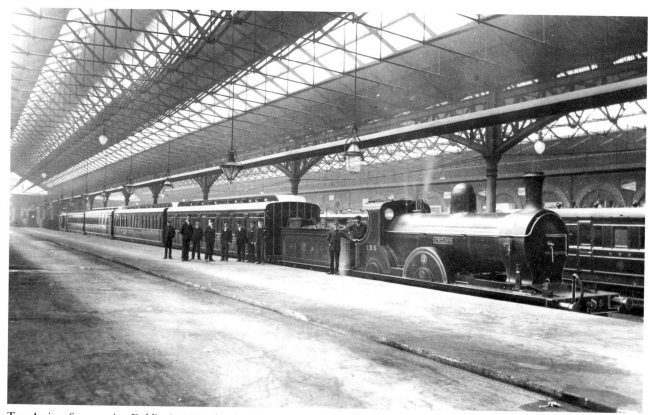

Top: Amiens Street station Dublin, in 1900, showing No 135 *Cyclops* with an early GNR corridor train. Note the original B1 tender without coal rails. The train comprises a semi-corridor composite, a dining car, a semi-corridor 2nd/3rd, a compartment third and a six-wheel brake.

R Welch, courtesy Ulster Museum

Bottom: Q class 4-4-0 No 124 *Cerberus* decorated for the GNR Royal Train of 1903, on the occasion of King Edward VII's state visit to Ireland. The nameplate is hidden beneath the board carrying the streamers along the boiler. The train travelled from Dublin to Belfast and hence to Newtownards (on the BCDR). By this time, GNR tenders were being fitted with coal rails, a practice introduced in 1902. No 124 was only a few months old in this view and looks immaculate.

L J Watson (WG 17)

Top: The complete Royal Train of 1903 posed near Dundalk. Another version of this photo, showing the engine without flags, was reproduced in Dr Patterson's book on the GNR. The seven coach train comprises M2 full brake No 240 (1901), F3 composite No 352 (1902), F6 composite No 338 (1895), B3 dining car No 427 (1900), A1 saloon No 326 (1900), A2 saloon No 400 (1893) and M2 full brake No 399 (1902).
L J Watson (WG 16)

Left: QL class 4-4-0 No 113 *Neptune* in original condition at Belfast. This engine was built by the North British Locomotive Company in 1904. No 113 was superheated in 1924 and scrapped in 1957.
Real Photographs 88129

One interesting feature, which can be seen on the diagram on page 78, is that, in contrast to the PPs, only the leading driving wheels had coil springs. The rear drivers had leaf springs.

The Q class were built by Neilson Reid of Glasgow, the first GNR engines to have been built by this company since 1863. The first batch comprised Nos 133 *Apollo*, 134 *Adonis*, 135 *Cyclops* and 136 *Minerva* and were delivered in September-October 1899. These numbers had previously been occupied by ex-UR F class double-framed 0-4-2s, which now became 109-112.

A second batch followed in January-Febuary 1901, comprising Nos 130 *Saturn*, 131 *Uranus* and 132 *Mercury*.

The names were attractive and inspired by classical mythology. Six more were added in the next three years as follows: Nos 124 *Cerberus* and 125 *Daphne* (1902); 122 *Vulcan* and 123 *Lucifer* (1903) and finally 120 *Venus* and 121 *Pluto* (1904). This last pair were built by Beyer Peacock, but the others were by Neilson Reid. Nos 122 and 123 were completed after Neilson Reid became part of the North British Locomotive Co, so they carried North British works plates.

Because of their 15½ tons axle load (compared to 14¾ tons on the PP class) the Q class were restricted to the main line and the Clones line until 1912, when the bridges on the Derry Road were strengthened. However, Clifford probably reckoned that the growing weight of trains would justify the numbers constructed. The later history of the class when

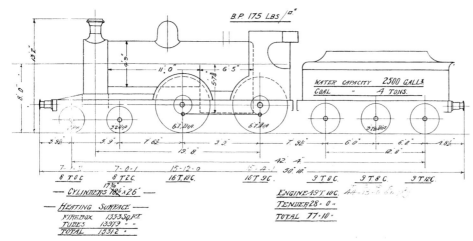

B.P. 175 LBS/□"

WATER CAPACITY 2500 GALLS
COAL   "   4 TONS.

CYLINDERS 18½"×26"
— HEATING SURFACE —
FIREBOX   133 SQ FT
TUBES   1397.9 " "
TOTAL   1531.2 " "

ENGINE 49 T 10 C. 44-13-0 &c %
TENDER 28 · 0 "
TOTAL 77·10 "

superheated is described in Chapter 8. Apart from No 134, withdrawn in 1951, the class remained intact until 1957 and one of the last survivors, No 131, has been preserved, though not active (see Chapter 13).

QL class 4-4-0 1904-10

The growing weight of main line passenger trains led Clifford to produce an even larger express passenger 4-4-0 in 1904. The QL class had the same cylinders and boiler pressure as the earlier Q class, so there was no increase in nominal tractive effort. However, they had larger 4'9" boilers which were pitched a full 6" higher than those of the Qs. This gave them a more modern appearance, with a shorter chimney. The Q chassis was lengthened at the rear to increase the coupled wheelbase from 8'8" to 9'3", in order to accommodate a larger 6'5" firebox with a 22.14 sq ft grate. The heating surface was 1,531 sq ft.

These changes increased the weight of the QL class to 49½ tons, or 3½ tons greater than the Q class. The axle load was almost 17 tons, which restricted their route availability. The QL class represented the peak of GNR express locomotive design, in the pre-superheating age, and it was to be 1913

before the S class ousted them from the principal main line trains.

The class was constructed as follows. The first seven were built by the North British Locomotive Company, Nos 113 *Neptune*, 114 *Theseus*, 156 *Pandora* and 157 *Orpheus* in 1904, followed by Nos 126 *Diana*, 127 *Erebus* and 128 *Mars* in 1907. In 1909, Beyer Peacock constructed an eighth member of the class, with strap big-ends instead of the solid fork type of the earlier engines. This was No 24 *Juno*, delivered in Febuary 1910. Soon after, it became the first GNR locomotive to have one of the new B2 tenders with outside springs. The B2 tender also had a low coping, in place of the earlier coal rails, and this was gradually applied to the earlier tenders as well.

PG class 0-6-0 1899-1904

Clifford did not build any new goods locomotives for several years after the last of the AL class was completed in 1896. The first of the PG class appeared in December 1899, when No 78 *Strabane* was completed at Dundalk. This engine was renumbered 151 in Febuary 1901. The PG class had 4'7" driving wheels, 18½"x 24" cylinders and an axle load of 14

tons. Although it is often claimed that Clifford's goods engines had the same boiler and cylinders as the corresponding passenger engines, this was not true of the PG class, which had a 4'6" boiler as opposed to the 4'3" boiler of the 1898 built PPs. The PG class was still a fairly small engine, with a wheelbase of 7'6"+ 8'1" and a total length of 46'8" over buffers. It was, therefore, only 4" longer than the AL class, though the B1 tender added a further foot. Tractive effort was 20,310 lbs and boiler pressure 160 lbs, though this was raised later to 175 lbs (22,215 lbs tractive effort).

A second engine, No 100, was built at Dundalk in June 1900. The engine was listed as *Clontarf* in a GNR list of 1901, but this is not supported by photographic evidence, and lists from 1903 on, give it as *Clones*. It also appears as such in photographs. Neilson Reid built Nos 101 *Balmoral*, 102 *Belleek* and 103 *Dunleer* in early 1901 and, finally, Dundalk added Nos 11 *Dromore* (1903) and 10 *Bessbrook* (March 1904). The last two were contemporary with the later QG class and are the only instance of two GNR goods types being built at the same time.

The policy of naming goods engines after counties was obviously abandoned with the PG class, presumably because

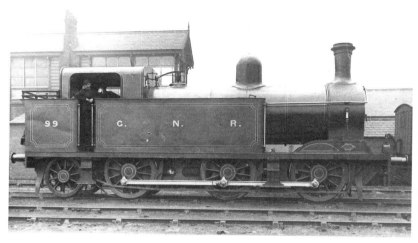

Left: QGT 0-6-2T No 99 at Belfast North cabin shortly after being built in 1905. Even shunting engines were painted in the fully lined-out green livery. Note the sanding gear fitted to the front and rear driving wheels. On the QG class only the centre driving wheel had sand.

H Fayle 16, courtesy IRRS

Bottom: LQG 0-6-0 No 158 *Ballybay* was the first of eleven goods engines with 4'9" boilers. GNR engines were now fitted with injectors rather than feed water pumps. Note the well-stacked tender. The engines built in 1908 had copings on the tenders rather than coal rails.

Maj Gen Sir Cecil Smith

there were only 32 counties and 29 of the names had already been used! The only ones not used were Westmeath, Offaly (King's County) and Leix (Queen's County).

All seven engines were superheated and all passed to the UTA in 1958, the last survivor being No 10 in March 1964.

QG class 0-6-0 1903-04

In September 1903, Clifford introduced his QG class goods engine. This class was equivalent to the Q class 4-4-0 and had 4'7" driving wheels, 18½"x 26" cylinders, a 4'6" boiler and 175 lbs boiler pressure. However, the boiler was pitched 3" lower than in the Q class, giving these engines a purposeful look. Coupled wheelbase was 7'10"+ 8'10" and the locomotive was 1'6" longer and 2 tons heavier than the earlier PG class. Tractive effort was 24,066 lbs but, despite this, they were put in the same power class as the PG 0-6-0s in 1908. The four members of the QG class were numbered 152-155 and were built by the North British Locomotive Company at their Neilson Reid works, two in 1903 and two in 1904. They carried the names *Lurgan, Scarva, Lambeg* and *Navan*, respectively. Like Clifford's other 0-6-0s, they were eventually superheated.

QGT class 0-6-2T 1905

The first GNR tank locomotives, built specifically for shunting, were delivered by Robert Stephenson and Co in 1905. Nos 98 and 99 were sturdy looking 0-6-2Ts, a type popular in Britain for shunting duties and adopted by Doncaster in 1906 for suburban passenger work. They had 4'7¼" driving wheels and 3'7½" trailing wheels on a radial truck. Cylinders were 18½"x 26", as on the QGs, but the boilers were of the 4'6"x 10'2" PG type, pitched at 7'3", and matched with a 5'10" QG firebox. The coupled wheelbase was 7'6"+ 8'6" which was somewhere between a PG and a QG. These locomotives had a tractive effort of 23,957 lbs. Both were initially allocated to Belfast but No 99 later shunted in Dublin. They carried 1250 gallons of water and 2 tons of coal and were superheated in the late 1930s.

LQG class 0-6-0 1906-08

The next development in goods locomotive design was the LQG class of 1906. These engines were, essentially, the QG class with a 4'9" boiler. They used the same chassis and cylinders as the QG class and had the same 5'10" firebox. In that sense, they were not really an exact equivalent to the QL passenger engines which had 6'5" fireboxes. The boiler centre line was at 7'9½", which was 6½" higher than the QG class but 2½" lower than the QLs. The heavier boiler increased the weight to 45 tons 3 cwt and the axle load to 16½ tons (QG figures were 41½ tons and 14¾ tons, respectively).

These locomotives were built by the North British Locomotive Company, with the exception of Nos 78 *Pettigo* and 108 *Pomeroy*, built at Dundalk in 1908. The North British engines were Nos 158-160 of 1906 (respectively, *Ballybay*, *Cootehill* and *Culloville*) and 110, 111 and 161-164 of 1908 (respectively, *Laytown*, *Malahide*, *Adavoyle*, *Ballyroney*, *Banbridge* and *Fintona*).

These names perpetuated the GNR custom of naming goods engines after stations and did not reflect the sphere of operation of the engines

concerned. It was ironic that these large and impressive engines were named after relatively minor stations (Banbridge excepted), whereas earlier and smaller A and AL class engines were named after larger stations like Belfast and Dundalk!

The LQG class were given the power classification 'C' in 1908, even though their nominal tractive effort was no greater than the QG class. These engines had long lives, all being superheated by Glover in the late 1920s. Those which passed to the UTA disappeared fairly quickly, apart from No 111, but most of the CIE engines lasted to the end of CIE steam in 1963.

Rebuilding work at Dundalk

Over these years, Dundalk was engaged in rebuilding the earlier standard engines. The B class 0-6-0s were modernised between 1896 and 1900, receiving 4'2"x 10'2" boilers with flush-topped 4'7" fireboxes. Likewise, the reboilering of the UR-designed C class 0-6-0s was completed in 1896-99, using slightly longer 4'2"x 10'3" boilers with 4'11" fireboxes.

The last of the G class were reboilered in 1899-1903 (4'2"x 9'9") and the H class in 1900-02 (4'2"x 10'3"). The J class 4-4-0s also received new 4'2"x 9'9" boilers between 1902 and 1907 and were gradually given 17"x 22" cylinders,

Above: Ex-D&DR 0-4-2 No 9 had been a casualty of the Armagh disaster in 1889. No 9 was built in 1858. The Works plate indicates that this photo was taken after its final rebuilding in April 1900. It entered the duplicate list in 1911, but was renumbered 201 in 1914 and scrapped in 1915. This would have been an ideal museum exhibit if it had lasted to the 1950s! *L J Watson (WG 1)*

Left: Ex-UR 2-4-0 No 129 *Connaught*, photographed shortly after its final rebuilding in June 1899, when it received a GJ class boiler. This view makes interesting comparison with the Builder's picture of the same class on page 42. The driving wheel springs were originally outside. No 129 went on the duplicate list in 1911 and was scrapped in March 1912.

L&GRP 88006

though not necessarily at the same time. This was followed by the rebuilding of the A class 0-6-0s, which commenced in 1905. These received 4'2"x 10'0" boilers with 4'7" fireboxes. Finally, eight of the tiny BT 4-4-0Ts were reboilered between 1906 and 1914, with 3'7"x 8'10¼" boilers.

By now, very few pre-amalgamation engines were receiving heavy work. The old ex-UR express 2-4-0s of 1863, Nos 126-129, received their final rebuilds in 1897-99, receiving G class boilers, as did old double-framed 2-4-0s Nos 114 *Lagan* (1897) and 121 *Dalriada* (1900). The last double-framed engines to be rebuilt were F class 0-4-2s Nos 109 *Shannon* (ex-133) and 112 *Donard* (ex-136) in 1901-02.

Ex-D&DR 2-4-0 No 12 was reboilered in 1897 and 0-4-2 No 9 in 1900. The only ex-INWR locomotives to be rebuilt in this period were L class 2-4-0 No 43 in 1901 and E class 0-6-0 No 37 in 1903. Apart from 0-6-0s of classes C, D and E, no pre-amalgamation types were rebuilt after 1902.

Above: In this view, on Amiens Street turntable, Dublin, H class 2-4-0 No 84 is paired with a 2000 gallon tender. This engine was built in 1881, rebuilt as shown in 1902 (with 17"x 22" cylinders) and withdrawn in 1932.

H Fayle, courtesy IRRS

Below: F class 0-4-2 No 109 *Shannon* (ex-133), after final rebuilding in October 1901 (compare page 43). The GNR monogram on the middle splasher was applied to goods engines, probably because there was insufficient room for a coat of arms. No 109 joined the duplicate list in June 1911 and was scrapped four months later.

Maj Gen Sir Cecil Smith

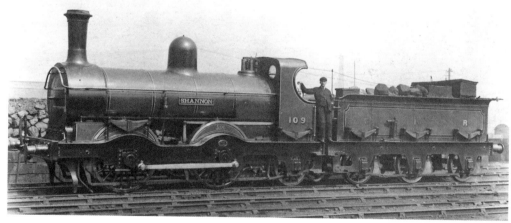

Left: Ex-UR 2-4-0 No 121 *Dalriada* was destined to be the last of the Ulster Railway's double-framed locomotives. It was rebuilt, as seen here, in Febuary 1901 with a GJ class boiler. No 121 joined the duplicate list in 1904 when the last of the new Q class was built. It was scrapped in October 1914, the end of an era.

H Fayle 142, courtesy IRRS

Above: This interesting snow-bound scene at Belfast shed shows No 135 *Carntual* on a turntable of the period. No risk of falling into the pit of this one! Above No 135's tender can be seen 2-4-0 No 126 *Ulster*, A class 0-6-0 No 146 *Wicklow* and an O class 2-4-0T, either ex-BCR No 95 or ex-NW&RR No 90. This dates the picture to be no later than 1898. Just visible beyond No 146, is engine No 122. If the photo was taken before 1895, this would be *Iveagh*, a Beyer 2-2-2. If taken after 1895, it is *Jupiter*, a UR built double-framed 2-4-0.

C P Friel collection

Below: This Belfast scene was photographed slightly further out the line, at the neck of Grosvenor Road goods yard. On the left is C class 0-6-0 No 144 *Vesuvius* and to the right of it is 2-4-0 No 108 *Lucifer*. Centre right are 0-4-2 Nos 139 *Tempest* and 104 *Owenreagh*, then 2-4-0 No 127 *Munster* and 2-2-2 No 111 *North Star*. All six are ex-UR locomotives and the combination of engines suggests a date of 1894.

C P Friel collection

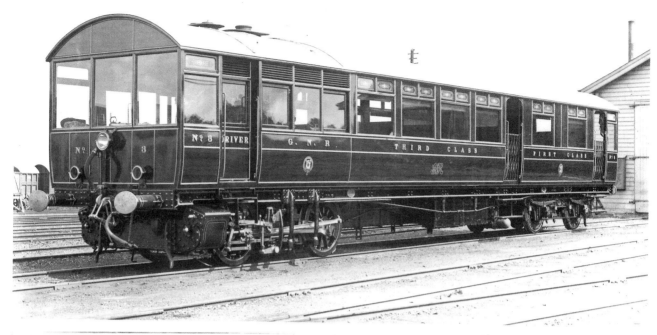

Above: Lisburn railmotor No 3, as delivered. This was one of three cars built by R & T Pickering in 1905 with North British engines and power bogies. Note the ornate livery with two crests and a monogram as well.

L J Watson, WG38

Left: The locomotive part of one of the Manning Wardle railmotors, identified as No 5 from the builder's plate, visible above the cylinder. Note the different shape of the cylinder block on the two types of railmotor. The heat generated by the boiler made footplate conditions very unpleasant for the crew, within the confined cab.

P Mallon collection

Lisburn and Howth railmotors 1905-06

Steam railmotors were the forerunners of diesel railcars and were designed to compete with urban electric trams on short-haul suburban runs. There had been a trend towards introducing this type of train on other railways at the time, and the GNRI was no exception. Indeed, all three railways radiating from Belfast introduced steam railmotors in 1905.

Railmotors consisted of a small locomotive (usually 0-2-2T, 2-2-0T or 0-4-0T) which was permanently articulated to a passenger carriage. The railmotor had an additional driving cab at the rear, so that it could be driven from either end, thus removing the need to use a turntable. The engine portion could be either separate from the carriage body or enclosed within the coach work. It could be either of the vertical boiler type (usually enclosed) or the more

conventional horizontal type.

The GNR railmotors were of the enclosed, vertical boiler, type. Three (Nos 1-3) were built in 1905 by the North British Locomotive Company for use on the Belfast-Lisburn service. They were 0-4-0Ts, with 3'7½" wheels, an 8'0" wheelbase and 12"x 16" outside cylinders activated by Walschaerts valve gear. This was the first use of Walschaerts valve gear on the GNR and the railmotors were the first outside cylinder engines to be built new for the company.

The small vertical boiler worked at 175 lbs pressure and was coned, with a diameter reducing from 5'11" to 4'5", and a height of 9'6", with 479 1⅛" tubes, giving a heating surface of 660.45 sq ft (47.33+ 613.12 sq ft). It had Aston pop safety valves. The engine carried 15 cwt of coal and 400 gallons of water. The entire vehicle weighed 44 tons 5 cwt. The carriage

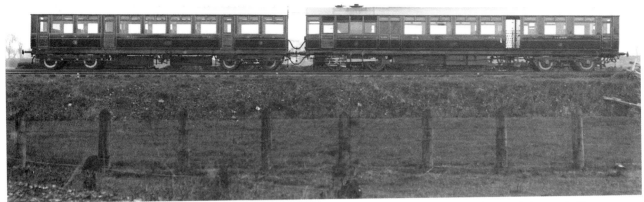

Top: In 1906 Brush built Nos 4-7, with Manning Wardle engines, for service on the Howth branch. In this posed shot, probably at Dundalk, railmotor No 4 is seen, attached to driving trailer No 11, a third class vehicle. Note that the engine portion of the railcar faces the trailer.
L J Watson, WG36

portions were built by R & T Pickering of Glasgow and had teak framing. They were very different from other GNR carriages at that time, being of the open saloon type, and were 9'6" wide (most GNR carriages were 8'9" or 9'0") with high arc roofs. The GNR, somewhat inaccurately, described them as 'high elliptical'. Each car seated 20 first and 39 third class passengers.

In 1906, four more railmotors (Nos 4-7) were built for service between Dublin and Howth. These were built by Manning Wardle of Leeds, with coach bodies by Brush of Loughborough and weighed 45 tons. The carriage style was similar to the Lisburn railmotors and the dimensions were

similar, with 3'9" wheels and 12"x 16" cylinders and Walschaerts gear. The boiler was of the vertical multi-tubular type with 653 sq ft heating surface, 175 lbs boiler pressure and 11½ sq ft of grate. The tractive effort was 8,960 lbs. Although often designated 'Howth railmotors', a photograph taken in 1909 shows No 4 operating into Belfast.

Around the same time, nine saloon coaches were built to operate as trailers. These carriages were of a similar body style to the railmotors and had driving cabs at one end. No 10 was a 1st/3rd composite with luggage compartment and Nos 11-14 were thirds. Nos 10-14 allowed five of the railmotors to have a trailer. When working with a trailer, the normal

Bottom: On the Belfast-Lisburn route, new halts for the railmotors were opened at Finaghy, Derriaghy and Hilden. In this view an unidentified railmotor and third class trailer are seen departing for Belfast from the newly opened Hilden halt. Note the short length of the platforms. In the background can be seen the goods shed at Hilden and what appears to be the tail end of an Up goods train.
R Welch, courtesy Ulster Museum

formation was for the engine end of the railmotor to face the trailing coach. The oft-repeated statement, that the Lisburn railmotors did not operate with trailers, is disproved by photographs (see opposite).

Nos 8 and 9 were 1st/2nd composites and Nos 15 and 16 were 1st/3rd composites. They were designed to operate with BT 4-4-0Ts as push-pull sets. In this arrangement the engine was sandwiched between two carriages.

The GNR experienced similar problems with its railmotors to those of other companies which adopted them. They gave a lot of trouble mechanically and were subject to vibration.

The enclosed engines were very hot to operate, especially in summer, and this may account for why they operated with the power bogie adjoining the trailing coach. The driver could drive from the cooler conditions in the other cab, though the fireman still had to endure the heat. In 1913, the railmotors were withdrawn and converted into ordinary coaches with driving cabs for push-pull operation.

The converted coaches initially ran as Nos 1-16 but, by 1916, had became Nos 201-216 in the carriage list. After 1913, they were usually operated with the tank engine at one end of a two coach set, rather than between the coaches.

Top: An early GNR push-pull train consisting of BT 4-4-0T No 97 *Lisburn* and trailers 9 (1st/2nd) and 15 (1st/3rd). The photograph is probably between Belfast and Lisburn around 1906 and is specially posed with no passengers in evidence. Cars 8 and 16 probably made up another push-pull set.
R Welch, courtesy Ulster Museum

Left: P5'6" 4-4-0 No 88 *Victoria*, coupled to a 1700 gallon tender from one of the earlier 4-2-2s. This engine was one of four built at Dundalk in 1905-06 with 4'6" boilers. Note the lubricator on the smokebox. Just visible in the left background is QL 4-4-0 No 24.
H Fayle, courtesy IRRS

More small passenger 4-4-0s

After constructing seventeen large passenger locomotives in 1899-1904, Clifford turned again to the P and PP types when more engines were required for lighter duties. In 1904, the two JS class bogie singles had been broken up and these were replaced by two new P5'6" 4-4-0s, built at Dundalk in 1905. These had the same numbers and names as the engines they replaced and, although nominally rebuilds, there can have been little of the original engines in the new locomotives. The bogies were probably re-used and the tenders were recycled – the photograph reproduced, shows No 88 with the same type of 1700 gallon tender as fitted to the 4-2-2 on page 61. Perhaps also, items like the safety valves were reused. One wonders if the ornate nameplates of the original *Victoria* and *Albert* survived.

Nos 88 and 89 were built with a new type of 4'6" boiler, in place of the 4'1" one used on Nos 51-53 of 1892. This was 10'2" long with a 5'0" firebox, giving a heating surface of 1,255 sq ft and a grate of 16.6 sq ft. This increased the weight to 41 tons 9 cwt, compared to 38 tons 15 cwt in the 1892 batch. Tractive effort was now 15,399 lbs (previously 13,199 lbs) due to the higher 175 lbs boiler pressure.

It is strange that Clifford retained 17"x 24" cylinders for such a large boiler. The U class of 1915 had 18"x 24" cylinders for a 4'3" boiler, as, indeed, did the later PP class engines. However, both these designs had larger fireboxes so that may have been the key. It is also odd that Clifford never built a 4-4-2T version of the P5'6" class.

In 1906 Dundalk turned out two more P5'6" engines, Nos

Left: PP class 4-4-0 No 107 *Cyclone*, built by Beyer Peacock in 1906. This engine and sister 106 *Tornado*, were built to operate the Derry Mail trains. Note the staff catcher fitted to the tender for single line working. In contrast to Nos 70-71 and 74-77, the 1906-11 PP engines had their sandboxes below the running plate.
Real Photographs 88112

Above: A class 0-6-0 No 28 *Wexford*, resplendent in green livery, probably photographed just after its rebuilding in October 1909. The 1700 gallon tender has had a coping added. Note the newly fitted power classification letter above the cab number.

L J Watson (WG5)

104 *Ovoca* and 105 *Foyle*. These names had originally been carried by ex-UR 0-4-2s. *Ovoca* should more correctly have been 'Avoca'. No 105 of this pair, was the first engine to receive Glover's black livery in June 1912. In 1906-07, Nos 51-53 were rebuilt with the 4'6" boiler, though No 54 retained its 4'2" boiler until 1916.

Clifford now turned his attention to the needs of the Derry Road. Until the bridges on this route could be strengthened, the Q class could not be used, so in 1906 Clifford built two new PP class engines for the Belfast-Derry mails. Nos 106 *Tornado* and 107 *Cyclone* had the same numbers and names as the two 0-4-2s they replaced. They used the same 4'3"x 10'2" boilers as the 1898 batch, but pressed to 175 lbs. They had only 18"x 24" cylinders, giving a tractive effort of 14,641 lbs. However, the axle load stayed within 14 tons 15 cwt.

These two engines looked slightly different from the 1896-98 engines, in that there were no large sandboxes on the leading splashers. The tenders were fitted with staff catching nets, to enable staff exchanges at speed on the single line sections of the Derry Road (see photo page 189).

Nos 106 and 107 worked the Derry mails until 1912. In 1909, Beyer Peacock supplied two more members of the PP class, again using names from former UR locomotives. These were Nos 45 *Sirocco* and 46 *Typhoon*, delivered in December 1909 and built alongside QL 4-4-0 No 24 *Juno*. They too, had staff catching nets and brought the PP class up to a strength of ten.

The power classification system of 1908

During 1907, the Locomotive Department was taking a considerable interest in the haulage capacity of its goods locomotives on various types of gradient. I have seen a large number of Dundalk documents on this theme, with calculations based on a goods train moving at 20 mph with 66% boiler pressure on gradients varying between 1 in 60 and 1 in 200. These figures were then related to the maximum gradients on particular routes, so that the load for particular types of engine between, say, Dundalk and Goraghwood, or Dungannon and Omagh, could be calculated.

However, this had to be translated into terms that engine drivers and Operating Department personnel could work with. In 1908, this led to the introduction of power classification letters on six-coupled tender engines. These consisted of cast iron upper case letters – A, B, C or D – mounted on the cabside, above the running number, and painted red. Train weights were translated into the number of wagons that each power group could haul on specific routes and these then appeared in the *Appendix to the Working Timetable*.

There were some anomalies in the system. A document of 1 January 1908 shows that the original intention was to put the QG class in the 'C' category, but this was changed to 'B'. 'C' would have made sense, for the tractive effort of the QG and LQG classes was identical. However, the smaller firebox on the QG class may have swung the decision in favour of class 'B'.

The other anomaly was that, whilst the engines with 4'7" wheels were classified A, B and C as their power increased, seven old locomotives with 5'0" wheels were classified 'D', even though they were less powerful than 'A'. This meant that when the SG3 class of 1920 were introduced, the old 'D' class had to be reclassified 'E'. The only explanation I can think of for this, is that, at the time, the 'D' class engines were not intended to survive more than a few years. In the event, four lasted until 1948!

In 1908, when the system was introduced, 'A' was by far the biggest category, with 41 locomotives of classes A, AL, B and C (Nos 26-36, 55-69, 79-81 and 139-150). There were

Opposite bottom: Photographed at the same spot as No 28, is C class 0-6-0 No 144 *Vesuvius* of 1876, also with an 'A' power classification. It has a much older UR-style tender with outside springs and toolbox, but, nevertheless, a coping has recently been fitted. This locomotive was withdrawn in 1924.

L J Watson (WG23)

This page: LQG 0-6-0 No 108 *Pomeroy* with its 'C' power classification just visible. This engine was one of the two Dundalk built examples of the class.

LPC 3160

Top: RT class 0-6-4T No 23, built by Beyer Peacock in 1908 and seen in its original green livery. When the ex-GNR locomotives, acquired by the UTA, were renumbered in 1959, No 23 was the only locomotive in the capital list to have the same UTA number as it had under the GNR. It was scrapped in 1963.
L J Watson (WG 4)

Fig 48 (below): Diagram of the RT class 0-6-4T. The cab and boiler mountings on this class were lowered to bring the overall height down to 11'8". This enabled the engines to operate through the Queen's Bridge tunnel in Belfast, but gave a false impression of the locomotive's size.

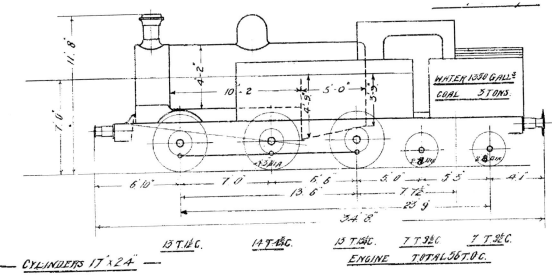

11 locomotives in class 'B' (PG and QG) and 11 in class 'C' (LQG). The class 'D' locomotives were Nos 37-39 (E class), 40, 41 (D class), 137 and 138 (C class). It is not hard to see how the use of A-D, for both engine class and train class, caused some confusion!

RT class 0-6-4T 1908-11

The RT class of 1908 was one of only two types built by Clifford, which were not a variation of 'P' or 'Q' class – the other being the JT class! These engines were specifically designed for working in the Belfast dock area, and trip working between Grosvenor Road goods yard and the cattle yards at Maysfields (where Belfast Central Station now stands). For this reason, they had reduced boiler mountings, the overall height being 11'8" (normally 13'2"), and small 4'3" driving wheels, with a wheelbase of only 7'0"+ 6'6". This, along with a rear bogie with only 2'8" wheels, allowed these locomotives to negotiate very tight dock curves.

The cylinders were 17"x 24" and the boiler pressure was 175 lbs, giving a tractive effort of 20,230 lbs. The boiler was 4'2"x 10'2", with a heating surface of 1,086 sq ft. In previous

publications this has been, erroneously, described as an 'AL class' boiler. However, the AL class boiler, although of the same diameter, was 10'3" long and had a different type of firebox. The RT firebox was 5'0" long and had a sloping grate, the front being a foot lower than the rear. This was to allow the rear of the firebox to sit *over* the rear driving axle, instead of *between* the axles, as was the normal practice.

It was this feature which enabled these 0-6-4Ts to have a coupled wheelbase of only 13'6". The locomotive carried 3 tons of coal and 1350 gallons of water, which enabled it to work a whole day without re-coaling. The axle load was only 14¼ tons and the whole engine weighed 56 tons. This was actually slightly greater than the QGT 0-6-2Ts, mainly because of the higher coal and water capacity.

Four locomotives of this class were built by Beyer Peacock, Nos 22 and 23 in 1908 and Nos 166 and 167 in 1911. None was named – indeed Clifford did not give names to any of his shunting tanks. When built, they had fully lined out green livery, as illustrated, but in Glover's day this gave way to black. They were rarely seen outside Belfast, apart from trips to Dundalk for repairs. In 1939, Nos 166 and 167

Right: PP 4-4-0 No 43 *Lagan* was one of only two of this class built at Dundalk. In this view of it at Amiens Street shed, it is paired to a new B2 tender.

Inspector A Johnston,

had their boiler pressure reduced to 165 lbs (tractive effort 19,074 lbs). All passed to the UTA and, apart from No 22 (withdrawn 1959), they lasted until 1963.

1911 – an important year

The year 1911 was significant in GNR locomotive history. No fewer than 17 new locomotives were placed in service instead of the usual four or so. In March, a brand new locomotive shed for Belfast, was opened at Adelaide and the old UR shed at Great Victoria Street was closed. The new shed cost £40,000 and was able to accommodate 55 locomotives in nine parallel roads. The shed had no turntable and engine turning was on a triangle. The following month saw the locomotive exchanges between the GNR and the GS&WR, of which more shortly. At Goraghwood a new ballast quarry came into operation in February 1911 and work was in hand on bridge strengthening on the Derry Road, which would soon allow the Q class to be used there.

The first new locomotives of the year were two PP class 4-4-0s built at Dundalk, Nos 25 *Liffey* and 43 *Lagan*. These were the only conventional-looking PPs built that year, differing from the earlier engines only in having a slightly different tube arrangement (192 tubes instead of the usual 206) and paired with two new B2 tenders built in 1910.

The 1911 locomotive exchange

The story of the locomotive exchanges of 1911 have been recounted in detail in the excellent article by the late R N Clements in IRRS Journal No 71 (October 1976) and there is not space in this publication to do more than summarise the main points. The initiative for the locomotive exchange came from the GNR. In December 1910, the Locomotive Department wrote to the GS&WR suggesting an exchange of locomotives. At first, the GS&WR were lukewarm about the idea, but it looks as if direct contact between the two company Chairmen cut through this problem and the exchange was agreed by the end of January 1911.

Clifford, at this point, was contemplating a new express passenger design and wanted to see the best GS&WR motive power at first hand. The GNR General Manager, Henry Plews, was more interested in the exchange of goods engines and this may go back to the work done on goods engine performance in 1907-08, when the power classification was introduced.

As it happened, the main classes of passenger engine exchanged were of the same age. The GNR QL class and the GS&WR 321 class were both introduced in 1904. They were broadly similar, both with 18½"x 26" cylinders and slide valves, but the GS&WR engine had a larger boiler, partly offset by lower boiler pressure, at 160 lbs compared to the QL's 175 lbs. Whilst both engines had 1½" steam ports, the 321 class had 3½" exhaust ports compared to the QL's 3¼". In theory, this gave the 321 class an advantage at high speeds.

Some concerns were raised about whether the 13'6½" tall GS&WR engines would foul the GNR loading gauge and at one point consideration was given to lowering the height of the GS&WR boiler mountings. This was avoided by putting restrictions on the platforms that the engine could use in Belfast, under the Boyne bridge.

The actual locomotives involved were GNR No 113 *Neptune*, driven by Robert Bruce of Belfast, and GS&WR No 322, driven by Jack Moloney of Inchicore. The engines were transferred on Monday 27 March 1911 and began work the following day. On the GNR, No 322 worked the 9.00 Down and 17.00 Up Limited Mail on Mondays, the 6.05 Down Limited Mail and 14.20 Up on Tuesdays, and the 10.45 Down and 17.30 Up on Wednesdays, the cycle being repeated on Thur-Saturday. On the GS&WR, No 113 was restricted by the relatively small 2500 gallon capacity of its tender (the GS&WR used 3345 gallon tenders). For this reason, it was not allowed to work the 6.40 Down Mail train.

Although the GNR used Killochan Scottish coal at Belfast and Tredegar Welsh coal at Dublin, the GS&WR insisted that, for the tests, their engine should be supplied with the

Below: GS&WR No 322 at Dundalk during the trials. The train is probably the 14.20 Up and this means the photo was taken on a Tuesday or Friday. The fireman is up on the tender shovelling coal forward. The train has been strengthened by two six-wheelers, the nearest being No 39A, a P5 first, dating from 1878. Next is a U2 third, the remaining vehicles being the normal clerestory-roofed five-bogie set, with six wheel clerestory brake on the rear.

L J Watson

Engine	Dates	Coal	Consumption (train miles)	Cost
322	April 3-8th	Tredegar/Nantyglo	42.35 lbs/mile	4.50d per mile
	April 11-27th	Nantyglo	41.10 lbs/mile	4.30d per mile
114	April 3-8th	Killochan (Scottish)	44.0 lbs/mile	3.19d per mile
	April 11-27th	Killochan	42.82 lbs/mile	3.10d per mile
136	April 3-8th	Tredegar	37.15 lbs/mile	4.01d per mile
	April 11-27th	Nantyglo/Tredegar	36.58 lbs/mile	3.89d per mile
24	April 11-27th	Nantyglo	38.41 lbs/mile	3.99d per mile

Engine (GS&WR main line)	Dates	Consumption (train miles)	Cost
307	April 4-May 18th	37.1 lbs/mile	3.55d per mile
GS&WR average	April 4-May 18th	37.9 lbs/mile	3.62d per mile
113	April 4-May 18th	40.9 lbs/mile	3.90d per mile

Right: The GNR locomotive selected to operate on the GS&WR was QL 4-4-0 No 113 *Neptune*. This view may be connected to the event, as it shows driver Robert Bruce on the footplate and 18 other men posed for what is obviously an important occasion. This may be 113 about to set off for Inchicore after preparation.
Maj Gen Sir Cecil Smith

Nantyglo Welsh coal normally used by the GS&WR.

For comparison with No 322, two GNR locomotives were tested on the GN main line, one using Welsh coal and the other Scottish. These were Q class No 136 (Welsh coal) and QL No 114 (Scottish). In one test, No 322 burned 38.9 lb of Welsh coal per mile and No 136 burned 34.2 lbs, working the same trains with similar loads and both using Nantyglo coal from the same wagon. The coal consumption figures on the GN main line are summarised in the first table opposite. Note that Scottish coal was 32% cheaper than Welsh coal.

Unfortunately, the GS&WR did not keep as good records of No 113's performance on the Dublin-Cork line. The GNR engine was assessed against GS&WR No 307, a '306' class locomotive of 1902. The lower table opposite shows that, as on the GNR trials, the 'away' engine performed less favourably. All engines used Nantyglo coal. The 'average' figure was an average of all engines on the Inchicore No 1 passenger link.

The GNR were rather disappointed with the southern results, but strange drivers working away from their home line would be less likely to do as well as men with years of experience on their own roads. The outcome of the tests had little impact on GNR locomotive policy. Only the removal of collars from the bogie axles could possibly be attributed to it. The expected trial of a GS&WR '368' class 2-6-0, against a Great Northern LQG 0-6-0, never took place, for reasons now lost in the mists of time. The GS&WR were impressed with the results obtained with Scottish coal and their implications for running costs. They even asked for drawings of the QL smokebox, brick arch and firebars, which Dundalk supplied. However, the tests made no obvious change to Inchicore practice either.

The 4-6-0 proposal

The GNR never built an express locomotive larger than a 4-4-0 but, in March 1911, Clifford looked at the possibility of building a 4-6-0. He wrote to the Civil Engineer asking, "What are the most liberal weights and dimensions you will allow in a 4-6-0?" The Civil Engineer replied on 25 March, as follows, "Dear Sir, A question has been raised as to the allowable wheelbase and axle loads for a 4-6-0 type engine. I have gone very carefully into the matter and bearing in mind the Boyne Viaduct and our rails, curves, etc, the most liberal weights and dimensions which we can give are shown on the accompanying diagram. Yours faithfully, etc."

In an article in the RPSI magazine *Five Foot Three* No 25 (1981), Paddy Mallon commented on the drawing and came to the following conclusions:

The total wheelbase of 29'0" was too long for the traverser, so the trailing coupled wheels would have needed to

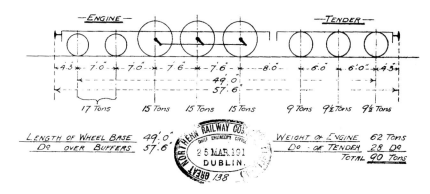

Fig 49: The Dundalk drawing for the acceptable weight distribution of a 4-6-0.
Courtesy P Mallon

be jacked up. The maximum length of the locomotive would have been roughly 37'0" without front buffers, assuming a short Clifford style cab. The erecting shop was 39'0" wide, so it would have just about fitted. The drawing seems to show 5'7' driving wheels, although the 7'6"+ 7'6" spacing would allow 6'7". Assuming an inside cylinder engine, the distance of 10'6" between the centre of the bogie and the leading drivers would have accommodated 19"x 26" cylinders comfortably.

In order to get a large enough firebox between the centre and rear drivers, a box with a sloping grate would have been necessary, so that part of the firebox would have been over the rear axle. To keep the axleload within the suggested 15 tons, a large diameter boiler would have been impossible, so the resulting engine would, probably, have looked like an elongated S class. The nearest equivalent in Britain was the GER B12 design of 1911, which had roughly the same length.

Leaving aside the length and axle load restrictions, the 62 tons weight of the engine could not have been lifted by the 40 ton overhead crane in the Erecting Shop. Even when the crane was upgraded to 60 tons in 1941, it could not have lifted the proposed engine, as the crane's lifting bogies could not have got close enough to the rear wall to get a vertical lift on the usual craning point in the cab floor, near the drag box.

For whatever reason, the proposal never went any further than this stage and when something larger than an S class was eventually built, it was a three cylinder 4-4-0.

Superheating

In the early 1900s, superheating was beginning to feature in British steam locomotive design, initially on the Lancashire and Yorkshire and Great Western Railways and, from 1909, on the Great Central. Before the days of superheating, steam was generated at a temperature

Top: PPs 4-4-0 No 12 *Ulster* was one of two fitted with the Phoenix superheater. The newly designed B3 tender had space underneath for the Drummond feed water heater. Note the very close spacing on the tender lettering. The superheater was a total failure and was removed in 1915. Beyer engines still had the ornate brass trim to the splasher but there was now a separate builder's plate.

L J Watson (WG 3)

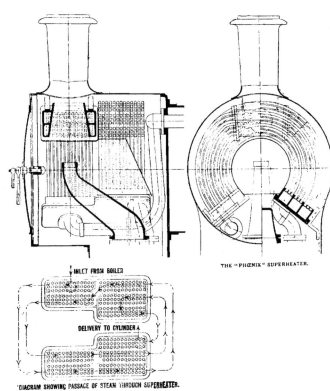

THE "PHŒNIX" SUPERHEATER.

↓INLET FROM BOILER

DELIVERY TO CYLINDER

DIAGRAM SHOWING PASSAGE OF STEAM THROUGH SUPERHEATER.

Above: The Phoenix superheater inside the smokebox of No 42.

Fig 50 (above right): The arrangement of the Phoenix superheater.

Both Beyer Peacock collection

Right: PP 4-4-0 No 50 of 1911 at Amiens Street, Dublin around 1915, in early Glover condition. This was one of three built with extended smokeboxes but never fitted with Phoenix superheaters. The long overhang is very evident in this view. Glover has removed the *Donard* nameplate, painted the engine black and lettered the tender 'Great Northern', but otherwise the locomotive is as built.

L&GRP 9154

governed by the boiler pressure. An ordinary kettle, at atmospheric pressure, generates steam at 100°C. A steam locomotive, working at 150 lbs boiler pressure, generates steam at 181°C, and at 225 lbs it is produced at 200°C.

Superheating involves heating the steam still further, by passing it back through the boiler tubes in pipes (called 'elements') until it reaches about 315°C. By raising the temperature of the steam, it expands still further. In a boiler working at 160 lbs pressure, a pound of saturated steam has a volume of about 2.6 cubic feet, but steam superheated to 315° would increase in volume to about 3.5 cubic feet. In other words, superheating effectively increases the volume of steam produced in the same boiler by about 35%. Some engineers took advantage of this, to lower the boiler pressure on superheated engines in order to reduce maintenance costs. When Clifford added superheaters to some engines in 1911, he reduced the pressure from 175 lbs to 160 lbs.

One disadvantage of superheating was that superheated steam lost the natural lubricating qualities of 'wet' saturated steam. Superheated steam is comparatively 'dry' and, when it was used, special arrangements had to be taken to lubricate the steam passages. In general, the old type of slide valves, then in vogue, did not work well with superheating and piston valves had to be used.

The best superheater on the market was the German-designed Schmidt apparatus, but railways in these islands were reluctant to use it. This was because it was protected by international patents which involved payments, not only for the superheater, but for the valve arrangements that went with it. These were about £50 per locomotive. To avoid this, British companies devised their own forms of superheating, notably, the GWR 'Swindon' type and the 'Robinson' superheater on the Great Central.

Superheated PPs

The GNR was the first Irish railway to experiment with superheating, though initially the experience was not a happy one. In 1910, 'Phoenix' type smokebox superheaters had been fitted to two Furness Railway 0-6-0 locomotives by the Superheater Co Ltd, who recommended a similar type for the

GNR. The FR locomotives concerned were Nos 14 (fitted 6/1910) and 18 (1/1910), both built in 1899, and later LMS Nos 12475 and 12479. As on the GNR, the experiment was a failure and the equipment later removed.

In April-May 1911, five new PP class locomotives were built for the GNR by Beyer Peacock, with specially extended smokeboxes to accommodate the Phoenix superheaters. The Phoenix superheater was a monster of a thing, consisting of a nest of about 300 pipes, which attempted to superheat the steam entirely within the smokebox. It was a total failure for several reasons.

Firstly, the smokebox is the coolest part of the boiler, so there was not much superheating achieved anyway. Secondly, in order to keep clear of the superheater, the chimney, and therefore the blastpipe, had to be at the front of the smokebox. This meant that the blast pipe could not be over the valve chest, which strangled the exhaust steam passages with two 45° bends. Thirdly, the enormous weight of the superheater added an additional 2¾ tons of weight to the front bogie, and increased the driving wheel axle load to 15½ tons.

The five new PP class 4-4-0s were (in order of construction) Nos 50 *Donard*, 129 *Connaught*, 44 *Leinster*, 12 *Ulster* and 42 *Munster*. All carried names of former UR locomotives. Phoenix superheaters were fitted only to Nos 12 and 42, which had 160 lbs boiler pressure and Drummond feed water heaters. The appearance of these engines, in their original green livery, can be judged from the picture of No 42 on page 146.

The superheater added 340 sq ft to the heating surface, giving a total of 1,459 sq ft. The other three had extended smokeboxes to accommodate the Phoenix superheater, should it prove satisfactory. In the event, this caution proved to be well justified. These three had 175 lbs pressure and exhaust injectors but remained saturated. All five had 3 feed Detroit lubricators.

The Phoenix superheaters in Nos 12 and 42 were so unsatisfactory that they were removed in 1915 and 1914, respectively, and their pressure restored to 175 lbs. The extended smokeboxes, and tortuous blastpipe, on all five remained until 1921-22.

Right: NQGs class 0-6-0 No 39 *Beragh* and sister No 38 *Kesh* had Phoenix super-heaters, which they retained only until 1914. No 39 is seen here as built, with B3 tender, boiler wash-out plugs and extended smokebox. Note that the power classification letter 'C' has not yet been fitted. In contrast to the 1903 QG class, note that the NQGs had sand to the front and rear drivers.

L J Watson (WG6)

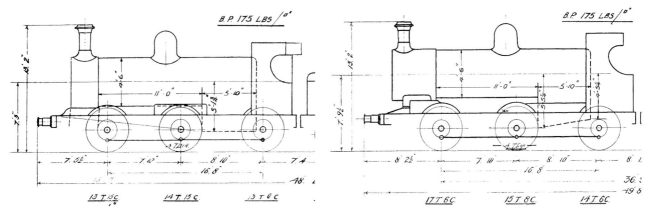

Fig 51 (above): The QG and NQG classes, to the same scale. Note how the NQG has a sloping grate, and a higher pitched boiler. The extended frames of the NQG, and the greatly increased weight at the front end, are also evident. Without the superheater, the load on the front axle was 16 tons.

Left: Nasmyth Wilson-built NQG class 0-6-0 No 109 *Moira*. The frames on this class were extended forward, which allowed the smokebox saddle to be centrally placed, resulting in a more pleasing appearance than the PP engines. Nos 9, 109 and 112 were not superheated. In this view, No 109 has already swopped its B3 tender for a second hand B1 type.

Inspector A Johnston,

Superheated NQGs

Later in the year, six 0-6-0s, designed for Phoenix superheaters, were built by the Leeds firm of Nasmyth Wilson. This was the first time that this firm had supplied locomotives for the GNR. Five were a new version of the QG class and the sixth, likewise, of the LQG class.

Of the former, Nos 9 *Kells*, 109 *Moira* and 112 *Keady* were built saturated, but with extended smokeboxes. Nos 38 *Kesh* and 39 *Beragh* were given the Phoenix superheaters, adding 340 sq ft to the heating surface (total 1,672 sq ft). The NQGs incorporated a number of other modifications to the QG design. The boiler was similar, but pitched 4½" higher, and the firebox was deeper, with a sloping grate and marginally bigger grate area. Because of the considerable overhang of the long smokebox, the frames were lengthened at the front by 9", a modification unnecessary on the PPs because they had a bogie.

Oddly, the class ran at first without the red power classification letters, possibly because the Operating Department were unsure of whether they should be 'B' or

'C'. I have seen one document where they were added to the list of 'B' engines. In the end, they became 'C', even though the QG class was 'B'. The Phoenix superheaters were removed from Nos 38 and 39 in 1914, but unfortunately the Diagram Book does not record when the extended smokeboxes were removed.

The solitary NLQG 0-6-0 was No 165 *Newbliss*. This had the 4'9" LQG boiler, pitched at the same 7'9½" centre line as in the NQGs. However, instead of the 5'10" LQG firebox with level grate, No 165 had a massive 6'7" firebox with sloping grate. This gave a heating surface of 1,430 sq ft and a grate area of 22.8 sq ft. The rear of the firebox was directly over the rear axle. Compared to the LQG class, the frames of No 165 were 9" longer at the front and 9½" longer at the rear. This allowed a deeper cab to accommodate the firebox. No 165 had an extended smokebox but did not receive a Phoenix superheater. All these locomotives had the distinctive Nasmyth Wilson triangular builder's plate on the leading splasher.

To run with these locomotives, eleven more outside spring tenders were built. Five were of the B2 type, introduced in

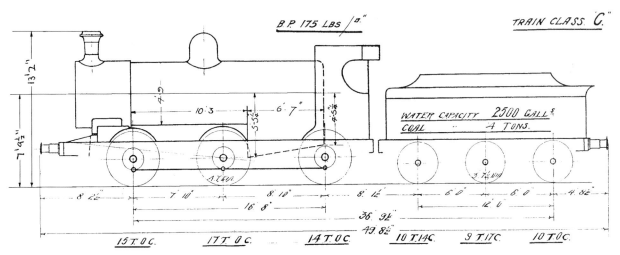

BP. 175 LBS /□" TRAIN CLASS 'C.'

Fig 52 (top): The weight distribution on the NLQG engine in this diagram is curious. Despite the larger boiler, the total weight is only 4 cwt heavier than the NQG type, which appears unlikely. Also the front axle load is given as 15 tons. Could this be a mistake for 16 tons? Glover has amended this diagram to include a high coping on the tender and an extended cab roof with hand rail.

Courtesy P Mallon

Right: An interesting view of No 165 around 1914. The engine is in black livery and the name *Newbliss* has been removed. The tender has received its high coping but the cab roof has not yet been extended. The tender has not yet been lettered 'Great Northern'. I retain a slight fondness for this engine as my grandfather, William Johnston, was Station Master at Newbliss from 1912 to 1918.

Inspector A Johnston

Bottom: QL class 4-4-0 No 157 *Orpheus*, ex-Works at Dundalk, and newly equipped with a B2 tender, a GNR built one, with the coping extended all the way to the back. The lubricator on the side of the smokebox is feeding oil to the bogie axleboxes.

L J Watson (WG 25)

Top: QGT2 0-6-2T No 169 at Dundalk, as running in the late Glover era in black livery. This engine and sister 168 spent the early part of their working lives shunting at Adelaide marshalling yard. However, after 1935 No 169 was transferred to Derry.

C P Friel collection

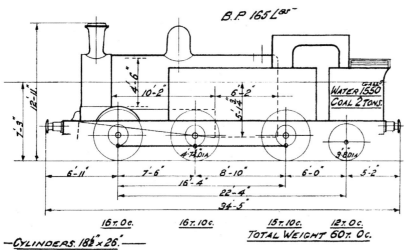

Fig 53 (left): The QGT2 0-6-2T design of 1911. These two locomotives had larger fireboxes and longer frames than the 1905 pair of QGTs. They were never superheated. As built, the engines had a boiler pressure of 175 lbs. Note that the water capacity was 1550 gallons, not 1250 gallons, as often misquoted.

1910, but Nasmyth Wilson built six B3 tenders, a new type, in which a section of the tank was below the bunker to provide a higher shovel plate. These were used on the superheated engines as they could accommodate another new device underneath. This was the Drummond feed water heater, used to warm the water slightly before it entered the boiler. The feed-water heater was designed by Dugald Drummond of the London South Western Railway, but was not a success. Externally, the B3 tenders differed from the B2 type of 1910-11, in that the coping extended to the rear of the tender. It would appear from photographic evidence, that some of the new 0-6-0s lost their B2 or B3 tenders to QL 4-4-0s (see the picture of No 157, page 99). Certainly, QL Nos 113, 126, 127 and 157 ran with the newer tenders, whilst 0-6-0s Nos 109 and 112 soon had the older B1 type.

It is often said of steam locomotive design that, if the engine *looked* right, it *was* right. The experience of the GNR Phoenix superheater experiment, bears out that the converse was also the case. If it *looked* wrong it *was* wrong! The NQG, NLQG, and modified PP, engines were undoubtedly the ugliest engines to emerge from the Dundalk drawing office –

indeed, they were the *only* ugly locomotives in a long line of handsome designs.

The QGT2 0-6-2Ts

Mention was made earlier that two more RT 0-6-4Ts, Nos 166 and 167, were built in 1911. They were followed by two more 0-6-2Ts, Nos 168 and 169, built by Robert Stephenson and Co. These were specifically designed for shunting the new marshalling yard at Adelaide, Belfast, opened at the same time as Adelaide shed. The QGT2 0-6-2Ts differed from the 1905 locomotives, in having 6'2" fireboxes and a grate area of 21.3 sq ft. The larger firebox was accommodated by increasing the wheelbase by 4" between the two rear driving axles. In addition, another 6" was added to the frames at the rear, increasing water capacity to 1550 gallons. The heating surface was 1,256 sq ft and tractive effort 23,957 lbs. They weighed 60 tons and had a 16½ ton axle load. The 0-6-2Ts, at 12'11" high, were 3" lower than main line locomotives. Both engines remained saturated and were withdrawn in 1957.

The S class 4-4-0s

Clifford's last project, before his retirement, was the design of a new express passenger locomotive to supersede the QL class. Locomotive design had progressed in leaps and bounds since 1904 and the S class would be thoroughly modern, with superheating and piston valves. It is to Clifford's credit that the unfortunate experiment with the Phoenix superheaters in the PP and NQG classes, described above, did not put him off superheating. This time, however, he went for the well-tried Schmidt type, regardless of the £50 royalty.

The main reason for building new express engines was the bridge-strengthening on the Derry Road. It was anticipated that, when this was completed, several Q class engines would be transferred to Derry road duties, thus creating the justification for new main line engines. The design of the new locomotives was completed in October 1911 and offered for tender. I should explain that, when the GNR drew up a new design, a Specification Book was printed, describing in detail the materials to be used and the way the locomotives were to be built. This book was then forwarded to any locomotive building firm which wanted to consider tendering for their construction. Tenders would be submitted and the Locomotive Committee, largely on cost grounds, would make recommendations to the Board as to which tender should be accepted. These books are very interesting and throw much light on the designs.

The original specification book for the S class 4-4-0 shows that it was to have been a much larger engine than was eventually built. Cylinders were to have been 20"x 26", driving wheels 6'7", and boiler 4'9"x 11'0" with a 6'7" firebox. There would have been 152 1¾" tubes, with an 18 element Schmidt superheater in 5¼" tubes. The cylinders were to be activated by 8" Schmidt patent piston valves, placed horizontally, on top of the inclined cylinders, and driven by rocker arms.

The locomotive would have operated at 165 lbs pressure and would have had a tractive effort of 18,463 lbs. The frames were to have been much stronger – 1⅛" compared to 1" on the earlier QL class – with the additional difference that they were to be 4'8" apart for the *full* length of the engine. Previously, the frames had narrowed to 4'5", from the motion plate forward. There would have been four slide bars, instead of the previous two, and strap big-ends, as in QL No 24 *Juno*. The wheelbase was to have been 23'0½", 6" more than the QL class. Most of the features outlined above, apart from the 4'9" boiler and the 20" cylinders, did of course appear on the final engines.

In a Board minute of 2 January 1912, there are hints of second thoughts on the weight of the new locomotives. The specification was altered to allow for a maximum axle load of 17 tons. The original drawing had estimated the weight at 53 tons but, given that the eventual weight of the S class was 52 tons 2 cwt, it is more likely that the original design would have weighed about 54½ tons. The design was altered to reduce the boiler diameter to 4'6" and the cylinders came down to 19"x 26". With these modifications, the tender from Beyer Peacock was accepted and five locomotives were ordered on 31 January 1912.

Clifford's retirement

Charles Clifford retired in May 1912 and was succeeded by George Glover. This led to further alterations to the design and the new engines will be dealt with in the next chapter. It should be added that five 0-6-0 locomotives, the corresponding SG class, were also ordered.

It is interesting to conjecture how Charles Clifford felt at the time of his retirement. His career on the INWR and GNR had spanned over fifty years. In that time, he had seen the design of steam locomotives change enormously, from the long boiler Grendon 0-6-0s of 1855-56 and small Beyer 2-2-2s of 1861, to the dawn of superheating. His locomotives were always aesthetically beautiful (the 1911 designs excepted) and, despite being a Victorian engineer, he had always kept himself abreast with the latest developments. In the appearance of his engines, he had remained true to the parameters established by James Park in the 1880s, even down to the inadequate Stirling cab. Thus, the resemblance to the English GNR was as strong in 1912 as it had been thirty years earlier. With the arrival of Glover, GNR locomotive design was on the threshold of change and 1912 was, in many ways, the end of an era.

Chapter 8
Building them in fives
George T Glover 1912-1933

Up to this point in the book, readers who were familiar with the GNR in the 1950s will have recognised many of the locomotives illustrated, but will be conscious that, in the early 1900s, they looked somewhat different from how they remembered them. This is because the 'look' of GNR locomotives in the mid-20th century was created by Glover in the years after 1912. George T Glover came from the North Eastern Railway, Gateshead Works, where he had worked with W M Smith, Chief Draughtsman. The reason for the title of this chapter is that, with two exceptions, Glover's locomotives were built in multiples of five.

The Glover era was to set the stage for GNR locomotive development during the remaining 46 years of the company's existence. With the exception of the first batch of 4-4-2Ts and the Hawthorn Leslie crane tank, all Glover's engines were built with superheaters. He subsequently superheated all earlier 4-4-0 locomotives (apart from the J class), the 4-4-2Ts mentioned above and most of the 0-6-0s as well. Among Irish railway companies, the GNR soon had the largest proportion of superheated engines in its fleet, though surpassed in this regard by the NCC in the late 1930s.

Glover soon changed the general appearance of the locomotives. In his view, the short Stirling cab offered little protection and, without altering the profile of the roof, he extended it backwards 18" to cover the whole footplate. Given that the NER had the largest locomotive cabs in Britain, this is not surprising. It is perhaps more surprising that Glover did not introduce side-window cabs, as on his native NER.

He was also against the general application of the ornate green livery. In June 1912, a month after taking over, he painted P5'6" 4-4-0 No 105 in lined black livery as an experiment and shortly afterwards decreed that this livery should be applied to goods engines, tank engines and small-wheeled passenger engines. He also felt that too many engines had names and they were quickly removed from all but the largest express engines. When the S class appeared in early 1913, they still had the

green livery, but the nameplates were curved and mounted on the splashers, rather than rectangular and mounted on the boiler, as before. From July 1914, Glover decided that all engines should be black with a vermillion line, even the express types, and only the S and QL classes were allowed to retain names. Even these had largely disappeared by 1920.

Three other subtle changes should be mentioned. Glover gradually fitted all tenders with a high coping, including those that had received the small coping from 1908 on. Tenders retained this new style right up to the end. Secondly, side handrails now stopped at the edge of the smokebox and a separate straight handrail was attached to the smokebox door on all new engines and, after 1920, on rebuilds. Previously, side handrails had curved round the top of the smokebox.

The third change came after 1920 and was probably the result of higher post-war labour costs. If you look at early GNR locomotives, the smokeboxes have a smooth outline. This was because of the use of counter-sunk rivets, which were then painted over. The disadvantage was that dismantling any part of the engine involved the time consuming job of drilling out the rivets. From September

Above: J class 4-4-0 No 118, formerly *Rose*, but now nameless and repainted in Glover black livery. It is seen here at Banbridge about 1914. This locomotive was sold to the SL&NCR in 1921, becoming *Blacklion*. It was scrapped in 1931.

Inspector A Johnston

Left: S class 4-4-0 No 170 *Errigal* brand new at Belfast in 1913. It was delivered in green livery but with a modified design of cab and new style B4 tender. The engine has Ramsbottom safety valves and only two lamp irons. The smokebox damper piston is clearly visible.

Inspector A Johnston

1923, Dundalk issued the General Order that all new smokeboxes were to use snap-head rivets. Snap-head rivets were easier to remove, as they were visible without having to strip back the paint. However, new construction from outside manufacturers continued to use counter-sunk rivets on smokeboxes right up to 1930.

The locomotive fleet in 1912

We last surveyed the locomotive fleet at the point when Clifford took over in 1895 (see page 75). In the intervening years, new construction had eliminated most of the older pre-1876 locomotives. By 1912, only seventeen remained, of which seven were 0-6-0s of classes C, D and E, which still had many years of life left in them. The other ten were made up of three 0-4-2s (No 9A, ex-D&DR, 109A and 112A, both ex-UR) and seven 2-4-0s. Three of these were old ex-UR double framed engines – Nos 114A, 121A *Dalriada* and 128A. Two more, Nos 44A and 45A, were ex-D&BJR H class engines and the other two were ex-INWR locomotives – Nos 22A (G class) and 43A (originally L class). The only other non-GNR locomotive was BP 4-4-0T No 96A of 1880, the last of the BCR locomotives, which was Dundalk station pilot and destined to last until 1950.

In 1912, the fleet consisted of 185 locomotives, comprising 169 in the capital stock and 16 duplicates. There were seventeen 2-4-0s, sixty-two 4-4-0s, three 0-4-2s, seventy-six 0-6-0s, thirteen 4-4-0Ts, six 2-4-2Ts, four 0-6-2Ts and four 0-6-4Ts. Traffic was expanding rapidly in the years just before World War One and within three years the fleet would expand to 204, its maximum size.

The S class 1913

The new S class locomotives were delivered in February 1913. They were the last new GNR locomotives to be delivered in the Doncaster green livery and were numbered and named 170 *Errigal*, 171 *Slieve Gullion*, 172 *Slieve Donard*, 173 *Galtee More* and 174 *Carrantuohill*. Nos 171

and 174 were allocated to Adelaide, whilst Dublin had 170, 172 and 173.

These engines included the various modifications already agreed by Clifford (see Chapter 7) and further modifications ordered by Glover. Changes included the omission of four longitudinal stays from the tubeplates, the fitting of ¾" piston rings in place of ⅝", changes to the diameter of the piston rods, and changes in the metal used for certain components. Glover naturally specified the new design of cab and changed the chimneys on these and subsequent engines, from built up to cast iron type. The nameplates, originally intended to be on the boiler as on Clifford engines, were on the splashers and were of a new type with black waxed letters sunk into the brass; previous plates had raised lettering.

The main dimensions, as built, were: driving wheels 6'7", bogie wheels 3'2", wheelbase 6'0"+ 7'6½"+ 9'6", cylinders 19"x 26" with 8" piston valves, boiler 4'6"x 11'0" at 165 lbs pressure, 134 1¾" tubes and 18 5¼" tubes (Schmidt superheater), heating surface 1,366 sq ft, firebox 6'7" long, grate area 22.9 sq ft, weight 52 tons 2 cwt with 17 tons axle load, tractive effort 16,663 lbs.

The piston valves were placed horizontally above the cylinders and driven by rocker arms. The engines were equipped with a new design of 2500 gallon tender, designated B4. These had a higher coping, and sides which were 5½" shorter, with a vertical hand pillar at the front instead of an outside grab-rail. Soon these higher copings were being fitted to earlier tenders too. In 1911, Watson had considered equipping the S class with 3500 gallon tenders, but this was abandoned, probably because the longer wheelbase would have required new turntables and because superheated engines were expected to be lighter on water.

Like most superheated engines of this period, the S class were fitted with pyrometers (to measure the temperature of the steam) and also superheater dampers. These were designed to prevent the superheater tubes being burnt when the regulator was closed. The piston operating these was fitted to the outside of the smokebox on the fireman's side

Top: A GNR express train of 1913. Note the bogie splasher and the Wakefield lubricator on No 172 *Slieve Donard*. By now two more lamp irons have been added to the front. In this view, No 172 is paired with a corridor train made up mainly of clerestory vehicles, consisting of N1 mail van No 9 (later 488), W1 6-wheel brake, F1 compo, B3 12-wheel dining car No 427, another F1 compo and M1 bogie brake, strengthened by an I3 tricompo and an L1 brake third.

R Welch, courtesy Ulster Museum

Centre: In this view, around 1920, No 174 *Carrantuohill* has been given the black livery with 'Great Northern' in Gill Sans style lettering. It now has Ross pop safety valves, and a Detroit lubricator, in place of the original Wakefield. Two steps have been added below the smokebox door to allow access to the top lamp bracket. However it still has bogie splashers and nameplates.

Courtesy IRRS

Bottom: A later view of No 171 at Adelaide in the early 1930s. Despite its express engine status, the engine has no lining whatsoever (abandoned in 1925) and is nameless. It has a snap rivetted smokebox with a smokebox tightening wheel instead of handle. The 'Great Northern' lettering on tenders was abandoned in 1928. In the background is LQGs No 164.

J D FitzGerald collection

and was connected to the regulator by a long lever which ran to the cab along the outside of the boiler. The piston was connected to the steam pipe and when the regulator was open the piston was forced back and lifted the dampers, closing them automatically when the regulator was shut off.

The S class had some teething troubles. The engines did not steam well until the blast pipe diameter was reduced from 5¾" to 4¾" and the blower ring altered. As delivered, the locomotives had the usual two headlamp brackets on the front running plate but, within a few months, Glover had them fitted with a centre bracket and a smokebox bracket. This allowed the full range of headlamp codes to be used and this alteration was gradually applied to the entire locomotive stock.

The S class and the SG 0-6-0s were the last new GNR engines to be fitted with Ramsbottom safety valves, as built. However, in 1914-15, the engines were amongst the first to be given the more modern Ross pop valves. These had the advantage over Ramsbottom valves that they could not be adjusted when the locomotive was in steam. This removed the temptation (occasionally fatal) for drivers, to screw down the valves when short of steam.

The superheater dampers proved troublesome and unnecessary and were removed in 1914-15 and the pressure was raised to 175 lbs (tractive effort 17,673 lbs). The piston tail rods and the pyrometers were also removed. On first repainting (around 1917) the S class received the lined black livery, with 'Great Northern' on the tenders, but retained their nameplates. These were removed in 1923-25, except for No 170, which retained its until May 1929. The Schmidt superheaters were replaced by the Robinson type as the elements became due for renewal (170 4/1922, 171 9/1922, 172 6/1922, 173 1/1924 and 174 11/1923).

When the S2 class were delivered in 1915, they were usually allocated to Belfast, and the original S class to Dublin. This may account for the consistently lower coal consumption of the five S class engines (averaging 39.2 to 41.4 lbs per mile, compared to 42.6 to 43.6 lbs for Nos 190-192 over the period 1920-36).

Several other alterations took place before renewal in 1938-39. Detroit lubricators replaced Wakefield after 1918 and bogie wheel splashers were removed after August 1921.

In June 1926, No 172 received an interchange S2 type boiler with 200 lbs boiler pressure, raising the tractive effort to 20,198 lbs. This proved very successful and the pressure was raised on the other four, using the existing boilers, but with new fireboxes. No 171, dealt with in December 1926, also had the valve travel increased from 3¾" to 4²⁵⁄₃₂" and this modification was made to the others, the pressure on which was raised to 200 lbs at the following dates: 174 4/1927, 170 7/1927 and 173 8/1928.

In August 1935, No 170 was involved in a locomotive exchange with NCC W class 2-6-0 No 96 *Silver Jubilee*, and ran trips between Belfast and Portrush and Belfast and Larne Harbour. Finally, mention should be made that, in March 1936, No 172 was experimentally fitted for oil burning and No 171 from July. Both reverted to coal burning in December 1936.

SG class 0-6-0 1913

The SG class incorporated the main features of the S class design – 19"x 26" cylinders, Schmidt superheaters, 4'6" boilers, etc. Like the passenger engines, they were conceived by Clifford and were originally intended to have 20" cylinders and 4'9" boilers, but following the same changes to the specification in Glover's first months, as Nos 170-174.

The introduction of the SG class heralded a change in driving wheel diameter for GNR goods engines, from 4'7" to 5'1". The reason for this was that 4'7" wheels had made it difficult to fit an efficient spring to the heavier LQG and NQG classes of 1906-11. A W Denniss, the Running Superintendent, recommended an increase in diameter of 6" to allow stronger springs, with the additional advantage that this would also make them better suited to cattle specials and excursion work – effectively making them mixed traffic engines. In any case, the GNR did not have the heavy mineral traffic which demanded 4'7" wheels on the larger goods engines of many English railways.

Initially, the SG class were allocated the numbers of the last five pre-1876 engines on the capital list – Nos 37 (E

Left: SG 0-6-0 Nos 177-179 were delivered as Nos 47-49 in March-April 1913. These were the first new locomotives to be delivered in black livery. Note the Ramsbottom valves, soon replaced by the Ross pop type.

J D FitzGerald collection

Left: Not the first member of the SG class, as the number might suggest, but the fourth. No 175 is seen at Dundalk shortly after delivery. It was April 1915 before these engines became train class 'C'. Note the superheater damper on the smokebox and the B4 tender with high coping.

L J Watson (WG 26)

Fig 54 (below): The original 1912 drawing for the front elevation of the first Glover 4-4-2Ts. Note the shape of the handrail round the smokebox.

Courtesy P Mallon

class), 40, 41 (D class), 137 and 138 (C class). The first engine was actually photographed by Beyer Peacock, in shop grey livery, bearing the number 37. However, just before delivery in March-April 1913, there was a change of plan, probably because Glover decided these older engines had more life in them. So, the new goods engines arrived as Nos 47-49, 175 and 176 (G class 2-4-0 Nos 47-49 joined the duplicate list). In October 1913, there was a further change of policy. Glover decided to abolish the duplicate list (initiated by Park in 1881), so the G class engines reverted to 47-49 and the first three SG engines became 177-179. This explains why the works numbers of Nos 175-179 appear out of sequence.

Initially, the SG class ran without train class letters but, in April 1915, they were classed 'C'. They were excellent engines and very popular with the crews, eclipsed only by the SG3 class of 1920-21. In later years, an SG engine was nearly always rostered for the nightly Belfast-Enniskillen goods. Unlike the S class, the SG boiler had a firebox with a sloping grate. During construction, Glover considered changing the firebox to the flat grated S type, so that the boilers could be interchanged. However, the plates had already been ordered and the alteration was not made. The wheelbase was 8'1"+ 8'10", with an axle load of 16 tons 16 cwt.

These engines were the first new locomotives to be delivered with lined black livery, but arrived lettered 'GNR' on the tender instead of the 'Great Northern' applied to subsequent Glover engines. They had superheater dampers but these were soon removed. The Schmidt superheaters were replaced by the Robinson type as the elements wore out, the dates being: 175 4/1925, 176 8/1923, 177 12/1923, 178 11/1925 and 179 1/1930. No 179 was, therefore, the last GNR locomotive to have a Schmidt superheater.

T class 4-4-2T 1913

The locomotive design most associated with George Glover, was his family of 4-4-2Ts, which eventually numbered twenty-five. By 1930, one engine in eight was a 4-4-2T. In 1912, the GNR certainly needed a good suburban tank. The railmotors were worn out, the 4-4-0Ts were too small and there were only six 2-4-2Ts. Most of Clifford's tanks had been shunting engines and the GNR still depended

too much on tender engines for short-haul passenger work.

Plans for Glover's new tank design were drawn up in October 1912. The main dimensions were: 3'2" bogie wheels, 5'9" driving wheels, a rear radial axle with 4'0" wheels, wheelbase 5'3"+ 6'10½"+ 8'3"+ 8'0" (total 28'4"), 18"x 24" inclined inside cylinders with slide valves, a 4'3" diameter PP class boiler with a 10'2" barrel and 5'5" firebox, a flat 18.3 sq ft grate, a boiler pressure of 175 lbs and a tractive effort of 16,763 lbs.

The D&SR had built a new 4-4-2T in 1911 – No 20 King George V – with 6'1" wheels and 18"x 26" cylinders, and Glover persuaded Wild (the D&SER Engineer) to display No 20 in Amiens Street one day, so that he could show the GNR Directors the type of engine he had in mind. Of course, the BCDR also had suburban 4-4-2Ts.

The 5'9" wheel diameter was new to the Great Northern but I have not seen any evidence as to why it was increased from 5'7". Glover specified a saturated boiler for the T class

Left: T1 class 4-4-2T No 185 as built in December 1913. These were the first locomotives to be lettered 'Great Northern' instead of 'GNR' They also got Ross pop valves and four lamp brackets. Note the short smokebox originally fitted to these saturated engines and the bunker coal rails. The T1 class had a much deeper rear cut out to their cabs than the later T2 class. To fit these locomotives on the traverser at Dundalk Works, the rear radial truck had to be jacked up.

V Welch, courtesy Ulster Museum

Right: No 185 passing Knockmore Junction with a mixed eight coach rake of six-wheelers and bogie stock in 1914. Surprisingly, these locomotives were not initially allocated to suburban traffic. The Banbridge and Newcastle line swings off to the left and the Antrim branch to the right.

Maj Gen Sir Cecil Smyth

and these were the only new main line engines after 1911 not to have superheaters. Perhaps, at this stage, Glover wanted to be satisfied with the new Schmidt-fitted engines before proceeding further. At any rate, it soon became evident that building them saturated was short sighted, a mistake rectified with the tender version in 1915. Another interesting feature of the 1912 drawing is that, the side handrail was carried over and round the smokebox door, as on the Clifford engines, but they were not actually built like this.

The original intention was to number the 4-4-2Ts 177-181 (following on from the SG 0-6-0s). However, in October 1913, plans were changed and they went into service as 185-189 in December 1913, arriving, at roughly weekly intervals, from Beyer Peacock. New numbers had been allocated as follows:

177-179 – renumbering of SG 0-6-0s 47-49
180-184 – new 0-6-0s, authorised
185-189 – new T class 4-4-2Ts
190-192 – new 4-4-0s, authorised
193-195 – renumbered duplicates 38A, 39A, 96A
196-200 – new construction, type to be determined

Some other modifications were made before delivery. Originally, the side tanks were to be smaller (425 gallons each and 4'0" high) and the rear tank 850 gallons. Beyer Peacock recommended that the rear tank should be 500 gallons and the side tanks 600 gallons each. This was to do with redistributing weight, transferred about a ton from the radial truck to the bogie and raising the side tank height to 4'7".

Other new features were Ross pop safety valves, oval buffers and the side tanks lettered 'Great Northern'.

Glover, obviously, had more than suburban traffic in mind for his new tanks. Instead of allocating them all to Belfast, two went to Clones and one each to Derry and Dundalk. The Clones engines may have been intended for the Cavan branch but one certainly worked, regularly, through to Belfast in 1914 (see above). Given that they carried 1700 gallons of water and 3½ tons of coal, Glover may have seen them as potential Irish North engines. However, with the arrival of the U class in 1915, they gravitated towards Belfast and Dublin for suburban duties.

The lack of superheaters was rectified in the 1920s. The first to be dealt with was No 186 in 1923. The boilers originally had 206 1¾" tubes with a total heating surface of 1,092 sq ft. On rebuilding with 16 element Robinson superheaters and 8" piston valves, the number of small tubes fell to 111 with a total heating surface of 1036 sq ft. Weight increased by 2 cwt to 65 tons 4 cwt. The others were rebuilt as follows: 185 3/1924, 187 4/1926, 188 6/1927 and 189 11/1926. As mentioned at the start of Chapter 6, the restricted width of the Dundalk erecting shop and traverser created major difficulties for the Glover tanks. One set of buffers had to be removed to create room to get past them when in shops.

Early changes to the fleet

Although a lot of new locomotives were being designed and delivered in 1912-15, Glover was already making

Left: The first engine to be numbered 202 was an ex-INWR 2-4-0, previously No 43A (see page 36), built in 1874. It was renovated by Glover in 1914 and lasted until 1921. Note the vacuum pipe tucked under the running plate.

Inspector A Johnston

Below left: H class 2-4-0 Nos 84 and 86 at Portadown shed on 8 August 1930. This illustrates engines with and without splasher sandboxes. They have the characteristic Glover extended cab and high tender coping. This class worked to Warrenpoint up to 1932, the last 2-4-0s on the GNR.

H C Casserley 7053

Opposite top: BT 4-4-0T No 1 with a Keady train at Irish Street halt, Armagh about 1909. The carriage is composite No 10, later L7 No 210. Note the pulleys, levers and wires for driving the engine from the coach in push-pull working.

J D FitzGerald collection

Opposite centre left: Hunslet 0-4-0ST No 203 at Portadown shed on 7 August 1930. This was the smallest locomotive on the GNR. with the possible exception of the old L&ER 2-2-0WTs. It was sold a few months after this picture was taken.

H C Casserley 7030

Opposite centre right: Hunslet 0-6-0T No 204 at Portadown. This was the second of the contractor's locomotives which originated from building the Armagh-Castleblaney line. The driving wheels were 3'4".

Real Photographs X 121

improvements to the existing fleet. Among the older locomotives thought worth retaining, C class 0-6-0 Nos 137 and 138 were rebuilt in 1912-13, ex-D&BJR D class 0-6-0 Nos 40 and 41 in 1913-15 and E class 0-6-0 Nos 193 and 194 (ex-38A and 39A) in 1915. All received new 4'2" boilers but with varying lengths of barrel and firebox, depending on the wheel-spacing and frames. They received the new black livery and, eventually, extended cabs and high copings to their tenders. The last three GNR 0-4-2s were soon eliminated, with the two ex-UR double-framed engines going in 1912-13. Only ex-D&DR No 9A had a reprieve. In 1914 it was repaired and renumbered 201, but was scrapped in 1915, its number then being given to H class 2-4-0 No 45A.

The last 2-4-0s

There were seventeen 2-4-0s in the fleet when Glover took over in 1912. Of these, H class 2-4-0 Nos 84-87 were reckoned to be worth retaining, even though due for replacement in 1920-21. They received extended cabs and other modifications and were given new fireboxes in 1914-19, enabling the pressure to be raised to 175 lbs and ensuring their survival until 1932, when they were the last GNR 2-4-0s. In their last years, they were mainly on the Warrenpoint branch and Portadown-Newry locals.

The First World War also ensured the survival of G class 2-4-0 Nos 47-49 which, in 1915, were patched up with new 16½" cylinders. Also reprieved was ex-INWR 2-4-0 No 43A, which, on account of the good state of its 1901 boiler, was given a heavy overhaul in 1914, with Glover modifications, and renumbered 202. These lasted until 1921.

Of the other 2-4-0s, most were beyond economic repair and were scrapped in 1913-14, but some doubt persisted over H class No 45A (ex-D&BJR, built 1866). It was nominally renumbered 201 in June 1915, but did no work after 1916 and may not actually have carried this number. Renumbering these older engines finally eliminated the old duplicate list, introduced by Park in 1881.

The Keady engines

The Castleblaney, Keady and Armagh Railway was one of the shortest-lived railways in Ireland. In 1900, a company called the Kingscourt, Keady and Armagh Railway proposed building a line to connect Armagh (firmly in GNR territory) with Kingscourt, terminus of a MGWR branch from Navan and Dublin. This proposal won Parliamentary approval and was financially backed by the MGWR.

To thwart this MGWR attempt at invading Great Northern territory, the GNR, at great expense, was effectively

obliged to buy off the KK&AR. For a financial investment of £350,000, the GNR persuaded the company to abandon the Kingscourt-Castleblaney part of the line and allow the GNR to work the Armagh-Castleblaney section.

Progress on what was now the CK&AR was slow and in 1908 the company took over the plant and works belonging to the contractor, Robert Worthington, and completed the construction themselves. The line was opened from Armagh to Keady on 31 May 1909 and from there to Castleblaney on 10 November 1910.

Initially, the Armagh-Keady section was operated as a branch from Armagh by a BT 4-4-0T and push-pull coach, but tender engines took over after November 1910.

In 1911 the CK&AR was vested in the GNR and among the assets of the company were two industrial tanks – *Kells* and *Mullingar* which were taken into GNR stock in March 1913, retaining their names. In 1915, the nameplates were removed and they were numbered 203 and 204 in capital stock.

No 203 was a Hunslet 0-4-0ST, built in 1904. It had 2'8½" wheels (the smallest on the GNR) and 10¼"x 15" outside cylinders. Its 3'0"x 7'10" boiler worked at 90 lbs pressure and the engine weighed only 16 tons. It was based at Portadown shed and, after transfer to Departmental use in 1921, was used on ballasting duties. However, with a tractive effort of only 3,709 lbs, it cannot have been much use for ballast work.

The second engine, No 204, was somewhat bigger. It was a Hunslet 0-6-0T, dating from 1889, with inside 15"x 20" cylinders and 3'4" driving wheels. Its boiler was 4'0"x 8'4" and worked at 100lbs. This locomotive weighed 28½ tons and had a tractive effort of 9,562 lbs. It too, was shedded at Portadown and, probably, shunted the goods yard there. In 1920, it was transferred to Departmental use and worked in the ballast and wagon department 1920-26. Both locomotives were sold in November 1930.

Rebuilding the P class

Despite the introduction of superheating for new locomotives, Glover continued to rebuild the existing engines with saturated boilers, at least until 1919. It would seem that he originally intended to superheat only the locomotives built after 1898. Glover's first major rebuilds were the P6'6" class 4-4-0s of 1892-95, which received 4'6" boilers in 1913-15.

The first two to be dealt with, Nos 83 (June 1913) and 82 (December 1913), were turned out in the full green livery, but were given such Glover features as an extended cab roof and high coping to the tender. At this point, only small-wheeled 4-4-0 engines were being painted black. However, the nameplates and the Beyer Peacock brass beading on the splashers were removed.

The 1895 pair were rebuilt in September 1914 (No 72) and June 1915 (No 73). By this time, black was being applied to *all* engines, so they were turned out in the new livery, with

Top: P6'6" 4-4-0 No 83, as rebuilt by Glover with a 4'6" saturated boiler in June 1913. As they had the larger size of driving wheel, Nos 83 and 82 (rebuilt December) qualified for the green livery. They must have been the last engines to get green livery, and the only ones (other than the new S class) to get green livery combined with Glover cab and tender.

L J Watson (WG 10)

Right: QL 4-4-0 No 128, as running about 1920, at Adelaide with nameplates removed. Apart from the livery it is still pretty much as built. Like all of the QL class, this engine had its cylinders bushed to 17¾" during the First World War.

Lens of Sutton

'Great Northern' on the tender. All the new boilers on the P6'6" locomotives were 4'6"x 10'2", with 5'0" fireboxes and 240 tubes, except for No 73, which had 216 tubes. As noted in Chapter 7, all the P5'6" locomotives, apart from No 54, had received 4'6" boilers in 1906-07. In 1916, No 54 was brought into line and received a new boiler identical to that fitted to No 73. The only other change to this class, before superheating in the 1930s, was the replacement of the splasher sandboxes by the under-frame type after 1927.

Bushing of cylinders

In late 1912 or early 1913, Glover appears to have done a detailed assessment of the locomotive fleet. New diagrams were prepared of all existing engines, but were not nearly as detailed as the earlier diagrams reproduced in chapters 1, 2 and 6. On several of the diagrams, hand-written comments by Glover can be found, such as "Useful class I.N.W. Over-cylindered at 18½"."

Glover appears to have concluded that some of the larger locomotives were 'over-cylindered' and, in 1913-16, he added bushes to reduce their cylinder diameter, the engines also requiring smaller pistons. A bush was basically a slieve, or lining, placed inside a cylinder to reduce its diameter.

The Q, PG and QG classes were bushed from 18½" to 17½" cylinders, but the QL class came down to only 17¾". Despite reducing the latter, he left the LQG class at 18½". Even more oddly, in 1917-19, he decided to reduce the cylinders of his own T class 4-4-2Ts from 18" to 17¼" and, in 1918, bushed the cylinders of LQG No 108 to 18". This last bushing brought no noticeable economy and no further engines of this class were bushed.

The reasons for the bushing have never been explained. Most writers simply stated that it was done. Glover's hand-written comments on the LQG diagram suggest that economy was the motive. It is significant that only the saturated engines were bushed and, certainly, when the engines concerned were superheated, they were restored to their former diameter or even larger.

It may also be that Glover was influenced by contemporary views on the relationship between cylinder volume and heating surface. Certainly, he would have been aware of G J Churchward's 1906 paper to the Institute of Mechanical Engineers on the subject of locomotive boilers, which began: "The modern locomotive problem is, principally, a question of boiler." Among other things, Churchward drew attention to the importance of increasing the diameter of boiler tubes to 2" or more, if the length of the boiler increased beyond 12 feet.

Right: Glover turned the A class 0-6-0s into quite attractive machines by adding the usual Glover features. In contrast to the AL class, the A class retained Ramsbottom valves and boiler side water feed. This view of No 146, ex-Works, was taken at Dundalk in August 1930. This engine was withdrawn in 1937.

H C Casserley 7038

Below right: In 1914 Glover commenced the rebuilding of the AL class, built in the 1890s. They received 4'6" saturated boilers working at 175 lbs. No 59, seen here at Enniskillen in May 1955, was rebuilt in April 1915. The ALs were excellent engines and remained in service right up to the demise of the GNR in 1958.

G W Sharpe, courtesy C P Friel

AL class rebuilds

By 1914, the rebuilding of the A class 0-6-0s was almost complete and Glover turned his attention to the AL class. This was the last class of goods locomotive to be rebuilt saturated. Like most rebuilds of the pre-1920 period, the ALs received 4'6" boilers, the first to be rebuilt being No 56 in December 1914. This engine and No 59 (April 1915) were given 228 tubes but the remaining nine got 216, with a slightly different tube arrangement. With 175 lbs boiler pressure and 18,758 lbs tractive effort, the AL 0-6-0s became popular and useful light goods and shunting engines. All of this class had been rebuilt by 1919.

The S2 and SG2 classes

Building on experience with the S and SG classes, new passenger and goods engines were ordered in 1913. These were SG2 0-6-0 Nos 180-184 and S2 4-4-0 Nos 190-192. The main changes to the earlier designs were that, Robinson superheaters (a GCR design) were fitted in place of Schmidt, and the cylinders had inclined valves and direct link motion, instead of horizontal valves and rocker arms. Inclined valves and direct drive had always been standard on the NER.

These locomotives were built new with 175 lb boilers (though initially specified for 165 lbs) and had 120 small tubes instead of the original 134. This reduced the heating surface from 1,366 sq ft to 1,296 sq ft. Other changes included: Ross pop valves; combined steam circulating valve and blower valve, in place of superheater dampers and Schmidt's patent circulating system, with automatic cylinder

by-pass valves. However, the latter were soon dispensed with. The top of the blast pipe was now 4⅞" dia (4½" on the SG2) in place of 5¾". Two footsteps were placed under the smokebox door, a modification soon made to all engines with a top lamp bracket.

Both classes were finished in lined black, with the 4-4-0s distinguished only by a small coat of arms on the leading splasher. When plans for these engines were been drawn up in 1913, the original intention had been to finish the 4-4-0s in green and name them *Lugnaquilla*, *Carlingford* and *Mount Hamilton*, respectively. However, this was changed with the decision in July 1914 to paint all engines black.

The abandonment of the plan for nameplates must have come quite late in the day, since the Beyer records refer to the engines as having names when delivered. Indeed, two plates for *Lugnaquilla*, and one each of *Carlingford* and *Mount Hamilton*, lay in the Dundalk stores for many years, confirming that they were delivered with the engines. Those for *Lugnaquilla* were actually used on 190, when it eventually named in 1939. The others were never used.

The name *Mount Hamilton* is a bit puzzling, as the others of the S/S2 class were named after mountains. Although *Mount Hamilton* sounds like a mountain, it isn't one. However, it was the name of Glover's house and the townland

111

Bottom: S2 No 192 arriving at Dublin around 1920 with an express from Belfast. The fourth vehicle is a B1 class dining car. In 1914, Glover had introduced modern high-elliptical roofed corridor stock and in 1916 a systematic classification system for carriages. No 192 would have been named *Mount Hamilton* if Glover had not decided to abolish naming engines.
LPC 88121

in which Dundalk station is built! The 4-4-0s were delivered in Febuary-March 1915 and the 0-6-0s in March-May. Like the S class, the S2 4-4-0s had their boiler pressure raised to 200 lbs as follows: 191 3/1928, 190 5/1929, 192 4/1930.

Between December 1924 and January 1925, a second batch of SG2 class 0-6-0s was delivered, the manufacturer on this occasion being Nasmyth Wilson. These engines were numbered 15-19, replacing five J class 4-4-0s. There were minor differences to the 1915 batch, mostly involving items like washout plugs and injectors, but nothing major. This batch were always recognisable by their triangular Nasmyth Wilson builder's plates.

U class 4-4-0 1915

The delivery of U class 4-4-0 Nos 196-200 by Beyer Peacock in April-May 1915, completed Glover's expansion of the locomotive fleet. Perhaps, the success of his new tank engines suggested that there might be a case for building a tender engine version for Irish North workings.

The U class were essentially a superheated tender version of the T class 4-4-2Ts. They had the same 18"x 24" cylinders and 5'9" driving wheels, but the boiler had 111 small tubes and a 16 element Robinson superheater, giving a total heating surface of 1,056 sq ft. Later, two tubes were replaced by stays and the elements were shortened. This reduced the heating surface to 1,031.6 sq ft. Unlike the slide valve tank engines, the U class had 8" piston valves with inside admission. According to the original (1914)

specification, the U class were to be painted green and to be named. It is not known what names were planned and no plates were cast. Like the S2 class, they were delivered in lined black livery.

Where this class scored over the T class, was in axle load. The tanks had a 16 ton 19 cwt axle load, but the 4-4-0s only 14 tons 14 cwt, with an engine weight of 44 tons 6 cwt against the tank's 65 tons 2 cwt. This meant that the U class had a universal route availability and carried the small white diamond which indicated this on the edge of their buffer beams. This feature was introduced in 1913 but was only supposed to be on the right-hand side of the buffer. Photographs, however, show them on either side and in practice they were on both.

The U class had the potential to become a fairly numerous standard small passenger engine. Up to 1930, passenger engines were replaced after forty years service. If this had happened to the P class and the earlier PP engines, a further 15 Us would have been built in 1932-38. There is also an intriguing pencil note on Glover's drawing of the saturated PP4'3" class – "Rebuild with 5'9" wheels?". This suggests the possibility of rebuilding the later PP class of 1906-11 as U class. After all, the PP class were exactly the same length and had the same wheelbase as the U class. They also had rather large wheels for the light branchline duties that were their domain after 1915.

If some PPs had been rebuilt as U class, and the older P and PP engines replaced by new U class, then there would, eventually, have been as many as 30 U class. In the event, it was to be 1948 before the class was expanded. In that era the 1915 engines received the famous blue livery and were named, but that story belongs to Chapter 9.

Before leaving the U class, there is the question of whether Glover, himself, planned a goods version. The UGs were not introduced until 1937, after Glover had retired. It is unlikely that the thought did not strike Glover, though there are no drawings to prove the point. Perhaps, with so many elderly small 0-6-0s still giving good service, Glover saw no immediate need for a modern engine in this power category.

Proposed T1 4-4-2T 1915

In 1915, Dundalk drew up a specification for a version of the Glover tank which was not in fact built. The 1913 saturated engines were designated T class and the 1921 superheated engines T2. The classification 'T1' was retrospectively applied to the T class on superheating, but was originally intended to be a slightly different 'animal'.

According to the specification book, the T1 class were to be superheated with a boiler identical to the U class, except that there would be ten longitudinal stays between the smokebox tubeplate and the boiler backplate compared to nine on the U class and the combined steam retarder and blower valve would be dispensed with.

The main difference was that the new engines were to have 18½"x 24" cylinders, which would have given a tractive effort of 17,708 lbs. However, it is possible that, although the cylinders were to be bored to 18½", this was to keep options open. A pencil note on the order says "cylinders may be 18ins, to bore to 18½ ins". The 8" piston valves were no longer to be Schmidt's patent and the Wakefield lubricator would be operated from the valve spindle, rather than the crosshead as before. The diameter of the piston valves was to be reduced from 4½" to 3½", a change incorporated in the later T2 class. The frames were to be 1" thick, compared to ¹¹⁄₁₆" on the earlier U class.

Five of these locomotives were ordered from Nasmyth Wilson in April 1916 and, in October, the numbers 1-5 were allocated to them. This indicates that they were intended to replace BT 4-4-0Ts and these numbers were actually used by T2 engines in 1921. In the event, shortage of materials during the war delayed construction of the T1s. In February 1919 the GNR had a change of heart and cancelled the order.

JT 2-4-2T rebuilds

Towards the end of the First World War, Glover turned his attention to the six small JT class 2-4-2Ts. Two types of rebuilding were carried out. Five were reboilered with new 4'2" boilers pressed to 175 lbs, the first to be treated being the preserved example, No 93, in 1917. The exception was No 92 (ex-14) which got a reconditioned boiler ex-90. In 1920 Nos 13 and 14 (the 1902 engines) became 91 and 92, exchanging their numbers with two BT 4-4-0Ts. The JT class were now neatly Nos 90-95.

At a different shopping, new 16½"x 22" cylinders were fitted, beginning with No 90, in 1918. Previously, these engines had different sizes of cylinder depending on the batch. The order in which the rebuilding was done, varied. Nos 92, 93 and 94 got their new boilers before the cylinders and the others vice versa. By 1925, the process was complete, except for No 92, which had to wait until 1930 to get its new cylinders.

Above: Rebuilt JT class 2-4-2T No 93 at Adelaide on 21 May 1924. No 93 is now at the Ulster Folk and Transport Museum, Cultra. *Ken Nunn collection*

Left: A rare view of PP class 4-4-0 No 70 with a saturated 4'6" boiler. No 70 waits at Adelaide, also on 21 May 1924. Note the splasher sandbox and continuous handrail, both removed in 1930. *Ken Nunn collection*

Rebuilding of PP Nos 70-71, 74-77

The final batch of engines to get new saturated boilers were the six original PP class 4-4-0s of 1896-98. In the period 1917-20 all six received 4'6" boilers. In this rebuilding, the cylinders were reduced to 17½"x 24", although Nos 75 and 77 had already been bushed to this in 1914. With a heating surface of 1,146 sq ft and 175lbs boiler pressure, this variation on the PP class had a tractive effort of 13,839 lbs. One odd feature of the rebuilds of this period is that the old Clifford style, of the boiler handrail continuing round the front of the smokebox, was retained. PP 4-4-0s with 4'6" saturated boilers were a short-lived version of the class and all had been superheated by 1931.

Enginemen's instruction car 1920

Another interesting innovation, now long forgotten, was the six-wheeled carriage fitted out in 1920, for the training of drivers, cleaners, firemen and others in the Locomotive Department. Numbered 8453 in the Departmental list, the vehicle had such useful visual aids as scale models of a cylinder and Stephenson valve gear, a Walschaerts valve gear, a model boiler and a model railway layout to teach signalling. There were also models of various components including lubricators, safety valves and injectors. This carriage could be delivered to the various engine sheds as required.

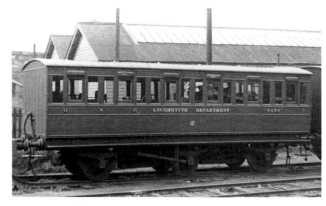

Above: Glover's Engineman's instruction car (No 8453) at Dundalk in April 1953.

H C Casserley 78349

Fig 55 (below): Interior layout of the Enginemen's instruction car. Note the model railway in the top right corner.

Railway Gazette 16 September 1921

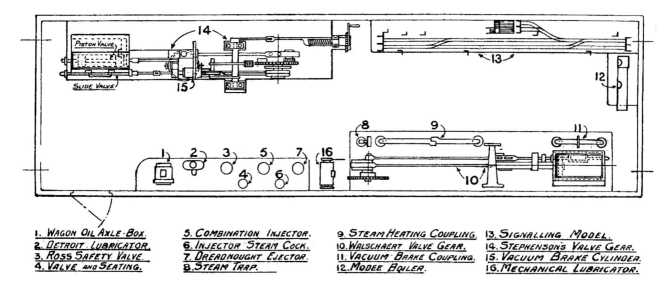

1. WAGON OIL AXLE-BOX.
2. DETROIT LUBRICATOR.
3. ROSS SAFETY VALVE.
4. VALVE AND SEATING.
5. COMBINATION INJECTOR.
6. INJECTOR STEAM COCK.
7. DREADNOUGHT EJECTOR.
8. STEAM TRAP.
9. STEAM HEATING COUPLING.
10. WALSCHAERT VALVE GEAR.
11. VACUUM BRAKE COUPLING.
12. MODEL BOILER.
13. SIGNALLING MODEL.
14. STEPHENSON'S VALVE GEAR.
15. VACUUM BRAKE CYLINDER.
16. MECHANICAL LUBRICATOR.

General Arrangement of Enginemen's Instruction Car, Great Northern Railway of Ireland.

SG3 class 0-6-0 1920-21

During the First World War the railways were placed under the direct control of the Government from 1 January 1917, with the proviso that they would be guaranteed the same level of earnings that they had enjoyed in 1913 and that, after the war, they would be paid a lump sum as compensation for arrears of maintenance. The GNR used this money for a major investment in twenty new locomotives in 1920-21. Fifteen of the locomotives were of a new heavy goods design, known as the SG3 class.

An early drawing of the proposed new engines, dated February 1918, shows that a number of changes were made before the locomotives were actually built. As originally conceived, the engines were to retain the 19"x 26" cylinders of the SG2 class but the firebox was to be 7'0" long, with a grate area

of 24.5 sq ft. The boiler would have had an 18 element superheater and, with 180 small tubes, would have had a heating surface of 1,610 sq ft. At this stage, it was assumed that the axle load would be the full 18 tons (on the driving axle) and that the overall weight would be 53 tons, 12 cwt.

In the event, they were built with 19½"x 26" cylinders and a 24-element Robinson superheater, giving a heating surface of 1,599.8 sq ft. The length of the firebox was reduced to the 6'7" of the SG2 class, with a 22.9 sq ft grate (sloping as on the SG2). The total weight of the engine in working order was 52½ tons (probably due to the smaller firebox) and the axle load was 17¾ tons. The other main dimensions were: driving wheels 5'1", wheelbase 8'1"+ 8'10", boiler 5'0"x 11'0" with 175 lb boiler pressure, tractive effort 24,107 lbs.

The GNR SG3 class ranked among the most powerful

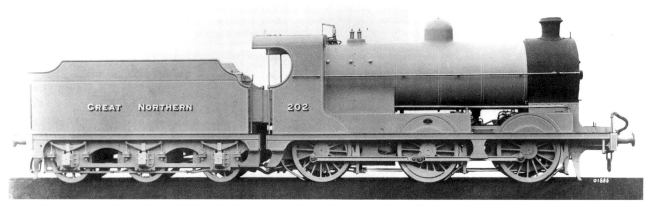

Above: Beyer Peacock Works photo of SG3 0-6-0 No 202, as built in March 1921. Reputedly, Beyer Peacock used the tender part of this photo to make up a Works photo of Compound No 87, which was built without a tender in 1932. If this is so, they were doubly clever, as the tender on No 87 displays a crest!

Duffner W125

0-6-0s in the British Isles, but the 17¾ tons axle load prohibited them from crossing the Boyne Viaduct at Drogheda, effectively meaning that they could not operate between Drogheda and Dundalk. Until the viaduct was strengthened in 1932, the class were largely active on the Belfast-Dundalk and Portadown-Londonderry routes, where they were put to good use on the steep banks.

All were built by Beyer Peacock and were delivered between November 1920 and May 1921. Their running numbers, in order of construction, were 6-8, 13, 14, 20, 47-49, 96, 97, 201, 202, 117 and 118. They replaced an assortment of BT 4-4-0Ts and G class 2-4-0s, as well as the last 2-4-0s of the D&BJR and INWR. When the U class of 1948 were built, Nos 201 and 202 were renumbered 40 and 41. The SG3s were classified 'D' for loading purposes, the earlier light 0-6-0s becoming 'E'.

A new design of tender appeared with this class. The D1 type was a slab-sided tender of 3500 gallon capacity and carried 6 tons of coal. It had a 13'0" wheelbase and weighed 38½ tons. Although built with the SG3 class, many of these tenders were transferred to passenger engines, particularly to the S class and the rebuilt Qs class 4-4-0s (see opposite). However, photographic evidence suggests that few transfers took place before 1928. Replacement tenders were usually of the 2500 gallon B1 or B2 type. When fitted with the D1 tender, the SG3 class weighed 91 tons.

Engine No 14 was involved in an incident early in its career. It was the train engine on a special for the 10th Hussars and their horses from Belfast to Dun Laoghaire on 24 June 1921, after the opening of the new Northern Ireland Parliament. The IRA blew up the train south of Newry at Adavoyle, killing the guard and five soldiers, as well as numerous horses. No 14 was undamaged.

Although the SG3 class were never rebuilt, No 117 received a new boiler in 1932, Nos 7, 13, 49 and 97 in 1948 and No 14, in 1949. A further seven new boilers were ordered from R Stephenson and Hawthorn, in 1952, five of these going on Nos 20 (1952), 8, 47, 40, and 41 (1953). This meant that, at the breakup of the GNR in 1958, the majority of the class had good boilers. Significantly, the first two casualties – UTA No 30 (ex-6) and CIE No 118N – had not received new boilers.

One SG3 class engine still survives today – a 16th member of the class, built at Dundalk as a sectioned working model. For many years, up to the closure of Great Victoria Street station in 1974, this model was displayed in a glass case

Opposite lower: In this August 1930 view, No 202 was simply lettered 'GNR'. The sheer bulk and power of these impressive machines is very evident in this view.

H C Casserley 7042

Right: The 16th member of the SG3 class, built at Dundalk by fitter Jimmy Webster and displayed at Great Victoria Street station until 1974.

Duffners

on the station concourse. The sectioned side faced the front and a mirror at the rear allowed the observer to see the painted exterior. When one old penny was inserted in the slot, the wheels turned and the pistons and valve gear operated. This model, which was of No 202, fascinated several generations of children.

I regularly took advantage of a wait for a train, by begging my mother for a penny "to see the engine work". The model was later moved to York Road station but was damaged in a bomb blast. Today it is being restored by a member of the RPSI when other more urgent work is not pressing and, perhaps, will one day be displayed again.

The Qs class 4-4-0 rebuilds

In Chapter 7, I described the building of Clifford's Q class 4-4-0s between 1899 and 1904. These locomotives were the first generation of the larger, 26" cylindered passenger classes on the GNR and were numbered 120-125 and 130-136. Useful engines in their day, they had been pushed to the sidelines by the QLs and newer superheated S/S2 class.

Up to 1919, Glover had made little change to the Q class other than bushing the cylinders to 17½" diameter, removing the nameplates and painting them black. Now they were to be the first class of Clifford engines to be superheated. Glover

Above: The most handsome 4-4-0 design on the GNR? Some enthusiasts would rate the Qs rebuilds even above the S class for good aesthetic proportions. No 120 is at Londonderry shed in this superb R G Jarvis study of 15 May 1937. Note the staff collecting apparatus on the tender.

R G Jarvis

made a superb job of the Qs class (superheated engines had a small 's' added to their classification) and the first rebuild to emerge was No 133, in December 1919. The other engines in the first series were completed in 1920-22 and Nos 120-125 followed in 1923-24.

Glover fitted these engines with new 4'6" boilers, operating at 175 lbs boiler pressure, with 120 small tubes (1¾" was standard) and an 18 element superheater, giving a total heating surface of 1,285 sq ft. The 18½"x 26" cylinders were restored and had 8" piston valves placed over the cylinders and driven by rocker arms. This required the centre line of the boiler to be raised by 10" compared to the original layout. The opportunity was taken to deepen the firebox by the same amount, resulting in a very free steaming boiler.

With modernised cabs and snap rivetted smokeboxes, the Qs class looked thoroughbreds and they were, arguably, the most handsome of the GNR two cylinder 4-4-0s (excepting the S class, of course!). The only weak point in the Qs class was the retention of the original shallow and rather inadequate frames. Although the crews loved these engines,

Dundalk had continuous work patching crackedframes.

The Qs class were mostly used on the Derry and Clones routes from Belfast, and were rarely seen south of Dundalk before 1958. In 1929 for example, ten were allocated to Belfast and one each to Portadown, Londonderry and Clones. Those on the Derry Road were fitted with staff collecting apparatus and, by 1930, all had the larger 3500 gallon tenders, some transferred from the SG3 0-6-0s and some newly built in the late 1920s. It was rare to see a Qs with a small tender. Nos 122, 125 and 133 regularly worked summer excursions to Portrush and were fitted with NCC-type tablet snatchers which, unlike the GNR apparatus, didn't have a net.

The first of the class to be withdrawn was No 134, in 1951, followed by Nos 120, 124 and 133, in 1957. The others survived into the CIE/UTA era, although only Nos 131, 132 (CIE) and 135 (UTA) did serious work after 1958. The survival of No 131, as a preserved example, was due more to accident than design and it remains the forgotten example of a preserved GNR 4-4-0.

Left: QL 4-4-0 No 127 in green livery, at Belfast in 1915, carrying the nameplates from PP No 76 *Hercules*.

Inspector A Johnston

Opposite top: A rare view of QLs 4-4-0 No 157, as first superheated in 1919. This was one of three engines initially rebuilt with slide valves and later rebuilt with piston valves. It is seen here at Dundalk. Note that, on first rebuilding, this engine retained the old style of handrail.

L J Watson

Opposite lower: Representing the piston-valved version, is QLs 4-4-0 No 114. It was initially superheated in 1920 retaining slide valves, but then got 6½" piston valves in 1923. This was the shortest-lived of the QL class by a long stretch. In 1932 it was, surprisingly, scrapped against one of the new three-cylinder Compounds.

Real Photos 88130

The QLs class 4-4-0 rebuilds

Whatever superlatives we may use of the Qs class, much less can be said in favour of the rebuilding of the larger QL type. This eight-strong class had been built in 1904-09 and were numbered 24, 113, 114, 126-128, 156 and 157.

At one time, these had been the principal GNR express type, but Glover seemed of two minds about their status. In 1913 he had decreed that all engine nameplates were to be removed, except on the QL and S classes. Then, in 1914, it was decided to remove the names from the QL class. In 1915, this was reversed again, but not before some plates had been melted down! New plates were apparently cast for No 157 *Orpheus*, but No 127 (previously *Erebus*) got the *Hercules* plates previously carried by PP 4-4-0 No 76.

Most of the names were removed later in the war, but were retained by No 126 *Diana* until 1919 and No 24 *Juno* until

early 1920. Like most of the later Clifford engines the cylinders of the QL class were bushed by Glover in 1914-16, in this case to 17¾".

By 1918, Glover saw no future for the QL class as main line express engines and he was not prepared to give them as expensive a rebuild as the Q class. The first three to be superheated, Nos 157 (1919), 114 (1920) and 113 (1922), retained their original boilers along with 17¾" cylinders and slide valves.

These three gave trouble with lubrication of the valve faces, so Glover went over to piston valves for the rebuilding of the remainder in 1923-28. The first three were brought into line in 1922-24. However, instead of the 8" valves placed over the cylinders, which he used on the Qs class, he chose the cheaper solution of 6½" piston valves for the QLs. These were placed between the cylinders but, as there was not enough space for

them to be side by side, they were at different heights, slightly over-lapping. This arrangement was made possible only by the extra width between the frames afforded by the 5'3" gauge in Ireland and meant that the boiler didn't have to be raised above its centre line of 8'0". The 18½" cylinders were restored on the piston-valved engines.

The first piston-valved QLs was No 157, in September 1922. It had also been the first to be rebuilt in the earlier form. Most of the others followed in 1923-24, with No 156 in 1925 and No 127 in 1928. These two, and No 128, got brand new boilers. The others retained the original boilers, apart from No 157, which, in 1931, got a reconditioned boiler, using the barrel from a boiler taken off LQG No 160.

The 6½" piston valve arrangement was ill-advised with cylinders as large as 18½", though it worked quite well with the smaller P and PP classes. The opinion of many drivers was that the engines were ruined by this rebuilding. It was difficult to get any speed out of them, as the small valves restricted the flow of steam. They actually had to be steamed down hill! In 1931, Glover, in a letter to J B Stephens, summed up the inadequacies of the QLs class as follows:

"The frames of these engines have always been too light, and were recommended for new frames in 1912, but modern methods of repair, oxy-acetylene welding, etc, have enabled this to be avoided, but they have never run on any continuous hard service until axleboxes commence to knock, frame bolts, etc, to loosen, long before the correct mileage of 60,000 miles between repairs is obtained. These engines have never been successful as stand-by express engines on present day service for above reason.

"If these engines are to be retained they must fall back onto local and INW services, and the company will be faced by a continual waste of coal (even if the cylinders and tractive effort of this class are reduced to save steam), as their grate area is large and must always be kept covered with coal, so that they never run any services under 40 lbs per mile, whilst No 200 class will save at least 5 lbs per mile in coal, or 70 tons of coal per annum, that is 350 tons per annum for five engines."

This just about sums it up – too weak in the frames for express work and too uneconomic for slow lighter trains. Had it not been for the depression of the 1930s, it is likely that the four QLs which still had old boilers would have replaced by Glover with brand new engines. Only No 114 suffered the fate of early scrapping and the other three (Nos 24, 113 and 126) limped on until 1957.

LQG 0-6-0 No 158

Although Glover concentrated his efforts on superheating the larger passenger engines in the early 1920s, he did some experimental rebuilding of goods locomotives. In August 1921, he fitted PG 0-6-0 No 151 with a new boiler and 18 element superheater, but otherwise left the engine largely unchanged with 17½" x 24" cylinders and slide valves, reflecting his treatment of the first three QL rebuilds.

Then, shortly afterwards, a more expensive rebuild was carried out on LQG 0-6-0 No 158. The rebuilding of this engine mirrored that of the Qs class. It received 8" piston valves placed above the cylinders, with frame stretcher

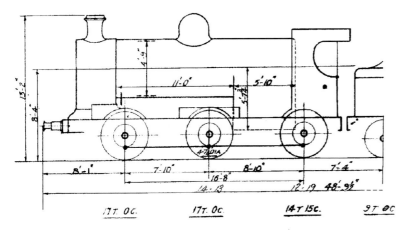

Fig 56 (left): The first LQG 0-6-0 to be rebuilt, No 158, in October 1921, was something of a guinea pig. It had its frames lengthened 7½" at the front and had a longer smokebox than the later rebuilds. No more were rebuilt until 1926 and then without lengthening the frames. In 1927 No 158 was altered to the new pattern.

Courtesy P Mallon

Below: T2 4-4-2T No 3 of 1921 outside Amiens Street shed, Dublin in the 1920s. The superheated version of Glover's 4-4-2T became the most numerous single class on the GNR, with 20 members by 1930.

Locomotive Publishing Co

rocking arm brackets, and the boiler centre line was raised from 7'9½" to 8'4". The cylinders, previously 18½"x 26", were increased to 19"x 26" and the frames were lengthened 7½" at the front, with a correspondingly longer smokebox.

As rebuilt, No 158 had a tractive effort of 25,385 lbs and was the most powerful locomotive on the GNR, in terms of tractive effort. It had an 18-element superheater, a total heating surface of 1,432 sq ft and weighed 48 tons 15 cwt. In March 1922, the rocking arm brackets were removed from the frame stretcher and attached to the motion plate. This locomotive

carried a white circle on its front buffer beam while in this condition. Although No 158 was a prototype for rebuilding the LQG class, the others were later superheated without lengthening the frames and No 158 was altered to conform in 1927.

T2 class 4-4-2T 1921-30

The most numerous class of locomotive on the GNR was the superheated version of the Glover 4-4-2T. Reference was made earlier to the five locomotives ordered from Nasmyth Wilson during the war, which were not built. A new specification, still incidentally designated T1 class, was drawn up in 1918. The 1916 order was cancelled, though a note in the Nasmyth Wilson order book, beside Works Nos 1115-1119, says "finished by Beyer Peacock".

Glover ordered five of the new version from Beyer Peacock in 1919 and, on delivery, they were known as the T2 class. The designation T1 remains a bit of a puzzle. When the S class were built in 1913-15, they were S and S2 (rather than S1 and S2, or S and S1) and the goods engines were SG, SG2 and SG3. So why were the tanks T1 and T2 in later years? It seems that T1 was used for the T class after superheating (A general order of December 1926 refers to T, T1 and T2, when

No 188 was still saturated) but that does not account for why the specification book uses T1 for what became the T2 class!

The T2 class, as we will call them from now on, differed only in details from the 1915 specification. The cylinders reverted to 18"x 24" and a Wakefield 4 feed mechanical lubricator was specified. The slidebars had one oil syphon instead of two. The main differences, from the original 1913 T class, were to do with superheating. The smokebox was slightly longer and the high section of the main frames, above the bogie, was extended rearwards by about a foot. There was a 16 element superheater and only 111 small tubes, giving a heating surface of 1,056 sq ft. Overall weight increased to 65 tons 15 cwt, but the extra weight was on the bogie and radial truck, leaving the maximum axle load unchanged.

The first five members of the class, Nos 1-5, were built by Beyer Peacock and delivered in August 1921, replacing five BT 4-4-0Ts of the same numbers. Ten more came from Nasmyth Wilson in August-October 1924. As there was a small gap in the Works numbers allocated, the GNR may have initially ordered five and then increased it to ten.

The Nasmyth Wilson engines had Detroit lubricators and the diameter of the top of the blast pipe was reduced by ⅛" to 4½". There were also 20 washout plugs in place of 16, but the

Right: Amiens Street shed, Dublin on 6 June 1932. The scene is dominated by the ubiquitous Glover tanks. From left to right we have T1 No 185, T2 Nos 4, 1 and 5 and, on the turntable in the right background, QLs 4-4-0 No 128.

H C Casserley 8764

Below: A delightful study of No 66, one of the 1930 Beyer Peacock batch, and the last 4-4-2T to be constructed. It is seen here at Platform 4, Great Victoria Street station, Belfast, on 17 May 1932, while still quite new.

William Robb

four washout doors were omitted. The ten Nasmyth Wilson locomotives were the last batch of GNR locomotives to have scattered numbers, arriving as Nos 21, 30, 115, 116, 139, 142-144, 147 and 148. They replaced six C class 0-6-0s, a B class 0-6-0 and three J class 4-4-0s. Nos 147 and 149 were renumbered 67 and 69 in 1948, to make way for new UG class 0-6-0s.

Finally, in December 1929-January 1930, Beyer Peacock delivered the last five members of the class, Nos 62-66, replacing B class 0-6-0s. These five had a number of modifications, including 200 lbs boiler pressure, which increased the tractive effort to 19,158 lbs. The higher pressure led to two longitudinal tubeplate stays replacing two tubes and reducing the heating surface to 1,021.6 sq ft. These engines also had steam sand in place of gravity and weighed

66 tons 8 cwt, an increase of 13 cwt over the earlier engines. They were sometimes referred to as the T3 class, though there is no official basis for this.

There is some uncertainty over the tank capacity of the 4-4-2Ts. The Dundalk diagram for the superheated engines originally stated 1700 gallons, but 1800 has been overwritten as a correction and a footnote says '1700 gallons for T1'. R N Clements noted that the 1918 specification stipulated 1700 gallons and likewise the 1923 spec. However, that for 1929 gives 1800 gallons, which Mr Clements considers a clerical error as there were no changes in the dimensions. The matter is unclear, as the extra weight for the 1929 batch more or less equals 100 gallons of water.

With 25 4-4-2Ts available by 1930, the GNR had ample power available for suburban traffic. Around ten of the type were normally allocated to the Dublin area for services to Howth and Drogheda. The remainder were allocated to Belfast, Portadown and Armagh (until 1933), working all but the heaviest suburban trains, until the arrival of diesel traction in the 1930s.

The interchange boilers put in Nos 1 and 2 in 1931-32 had 200 lbs pressure, but, in 1939, the pressure on all the tanks reverted to 175 lbs. In July 1940, No 147 was fitted with an experimental boiler with a welded steel firebox, 54 'Sinuflo' tubes, 2⅛" in diameter, 10 standard tubes and 16 large tubes, giving a heating surface of 895.6 sq ft. In 1941, No 142 was the subject of unsuccessful experiments with turf burning and, in late 1946, several tanks were temporarily equipped for oil burning (see page 135-136).

The Ps5'6" 4-4-0 rebuilds

The next class of passenger engine to be superheated by Glover was the eight-strong P5'6" class which, after the withdrawal of the J class, were the smallest type of GNR 4-4-0. This class consisted of Nos 51-54, built in 1892-95 (but rebuilt with 4'6" boilers in 1906-16), and Nos 88, 89, 104 and 105, built new in 1904-06 with this type of boiler.

These engines were all superheated between 1923 and 1927, using the existing boilers with 18 element superheaters and 120 small tubes. Like the QLs class, they had 6½" piston valves, placed one above the other between the cylinders. However, as no feats of speed were expected of the Ps5'6" class, this arrangement worked fine. Up to 1923, the cylinders on this class had been 17"x 24", but Glover increased them to 18" on the superheated engines, resulting in a tractive effort of 17,264 lbs, with the boiler pressure unchanged at 175 lbs.

In their superheated form, these locomotives weighed 42 tons 2 cwt and had 2500 gallon tenders of type B2 or B3. The first to be rebuilt was No 88 and the last, not unnaturally, No 54, which had a 1916 boiler. The Ps5'6" class would not have ranked as the best of the GNR 4-4-0s but, with their small 5'7" driving wheels, they were useful on the Newcastle line, the Irish North, and the Bundoran and Oldcastle branches.

Above: Ps5'6" 4-4-0 No 105 at Adelaide shed, Belfast, on 16 May 1937. The engine is rather dwarfed by its 3500 gallon tender, an unusual type for this class. With a buffer missing, No 105 is not going far. This engine was destined to be the last survivor of the type and was scrapped in 1960 by CIE. Its last working days were spent in the Clones area.

R G Jarvis

Above: PGs 0-6-0 No 103 at Enniskillen shed. This was the first class of 0-6-0 to be superheated by Glover, albeit with slide valves – No 151 experimentally in 1921 and the others in 1924-29. No 103 was the last to be rebuilt and was withdrawn in 1960. All seven of this class passed to the UTA.

Real Photographs X 60

Nos 51-54 were withdrawn in 1950 (though not immediately scrapped) and Nos 88, 89 and 104 in 1956. Only No 105 outlived the GNR. It had been overhauled in November 1956, receiving new superheater elements and, allegedly, the best bits of several engines. It passed to CIE and was scrapped in 1960.

PGs class 0-6-0 rebuilds

Up to 1924, Glover concentrated his efforts on the passenger engines but now he began to extend superheating to Clifford's goods locomotives. As described earlier, LQG 0-6-0 No 158 and PG 0-6-0 No 151 had already been experimentally superheated in 1921. The rest of the PG class now followed – Nos 11 and 100 in 1924, No 10 in 1925 and Nos 101-103 in 1927, 1928 and 1929 respectively. These all received brand new 4'6" boilers with 120 small tubes and 18 large, giving a modest heating surface of 1,116 sq ft.

Although lacking piston valves, the PGs 0-6-0s seemed satisfactory engines, employed largely on light goods work in the Belfast and Drogheda areas and on the Bundoran branch goods. According to most sources, including Mr Clements' notes, they had 17½"x 24" cylinders but one Dundalk drawing gives 18"x 24". This may have applied to Nos 101-103, which received new cylinders. All outlived the GNR, but the majority were scrapped in 1960-61, only No 10 lasting until April 1964.

QGs class 0-6-0 rebuilds

The rebuilding of the PGs was followed by that of the QG 0-6-0s. Nos 152 and 155 were rebuilt in 1926 and Nos 153 and 154 in 1928. Again, these locomotives were a fairly cheap rebuild, receiving new 4'6" boilers with 18 superheater elements and 1,257 sq ft of heating surface, but retaining slide valves.

The cylinders, originally 18½"x 26", had been earlier bushed to 17½", and were now altered to 17¾" in the superheated version. This produced a tractive effort of 22,054 lbs in rebuilt form. This was a very small group of locomotives, but were widely distributed. In 1940, Adelaide had No 152, Cootehill No 153, Dundalk No 154 and Clones No 155. Both the PGs and QGs classes were in power class 'B'.

Above: QGs 0-6-0 No 155 at Dundalk in September 1949. As was the case with most of the goods engines, it has a B1 tender with inside springs. Like the PGs, these engines retained slide valves when superheated in 1926-28. All four passed to CIE and lasted to the end of steam in 1963.

Kelland Collection

Below: LQGs 0-6-0 No 108 ex-Works at Dundalk after rebuilding in June 1928. The engine has been given a special paint job with burnished buffers for display at a Dublin exhibition. Some LQGs were given 3500 gallon tenders around this time.

L J Watson

LQGs class 0-6-0 rebuilds

Following the experimental rebuilding of No 158 in 1921, the LQG class remained unsuperheated for another five years, but rebuilding of this eleven-strong class began in earnest in November 1926, with No 160. This time the frames were left unaltered, but the addition of 8" piston valves with rocker arms, 19"x 26" cylinders and new 4'9" boilers, turned these locomotives into excellent freight engines. In February 1927, the frames of No 158 were shortened again to the original length and the rebuilding of the other nine quickly followed – Nos 162, 163 (1927), 108,

111 (1928), 78, 159, 161 (1929), 110 and 164 (1930).

Although No 158 had remained power class 'C' at its earlier rebuilding, the entire class joined the SG3s in power class 'D' in 1927. In driver parlance the SG3 were 'Big D' and the LQGs 'Rebuilt D'. Although not as good as the SG3s, the smaller 4'7¼" wheels of the LQGs type sometimes gave them the edge. They could be found on the heaviest freight workings of the GNR main line and the Irish North. With their tractive effort of 25,385 lbs, they were the most powerful 0-6-0s, not only on the GNR, but in the whole of Ireland.

The 0-6-0 crane tank

One of the more unique locomotives in the GNR fleet was the Hawthorne Leslie crane tank of 1928. This engine was built as the Dundalk Works shunter and was a typical Hawthorne Leslie industrial tank. Glover looked at various options, including a Beyer Peacock scheme for a slightly larger 0-6-0T. The engine was ordered in October 1927 and delivered in March 1928. It was numbered 31, replacing a B class 0-6-0. It had 3'4" driving wheels with a 5'0"+ 5'0" wheelbase. The outside 14"x 20" cylinders had Walschaerts gear and the original boiler pressure was 190 lbs (tractive effort 15,827 lbs), later raised to 200 lbs (tractive effort 16,660 lbs).

The boiler was 3'4⅛"x 8'1" and was saturated (the last GNR engine to be so built). It had 152 tubes, giving a heating surface of 637 sq ft. The firebox was 4'5' long with a sloping grate. The coal capacity as built was 11 cwt but, in April 1951, a coal bunker was added behind the cab, raising the capacity to 25 cwt and, presumably, the overall weight to 45 tons 14 cwt. The dimensions of the crane can be ascertained from the accompanying diagram (Fig 56). Note that the axle loads on the diagram reflect the original weight of 45 tons.

On the split up of the GNR in October 1958, neither CIE nor the UTA got the crane tank. Instead, it passed to the Dundalk Engineering Works (as the Works became). However, they had little use for a locomotive once their last railway work was completed in June 1960, so the engine was sold to CIE on 7 July 1960. This was, of course, the last steam locomotive to enter CIE stock. It was renumbered 365A (a Departmental number) in April 1961 and was eventually scrapped at Inchicore in 1965.

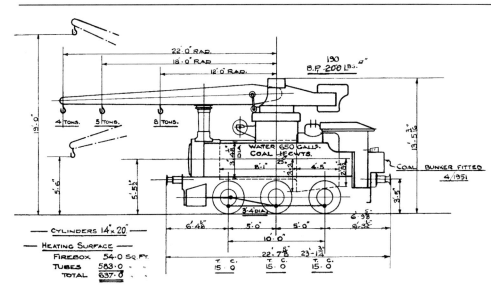

Fig 57 (left): Dundalk Works drawing of the 0-6-0 crane tank. It shows the small coalbunker added by Paddy Mallon and Pearse McKeown in April 1951.

Below: GNR crane tank No 31 at Dundalk Works on 11 July 1955. This engine was a standard Hawthorne Leslie industrial tank design and had little in common with other GNR locomotives.

L G Marshall

The PPs class 4-4-0 rebuilds

The 17 PP class locomotives can be a confusing group of engines, because the construction of the class stretched over 15 years and the design went through several stages of evolution. In 1926, the class could be divided roughly into three main groups. The original six engines of 1896-98 (70, 71 and 74-77) had sand boxes on the front splashers and had been rebuilt in 1917-20 with 4'6" boilers. Another six (25, 43, 45, 46, 106 and 107) dated from 1906-11 and had 4'3" boilers with plain splashers. The remaining five (12, 42, 44, 50, 129) also had 4'3" boilers but, originally, had extended smokeboxes, in connection with the Phoenix superheater experiment of 1911. The Phoenix superheaters had gone in 1914-15 and in 1921-22 the extended smokeboxes were removed.

Glover succeeded in turning this class into excellent branch line passenger locomotives by superheating them with 6½"

piston valves (like the Ps5'6" class) and 18"x 24" cylinders, giving them a tractive effort of 14,641 lbs. However, depending on which size of boiler was fitted in rebuilt form, they were designated PPs 4'3" or PPs 4'6". All the 4'3" engines had 18 element superheaters fitted in the existing boilers in

Right: Another charming R G Jarvis portrait at Londonderry shed. The subject of this May 1937 view is PPs 4'3" 4-4-0 No 43 and her crew. No 43 was built at Dundalk in 1911, superheated in 1928 and received a new 4'6" boiler in February 1941. It was scrapped by the UTA in 1960.

R G Jarvis

Below right: An atmospheric study, by Hamilton Ellis, of No 50 blowing off at Enniskillen, in the 1950s. This shot represents the 4'6" boilered version. No 50 was built by Beyer Peacock in 1911, superheated in 1929, and received its larger boiler in 1939. Note the indentation in the boiler cladding to accommodate the elbow joint of the reversing lever.

National Railway Museum (IR 7)

1927-30 (with a boiler change in most cases), except for Nos 45 and 107, which got *new* superheated 4'6" boilers, in 1928 and 1929 respectively.

The engines which *already* had 4'6" saturated boilers (Nos 70, 71, 74-77) had superheaters fitted to them in 1930-31, except for No 76, which got a *new* superheated boiler, and No 71, whose exchange boiler, ex-No 42, was a 4'3" one. A spare 4'6" boiler was fitted in No 25 in 1932, by which stage all were superheated, eight with the 4'6" boiler and nine with the 4'3" type, with one of each type of boiler spare and one 4'3" one scrapped. The 4'3" engines weighed 42 tons 12 cwt and the 4'6" engines 45 tons.

In this form, the PPs class put in excellent work on Irish North services, the Bundoran and Oldcastle branches, stopping trains on the Derry Road and services from Belfast to Banbridge, Newcastle, Warrenpoint and Antrim.

A further bout of rebuilding took place during the Second World War, when seven new 4'6" boilers allowed the 4'3" type to be replaced in all of the class, except No 129, which remained PPs 4'3" until scrapped in 1957. The position can be rather confusing due to changes of boiler. The dates of alteration to PPs 4'6" were 50 (1939); 43 (1941); 42 (1942); 12, 71 (1943); 44, 106 (1944) and 46 (1945). However, the boilers which went into Nos 42, 46 and 50 were second-hand, whilst Nos 74 and 75 got brand new boilers in 1941 and 1944, respectively.

At the end of all this, the seven new boilers were in Nos 12, 43, 44, 71, 74, 75 and 106. The 1928-29 boilers were in Nos 25, 76 and 107, whilst the older boilers of 1917-20 were

in Nos 42, 45, 46, 50, 70 and 77. This would explain why someone at Newry shed, in 1960, was horrified that 74 was going to be scrapped rather than 42, and switched the numbers!

LNQGs and NQGs class 0-6-0 rebuilds

The 1911 Nasmyth Wilson 0-6-0s were oddities and also had been part of the ill-fated Phoenix superheater experiment. They were also the last Clifford goods engines to be superheated and retained their extended smokeboxes, even though the Phoenix superheaters in Nos 38 and 39 had been removed in 1914.

The first to be rebuilt was No 165, the solitary NLQG 0-6-0. Essentially, this engine was rebuilt as an LQGs but, because it retained its longer frames, it was classified LQGNs (*not* LNQG as sometimes stated). It was easily recognisable by its larger cab, and the greater distance between the smokebox and the front buffer beam. This engine weighed 49½ tons, 8 cwt more than the LQGs type.

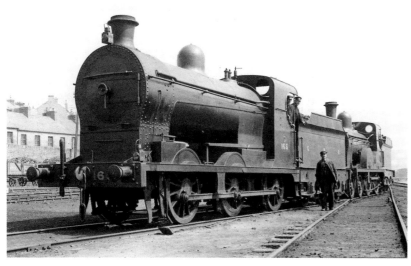

Left: On his fruitful 1937 visit to Londonderry, R G Jarvis captured this shot of the unique LQGNs No 165 of 1911. No 165 retained its longer frames when superheated in 1929.

Below left: The other Nasmyth Wilson engines were the five NQG type. Four were rebuilt as NQGs, like No 38, seen here at Drogheda. However, the fifth, No 109, got a 4'9" boiler making it LQGNs.

J D FitzGerald collection

Opposite top: Ps6'6" 4-4-0 No 73 at Kells on 27 June 1939. In 1892-95, these were the first express 4-4-0s on the GNR and were superheated in 1931-32. No 73 was finally withdrawn by CIE in 1959. The large disk-like protrusion on the side of the smokebox is a snifting valve.

W A Camwell

The five members of the NQG class were rebuilt in 1930-31. Nos 9, 38, 39 and 112 became the NQGs class and were known as the 'Rebuilt Cs'. They got new 19"x 26" cylinders with 8" piston valves, but the 4'6" boiler was retained, with the centre line raised 1½" to 7'11". With an 18 element superheater, they had 1,243 sq ft of heating surface and a tractive effort of 25,385 lbs. These locomotives weighed 47 tons 12 cwt. No 109 was rebuilt in 1930 with a new 4'9" boiler pitched 5" higher, as on the LQGs class. However, although classed LQGs, it was more correctly LQGNs, as it still had the longer frames. The NQGs class was concentrated at Drogheda, after rebuilding, to work heavy cement trains over the steeply-graded Navan branch. As NQGs engines became due for new boilers, the replacements were of the 4'9" type. Therefore, No 9 became LQGNs in 1945 and No 39 as late as March 1956. By 1958, only Nos 38 and 112 were still NQGs.

The proposed 2-6-2T

One of the more intriguing 'might-have-beens' to emerge from the Dundalk archives is the proposal for a 2-6-2T in 1929. Apparently, when seeking tenders for the last batch of 4-4-2Ts, Glover asked the North British Locomotive Co to cost a 2-6-2T alternative. This would have been an outside cylinder mixed traffic design, using the same boiler as the 4-4-2Ts. The decision in favour of the 4-4-2T came down to price, at that time of economy. Nothing else is known about the proposal, which only came to light in 1965.

Since a 2-6-2T would be subject to the same restrictions in length as the 4-4-2Ts were, the wheel arrangement would have had to fit into a 28'4" wheelbase. In my view, this would have precluded using 5'9" wheels, but would have worked with 5'1" wheels, creating something like a GWR '4500' class 2-6-2T, or one of the later LMS Ivatt tanks.

This proposal is particularly interesting because it has often struck me that a light outside-cylindered GNR 2-6-0 could have performed the duties of both the U and UG classes. If the 2-6-2Ts had been built, there would have been the possibility of a 2-6-0 version at some stage, though, on the other hand, the Dundalk designers did not like leading pony trucks.

The Ps6'6" 4-4-0 rebuilds

The last class of engines to be fitted with superheaters were the P6'6" 4-4-0s of 1892-95. Probably Glover had not initially intended them to last beyond 1932-35, when they would have been 40 years old. They had already been rebuilt in 1913-15 with saturated 4'6" boilers. However, by 1930 there was little prospect of replacing old engines, given the financial state of the GNR in the face of the Depression and the development of road competition for the railways. From 1930 on, keeping the old engines going became the main policy, so Glover decided to superheat the P6'6" class.

The rebuilding mirrored that of the PPs, with 6½" piston valves placed one above the other between the cylinders. New 18"x 24" cylinders were fitted, raising the tractive effort to the 14,641 lbs of the PPs's, though the P6'6" class were slightly shorter, and lighter, at 44 tons 8 cwt. Externally, these engines were hard to distinguish from the PPs class, but the slightly shorter coupled wheelbase gave them away. In service, they worked turn about with each other.

Nos 72, 73 and 83 were rebuilt in 1931 and No 82 in 1932. With the pending arrival of the Compounds (see below), Nos 82 and 83 were renumbered 27 and 26 respectively in May 1931. No 26 was withdrawn in 1957. The other three passed officially to CIE, but were withdrawn in 1959 and broken up at Dundalk the following year.

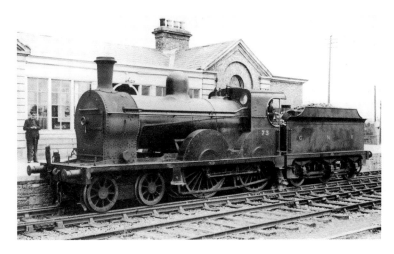

V class 4-4-0 1932

Glover's most famous class was the 4-4-0 compound design of 1932. These engines aroused considerable interest in the railway press at the time and brought the GNR to the notice of many English railway enthusiasts, particularly those who made a hobby of logging locomotive performance.

They were the first three-cylinder engines in Ireland, as well as on the GNR, and they were the only GNR compounds. With a total weight of 103 tons 11 cwt, including tender, they were, by a long way, the largest engines on the GNR, up to that time. The only slightly dated things about them were the round-topped boilers and the continued use of Stephenson gear. Only the LNER, among the major British companies, remained faithful to round-topped boilers.

The background to the introduction of the Compounds was the public pressure, in the early 1930s, for faster schedules and greater comfort. The eight S and S2 locomotives of 1913-15 were giving bother, particularly with broken crank axles. Raising their boiler pressure to 200 lbs had increased their power, but was playing havoc with maintenance costs and would soon have to be reduced to 175 lbs again. Glover, nevertheless, was looking for ways to get more out of them. In March 1931, he considered raising the pressure on the 5'0" SG3 boilers to 200 lbs and asked Watson to look at whether such a boiler could be fitted on the S class. Watson replied, listing major alterations that would be necessary, including raising the expansion and steadying

brackets, fitting a new smokebox and a new cab front and deciding what to do about the sloping grate. To make matters worse, the QLs class were regarded as no longer fit for heavy main line work. Only three of them had been reboilered, though No 157 was in process, and, in the memo to J B Stephens on 15 September 1931 (referred to in the QLs section, page 119), Glover was of the view that the £1,000 each needed to reboiler Nos 24, 113, 114 and 126 would not be justified, in view of their poor frames and heavy coal consumption, and that they should, therefore, be scrapped.

Glover became convinced that a completely new design was needed, but selling this idea to the Directors was a challenge. The Depression was in full swing and the GNR was in the mood for economy. Engine livery was becoming more austere. In 1925 all lining out on engines was stopped. In 1928, the 'Great Northern' lettering on engines was reduced to 'GNR' and from October 1930 engines ceased to be lettered at all. This was reversed in June 1931.

Glover wrote a letter to the Board, on 18 September 1931, to explain the need for the new engines. To sweeten the pill, he stressed that prices were low, due to the depression and that the engines could be procured for £5,500 each. Furthermore, five old engines would be scrapped against them, so they could be charged to the Renewal Fund (not the Capital), and no new tenders would be required as, with the tender renewal programme of two a year, sufficient 3500 gallon tenders were in stock.

He was partly right about price – the SG3s of 1920-22 had cost £8,741 each, including tender – but the Compounds still cost £5,847 apiece. Glover also favoured

Left: V class 4-4-0 No 84 *Falcon*, brand new at Amiens Street, Dublin on 4 June 1932. The tender carries the original small company crest. The engine appears to be reversing up to its train.

H C Casserley 4632

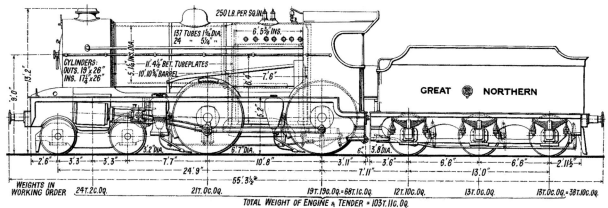

250 LB. PER SQ. IN.

137 TUBES 1¾" DIA.
24 " 5¼"

6. 5⅜" INS.

CYLINDERS:
OUTS. 19"x 26"
INS. 17¼"x 26"

11' 4½" BET. TUBEPLATES
10' 10¾" BARREL

7'.6"

GREAT ⊕ NORTHERN

5' 1¼" INS. I.D.

15'.2"

9'.0"

6.4"

5'.2"

3.2" DIA.

6'.7" DIA.

6". 3'.8" DIA.

2'.6" 3'.3" 3'.3" 7'.7" 10'.8" 3'.11" 3'.6" 6'.6" 6'.6" 2'.11½"

24'.9" 7'.11" 13'.0"

55'.3½"

WEIGHTS IN
WORKING ORDER 24T.2C.0Q. 21T.0C.0Q. 19T.19C.0Q.=68T.11C.0Q. 12T.10C.0Q. 13T.0C.0Q. 13T.0C.0Q.=38T.10C.0Q.

TOTAL WEIGHT OF ENGINE & TENDER = 103T.11C.0Q.

NEW THREE-CYLINDER COMPOUND LOCOMOTIVE FOR ACCELERATED SERVICES, GREAT NORTHERN RAILWAY OF IRELAND.

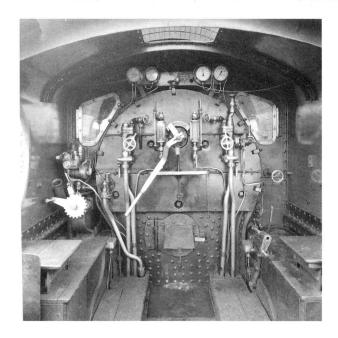

building compounds. At Gateshead, he had worked with W M Smith, who was well-known for his compound designs for the NER. John Bagwell, the GNR General Manager up to 1926, had earlier been on the Midland Railway (England), also well-known for using Smith compounds. Indeed, the LMS, successor to the Midland after 1923, had built a modified version of the Midland design in large numbers. Glover, in his letter to the Board, offered three arguments for using three-cylinder compounds:

1) A modern 4-4-0 type locomotive is sufficiently powerful for all our work. The six-coupled type is, therefore, not recommended, particularly as such an engine would not only cost £800 more per unit, but would require the entire remodelling of Dundalk erecting shop before it could be repaired there.

2) Present '170' class 4-4-0 type cannot be increased in power without increase in weight, particularly for adhesion. To increase the weight of a two cylinder locomotive would add undue stresses on the permanent way and, therefore, with the approval of the Civil Engineer, the three cylinder principle is

recommended as, with this type, a greater adhesive weight can be provided at a less stress on the permanent way than with our present type of locomotive.

3) The compound principle is strongly recommended, as by this means the maximum efficiency of high pressure steam can be obtained. The type recommended is not in any way experimental, as 245 such locomotives are in use on the LM&SR, and additions still continue to be made to this number.

(This last statement was not quite accurate. The number in use on the LMS was 235, the newest built in 1927 and, although five more (Nos 935-939 of 1932) were on order, these would be the last.)

While the new compound design was being prepared, the GNR Running Inspectors and Draughtsmen were sent over to the LMS, the latter to Derby Works and the former to Carlisle for footplate experience on the LMS compounds.

The main dimensions of the LMS design were: 6'9" driving wheels, one high pressure cylinder 19"x 26" and two low pressure cylinders 21"x 26", 200lbs boiler pressure, 22,649 lbs tractive effort and 61 tons 14 cwt weight. In contrast, the GNR design had 6'7" driving wheels, 17¼"/19"x 26" cylinders, 250 lbs boiler pressure, 23,762 lbs tractive effort and weighed 65 tons 1 cwt. Although the Glover design had smaller cylinders than the LMS one, this was compensated for by the higher boiler pressure and slightly smaller wheels.

One highly unusual feature, common to both the LMS and GNR compounds was that the coupling rods were *outside of* the connecting rods. The only other 20th century British outside cylinder locomotives to have this feature, were the NER V and V1 class 4-4-2s.

In order to allow for a very deep firebox and level grate, the V class had a 10'8" coupled wheelbase, certainly the largest ever used in the British Isles (The LMS compounds used 9'6"). The boiler was a massive 5'1¼"x 10'10¾", with 137 small tubes and a 24-element superheater, giving a heating surface of 1,534 sq ft. The 7'6" long firebox was round-topped with a grate area of 25.22 sq ft. The bogie used on the V class was of a new type, with 3'2" diameter wheels

Fig 58 (0pposite top): **Fig 58 (0pposite top):** General arrangement drawing of a GNR V class 3-cylinder compound, as built.

Opposite lower: The cab and footplate fittings of a GNR 4-4-0 compound. Note the screw reverse and the long handle regulator.

Duffner W106

Right: QGTs 0-6-2T No 98 at Adelaide on 19th June 1938. This locomotive was built in 1905 and superheated in 1932. Sister engine No 99 was shunter at Dublin.

H C Casserley 40828

and a 6'6" wheelbase. The adhesive weight was 40 tons 19 cwt, with a maximum axle load of 21 tons.

The locomotives were ordered from Beyer Peacock and delivered at weekly intervals between 9 April and 5 May 1932. They were numbered 83-87. H class 2-4-0s Nos 84-87 and QLs 4-4-0 No 114 were scrapped, the latter as recommended in Glover's memo of September 1931 (see earlier). However, the recommendation to scrap QLs Nos 24, 113 and 126 was cancelled. These engines soldiered on with their old boilers, until scrapped in 1957.

Glover agreed that the prestige of these superb engines demanded something more than the now universal GNR unlined black. The engines were, therefore, given ¼" red lining and a small company crest was displayed on the tender, flanked by the words 'Great Northern'. In a further reversal of Glover policy, the locomotives were graced with names. The brass plates were cast at Dundalk and were on the theme of birds of prey, the locomotives becoming 83 *Eagle*, 84 *Falcon*, 85 *Merlin*, 86 *Peregrine* and 87 *Kestrel*.

Beyer Peacock produced a clever Works photo of No 87, named, in 'shop grey', showing a 3500 gallon tender, even though the tenders were built at Dundalk! Allegedly, this was done by adding to the photograph a fake name plate, and the tender from the 1921 Works photo of SG3 0-6-0 No 202 (see page 116)!

Returning, for a moment, to technical matters, one feature of the Compounds was that, whilst the inside cylinder had an 8" piston valve, the low pressure cylinders had balanced slide valves. Probably in 1933, these were altered to unbalanced. Live steam could be used in the low pressure cylinders when starting. This could only be done by opening the regulator slightly, so that a port directing steam to the LP cylinders was lined up. Once under way, the lever was moved over further and shut off steam to the LP cylinders, which then were fed by the steam exhausted from the HP cylinder.

The Compounds arrived in time for the introduction of the faster schedules of June 1932 for the 112½ mile Dublin-Belfast main line. This involved an average reduction of 14 minutes off the Down schedule and 22 minutes off the Up schedule, with 60 mph start to stop timings between Dublin and Drogheda on certain workings. In the first two years, there were maintenance problems associated with these

punishing schedules. These involved hot boxes and hot connecting rods and the boilers were ready for retubing as well! As a result, the boiler pressure was reduced to 200 lbs in 1934, reducing the tractive effort to 19,009 lbs. Later, however, the pressure was raised, though never again to 250 lbs, but that story belongs to Chapter 9.

Superheating the QGT 0-6-2Ts

The last class of engines to be given superheaters were Clifford's heavy shunting QGT 0-6-2Ts. Glover did not superheat shunting engines as a rule, but he made an exception in this case. No 98 was rebuilt in September 1932 and No 99 in December 1935, after Glover's retirement. They got similar 4'6" boilers to the original, but with 18 element superheaters and 116 small tubes, giving a reduced heating surface of 1,121 sq ft. Slide valves were retained. No 98 was allocated to Belfast in the 1930s, and 99 to Dublin.

The end of the Glover era

When Glover retired in 1933, the locomotive fleet was in very different shape to the one he had taken over in 1912. At that time, there had been 185 locomotives. This figure had risen rapidly to 204 in 1915 and had stayed at that level until 1930. Withdrawals of some shunting tanks and old 0-6-0s had reduced the fleet to 199 by 1933. The last 2-4-0s had gone in 1932 and the fleet now consisted of 67 4-4-0s (all superheated), 90 0-6-0s (58 superheated), 25 4-4-2Ts (all superheated), six 2-4-2Ts, four 0-6-2Ts (one superheated), four 0-6-4Ts, two 0-6-0Ts and one 4-4-0T. In all, there were 151 superheated engines, or 76% of the fleet, compared to only the four Phoenix-fitted engines in 1912.

If we use the normal yardstick, of 40 years life expectancy for a passenger engine, 45 years for a passenger tank and 50 years for a goods or shunting engine, only four 4-4-0s and twelve 0-6-0s were beyond their normal life span. All this was to change drastically in the next 25 years, as economic circumstances prevented the company from replacing locomotives at their normal life expiry dates.

Chapter 9
Rhapsody in Blue
The last years – 1933-1958

The first GNR Locomotive Engineer, after George Glover's retirement, was George B Howden, who held the post until 1939. Howden was an internal appointee and had been the Chief Civil Engineer since 1929. He became Chairman of the GNR in 1939, a post he retained until 1958, after which he became Chairman of the UTA.

The blue livery

The unrelieved black livery of the Glover era had been practical, but austere and uninspiring. Glover had tried to brighten up the Compounds of 1932 with nameplates and extra lining, but they were still very plain and impressed more despite their livery than because of it. The black livery of the Compounds was slightly modified by Howden in 1934. The lining was increased to ½", the tender was given a larger crest and the small crest was moved to the leading splasher. However, study of contemporary photographs suggests that these changes were only applied to Nos 83, 86 and 87, before the introduction of the blue livery in 1936.

The reasons for the introduction of the new GNR livery were probably to do with the mood of the era. The neighbouring Great Southern Railway, which

rubbed shoulders with the GNR at Dublin, Navan and Cavan, offered little competition with its plain black (unrelieved even by company initials), nor did the BCDR with its dark green. However, the LMS (NCC) had introduced a bright red livery for locomotives in 1924 and, in 1930, had commenced a policy of naming virtually all of its passenger locomotives. Similarly, in England, bright liveries and named locomotives were renewing interest in trains and romanticising the railways in popular perception. The Depression was ending and the public wanted brightness and romance to replace the drabness of the 'hungry thirties'.

The colour selected by Howden was appropriate and attractive. The GNR had already begun to use a livery of

Above: V 4-4-0 No 86 *Peregrine* in the modified black livery introduced by Howden in 1934. This had a small crest on the splasher and a larger one on the tender. No 86 is at Adelaide, where all the Compounds were shedded at this time.

J D FitzGerald collection

Left: V 4-4-0 No 87 *Kestrel* in the early version of the blue livery, with the large 'GN' letters above the buffer beam. The addition of the high curved sides on Compound tenders coincided with the change of livery.

L&GRP 7595

Above: Official portrait of No 87 after the engine number had been repositioned to the front of the running plate above the buffer beam. The number is just visible in the shadow of the vacuum pipe.

Duffner W107

Oxford blue and cream for its fleet of road buses and the new diesel railcars. Therefore, blue was the obvious colour to use, as other railways were using red or various shades of green. The shade is usually described as 'sky blue', the locomotives being lined out in black, edged with white. This livery was reminiscent of that on the old Caledonian Railway before 1923, though not quite so purple. The tender was particularly attractive, with a large 18" crest surmounted with the letters 'G' and 'N' in 12" gold lettering, shaded with black and a fine white line. Only the Compounds received the new livery and both the bufferbeam and the front of the locomotive running plate were painted vermilion. The first locomotives to be repainted, Nos 87 and 84 (in that order), also received the large 'G N' on the front of the running plate, with the number placed below on the buffer beam. However, this was not repeated on Nos 83, 85 and 86, and the number was moved up to the higher position. Nos 84 and 87 were later modified to conform.

The combination of blue livery and names inspired by birds of prey was not lost on enginemen and other staff. In view of the exploits of the

famous Donald Campbell and his record breaking 'Bluebird' cars, the Compounds were soon nicknamed 'Blue Birds'. Around 1936, the tenders of the Compounds were modified to carry more coal, by fitting a high curved coping. This further improved the appearance of the engines. However, it was not unknown, in later years, for Compounds to be seen running with flat sided tenders. Certainly, Nos 83 and 85 were photographed with them in the 1950s.

UG class 0-6-0 1937

The only brand new locomotives built by George Howden were the five UG class 0-6-0s of 1937. Back in 1912, the GNR had a fleet of 48 small 0-6-0 locomotives with 17"x 24" cylinders. Fifteen of these had been scrapped

Right: B class 0-6-0 No 34 at Dundalk. This was one of the last engines to retain the old style of square cab and still has Ramsbottom valves. This engine was scrapped in 1932 but No 149, of the same class, lasted to 1938.

J D FitzGerald collection

Top: Official photograph of UG 0-6-0 No 79, built at Dundalk in April 1937. Surprisingly, the tender was given a company crest, unheard of for a GNR goods locomotive either before or since. No 79 became an Adelaide engine.

Duffner RL101A

Centre: UG 0-6-0 No 79 waiting to depart from Belfast with the 6.40 pm Belfast-Goraghwood on 17 July 1937. At this date the engine was only three months old and Nos 81 and 82 were still under construction.

W Robb 65

Bottom: D class 0-6-0 No 41 at Adelaide on 8 August 1930. This was one of the last pair of former D&BJR locomotives and bears the power classification letter 'E'. It was scrapped in 1934 and sister No 40 in 1937.

H C Casserley 7062

Opposite top: C class 0-6-0 No 137 was scrapped in 1938. This was a former Ulster Railway locomotive, built in 1872. Sister No 138, which still had brass beading on the splasher, was saved by the outbreak of War and lasted until 1948.

Real Photographs X 76

in the Glover era, so that, by 1932, there were only 33 of them left, none superheated. These comprised 13 A class 0-6-0 of 1883-91 (two others had been sold to the SL&NCR), 11 AL class of 1893-96, two B class of 1879-80, two ex-UR C class of 1872-73, two ex-D&BJR D class of 1872 and three ex-INWR E class of 1871-76.

Further withdrawals soon followed. B class 0-6-0 No 34 went at the end of 1932, D class No 41 in 1934, and A class Nos 61 (1935), 80 and 81 (1936). BT class 0-6-0T No 119 was also scrapped in 1935.

UG 0-6-0 Nos 78-82 replaced a further five of this type in 1937, namely A class Nos 67, 69, 145 and 146 and D class No 40. The UG class were fairly conventional small superheater 0-6-0s. They had 5'1" driving wheels, 18"x 24" cylinders, with 8" piston valves, and 200 lbs boiler pressure (later reduced to 175 lbs). The 4'3" diameter U class boilers had 109 small tubes and 18 large, giving a heating surface of 1,022 sq ft and a tractive effort of 21,671 lbs (later 18,962 lbs). The boiler centre line on the 1937 batch of UGs was at 8'0½", very slightly higher than the 1915 U class, but 2¾" lower than the 1948 UGs. The weight of the locomotives in working order was 45 tons 12 cwt. The chassis was perfectly balanced, with exactly 15 tons 4 cwt on each axle.

The locomotives were built at Dundalk, the first to be constructed there since 1911. This was primarily on cost grounds. The cheapest outside tender had been £6,475 per engine, but Dundalk built them for £4,893. No 78 was completed in March 1937, Nos 79-82 emerging in April, June, August and October, respectively. To clear these numbers, LQGs class 0-6-0 No 78 was renumbered 119, and A class 0-6-0 No 79 became 69.

The new engines were painted in lined black and the large D2 type 3500 gallon tenders were given the same 12" 'G N' letters and 18" crest as the Compounds. When repainted during the Second World War, the tenders received the more conventional small 'GNR' lettering. The tenders were far larger than the work performed by the engines could justify and, in the 1950s, they were mostly replaced by B4 2500 gallon ones. In 1958, the five tenders originally built for the UGs were being carried by engines 112, 125, 135, 172 and 174.

Apart from the tenders, the most striking feature of the UGs was the new design of cab. Instead of the usual cut-out, the cab had a rectangular side window, the glass of which was a sliding pane that could be pushed forward in warm weather. The rear of the cab roof was also cut back at the corners. On the 1937 batch, there was just a hint of a cut-out on the cab side sheets, a feature not repeated on the 1948 engines. I think I am right in saying that, during the War-time blackout, the sliding glass was replaced by a metal plate. The UGs were unique in being the only class of 0-6-0 not to be

given Train Class letters, though for loading purposes they were B class.

The UGs were really mixed traffic engines and were used for a wide variety of duties, from light goods and shunting to suburban passenger and they were popular for excursion work. In April 1940, Nos 79 and 81 were shedded at Adelaide, No 80 at Portadown and Nos 78 and 82 at Dundalk. No 80 was a regular performer on the Keady branch. Further withdrawals of old 0-6-0s continued up to the War. The last B class (No 149) went in 1938, followed by C class No 137 (1939). Finally, A class No 69 was sold to the SL&NCR in 1940, leaving only 20 saturated 0-6-0s (5 x A, 11 x AL, 1 x C, 3 x E). This reduced the locomotive stock to 191, and it stayed at that figure until 1948.

Renewing the S class 1938-9

The arrival of the Compounds in 1932 had taken the heaviest work off the S and S2 class 4-4-0s. In 1937, Howden decided to renew all eight members of the class with new deeper frames and in most cases new boilers as well. In the late 1920s, the engines had been fitted with long travel valves, the maximum travel being increased from 3¾" to 4²⁵⁄₃₂". This was retained on renewal and allowed the locomotives to be run on 25% cut-off, without reducing the width of the port open to exhaust.

The first locomotive treated was No 173, in May 1938 and, to the delight of enthusiasts, it was turned out in the same blue livery as the Compounds and its nameplates were restored. The rest of the class were turned out similarly in the next 16 months and the S2s got names for the first time.

No 190 received the *Lugnaquilla* plates delivered with the engine in 1915, but the others got new names, becoming 191 *Croagh Patrick* and 192 *Slievenamon*. The 1915 nameplates on *Lugnaquilla* differed from the others, in having a line round the outer edge, filled with black wax. Incidentally, the mountains after which the S/S2 engines were named were all over the island of Ireland and not just in GNR territory. Although GNR locomotives were named after mountains,

Above: Renewed S class 4-4-0 No 171 *Slieve Gullion* departing from Derry with an evening express for Belfast on 9 July 1955. The leading carriage is No 197, the only F17 side corridor composite. This carriage had its corridor on the opposite side to that on the F16s.

L G Marshall 1741

Left: S2 class 4-4-0 No 190 *Lugnaquilla*, with its unique built-up tender (explained on page 191), at Adelaide on 10 July 1955. *Lugnaquilla's* nameplates were cast in 1915 but not used until 1939. They were different in style to those on the other engines of this class.

L G Marshall 1775

rivers, loughs, etc, they are *never* called 'Mountain class', etc. The names and renewal dates were as follows:

June 1939	170	*Errigal*
September 1938	171	*Slieve Gullion*
October 1938	172	*Slieve Donard*
May 1938	173	*Galteemore*
October 1939	174	*Carrantuohill*
July 1939	190	*Lugnaquilla*
June 1939	191	*Croagh Patrick*
June 1938	192	*Slievenamon*

Returning to the details of the renewals, the heavier frames raised the weight of the locomotives from 52 tons 2 cwt to 53 tons 6 cwt. Although rebuilding raised the axle load to 18 tons, this didn't matter, since the main limitation previously had been the Boyne Viaduct, which had been renewed in 1932. All the engines, except for Nos 170 and 190 (which worked through to Warrenpoint), were now fitted with the larger 3500 gallon D1 tenders. The superheaters fitted were of the ball-joint type and they had the latest type of Davies and Metcalfe exhaust injectors. From 1939 to late 1940, No 172 was again fitted for oil burning.

From renewal in 1938-39, the S/S2 class returned to their full share of main line work, prompting R N Clements to comment that they were doing harder work than any comparable inside-cylinder 4-4-0 in the British Isles, and as heavy as that performed, at the time, by the larger LNER 'Directors'. Nos 170-174 were shedded at Dublin. Belfast had Nos 190 and 191, as well as all five Compounds. No 192 was based at Dundalk and had a D1 tender with high side sheets.

Right: In 1943 the Dublin 0-6-2T, QGTs No 99, was fitted with a new bunker to increase its coal capacity to 3 tons. With a shunter's pole resting on its buffer, No 99 rests between duties beside Amiens Street cabin in 1949.

Kelland collection

Below right: T2 class 4-4-2T No 1 at Dundalk while running as an oil burner in 1946-8. Its coal bunker has been altered to carry oil. Note the ventilation pipe.

Duffner

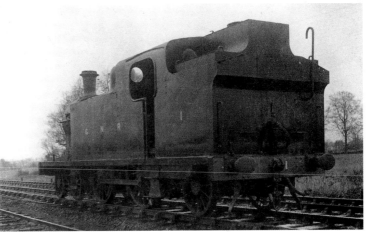

The War years 1939-45

Although G B Howden had been Locomotive Engineer since 1933, in practice he delegated responsibility for locomotive matters to H R McIntosh, the Scotsman who was his assistant. In 1939, Howden became General Manager, and McIntosh replaced him as Locomotive Engineer, a post he held until 1950. With the Second World War looming, McIntosh's moment as a locomotive designer did not come until 1948.

The outbreak of war in September 1939 put the GNR in the unique position of having part of its line in a neutral country (Éire) and part of it in an Allied country (the United Kingdom). This put some unusual strains on operations. Northern Ireland played a very active part in the war, acting as host to large numbers of Allied soldiers and airmen, particularly after 1942. This resulted in heavy troop trains at all times of the day or night, but these were restricted to routes *totally within* Northern Ireland, as uniformed service personnel could not enter neutral Éire. This meant that troop trains to Fermanagh could not be routed via Clones and had to go by Omagh. Troop trains to Londonderry had to go via the NCC route, as parts of the Strabane-Londonderry section were in Éire.

In 1942, the heavier loads of the war years led to the S class appearing on the Derry Road for the first time, and some were fitted with staff catching nets on their tenders. Because of their more flexible frames and shorter wheelbase, some drivers still preferred the older Qs class for the curves and banks of this difficult road.

Because Éire was neutral, it had very low priority for getting coal supplies from Britain, whilst railways in Northern Ireland were given ample supplies. Thus, whilst sheds in Éire were always short of coal, those north of the border had plenty. The GNR had an interesting way of getting round this problem. North-bound main line trains were double-headed, the pilot engine having a virtually empty tender. The pilot then came off at Goraghwood and ran light to Newry, where it coaled up and returned to Goraghwood to pilot a south-bound train. This procedure kept Dundalk well supplied with coal, some of which was passed on to Dublin and Drogheda. Thus the GNR sheds in Éire always had more coal than the GSR ones. If the Northern Ireland authorities knew what was going on, they turned a blind eye to it!

An interesting insight into the allocation of locomotives in the early part of the War is given in an article by R G Bateman in the *Railway Observer* in the spring of 1940. This indicates what was where on 14 April 1940. Particularly interesting is the wide distribution of PPs 4-4-0s, with allocations to Belfast (2), Portadown (2), Newry (1), Dundalk (1), Drogheda (2), Oldcastle (1), Clones (1), Enniskillen (1) and Londonderry (4). There was no attempt to concentrate even relatively small classes. The four Ps6'6" engines were at four different sheds, as were the PGs and QGs 0-6-0 classes! On the other hand, all the U class, except No 199, were at Dundalk. Despite the strengthening of the Boyne Viaduct, only one SG3 was stationed south of the Boyne, and ten of them were allocated to Belfast. The SG2s were equally divided between Belfast and Portadown.

The Glover 4-4-2Ts were concentrated at the northern and southern extremities of the main line. Dublin had Nos 1-5, as well as 147, 185 and 186. Drogheda had No 187. Most of the other T2s were at Adelaide, or Portadown, the latter also having T1 No 188. Newry had Nos 21 and 62. Most of the JT 2-4-2Ts were at Dundalk for DN&GR working, but

Clones had No 90 for the Belturbet branch. All the RT 0-6-4Ts were at Belfast, which also had 0-6-2T Nos 98 and 168. Dublin had No 99 and Londonderry No 169.

The War put a heavy strain on locomotives and men. Surprisingly, the thirteen blue engines remained blue throughout these years. As noted in Chapter 8, quite a few of the PPs 4-4-0s received new 4'6" boilers in 1939-45 and NQGs 0-6-0 No 9 was rebuilt as an LQGNs in 1945. In 1943 the Dublin shunter – QGTs 0-6-2T No 99 – was rebuilt with a much larger bunker, capable of holding 3 tons of coal. Apart from these examples, no major rebuilding work was done during the War.

Just after the end of the War, there was a further bout of fitting locomotives for oil burning, on this occasion due to post-war fuel shortages. The locomotives concerned were S class 4-4-0 No 172 (10/1945), LQGs class 0-6-0 No 159 (10/1945 to 4/1948) and T2 4-4-2Ts Nos 1 (12/1946 to 6/1948), 2 (11/1946 to 10/1948), 115 (9/1946 to 12/1948) and 116 (12/1946 to 3/1948).

Rebuilding the Compounds

The War years took a heavy toll on the Compounds. As the most powerful 4-4-0s on the main line, they were expected to haul prodigious loads – often twelve or fourteen bogies over the heavily graded Dundalk-Goraghwood section. Wartime coal was poor and by 1945 the fireboxes were in need of renewal. In December 1946 No 87 *Kestrel* was rebuilt with a new Belpaire firebox boiler, supplied by Harland and Wolff of Belfast. This was the first main line GNR locomotive to have a Belpaire firebox, the boiler remaining unique compared to the other Belpaire boilers, because of its double row of firebox crown stays visible along the sides. Boiler pressure was now 215 lbs, compared to 200 lbs for the unrebuilt engines.

The other engines were rebuilt using existing barrels with new fireboxes – this time without the crown stay feature. The first to be dealt with was No 84 *Falcon* in September 1947, receiving 87's old boiler. The other three followed after the VS class had arrived – 86 *Peregrine* in November 1948, 83 *Eagle*

in July 1949 and finally No 85 *Merlin* in May 1950. The old boiler from No 85 was then rebuilt and provided a useful spare, which could be used on both the Compounds and the newer VS class 4-4-0s (see pages 140-142). Eventually, the unique Harland and Wolff boiler ended up on No 84.

The 'Enterprise' express

In August 1947, the GNR introduced a non-stop express between Belfast and Dublin. Traditionally, GNR express trains had changed engines at Dundalk, but the division of Ireland in June 1921 added the further delay of lengthy customs examination at Goraghwood and Dundalk. To get round this problem the GNR introduced customs examination at special platforms in Belfast and Dublin. The new service was dubbed the 'Enterprise' and the inaugural run from Belfast was on 11 August 1947, hauled by No 83 *Eagle* which, with a restricted load of seven bogies, was able to run the 112½ miles non-stop, with 3500 gallons of water.

One interesting feature of the 'Enterprise' was that the dining car had two drinks cabinets, because of the differing excise duties in the North and South. On crossing the border, one was closed and the other opened, by transferring a shutter which effectively unlocked one and opened the other! On 31 May 1948, a Dublin-based set was introduced, also inaugurated by No 83, still with a round-topped boiler. The initial plan was to name this train 'Endeavour' but 'Enterprise' had already caught the public imagination and the plan was dropped. The Dublin set was less well loaded and was soon given over to the S class. The new VS class took over the bulk of both workings after September 1948.

From 1950 to 1953 the Belfast-based 'Enterprise' was extended to Cork, a run of 278 miles, requiring two sets of carriages, one GNR and the other CIE (see page 141).

Modified U class 4-4-0 1948

In 1947, McIntosh found himself in the happy position of being able to order fifteen brand new locomotives. This was made possible by the much improved financial position of the Company, due to the vastly increased traffic in the War years and the period immediately after. The new locomotives

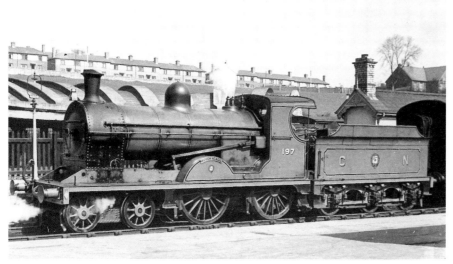

were of three different types. The first to arrive were U class 4-4-0 Nos 201-205, built by Beyer Peacock in 1947, for £15,896 each (including the tender), and delivered in the first two weeks of January 1948. These were the last new inside cylinder 4-4-0s to be built in the British Isles, certainly in Europe and, probably, in the world. The last inside cylinder engines of this wheel arrangement to be built in Britain were LMS 2P 4-4-0 Nos 666-700 in 1932. In Ireland the last examples up to 1948 had been LMS (NCC) No 87 of 1936 and GSR Nos 342-346, also in 1936.

Nos 201-205 joined the ranks of engines finished in the striking GNR sky blue livery and were named after counties (*Meath, Louth, Armagh, Antrim* and *Down*, respectively). In the 1880s, GNR goods locomotives had borne these names. To allow the new locomotives to run in sequence with Nos 196-200 of the same class, SG3 0-6-0 Nos 201 and 202 were renumbered 40 and 41. The 1948 U class were the only GNR passenger locomotives to have the square window cabs used on the UG class, a point I noticed at an early age, when I travelled behind this class in Fermanagh. I often thought that Nos 204 and 205 could have been more appropriately named *Fermanagh* and *Donegal* in view of their use on the 'Bundoran Express'.

The earlier U class of 1915, hitherto in black livery, now received the sky blue livery to match, the first to be treated being Nos 198 and 200 in April and July 1947. In May 1949, it was decided to name the 1915 engines after Irish lakes, the first to be named being No 197 *Lough Neagh* in May 1949 (see frontispiece). Incidentally, lakes are called 'loughs' in Ireland and 'lochs' in Scotland. The others were named as follows: 196 *Lough Gill*, 198 *Lough Swilly*, 199 *Lough Derg* and 200 *Lough Melvin*. If the dates in the diagram book for the repainting of Nos 198 and 200 are correct, then these two engines ran in blue, but unnamed, for two years, although I have seen no photographs to confirm this.

The 1948 engines differed from the 1915 batch in several respects. They had three boiler inspection plugs on each side of the firebox. These had long been removed from the 1915 batch. The cylinders were placed 2¾" closer and the boiler

centre line of 8'2½" was 2½" higher than previously. The boiler had 111 small and 16 large tubes. Although pressed for 200 lbs pressure, it operated at 175 lbs, giving a tractive effort of 16,763 lbs. The most striking visual change from the original U class, was a very modern design of tender, inspired on the LMS Stanier shape of the late 1930s. These E type tenders had Hoffman roller bearing axleboxes and were much taller than earlier types, allowing a high coal capacity. They held 2500 gallons of water and 6 tons of coal and were adorned with the GNR crest and large 'G N' letters.

The new locomotives entered service on the Irish North services, being shedded mainly at Dundalk, Clones and Enniskillen. On weekdays, two U class engines (of either batch) virtually always worked the Up and Down 'Bundoran Expresses', which crossed at Pettigo. The blue Us quickly endeared themselves to railway enthusiasts and passengers alike, and those photographers equipped with the new Kodachrome colour films of the 1950s, were attracted to the Fermanagh routes, like bees to a honeypot. When the GNR was divided between the UTA and CIE in 1958, the UTA got Nos 201, 202 and 205. It was rather ironic that CIE got Nos 203 *Armagh* and 204 *Antrim*, both counties in Northern Ireland, whilst *Meath* and *Louth* passed to the UTA!

Modified UG class 0-6-0 1948

The second batch of new engines were additions to the successful UG class of light mixed traffic engines. It was a measure of Wartime inflation that the 1948 UGs cost £15,993 each, compared to £4,893 for the 1937 engines. Nos 145-149 were also built by Beyer Peacock, and arrived in February 1948, their works plates bearing the date 1947. They allowed the withdrawal of the last ex-UR locomotive – C class 0-6-0 No 138 of 1873 – and the last ex-INWR locomotives – E class 0-6-0 Nos 37, 193 and 194 of 1871-76 – as well as A class 0-6-0 No 68 of 1886. To clear numbers for the new engines, T2 4-4-2T Nos 147 and 148 were renumbered 67 and 69, respectively.

The changes from the 1937 batch reflected those in the U class. The boiler was pitched slightly higher at 8'3¼" and the

Right: UG 0-6-0 No 147 on one of the popular summer excursions to Bangor, with which this class is associated. The oldest coaching stock was turned out for these specials and, in this June 1956 view near Craigavad, the stock is mainly clerestory roofed, or the low elliptical stock of the late 1890s.

A Donaldson

distance between the centre of the cylinders was reduced from 2'7" to 2'4¼". There were 111 small tubes instead of the previous 109, increasing the heating surface to 1032 sq ft.

There was a slight change to the shape of the cab, only discernable from close study of contemporary photographs. The beading on the edge of the cab terminated just below window level, with a separate bracket at that point to hold the vertical handrail. On the 1937 engines, the beading curved round to form the bracket. In contrast to the 1937 engines, Nos 145-149 had three inspection plugs on each side of the firebox casing. Like the new U class 4-4-0s, the 1948 batch of UGs had the new E type tenders, making them easily distinguishable from the 1937 engines.

The 1948 batch of UGs were shedded mainly at Dundalk and Adelaide and performed a wide variety of duties, sometimes even deputising for a U class on the 'Bundoran Express' between Dundalk and Clones. Nos 146 and 149 (as UTA Nos 48 and 49) were the last GNR engines in active use, still steamed daily as late as 1966.

Enthusiasts of the mid-1960s particularly associate them with the Sunday School excursions from Portadown and Lurgan to Bangor, on Saturdays in June each year. Their low axle load meant that they were the only class that could be used to cross the Lagan Viaduct (since replaced, but known then as the 'Shakey Bridge').

VS class 4-4-0 1948

The VS class were McIntosh's masterpiece and unique in many respects – the last new design of 4-4-0 in these islands, and, indeed, the last new 4-4-0s built in the whole world. They were the only locomotives in Ireland ever to have smoke deflectors (apart from GSR No 409, briefly) and the only GNR locomotives to carry number plates. They were the only GNR express locomotives with Walschaerts valve gear, and the only GNR locomotives built new with Belpaire fireboxes – I could probably go on. To me, when I first saw them, as a child, the VS class were the essence of glamour and power. I was brought up on picture books of Britain's steam locomotives in the early 1950s and, to me, the front end shape of the VS class made them look like scaled down LMS Duchesses!

The decision to build five more large 4-4-0s was made on the grounds of exceptionally heavy main line traffic in the early post-war years. Certainly, five Compounds alone could not handle it, but it is doubtful whether *ten* big engines were really justified. At the Board meeting which was going to approve their purchase, McIntosh was looking just a little keyed up, as the Board sanctioned various items of expenditure, but didn't mention the Beyer Peacock tender for the VS engines. Reputedly, Lord Glenavy, the Chairman, leaned over and said, "Don't worry Mr McIntosh, you are going to get your Simples!"

McIntosh based his design on the well-tried Compounds, but he did not think compounding had brought the economies that Glover had promised. Three simple cylinders and Walschaerts gear brought the design up-to-date. The new engines also had self-cleaning smokeboxes, hopper ashpans, rocking grates, spark-arresters and steam chest pressure gauges (all except the latter were new to the GNR fleet).

The vital statistics of the new locomotives were as follows;

Driving wheels 6'7", bogie wheels 3'2", three cylinders 15¼"x 26", three sets of Walschaerts valve gear, boiler as on the rebuilt Compounds, but pressure 220lbs, heating surface 1527 sq ft, grate area 25.2 sq ft, tractive effort 21,469 lbs, axle load 21 tons, total weight in working order 66 tons 6 cwt (110 tons with tender), total length over buffers 56'8¾", total wheelbase 46'4¾", water capacity 4000 gallons, coal 6 tons. The F type tenders were a new type, similar in style to the 2500 gallon E type, and fitted with Hoffman roller bearings. Both had a 13'0" wheelbase but the F type had longer frames.

Few people are aware that the VS class were not originally going to be Nos 206-210. I have in front of me a memo from the Works Manager (R W Meredith) to the foreman at the Schedule Office (W McGowan) on 20 May 1947, when the engines were being planned. This allocated them 211-215, which I presume was to leave open the possibility of adding to the U class. However, the same document has the proposed numbers scored out and the comment "? 206-210 incl" added. It would also appear from this, and another similarly dated memo by H E Wilson, that the big tenders were initially to be 3500 gallon. By July 1947, 4000 gallons was specified.

The locomotives were built by Beyer Peacock at a cost of £21,890 each and were delivered to Dublin in August-September 1948. They were finished in the now standard express passenger blue livery which, when the repainting of the U class was completed, was now applied to 28 locomotives (15% of the stock), truly a 'Rhapsody in Blue'. The names chosen were of major rivers on the GNR system – 206 *Liffey*, 207 *Boyne*, 208 *Lagan*, 209 *Foyle* and 210 *Erne*. As it happened, the only river of the five that the GNR main line actually *crossed* was the Boyne, though the VS class came *close to* the Lagan and the Liffey!

There were minor cosmetic differences between the V and

Opposite left: Official GNR photograph of VS class 3-cyl 4-4-0 No 206 *Liffey*, as delivered by Beyer Peacock in August 1948. There were no smoke deflectors as built and No 206 still had no front number plate.

Duffner RL101B

Top right: A rare view of No 206, running without smoke deflectors, but with a front number plate, in May 1949. She is climbing out of Drogheda with the Up 'Enterprise'.

C P Friel collection

Centre right: No 210 *Erne* with the smaller size of deflector plate, at Dundalk in May 1950.

Kelland Collection

Bottom right: No 209 *Foyle*, with the taller type of plate, on the 10.30 Up 'Enterprise', when it was running through to Cork. It is passing Adelaide on 26 May 1953 with a rake of CIE carriages, strengthened at the front by a GNR K15. This picture has also been used as our end-paper shot.

Neil Sprinks

VS classes. The VS class had outside steam pipes and much longer smokeboxes. It is odd that McIntosh did not give his new engines more modern cabs. Instead of the side window type used on the U and UG classes, he had the traditional 'cut-out' and made it smaller than the one on the V class cab. On the forward side of the cut-out was a small hinged piece of glass, designed to enable the crew to see ahead without worrying about cinders.

In contrast to most contemporary LMS and LNER designs with Walschaert's gear, the centre line of the piston valves on the VS class was not directly above the centre line of the main cylinders, so that the cylinder block appeared at an angle to the vertical. I always thought that this detracted from the aesthetics of the design and made the engines appear slightly ungainly when in motion.

The explanation for this feature is probably to do with the fact that (as on the V class Compounds) the coupling rods was placed *outside* the connecting rods. Since the eccentric rod for the valve gear was *outside* the coupling rod, the width of the coupling rod lay between the eccentric and connecting rods, thus forcing the pistons out of vertical alignment. As far as I can see, the VS class was the only modern Walschaert's valve gear design in the British Isles to have the connecting rods on the inside.

Another curious feature was that the expansion link and reversing shafts on the valve gear had their own splasher. On the SR 'Schools class' 4-4-0s, the link simply passed through a slot in the running plate, but had no protection. The cast numberplates were an interesting touch. They had never featured before in GNR practice. Oddly, the official photograph of No 206, as delivered (see page 140), shows that it arrived without a front number plate.

As with many other large-boilered engines in Britain, smoke deflectors had to be fitted after a few months. The deflectors on Nos 207, 208 and 210 were the first to be fitted, and the top of them was attached to the boiler handrail. In an attempt at improving the design, those fitted later, to Nos 206 and 209, were modified so that the plates extended above the handrails and had a more pronounced curve on the upper front corner. The smoke deflectors greatly enhanced the appearance of the VS class but, although the Compound boilers gave similar bother with drifting smoke, no smoke deflectors were ever fitted to them.

The new locomotives soon took over the 'Enterprise' workings and shared the main line duties with the Compounds. With their arrival, more S class engines were available for the Derry Road. The VS class were regarded as stronger than the Compounds, but not as fast. In 1950, the arrival of the AEC diesel railcars allowed the Dublin-based 'Enterprise' to be dieselised. Lighter traffic in the 1950s, compared to the War years, meant that the VS class were never as severely taxed as the Compounds had been in their heyday and never got the chance to show how well they could perform. The arrival of the BUT railcars in 1957-58 took away many of their duties and, by 1958, a number of the big engines were laid up. No 84 was acting as a stationary boiler at Dundalk and No 206 was in poor shape. Sadly, there was not enough work for ten big engines and, even if the GNR had survived beyond 1958, their prospects were not bright.

Dieselisation and other matters

The story of GNR dieselisation is told in full in Chapter 10, but the arrival of the AEC railcars in 1950-51 rendered many locomotives surplus to requirements. Oddly, no locomotives were scrapped against the U and VS class engines of 1948, so the net result of the arrival of Nos 201-10 was an increase in stock to 201, from the war-time total of 191. In 1950, Ps5'6" 4-4-0 Nos 51-54 (of 1892-95) and BP 4-4-0T No 195 (1880) were withdrawn. The tank engine had been Dundalk pilot since 1905 and was the last engine of the old Belfast Central Railway.

Nos 51-54 were not immediately cut up and were used for spares. Similarly, although Qs class 4-4-0 No 134 was officially withdrawn in 1951, it too lingered in the Dundalk 'bank' and its frames went to fellow Qs No 122 in 1956. No more withdrawals took place until 1955, though many older engines were doing little work. In 1952 McIntosh retired and

R W Meredith, the Dundalk Works Manager, replaced him as Locomotive Engineer.

One interesting episode in 1952-53 was the extended loan to the GNR of two ex-NCC locomotives, U2 class 4-4-0 No 81 of 1925 and WT class 2-6-4T No 57, built as recently as 1951. Both stayed on the GNR for about a year, the 4-4-0 working regularly to Clones and Cavan, Although the Derby-built 2-6-4T was a novelty at the time, this class of locomotive was to become commonplace on the former GNR after 1959.

The proposed SG2 0-6-0 of 1952

Although the VS class were the last new GNR steam locomotives, there was a little-known proposal in 1952 to build ten more members of the SG2 class. The most striking visual changes in the specification were the fitting of a large sliding window on each side of the cab, and the equipping of the new engines with 4000 gallon, Type F tenders, with roller bearings. It is interesting that it was the SG2 type of 0-6-0, rather than the SG3 type, that was the subject of this proposal. Perhaps, with 15 'Big Ds' and 14 'Rebuilt Ds', it was felt that there were enough big goods engines.

Other changes to the design were mainly to do with fittings, and the type of rivets used. However, the engines were to have all-welded steel fireboxes with ¾" Monel stays. There were to be 116 small tubes and the large tubes were to be reduced to 3¾" at the firebox end. The outside of the smokebox was to have countersunk rivets. The livery was to be plain black, with no mention of lining, but the inside of the frames would have been vermilion. The proposal never went beyond drawing up a specification. Probably, the financial state of the company was deteriorating so fast in 1952 that finance was not available. It may also be that the decision in 1952, to order seven new SG3 boilers, was linked to this scheme. Five were fitted in Nos 20 (1952), 8, 47, 40, 41 (1953).

Developments under the GNR Board 1953-58

The deteriorating financial situation of the GNR came to a head in December 1950, when the Directors announced their intention to close the railway and wind up the Company. In essence, this was a ploy to force the two governments in Ireland to give the GNR financial support and it worked perfectly. Throughout 1951 and 1952, the railway was subsidised heavily to keep it open.

Then, in 1953, the company was jointly purchased by the two Governments – effectively nationalised – and the Great Northern Railway Board, consisting of ten members, five from each part of Ireland, took over from 1 September 1953. In operating terms, little changed and Meredith remained in charge of mechanical engineering matters. Naturally, much of Meredith's energy was directed towards advancing the dieselisation plans of the Board (Meredith had been closely involved with the railbus project in the 1930s).

Meredith retired in 1957 and the very last Locomotive

Left: Last days of the QLs. No 127 receives attention at Adelaide in the 1950s.
J D FitzGerald collection

Below: SG3 0-6-0 No 20 received a new boiler in 1952 and, in this September 1957 view, is fitted with a new E type roller-bearing tender. It is on Dundalk turntable, with the running shed in the background. This locomotive was later UTA No 33.
N C Simmons 2253A

Engineer of the GNR was H E Wilson, who had been chief draughtsman at Dundalk since 1933. H E Wilson joined the staff of CIE at the break up, in 1958.

However, there were still some developments in relation to steam traction. Seven more of the E type 2500 gallon roller bearing tenders were ordered in 1954. Three were completed in 1955 and four in 1956, though my recollection is that all were dated '1954'. In fact, I remember this confusing me as a child, when I started noting dates from engine builder's plates. I thought SG3 No 20 was built in 1954! These tenders were fitted to various engines, including PPs 4-4-0s

and SG3s. In 1958, five were running with 0-6-0s Nos 20, 110, 148 and 163 and U class 4-4-0 No 198. The other two were spares. In March 1956, NQGs 0-6-0 No 39 was reboilered as an LQGns.

However, apart from this, steam was in decline. As well as the advancing tide of dieselisation, there were successive closures in 1955, 1956 and 1957, all of which drastically reduced the demand for steam rosters in the Operating Department. Nevertheless, the GNRB was slow to actually scrap locomotives and, surprisingly, even continued to give major overhauls to some of the older types. Thus, PPs 4-4-0 Nos 44, 50, 76 and 106 were overhauled in 1956 and Nos 42, 43 and 74 as late as 1957. Similarly, Qs 4-4-0 No 123 was overhauled in 1955, Nos 121, 122, 125 and 132 were overhauled in 1956, 135 in October 1957 and 131 was in the Works in 1958. Even Ps6'6" No 27, Ps5'6" No 105 and QLs Nos 127, 156 and 157 received attention.

Among the older goods locomotives, 1956 saw the shopping of Nos 10, 11, 151 (PG), 39 (LQGns), 119 and 160 (LQGs). In 1957, Nos 150 (A class!), 29, 32 (AL), 100, 102, 103 (PG), 154 (QG), 38 (NQGs), 162 (LQGs), 109, 165 (LQGns) were shopped. Even in 1958, overhauls were

carried out on 153 (QGs), 111, 161, 163 (LQGs) and 9 (LQGns). This activity enabled some of these engines to continue working after the great cull of 1959.

The first locomotives to fall to the cutter's torch were the JT class 2-4-2Ts, made redundant by the closure of the DN&GR in 1951. In 1955-57 all were withdrawn except for No 91, which was overhauled in May 1956 and retained to work the Belturbet branch. However, No 93 was presented to what was then the Belfast Transport Museum, and was saved for posterity.

In 1956 A class 0-6-0 No 28 and three more Ps5'6" 4-4-0s were scrapped, leaving only No 105 to soldier on until 1959. A more extensive cull took place in 1957, a delayed response to the closures of 1955-56 and the earlier arrival of the AEC diesel trains. The bulk of the twenty locomotives scrapped were passenger types – Ps 6'6" No 26; PPs Nos 25, 45, 70, 77 and 129, Qs Nos 120, 124 and 133, QLs Nos 24, 113, 126 and 128, as well as JT No 90, mentioned earlier.

The only goods engines to go in 1957 were AL class 0-6-0 Nos 36, 140 and 141 and 0-6-2T Nos 98, 168 and 169. Of course, many of these engines had been in store, some for up to two years. More locomotives were made redundant by the

Left: On 9 June 1958, QGs 0-6-0 No 155 attaches two container wagons to the rear of a diesel train, at Strabane. Visible on the left is the CDRJC station, with railcar 20 about to set off on the 11.00 am for Donegal town.

John Langford, JP 30/8

Right: On 12 June 1958, the crew of T2 4-4-2T No 3 relax between duties at Dundalk. This locomotive had left the Works only three weeks earlier, and is probably still on running-in trials. On the left are the Carriage Shops, whilst visible in the distance is the Smith's Shop. No 3 passed to CIE a few months later and lasted to the end of steam.

John Langford, JP 35/3

closure of most of the Irish North section in October 1957 but, just in case these lines could be reopened in some form, no more engines were scrapped in 1958, leaving the steam locomotive stock at 167.

The end of the GNR 1958

The experiment of the Great Northern Railway Board was short-lived. The Northern Ireland Government pushed for the GNRB to be wound up, and its assets split between the UTA and CIE. Eventually, the Éire Government agreed to this. The actual division of the locomotive stock was worked out in a series of meetings at Dundalk between Norman Topley and H E Wilson. The more modern classes were split evenly, CIE getting three VS class and two Compounds, for instance, and the UTA getting three Compounds and two VS class. The older engines were divided up proportionally, according to monetary value, based on age, condition, etc.

All this generated much correspondence and paper work between May and September 1958. Much of this is presently on my desk as I write, on loan from Paddy Mallon of Dundalk. As the division was finalised, in September 1958, locomotives and other items of rolling stock had 'UT' or 'CIE' stencilled on their buffer beams. The division came into effect on 1 October 1958, ending the independent existence of the GNR after over 80 years.

GNR Locomotives in Colour

Above: PP class 4-4-0 No 42 *Munster*, as built by Beyer Peacock in May 1911. This was one of the two locomotives, in this batch of five, that were fitted with Phoenix smokebox superheaters. This plate was originally produced in a magazine of that period, and serves to illustrate the 'Doncaster Green' livery applied to GNRI locomotives between 1881 and 1913. The nameplates had raised brass lettering against a red background.

J D FitzGerald collection.

Below: The same locomotive, many years later, simmers at Enniskillen shed in the summer of 1956, with another of the same class alongside. Originally fitted with a 4'3" diameter boiler, this locomotive had been superheated in 1929 and, subsequently, fitted with a 4'6" boiler in 1942.

No 42 passed to the UTA in 1958 and was scrapped in March 1960. Some may swear that they saw it running as late as 1963. However, *that* No 42 was really No 74 in disguise! The staff at Newry shed swopped the numbers in 1960, when they heard that the UTA had sold No 74 for scrap. The engine seen here was scrapped as No 74!

ColourRail, IR 94

Above: By 1956, No 105 was the last active member of the Ps5'6" class, which was originally eight strong. These locomotives differed from the other small black GNR 4-4-0s, in having 5'7" driving wheels, instead of 6'7". In this view, No 105 is seen at Cavan, where the GNR made a head-on junction with the 25 mile long CIE goods-only branch from Inny Junction. Note the CIE cattle wagon on the left. No 105 was built in 1906 and scrapped by CIE in 1960. The other seven were withdrawn in 1950-56.

ColourRail, IR 93

Below: The QLs class 4-4-0s were rarely photographed in colour, so it is also especially pleasing to see No 157 so clean. In this July 1956 view, No 157 is easing up to the front of Adelaide shed, Belfast. It had received its last heavy overhaul the previous December. Five of this eight strong class were scrapped by the GNR. Nos 127, 156 and 157 passed to the UTA. No 157 was broken up in December 1959 and the other two the following March.

K R Photographics, C187

Above: A delightful study of blue VS class 4-4-0 No 207 *Boyne* pounding out of Amiens Street station, Dublin, with an express for Belfast in May 1957. Most of the carriages are in the attractive GNR mahogany paint finish, though the buffet car is in cream and blue, because it is part of the diesel railcar stock.

ColourRail, IR 178

Below: Another rare class to see in colour was the Ps 6'6" 4-4-0. This was the first design of express 4-4-0 on the GNR and, in fact, No 27 was the first one built, as far back as 1892. In July 1956, it is standing at the top of Dundalk shed yard. There were only four in this class, compared to seventeen of the slightly larger PPs.

K R Photographics, C40

Above: In July 1956, V class 4-4-0 Compound No 83 *Eagle* waits quietly outside Dundalk shed on a July afternoon in 1956. Despite the headboard, it had been nowhere near Bundoran on this, or any other, day! It was common for Compounds to work the first leg of the Down 'Bundoran Express' from Dublin to Dundalk, where a U class 4-4-0 would take over for the Irish North section. No 83 is waiting to take over the Up Express which will arrive later that afternoon.

K R Photographics, C153

Below: This study of VS class 4-4-0 No 209 *Foyle* at Adelaide shed, Belfast, is taken from almost the same perspective as the picture above of No 83, and enables us to see the similarities and differences between the two three-cylinder GNR designs. Most striking is the absence of Walschaert's valve gear and smoke deflectors on the Compound. Note also the more rounded corners on the VS firebox and the modern looking Stanier style tender. This picture was taken on 8 June 1957. No 209 was built in 1948 and withdrawn in 1960.

Ken Cooper, ColourRail

Above: Another interesting comparison is afforded by these two views of a Qs 4-4-0 and an S class 4-4-0. Many fittings were obviously common between the two classes and both have D1 type 3500 gallon tenders. There were 13 members of the Qs class, built in 1899-1903 and rebuilt in 1919-24. No 123 is at Grosvenor Road goods yard in July 1956. It was last overhauled in December 1955 and was scrapped by CIE in 1960.

K R Photographics, C68

Below: Apart from the contrast between the blue livery of the S class and the plain black of the Qs, the shallow frames of the Qs class look very inadequate beside those on the S class. This view of No 173 *Galtee More*, on Portadown turntable, was taken in July 1959. The engine was in UTA ownership by this time and was shortly to be renumbered 61. The stencilled 'UT' can just be seen on the buffer beam. Portadown and Clones had round-house sheds.

K R Photographics, C73

Above: In another example of the striking GNR sky blue livery, S2 class 4-4-0 No 191 *Croagh Patrick* is photographed at Adelaide shed at an unspecified date in the mid-1950s. This engine has a staff catching net for use on the single-track Derry Road. It passed to CIE in 1958 and, in 1960, was the first of the S/S2 class to be withdrawn. It is, therefore, a rare engine to see in colour. In the background is an LNWR-pattern side corridor third, one of a batch purchased from the LMS in 1947.

ColourRail

Below: Now preserved, V class 4-4-0 No 85 *Merlin* sits outside Dundalk shed in late July 1956, with blue U class 4-4-0 No 198 visible in the background. *Merlin* is just ex-Works here and has not yet had its tender crest applied. Note how the coupling rod is outside the connecting rod, a feature also seen on the VS class, but very rare on outside cylinder engines. Dundalk and Dublin had identical four-road engine sheds, but that at Dundalk had a clock, mounted as shown.

K R Photographics, C28

Above: The earliest of our colour pictures is this view of U class 4-4-0 No 199 *Lough Derg*, at Adelaide shed, Belfast in May 1950. These engines were from the first batch of U class, Nos 196-200, built by Beyer Peacock in 1915. They spent most of their lives in black livery and were only painted blue, and named, in the late 1940s. In blue, they were most attractive. The class were common on Irish North passenger services and on the Banbridge/Newcastle line. They had 5'9" driving wheels and 18"x 24" cylinders.

ColourRail, IR 278

Below: The second batch of U class, Nos 201-205, were built as late as 1948 and were blue from new. In contrast to the first batch, they had side window cabs, higher pitched boilers and the more modern E type 2500 gallon tenders. Making an interesting contrast to No 199, in this 1956 view at Clones, No 202 *Louth* sits at the head of a Down Dundalk to Enniskillen train. No 202 became UTA No 67 and worked until early 1965.

ColourRail, IR 133

Above: Very popular with enthusiasts was 2-4-2T No 91, the last active member of the JT class, which was retained to work the branch from Ballyhaise to Belturbet. In July 1956, No 91 waits at Belturbet with its clerestory coach sitting under the overall roof. The engine is only two months out of shops here. It survived to 1963.

K R Photographics, C14

Below: Enniskillen shed was renowned for keeping its steam engines clean, and this extended even to humble goods locomotives, like No 59 here, the resident shunter. The GNR black livery was originally lined in red but lining was largely abandoned in the 1920s. No 59 was a member of the eleven strong AL class.

ColourRail, IR 92

Above: The GNR 0-6-0 locomotives carried red train class letters on their cabs. These indicated the power of the engine, C being roughly equivalent to LMS/BR class 3F, and D equivalent to 4F. Here SG class 0-6-0 No 179 simmers in the sun while on station pilot duty at Amiens Street in June 1959. There were 15 members of the SG/SG2 class, built in 1913-24. The SG class was the goods version of the S class. No 179 was withdrawn in 1963.

A G Cramp. ColourRail, IR 91

Below: With crews, the most popular of the GNR 0-6-0s were the SG3 class, 15 of which were built in 1920-21. These were an enlarged version of the SG class seen above. They had 5'1" driving wheels. 19½"x 26" cylinders and 5'0" boilers, compared to the 19"x 26" cylinders and 4'6" boilers of the SG class. Here, No 48 sits alongside Amiens Street signal box in June 1961. Although owned by CIE in these pictures, both engines carry full GNR livery.

K R Photographics, C215

Above: With a full head of steam, QGs 0-6-0 No 152, on a local train out of Belfast, slows for its first stop, at Adelaide, in July 1956. The capuchlon is missing from No 152's chimney. This class of four was built in 1903-04.

K R Photographics, C198

Right: The last 0-6-0s built for the GNR were five of the UG class in 1948, Nos 145-149. With their low axle load, these engines were a popular choice for GNR excursions to Bangor, on the neighbouring UTA system. On a sunny June evening in 1953, No 145 buffers up to its train at Bangor.

J Jarvis, ColourRail, IR 313

Left: The GNR had relatively few tank loco-motives specifically built for shunting, and virtually none of the 0-6-0T wheel arrange-ment, so common in England. Instead, there were four 0-6-2Ts and four 0-6-4Ts.

The 0-6-2Ts were of two classes. Nos 98 and 99, built in 1905, were the QGTs class and were eventually superheated. Nos 168 and 169, of 1911, were QGT2 class, and were not. Here, QGTs 0-6-2T No 99 shunts at Dublin in May 1957.

ColourRail, IR 173

Top: The four 0-6-4Ts built for shunting were the RT class. Nos 22 and 23 were built in 1908 and Nos 166 and 167 in 1911. This class was designed with low boiler fittings for use on the Belfast dock lines, which had a restricted tunnel under the Queen's Bridge. They had a total coupled wheelbase of only 13'6". All four passed to the UTA and lasted until 1963, except for No 22, seen here shunting at Grosvenor Road goods yard, in July 1956. No 22 was scrapped in 1959.

K R Photographics, C46

Centre: The GNR also had a fleet of 25 4-4-2T locomotives for suburban passenger work, all superheated. The earliest were the five T1 class, Nos 185-189, built in 1914. No 186, of this class, is posed on the turntable at Amiens Street shed, Dublin, in May 1957.

CCQ 1829

Bottom: The other 20 4-4-2Ts were the more numerous T2 class, built in 1921-30. In August 1961, well into the CIE era, two of the class appear in this view at Dublin. Nearest the camera is No 3. although it carries the buffer beam from No 65! Note the S class 4-4-0.

Don Beecroft, K R Photographics, C298

Above: In this very atmospheric scene, at Belfast, Great Victoria Street, in July 1956, examples of both GNR three-cylinder express types are on view. Just pulling out of Platform 3, is VS class 4-4-0 No 210 *Erne* with an express for Dublin, whilst V class No 86 *Peregrine* blows off at Platform 2. At Platform 5 is the stock of another mainline express. Crossing the platforms is the Boyne Bridge, which carries Sandy Row over the station.

K R Photographics, C44

Below: When CIE took over the southern portion of the GNR system, in October 1958, they made the surprising decision to overhaul Qs class 4-4-0 No 132, then almost 60 years old. No 132 entered the Works on 8 December and emerged on 10 April 1959. Here the engine is seen at Amiens Street shed in June 1961, looking absolutely immaculate in the sunshine. Alongside, is S class 4-4-0 No 174 *Carrantuohill*.

K R Photographics, C90

Above: CIE continued to overhaul GNR locomotives until mid-1960. These were painted in GNR colours, but not lettered. The very last engine to be put through the old GNR Works at Dundalk, S class 4-4-0 No 174 *Carrantuohill*, emerged on 15 June 1960. To mark the occasion, this engine was given full GNR livery, including the crests and letters. No 174 is seen at Dublin in June 1961.

K R Photographics, C15

Below: GNR locomotives which passed to the UTA in 1958 were renumbered into UTA stock, except for the older types, which had an 'x' added to their GNR numbers. Many of the engines taken into UTA stock were overhauled at York Road, Belfast, and repainted into UTA black. UTA black was much more ornate than GNR black, as seen in this view of SG3 0-6-0 No 33 (ex-GNR 20) at York Road on 13 July 1963, being run in after overhaul.

Derek Young

Above: One of the most popular of the preserved GNR locomotives has been S class 4-4-0 No 171 *Slieve Gullion*. Until 1995, this locomotive ran in the striking GNR sky blue livery. In that year, it was painted black, due to the engine featuring in Neil Jordan's film *Michael Collins*. This represented its 1922 appearance, when it was black and nameless. In this view, it is seen at an accommodation crossing near the summit of Ballyboyland bank, between McFinn gates and Ballymoney station, on a return RPSI 'Atlantic Coast Express' on 16 September 1995.

C P Friel, 20363

Below: In 1993, the old Belfast Transport Museum in East Belfast was amalgamated with the Ulster Folk and Transport Museum at Cultra, Co Down, and the exhibits moved to a new purpose-built Railway Gallery at Cultra. One of the engines moved to Cultra, was ex-GNR JT class 2-4-2T No 93. It is seen outside the old museum, on 6 February 1993, en route to Cultra. This view shows the appearance of the GNR black livery when the locomotive was lined out with vermilion, a style generally applied only up to 1925, though used for new locomotives, such as the Compounds in 1932 and the UG class of 1937-48.

C P Friel, 19139

Top: GNR diesel multiple unit trains were introduced in the 1950s. The first type consisted of 20 AEC cars, numbered 600-619. Here, railcar 618 is on the tail of a three-car set at Amiens Street, Dublin, in May 1957.
F W Shuttleworth, ColourRail

Centre: In 1957, a slightly more powerful fleet of BUT railcars was introduced. These were designed to operate in six or eight-car sets. These trains enabled the Belfast-Dublin and Belfast-Derry expresses to be dieselised. Sixteen cars, numbered 701-716, were fitted with small driving cabs and corridors at both ends. Here No 706 heads the 15.50 Derry-Belfast into Strabane on 2 August 1958. The fourth vehicle is the buffet car. No 706 illustrates the very unusual corridor connections on these trains.
E S Russell, ColourRail

Bottom: Eight cars, Nos 901-908, resembled the earlier AEC cars in having full width cabs. One of these was usually on one end of each set. Here, No 902 heads a six-car set out of Great Victoria Street, Platform 5 in the summer of 1958. The GNR diesel livery, of Oxford blue and cream, was very attractive.
R C Ludgate, ColourRail

Chapter 10
Diesel Traction
1932-1958

The GNR was a very significant pioneer of diesel traction in the British Isles as a whole. Experiments with diesel traction began in 1932 and, by the break up of the GNR in 1958, diesel traction was well on the way to becoming universal for passenger traffic. Although the main theme of this book is the development of steam locomotives, the GNR was primarily a business concern and by no means looked at steam traction through rose-tinted spectacles. If the company had survived into the mid-1960s, the complete dieselisation of all passenger services would have been highly likely, funds permitting.

As well as being a major operator of diesel trains in its own right, the GNR acted as technical consultant for the development of diesel traction on neighbouring railways. Its clients in this regard were the Dundalk, Newry and Greenore, the County Donegal, the Clogher Valley and the Sligo, Leitrim and Northern Counties Railways and, briefly in 1930, the Castlederg and Victoria Bridge Tramway. Consultancy included not only advice with design, but quite often, the actual construction at Dundalk of rolling stock for these railways, and its subsequent repair. In some cases, the smaller companies had not the facilities, or expertise, to do the work themselves. GNR influence in modern traction even extended to the much larger CIE organisation, which ran the main railway network of the Republic of Ireland after 1945. The diesel multiple-unit trains introduced on CIE in 1952 were virtually identical to the Park Royal/AEC fleet ordered for the GNR in 1950.

Early experience with diesel traction

The County Donegal Railways, mentioned above, were jointly owned by the GNR and the LMS (NCC) and, in the late 1920s, the CDR had introduced a number of petrol driven railcars. Two of these, Nos 4 (1928) and 6 (1930), were built at Dundalk. In 1930-31, the GNR constructed CDR Nos 7 and 8, the first diesel-engined railcars to operate in the British Isles. These went into service in 1931 and had Gardner 6L2 diesel engines, with bodywork by O'Doherty's of Strabane.

In 1932, a more sophisticated, articulated diesel railcar was built for the Clogher Valley Railway, also with a Gardner 6L2 engine. The traction unit for this car was built by Walkers of Wigan, but the GNR built the passenger bodywork at Dundalk. In addition, by 1932 the GNR had amassed considerable experience in internal combustion by the development of an extensive fleet of road motor buses and lorries.

Railcars A and B

It was natural that, with this experience, the GNR should soon construct vehicles for their own railway system. The first two railcars, A and B, were put into service in 1932. They were designed to be capable of 50 mph on the level, reducing to 40 mph if hauling 7 tons (one loaded wagon), and 35 mph if hauling 14 tons (two). The railcars had similar bodies and were roughly two-thirds the length of a railway carriage. Both were single-unit, twin-bogie vehicles with a driving cab at each end and were constructed to full railway standards in terms of seating, frames, buffers and draw gear. Both seated 32 passengers in 2+2 seating. The passenger compartment had end doors on each side and eight square-shaped windows, which resembled the windows in contemporary AEC Regent I and Leyland Titan TD1 double-deck buses. These, and all subsequent diesel trains, were painted in an attractive Oxford blue and cream livery, as used on the omnibus fleet (see opposite).

However, the two cars differed in their mechanics. Railcar A, which entered service in July 1932, had a 130 bhp 6 cylinder AEC engine and mechanical transmission. It had an AEC type radiator at the front end and was 40'0" long over body. It had bogies with 3'5" wheels and a wheelbase of 6'6". Overall weight was 18 tons 15 cwt.

Railcar B had diesel-electric drive, with a 120 bhp Gleniffer engine and a Tilling-Stevens generator. Because of the diesel-electric transmission, this car was heavier (21 tons) and had to be two feet longer (42'0") and the front (power) bogie had an 8'0" wheelbase. Both these cars went into service in the Portadown area and were a familiar feature on the Scarva-Banbridge branch. They gave fuel consumption figures of 8-10 mpg and were able to operate at a running cost of 4d (1.7p) per mile.

Some alterations were made to the cars in later years. After experience gained with the articulated railcars, the seating on Railcar A was altered to 3+2 with five rows facing forwards at the front end and five facing backwards at the rear, giving a total of 50 seats. Without a diagram, I cannot be certain of the reseating in Railcar B, but it had 40 seats, suggesting a similar arrangement with 2+2 seating. In 1940, a two-bench seat was removed from each, reducing seating to 48 and 38, respectively.

Railcar A later received a 102 bhp Gardner 6LW engine in place of the AEC one. A radiator was fitted to the roof and the earlier AEC radiator removed. It covered 893,000 miles up to June 1956 and passed to the UTA in 1958.

Railcar B had a more chequered career. It was taken out of passenger service during the War and, in 1942, was in use

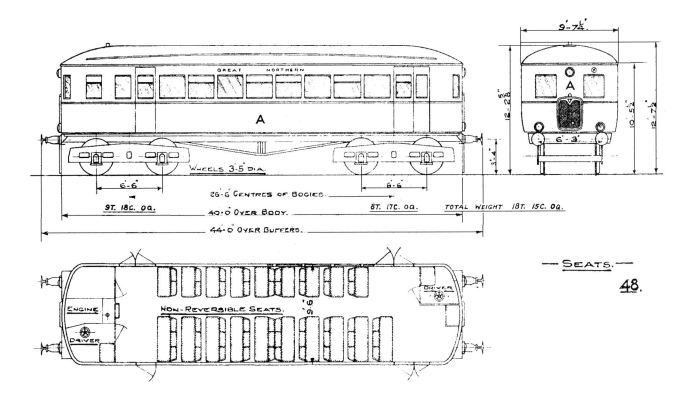

Fig 59 (above): Railcar A, as running about 1940. The front elevation shows the AEC radiator originally fitted to both ends of this car. The seating was originally for 40, arranged 2+2.

Right: Railcar B at Scarva. This car was two feet longer than 'A' but had a similar body. This view is from the opposite end to the view of 'A' above. The driver is Joe Graham or Bertie Lyttle.

Real Photographs X 124

Fig 60 (opposite top): The internal layout of railcar C1.

Left: Railcar A as later altered externally after the fitting of a Gardner 6LW engine. Steps (the nearer set vacuum operated) have been added for use at level crossings and the radiators replaced by a cooling apparatus on the roof at the near end. Note the destination blind.

Duffner R577

Right: Railcar C1 out of use at Dundalk showing the rather odd rear end. Did the GNR intend fitting driving controls to this end? This car was built in 1934 and had a Gardner 6LW engine. It passed to CIE in 1958.

D Anderson

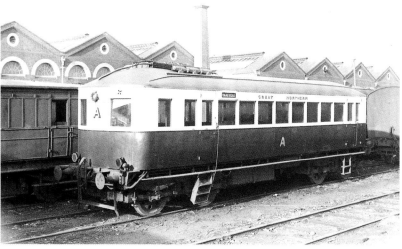

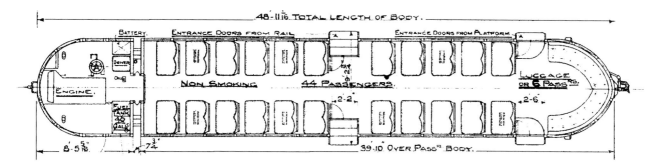

on the Dublin-Belfast newspaper trains. Then, in October 1946, the engine was removed and the car entered the carriage stock as coach No 500. It was used on the Irish North section, though I have seen no photographs of this. Finally, in 1949, it was scrapped. Apparently, the diesel generator was too heavy for the available springs and, in any case, parts for the Gleniffer engine and the Tilling-Stevens generator could not be acquired during the War. As it was non-standard anyway (the other railcars having Gardner engines), it was simpler to withdraw it.

Railcar C

The success of the Gardner engined CVR railcar No 1 of 1932 and of the similar, but larger, CDR railcar No 12 of 1934 – also built at Dundalk – encouraged the GNR itself to experiment with articulation. The result was Railcar C, which emerged from Dundalk works in November 1934. On this vehicle, the main body was articulated onto the rear of the driving unit (supplied by Walkers of Wigan) and movement from one to the other was possible through a bellows connection and door. The diesel engine was a 96 bhp 6LW Gardner, driving through a four-speed gear-box to a coupled 7'3" wheel-base bogie. The driver sat to the right of the engine and had a clear forward view through five large windows. The passenger compartment seated fifty, 44 in bus-type seats arranged 2+2 and facing forwards, and 6 on a horseshoe shaped bench seat at the rear.

Both ends of the railcar were rounded, the rear resembling a bullet in shape. The side and rear windows were slightly arched, giving the vehicle a rather French look. CDR Railcar

14, built in 1935, also had this style of window.

The overall length of Railcar C was 48'1¹¹⁄₁₆", but it was only 8'0" wide and 10'5⅛" high. It did not have normal carriage buffering, the body construction owing more to bus technology than railway carriage design. It was, therefore, rather different from Railcars A and B, which had the usual carriage width of 9'6" and height of 12'7½". It weighed only 14 tons 15 cwt empty and used fuel at the rate of 12 mpg.

This car was used on the Enniskillen-Bundoran service, though replaced by a steam train on summer weekends. The principal disadvantage, compared to railcars A and B, was that the car had only one cab and needed to be turned at the end of each journey. The rails on the Bundoran turntable were extended to suit. However, the need to turn was less of a problem on the 43 mile Enniskillen-Bundoran run, than it would have been on the 6¾ mile Scarva branch. Railcar C became C1 in 1935 and ran 819,000 miles up to June 1956. It passed to CIE in 1958. For a time in 1959, it was used on the daily mail service between Dundalk and Cavan.

Railcars C2 and C3

The next step, was to design a diesel train with sufficient passenger accommodation for suburban work, where off-peak loadings could be more economically worked by diesel trains. Dundalk tried to achieve this by placing two articulated railcars back to back. Railcars C2 and C3 emerged in June 1935 and were put to work as a two coach train on the Dublin-Howth route, with some runs to Balbriggan on the main line.

In design, the cars were similar to Railcar C, with the same overall dimensions. Each weighed 15 tons empty so that, despite the two heavy diesel engines, the entire train weighed about the same as a mainline carriage. There was no corridor connection between the two vehicles and the rear of each car was flat, rather than rounded, to enable them to be coupled. Railcar C2 seated 52 third class passengers, though four seats at the rear were removed in 1940 to make way for luggage. Railcar C3 seated 32 thirds at the front, 8 seconds at the rear and 6 first class passengers in a small 6'6" saloon at the centre. In all, the entire train seated 98 people.

Mechanically, Railcars C2 and C3 had

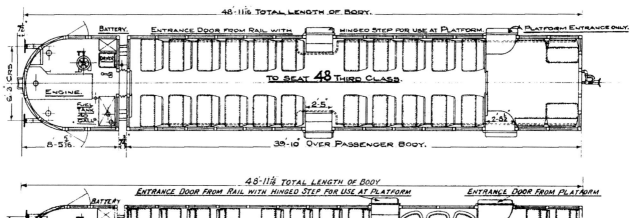

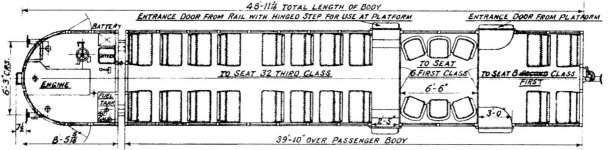

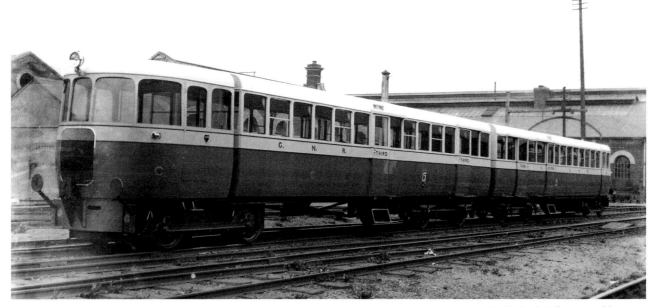

Fig 61 (top): The internal layout of railcar C2.

Fig 62 (second from top): The internal layout of railcar C3.

Centre: Railcars C2 and C3 at Dundalk when new, showing them as a two car unit. C2 (nearer the camera) was all third and C3 was tri-composite.

Duffner W85

Left: Railcar C3 running as a single unit with a small luggage trailer, at Platform 3 Portadown on 3 July 1957, probably about to set off for Omagh. Behind it is an AEC diesel train.

Kelland collection 105

Right: Railbus F at Dundalk Works after conversion from a road bus in January 1935. It became F3 in 1938 when railcar F was built.

Duffner W74

slightly higher rated 102 bhp Gardner 6LW engines and were capable of 48 mph. When running as a two-car set, only the power bogie of the leading car was used, the driver having no method of driving both engines from one end.

The operation of C2 and C3 as a two-car unit was not considered a success and, in August 1937, the articulated twins were separated. The second class compartment in C3 was redesignated 'first' so that the seating became 14/32. C2 remained a one-class car. In their separated form they were transferred to Irish North services, where they worked regularly between Dundalk and Omagh, Enniskillen and Clones and Omagh and Portadown. Small 2¾ ton luggage wagons were built to run with them. On my childhood travels in Fermanagh, I used these railcars quite often, as one of them was frequently on the 6.35 pm Enniskillen-Clones. C2 covered 696,000 miles up to 1956 and went to CIE in 1958. C3 covered 690,000 miles and passed to the UTA. Neither company had traffic to suit them and they lay idle for several years before being scrapped.

Railbuses

Contemporary with the introduction of the C series of railcars, the GNR was developing another category of motorised rail vehicle, by adapting actual road buses for rail use. As mentioned earlier, the GNR had built up an extensive bus fleet and was busy constructing Gardner-engined buses at Dundalk works, to its own designs. These, in turn, were making older buses redundant and it was realised that, if some of these were fitted with railway wheels, they might provide an even cheaper solution than railcars, on some lines. Already, in 1933, two petrol engined buses had been converted at Dundalk for service on the narrow gauge CDR, where they became Nos 9 and 10.

Two GNR engineers and the Dunlop Rubber Co collaborated to design a pneumatic tyred railway wheel which was patented as the Howden-Meredith wheel. This had a bus wheel hub with a pneumatic tyre which was gripped by a steel outer rim, profiled on the outside like a railway wheel and on the inside to correspond to the threads on the tyre. The rim was held on by tension, being of a slightly smaller diameter than the tyre. This system was first tested on two permanent way lorries in 1933-34. These experiments identified the need for a slightly squatter type of tyre on passenger vehicles and Dunlop helped by making a suitable wheel hub.

It is not my intention, in this publication, to go into details about the particular types of bus converted. Naturally, all the railbuses were single deck vehicles and the first was ready for use on the GNR in September 1934. It was designated 'D' and was rapidly followed by 'E' (October 1934) and 'F' (January 1935). 'E' was used on the Scarva branch and another on the lightly used Oldcastle branch from Drogheda. One also operated between Dundalk and Enniskillen. When railcars D, E, F and G were placed in service in 1936-38, the railbuses were renumbered D1, E2 and F3, respectively. At first the railbuses had pneumatic tyres on all four wheels. However, these could not operate the signalling track circuits, so later the front end reverted to ordinary wagon axles.

Other neighbouring companies soon realised the potential of this new type of vehicle. Although the CDR did not develop the type further, two were converted for use on the DN&GR in 1935 (their Nos 1 and 2). The GNR had taken over the working of this railway in 1933. Another was supplied to the SL&NCR in 1935 (their railbus A) and a second in 1938 (railbus 2A). In 1939, GNR railbus D1 was sold to the SL&NCR to replace railbus A, which had been destroyed in an accident the previous year.

In 1944, F3 was damaged in an accident at Dundalk and another road bus (also F3) was converted to replace it. In 1947, E2 and F3 were renumbered 1 and 2, and the DN&GR pair were taken over in 1948, becoming GNR Nos 3 and 4. Of these four, No 3 was scrapped in 1955 and Nos 1 and 4 were transferred to departmental use in 1956 (as 8178 and 8177, respectively), leaving No 2 as the only operational railbus. This vehicle (and 8177) passed to CIE in 1958. The UTA got 8178, which continued in departmental use until 1963 and is now preserved and restored as railcar 1 at the Ulster Folk and Transport Museum, Cultra, Co Down.

Railcars D and E

In the late 1930s, the GNR continued to construct single-cab articulated railcars for the CDRJC, producing five more up to 1940 – Nos 14 (1935), 15 (1936), 16 (1937), 17

Left: The engine compartment of railcar E , showing the Gardner 6L3 diesel engine. To the right is the air reservoir for the compressor which is itself visible opposite the door. The dynamo is also visible, on the left, wired to the switchboard.

Duffner W90

Below: The interior of railcar E showing the rather odd rearward-facing seats on either side of the driver's compartment. The 3+2 seating was not reversible. This picture is inside Dundalk Works and railcar A, with its AEC radiator, can be seen through the front windows.

Duffner W118

Opposite page, top: Railcar E at Amiens Street, Dublin, while on the Howth service. Note the open door of the engine compartment. This end of it housed the gearbox, reverse box and luggage and doubled as a guard's van! Another point of interest is that one of the coupling rods is missing.

Kelland collection 116

Fig 63 (opposite left): Diagram of the engine compartment of railcars D and E.

Fig 64 (opposite right): Diagram of the engine compartment of railcars F and G.

corridor connection between the three parts of the train but, as this was routed through the engine compartment, it was only for the use of the crew.

The two coach bodies were very modern, with large windows, and had full width three-window cabs, with a forward view for the passengers. Although lower in height than a normal carriage, the railcars had full 9'6" wide bodies and seating was in a 3+2 arrangement. In one coach there were 82 third class seats, with those at the outward end facing the cab and the rear section facing the engine. The other coach was tri-composite, with 19 thirds next the engine (naturally!) but, rather oddly, it was the second class which had the benefit of the front view – though only 20 of the 50 second class seats faced that way. Indeed, the front end of this portion had two bench seats in the window corners, with their backs to the front! The 8 firsts were in 2+2 seating with their own self-contained compartment separated from the seconds and thirds by internal doors. In all, the train seated 159 and had an overall length of 124'5" over buffers, about the same as two main line carriages. However, the weight was only 39½ tons empty and 50 tons loaded.

Railcars D and E went into service on the Dublin-Howth route and handled the bulk of traffic, except during the morning and evening rush hours, when the 4-4-2Ts dominated. Up to 1956, they covered 555,000 and 628,000 miles, respectively (considerably less than railcars F and G which followed). After 1938, they graduated north, one working on the Newry-Warrenpoint branch and the other in the Belfast area. Railcar D passed to the UTA in 1958 and

(1938) and 18 (1940). However, for their own purposes they moved to a different formula in railcar design. Railcars D and E of May and June 1936 were a major advance towards producing a self-contained diesel train, suitable for suburban traffic. It should be borne in mind that, at this time, the GWR, LMS and LMS (NCC) were still developing the concept of single unit railcar, sometimes hauling a trailer. It was to be 1938 before the LMS produced its own light-weight articulated diesel train.

Railcars D and E comprised a centrally placed engine section, at each end of which, a passenger coach, with driving cab, was articulated. The engine was a Gardner 6L3 unit, rated at 153 bhp at 1,200 rpm. Transmission was by a fluid flywheel and Wilson 4 speed epicyclic gearbox, with electro-pneumatic remote control for the gearbox and reverse box. The engine section was 16'5½" over body and mounted on a six-coupled chassis, on 3'0" wheels, with a 7'3"+ 7'3" wheelbase. It was divided into two compartments, one of which contained the engine, compressor and dynamo, and the other the gearbox and reverse box.

This section also served as a luggage compartment and, in theory, the guard was accommodated in the engine compartment. This was more honoured in the breach than the observance, as the reader can well imagine! There was a

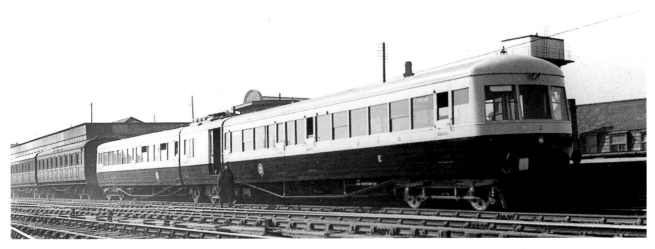

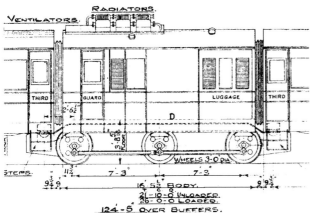

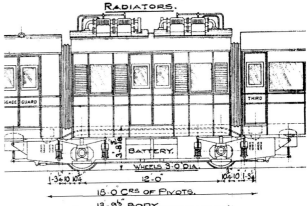

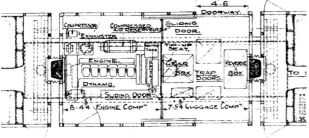

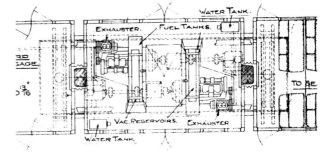

worked at Newry until 1963. Railcar E went to CIE, but did little work, and was sold to the UTA in 1961, to be cannibalised for spares.

Railcars F and G

One problem with railcars D and E was that they were underpowered, compared to cars A-C3, and were capable of only 42 mph in 4th gear. This was rectified in railcars F and G of March/April 1938, which were built to a modified design, in the light of experience gained with D and E.

Firstly, the single 153 bhp 6L3 engine was replaced by two Gardner 6LWs (as used on the C cars), developing 102 bhp at 1,700 rpm. These sat at either end of a slightly smaller 13'9½" central section. The six-coupled chassis was replaced by two axles on a 12'0" wheelbase, each engine driving a different axle through a Vulcan-Sinclair hydraulic coupling. There was now a 5-speed Wilson epicyclic gearbox with

vacuum electric control for the gearbox. With 204 bhp on tap, the top speed of F and G was a more respectable 48 mph, with slightly greater hill-climbing ability.

Although the new cars resembled those of 1936, there were differences. They were slightly longer, at 125'9½" overall and weighed 41 tons 5 cwt empty and 52 tons loaded. Although the engine portion was shorter, the passenger sections were about 2 feet longer, allowing the guard and luggage to be allocated a small 7'0¹³⁄₁₆" van in the third class section; a much more sensible arrangement. Even with the removal of the central entrance, this was at the price of slightly less knee room for the passengers but, at least, the guard wasn't deafened.

There were minor changes to the seating arrangements. At both ends of the train there were two small transverse bench seats, each seating two. These faced the driver (no doubt an unwelcome feature for him), but allowed the four

Top: A broadside view of railcar F, giving a very clear view of the articulation of these cars. Railcars F and G spent most of their working lives on the Howth service but were transferred to the Warrenpoint branch in the 1960s.
Real Photographs 88159

Left: Railcar G heading out for Howth in August 1957, with the rear passengers enjoying a good view of Amiens Street station. Note the white tailboard, indicating 'train complete'. In the distance, a Glover tank waits between duties.
N C Simmons 2217B

Below: First class compartment of an AEC diesel train, showing the superb forward view for the front six passengers. This posed shot is probably in Dundalk yard. *Duffner 630C*

passengers a sideways view out of the front (or rear) – an improvement over the 1936 cars. The overall seating was 164 (51 second/8 first/24 third at one end, and 81 third at the other). Later, when second class was abolished, the seconds were redesignated first class in all four articulated sets, but this left rather more first class accommodation than was needed.

Railcars F and G covered 1,006,000 and 1,061,000 miles, respectively, up to 1956. They spent most of their working lives on the Howth branch, but in 1958 Railcar F went to the UTA, where it spent its remaining days on the Warrenpoint branch. It was joined there by railcar G, which had gone to CIE, but, in 1963, was sold to the UTA.

AEC diesel trains

By 1939, the GNR had more experience with diesel railcars than any other railway in the British Isles, save the GWR. It had built nine railcars for its own use, as well as ten for the CDRJC, one for the Clogher Valley Railway and ten railbuses for itself and various other companies, as outlined above. There is no doubt that, but for the intervention of the War, diesel traction on the GNR would have developed much sooner in the direction of multiple unit trains. The GWR had worked closely with the AEC Co of Southall to produce its single-unit railcars and, after the War, AEC produced a transmission system that allowed two power cars to be operated by one driver, with an intermediate non-powered

coach. The DMU was born and the first experimental units, built for the GWR in 1947, provided the basis for the post-war plans of the GNR.

In 1948, the GNR placed an order for 20 power cars with AEC Ltd, with the railcar bodies to be built by Park Royal. When these were delivered between June 1950 and April 1951, they immediately became the largest fleet of diesel multiple-unit trains in the British Isles. One odd thing is that the abbreviation 'DMU' never came into use in Ireland. These, and other multiple-unit trains, were usually referred to as 'railcars' and I think this goes back to the widespread use of railcars in Ireland before the Second World War. However, in the GNR working timetables, the AECs were called 'diesel trains' and the earlier vehicles 'railcars' or 'railbuses'.

The AEC cars were built to main line standards, in terms

Top: A publicity shot of a complete three coach train near Dundalk on 13 May 1950. The set is made up of 601-188-600, the centre vehicle, in this instance, being a K23 buffet car.
Duffner R629B

Left: An AEC train at Portadown platform 3 on 3 July 1957. In the distance is a UG 0-6-0 with a nearly empty tender. The intermediate coach is a 70-seater K15 open third. Comparison with the previous 1950 photograph shows detail changes to the livery. On first repainting, in 1955-56, the running number was added to the front end and the side number was near the rear door.
Kelland Collection 118

of seating, and were certainly not suburban cars. The 62'6"x 9'6" bodies had attractive full width cabs with two large front windows and a small centrally placed headlamp just below the cantrail. Behind the driver was a first class compartment, affording most of the 12 passengers a panoramic forward view in comfortable 2+1 Pullman seating. Across a toilet-equipped vestibule, the third class section seated 32 in 2+2 seating, with another vestibule leading to a luggage compartment, cum guard's van, at the corridor end. The guard's compartment of even-numbered cars was equipped with a Vapor-Clarkson oil-fired boiler for steam heating. The cars were numbered 600-619 in the coaching stock series.

Mechanically, the cars had two under-floor 125 bhp AEC 9.6 litre engines. These were six cylinder direct injection compression ignition diesel engines, with transmission by fluid flywheel and five speed, pre-selector, epicyclic gearboxes. One engine powered the front bogie and the other the rear. The power bogies had a 10'0" wheelbase with 3'2" wheels. Each car weighed 38 tons 5 cwt empty, the boiler in the even-numbered cars adding a further 24 cwt. Each car had two 50 gallon fuel tanks. With an intermediate car weighing 30 tons approximately, a three car train had 500 bhp available for a 108 ton train. This compares with 204 bhp, for a 52 ton train, in railcars F and G.

The intermediate coaches for the AEC cars were of four types, all conversions from existing main line stock, or built new by the GNR. Five were K15 open thirds, seating 70.

These gave an overall seating capacity, for the three coach set, of 24 first and 134 third class seats. Two were similar K31s, built by the GNR in 1954. These differed in having 72 seats and a small driving cab, so that a two car set, seating 12/104, could operate, if a power car was under repair. Four sets were paired with K23 buffet cars. These allowed tea, drinks and light snacks to be served on the train, but seated only 54 at tabled seats. In K23-fitted sets, the seating was 24 first and 118 third. Finally, two L12 brake thirds, seating 39, were AEC fitted. These normally ran on four-car sets and were intended for workings like the nightly Dublin-Belfast newspaper train, which required additional van accommodation.

All AEC-fitted intermediates had vacuum and corridor connections compatible with steam-hauled stock, so it was not uncommon for blue and cream railcar intermediates to be marshalled in steam trains. Sometimes, indeed, three coach diesel trains were augmented by an older mahogany-painted coach attached to the rear at times of peak traffic, although this adversely affected performance. It was also common for diesel trains to haul 4-wheel 'Y' vans.

The GNR made very wide use of its ten new diesel trains, concentrating them on services where passenger traffic was under threat from competitors. They took over most services on the Banbridge and Newcastle line and were commonly used on outer suburban workings from Dublin. However, the GNR cleverly used them to develop new traffic. The Dublin-based 'Enterprise' express went over to diesel operation, the first inter-city diesel express in the British Isles. A new direct Belfast-Enniskillen diesel service was inaugurated, removing the need to change trains at Clones and diesels were also made available for excursion work, complete with buffet car refreshments. Well aware of the dated appearance of many of its steam trains, the GNR spread the 'diesel experience' far and wide so that, on virtually every route, diesel traction was available on some services. This was good for morale and made the company appear progressive.

MAK diesel locomotive No 800 *DA CLASS 265*

The Great Northern Railway Board, which took control of the railway from the old company on 1 September 1953, wisely focused its dieselisation plans on the passenger services. Customers with freight to be delivered didn't particularly care what hauled the train, as long as it got there and didn't cost too much. Passengers were much more sensitive to the differences between 'modern diesels' and 'dirty old steam trains' – stereotypes that were reinforced by the conversion of the modern, big-windowed hauled-stock into railcar intermediates. The argument in favour of diesel traction for shunting and haulage of freight, was dominated more by factors relating to operating costs. The main difficulty was that, in the British Isles, diesel locomotives had not been developed with the same enthusiasm as railcars and the only really well-tried type was the 350 bhp English Electric 0-6-0 shunter. In 1953, British Railways had only six main line diesels and CIE only two.

Nevertheless, the GNRB considered two diesel locomotive types – shunters in the 350-400 bhp range and 800-1000 bhp light freight locomotives. At the time, BR were trialling an 800 bhp Bo-Bo built by British Thompson Heuston, which was considered. In April 1954, tenders were invited for locomotives in the above power ranges. High capital cost made most of the tenders prohibitive, but a tempting offer came from a German firm – Maschinenbau A-G of Kiel – who were willing to construct, and ship at their own expense, an 800 bhp diesel-hydraulic locomotive for trial on the GNR. This offer was accepted and the locomotive arrived at the North Wall, Dublin on 14 December 1954. It was painted in a blue livery, relieved by a horizontal white band just below bonnet level.

By any standards, the MAK, as it was soon dubbed, was an unusual 'animal'. Germany was the biggest user of Voith hydraulic transmissions and the engine certainly looked German. It weighed 57½ tons and was unique for a diesel engine in these islands, in having eight coupled wheels instead of four wheel bogies. In essence it was really a very

Above: The MAK, still unnumbered, and without headlamps, being tested on a Down goods train at Malahide in 1955. The No 2 end is nearest the camera. The men in this view are Hugo Kemphe (German driver), 'Pappy' Fox (guard) and Billy Gargan (pilot driver).

C P Friel collection

Left: The No 1 end of the MAK, being inspected at Drogheda, on 3 June 1957. On the engine are John Brennan (charge hand fitter) and Matt Farrelly (fitter). Looking on are Paddy Mallon, P McKeever (loco inspectors) and Johnnie Deery (driver).

F W Shuttleworth, AU26

Opposite top: A later view of the MAK diesel, now numbered 800, at Dundalk platform 1, with the No 1 end nearer the camera. The headlamps were fitted by Paddy Mallon.

C P Friel collection

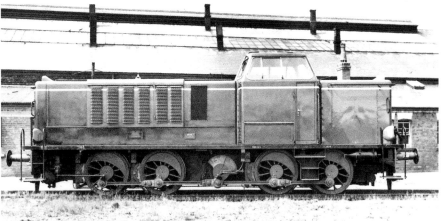

Right: Side profile of the MAK diesel at Dundalk. This view shows how the final drive was to the jackshaft and was transmitted to the wheels by coupling rods.

Duffner L1143C

powerful shunter, rather than a serious main line locomotive. Without bogies, it would never have been capable of high speed. It ran trials, without bearing any number, for most of 1955, mainly on freight workings on the main line and Portadown-Londonderry, but was also tried on outer suburban passenger services out of Dublin. The Germans sent over two engineers, one of whom was Hugo Kemphe, and, such was the skill necessary to drive it, only a small number of the men got the experience. Paddy Mallon was the GNR fitter who accompanied the locomotive on its trials.

The MAK also did some trials on the UTA lines before the Board decided to purchase it for £29,500, but no more were built, although the Board pushed for a follow-up order. However, by this time, the Governments were wary of more expenditure on the loss-making GNR and it was hard enough persuading them to finance the proposed BUT railcar fleet,

let alone freight locomotives. The MAK entered GNR stock as No 800 (rather than No 211), reflecting the locomotive's horse power and distancing it from the steam locomotive fleet. It remained something of a white elephant and passed to CIE in 1958. With the exception of the crane tank, the MAK was the only item of GNR stock to be actually renumbered by CIE, becoming K801 in 1959.

Before moving on from the MAK diesel, I should mention that there was a *second* GNRB diesel locomotive. This was one hired from Harland and Wolff of Belfast in 1957. It was built, as BCDR No 28, in 1937, to operate the Ardglass branch. It had later run on the NCC in 1947-51, also as No 28. The GNRB used it to shunt at Grosvenor

Above: Side profile of No 701, the first BUT car, on 25 April 1957. The three small windows on the left mark the driver's compartment and the large frosted one on the right is the toilet. On the opposite side, the positions were reversed. The two BUT 150 bhp diesel engines were covered by a wire grill, whereas the earlier AECs had valances.

Duffner L1177

Left: Interior of 701, inside Dundalk Works after completion. The saloon had end doors only. Whilst the seats were comfortable, tables would have been appreciated.

Duffner R500H

Below: Publicity shot of the new 'Enterprise Express' near Dundalk on 25 April 1957. The cars are 701-702-232-88-227-703, the intermediates being, respectively, a side corridor brake first, a diner, and a side corridor first.

Duffner L1177A

Road goods yard, Belfast. By coincidence, the scrapping of A class 0-6-0 No 28 in 1956 allowed the diesel to retain its ex-BCDR number when operating on the GNR. No 28 was a 500 bhp diesel-electric, with a unique A1-1A wheel arrangement. The hire arrangement was taken over by the UTA in October 1958, who, incidentally, retained the number 28, as did NIR, when they took it over in 1968! This must be some sort of record, as this locomotive occupied the same number when in the fleets of five different railways.

BUT diesel trains

The AEC fleet had been a tremendous advance for the GNR, who took maximum advantage of them in company publicity. However, they had operational limitations, the main one being that they were restricted to three or four coach sets. Later, the UTA adapted the cabling on those they inherited, to allow six (or eight) car sets, but, due to the full-width cabs, no corridor connection between the sets was possible. After the GNR Board was set up in 1953, the company was dependent on the two governments for funding to modernise. Nevertheless, the GNR set about designing the next generation of diesel trains. By this time, AEC had become absorbed into the British United Traction Company, so the new trains were known as BUT railcars.

The BUT trains were designed to completely dieselise the inter-city services of the GNR, even though modern three-cylinder steam locomotives had been built for this work as recently as 1948. That such a move was contemplated in 1954 is a measure of how desperate the GNR was to reduce its escalating operating costs. The new fleet would comprise 24 power cars of two types. They would allow full corridor connections in six or eight coach trains and would enable a six-car set to be augmented to eight without re-forming the set. As conceived, there would have been two 6 or 8-car sets for the Dublin-Belfast services, two 6-car sets (8-car on Saturdays) for the Belfast-Londonderry route, and four 4-car sets for the Irish North and other secondary routes or as spares. With AEC trains cascaded to other routes, this plan would have allowed diesel trains to operate the bulk of GNR passenger services, with steam restricted to peak time and seasonal traffic.

Each train was to have one power car with a full width cab and up to three power cars with small cabs, and corridor connections, at each end. There were to be 8 of the former and 16 of the latter. Advantage was taken of new larger AEC engines being developed for use on British Railways' DMUs. These were 11.3 litre and developed 150 bhp at 1,800 rpm. Thus a six-coach train would have 900 bhp and an eight-coach set, 1,200 bhp of power. They had 4-speed gearboxes which were not pre-selective and BUT trains were capable of 85 mph.

The intermediate coaches were all conversions from main line stock built in the 1930s and 1940s. The types are too numerous to describe, but included full dining cars and first and brake-first side corridor stock. There were two significant changes from the AEC fleet. Firstly, although heating was by means of the engine cooling water, this had to be supplemented by steam heating boilers. These were placed in the guard's van of a brake/first or brake/second vehicle (the GNR had no third class after 1950). This meant that every train had to have a trailer with a large guard's van, although a single power car could form a train on its own, using only the heat from the engine cooling system.

Secondly, although the trains were vacuum braked and steam-heated, the corridor connections were incompatible with the AEC cars and hauled stock. Indeed, they were unique and I have never seen them on any other diesel train. The top and sides consisted of ¾" thick rubber moulded to give a convex outer surface about 10" wide. When pressed against a similar moulding on a neighbouring car, this made a firm, virtually draught-free, connection (see centre photo, page 159).

It took a long time for the two governments to approve funding for the proposed fleet and it was April 1957 before the first cars were completed. The chassis and structural members for the bodies were supplied by BUT from September 1956, but were actually assembled at Dundalk. The cars emerged over a year or more, at roughly three-weekly intervals. The first sixteen cars (701-716) had half-width cabs at each end and were 65'6" long. A single second class compartment seated 56, and, at each end of the vehicle, there was both a driving cab and a toilet, placed on opposite sides of the corridor with the cab on the left from the driver's perspective.

The eight cars with full width cabs (901-908) resembled the AEC cars in appearance and layout, except that they had no guard's van and their headlamps were larger and mounted above cant rail level. They were 65'0" long and seated 12 first class in luxury armchair seats facing forwards and 44 in a second class compartment with 2+2 seating. In the first class, the second and third rows of seats were slightly tiered to give a better forward view.

The first four cars were ready for service at the end of June 1957 and went into service on the Belfast based 'Enterprise' working, initially as a six-car set with power cars 701-703. I was in hospital at the time, close to Balmoral station, and remember this train on trials during May. Two more cars were ready in July and one was used to introduce a new morning express service from Enniskillen to Belfast via Omagh. This was a short-lived service, as the Fermanagh routes closed at the end of September 1957. At the end of 1957, ten cars were available, sufficient to turn the Dublin based 'Enterprise' over to a BUT set and to commence dieselisation of the Belfast-Londonderry route. All the 700 series cars were completed before construction of the 900 series began. At this stage, therefore, first class passengers had to be accommodated in side corridor intermediate stock.

It was May 1958 before the last of the 700 series entered service, and July before the first of the 900 series cars was completed. By this time, the days of the GNR were numbered, with the Northern Ireland Government determined to end this early example of a 'Cross-Border Body' and split the GNRB between the UTA and CIE. Consequently, the full potential of the BUT fleet was never realised, as many of the lines for which they were intended had closed in 1957. The last cars were completed during the death throes of the company and No 908 was actually delivered in the green livery of its new owners, CIE, in October 1958.

However, had the GNRB survived after 30 September 1958, there would have been a major transformation in passenger train operation, which would have sounded the death knell for steam in any case. The combined effect of the widespread closures of 1956-57, and the introduction of the new diesel fleet, would have drastically curtailed the number of steam operated services to the morning and evening rush hours on suburban routes and heavy loadings at weekends.

Chapter 11
Under the UTA and CIE

The end of the GNR, on 30 September 1958, has been described in Chapter 9. This was a very traumatic time for employees of the old company, as their GNR identities were hidden beneath the uniforms of CIE and the UTA. Absorbtion into larger companies have been common place in railway history. Rarely, at least until the privatisation of British Rail, have railway employees found themselves split into different companies, with former colleagues working for another organisation. Old loyalties were not so easily forgotten, however, and for years to come, the GNR men who continued in railway service retained a strong GNR identity. Today, even after over forty years, reunions of ex-GNR men attract an enthusiastic response.

In a sense, the division was three way, because the Locomotive, Carriage and Wagon Works at Dundalk became a seperate entity called the Dundalk Engineering Works. Although Dundalk was within the Republic of Ireland, CIE did not want another major engineering works to add to Inchicore. The theory behind turning the Works into an independent company was that it could tender for railway work from both CIE and the UTA and could diversify into other branches of engineering. In practice, the DEW did no work for the UTA, after the last UTA-allocated locomotives left the Works in 1958, and very little for CIE after 1960. Dundalk Engineering Works retained the Works shunter, 0-6-0 crane tank No 31, up to 1960.

The GNR locomotive fleet was divided up as shown below. Those locomotives in heavy type are the ones which remained in service after the mass scrapping of 1959-60, when 78 steam locomotives were cut up.

Class	CIE	UTA
4-4-0		
VS	206 **207** 209	**208 210** (UTA 58 59)
V	84 **85**	83 **86** 87
S	**170 171 174**	**172 173** (UTA 60 61)
S2	191	**190 192** (UTA 62 63)
U	**197** 198 **199 203 204**	**196 200 201 202 205** (UTA 64-68)
QLs	–	127 156 157
Qs	123 130 **131 132** 136	121 122 125 **135**
PPs	12 44 71 75 106	42 43 46 50 **74** 76 107
Ps6'6"	27 72 73	–
Ps5'6"	105	–
0-6-0		
SG	177 178 179	175 176 (UTA 43 44)
SG2	**15** 19 **180 181 184**	**16 17 18 182 183** (UTA 38-42)
SG3	**8 14** 47 48 96 **117** 118	**6 7 13 20** 40 41 49 **97** (UTA 30-37)
UG	80 81 145 147 148	78 79 82 146 149 (UTA 45-49)
LQGs	110 **158 159 161 163 164**	108 **111** 119 160 162
LQGNs	–	9 39 109 **165**
NQGs	38 112	–
QGs	**152 153 154 155**	–
PGs	–	**10 11 100** 101 102 103 **151**
AL	29 35 55 57 58 59	32 56
A	33 60 **150**	–
Tanks		
T1 4-4-2T	188	185 186 **187** 189
T2 4-4-2T	1 **3** 62 63 65 67 115 **116** 139 **143** 144	2 **4 5** 21 **30** 64 66 69 142
JT 2-4-2T	**91**	–
RT 0-6-4T	–	22 **23 166 167** (UTA 22x 23-25)
QGTs 0-6-2T	99	

*Numbers in **heavy type** indicate locomotives which survived after 1960.*

Above: Ex-GNR locomotives awaiting scrapping at Dundalk in 1959. The line up includes 4-4-2Ts, SG3 0-6-0s, PPs 4-4-0 No 44 (extreme left), Ps6'6" No 73 (foreground) and Qs No 136 (behind 73). Just beyond No 136, is a SLNCR 0-6-4T and, in front of No 73, is a tender from one of the V class Compounds. Forty ex-GNR engines were scrapped by CIE in 1959-60.   *Jenks 1475*

GNR locomotives under CIE

We will now look at how the survivors of the GNR fleet fared under their new owners, from 1 October 1958. Theoretically, CIE added an 'N' suffix to ex-GNR locomotives to make a distinction, for instance, between 182 (ex-GSR) and 182N (ex-GNR). However, this was not applied in practice, so it was possible to photograph locomotives south of the border with GNR numbers, and livery, up to 1963. Those locomotives which were overhauled at Dundalk Engineering Works in 1958-60 continued to be painted in GNR liveries, but the crests and GNR lettering were generally omitted.

One difference between CIE and the UTA was that CIE made no real distinction between the older and newer locomotives when it came to overhaul and scrapping policy. Thus, Qs 4-4-0 Nos 131 and 132 were fully overhauled in 1958-59, despite being 57 years old. Conversely, VS 4-4-0 Nos 206 *Liffey* and 209 *Foyle* were withdrawn in 1960, though only twelve years old. The same fate befell UG 0-6-0 Nos 81 and 147 and S2 4-4-0 No 191 *Croagh Patrick*.

For the first year after the takeover not a lot changed. There were enough AEC and BUT diesel railcars to handle most of the passenger traffic. Both 'Enterprise' sets – the 11.00 Down/16.45 Up (CIE) and the 10.30 Up/17.30 Down, (UTA) – were BUT railcars. The 7.30 Down/15.00

Up and 9.00 Down/18.10 Up were officially CIE diesel, but steam reigned supreme on the other main line workings – the 8.15 Up/14.30 Down and the 12.00 Up/ 18.25 Down. These trains changed from UTA to CIE locomotives at Dundalk. Sometimes steam deputised on the 7.30 Down, in which case a Dublin engine worked through to Belfast and back.

Main line steam

For the main line steam workings, the motive power was initially VS 4-4-0 Nos 206, 207 and 209, all in poor shape, and S Nos 170, 171, 174 and 191. At this time, No 85 was in shops and 132 was waiting to go in. No 131 was fresh from overhaul jn September 1958. No 132 (at Derry up to October) joined 85 in the Works on 8 December. No 85 became available in February 1959 and 132 emerged in April. It was then the turn of Nos 170, 171 and 207 to enter shops. By now, 206 and 209 had turned their last wheel, and most of the main line work was in the hands of the inside cylindered engines – 131, 132 and 174. No 85 was commonly on the local 12.45 Dundalk-Dublin and the heavy 17.35 return.

The summer of 1959 brought an influx of CIE A class Metro-Vick diesel power for main line workings and there was less demand for steam. Nevertheless, No 170 emerged from Dundalk in June 1959 and No 171 in September. VS

Left: Qs 4-4-0 No 131 was overhauled at Dundalk, emerging in September 1958. It is seen here at Dublin, Amiens Street, shed on 26 August 1960, coupled to the 2500 gallon E type tender with which it was later preserved.

J D Fitzgerald

Below: S class 4-4-0 No 171 *Slieve Gullion* at the Dundalk shed on 11 May 1962. This locomotive had been overhauled in September 1959 and was eventually preserved.

J Oatway 27/1

Opposite: LQGs 0-6-0 No 164 with 'CIE' stencilled on the tender. Goods services continued on the truncated Irish North for nearly two years. In this 1959 view, No 164 is at Monaghan.

A Donaldson

class 4-4-0 No 207 was undergoing a protracted overhaul, which took until January 1960. The fate of No 174 hung in the balance for a while but, fortunately, in October 1959, it was decided to proceed with overhaul.

Hitherto, these engines had emerged with no GNR decals on their tenders but, when No 174 *Carrantuohill* left the Works in June 1960, it was given the full treatment, even down to the tender crest (see page 157). This was a fitting gesture for the very last locomotive to be overhauled at Dundalk Works.

Other steam classes

The takeover of the southern half of the GNR system had delayed completion of the CIE programme of dieselisation. Indeed, if the early CIE diesel fleet had proved reliable, steam would have disappeared on CIE around 1959. The unreliability of the Metro-Vick fleet led to some run-down CIE steam locomotives being retained for goods workings and seasonal passenger traffic. Officially, some 150 were still on the books, mostly 0-6-0 types, though many of these did not turn a wheel after 1959.

As most of the ex-GNR steam locomotives were in better shape than the CIE ones, some GNR goods locomotives were transferred to other areas. In 1959, UG No 148, SG No 179 and SG2 Nos 180, 181 and 184 were transferred to Broadstone shed, to assist with passenger turns to Bray.

Some GNR goods engines were even overhauled at Dundalk. SG3 0-6-0 Nos 8, 96 and 117 had just been run in, after being shopped in June-July 1958, and No 14 was in the Works when CIE took over. It emerged in January 1959. LQG 0-6-0 Nos 158 and 159 both entered Dundalk Works

for overhaul in November 1958, emerging respectively, in March and February 1959. No 158 and 163 also both went to Broadstone for a spell. The remaining GNR 0-6-0 types still found useful employment on GNR area goods workings, shunting, passenger workings to Howth, and cement trains down the Navan branch to Drogheda.

The Glover 4-4-2Ts were less fortunate. Only No 143 received a heavy overhaul under CIE (December 1958 - April 1959), though No 116 was pretty fresh and No 3 got a light overhaul in early 1960. With so many diesel railcars available, there was little suburban work for them, so the others had gone by 1960 and No 116 followed in 1961, leaving only Nos 3 and 143. Both did spells at the Broadstone (as it was termed). The only other tank engine to survive beyond 1960 was JT 2-4-2T No 91 of 1902, which was still in excellent condition. In September 1960, it was transferred to Liffey Junction as the wagon yard pilot. It remained there until Broadstone shed closed on 8 April 1961, and survived until 1963.

CIE seems to have found little suitable work for the five blue U class 4-4-0s, now that the Irish North was closed. They received Nos 197-199 (1915), 203 and 204 (1948).

Above: V class 4-4-0 No 85 *Merlin* at Dundalk on 8 September 1962. It is about to work the 12.45 pm Dundalk to Dublin. The leading carriages on the train are an L12 brake/2nd and an F16 1st/2nd composite. Note the F type 4000 gallon tender.

J D FitzGerald

No 132 at Platform 2, a Glover tank (probably No 3, but the number is illegible) on a Howth train and A57 (CIE) at Galway on the Radio Train. (If you're still out there Martin, get in touch!)

By summer 1961, the first fifteen GM diesels, B121-135 with single cabs, had arrived, as the first phase in the final plan to oust steam. This spelt the end of BUT power on the CIE 'Enterprise', as the train now became a hauled set, with a GM running right through to Belfast. The other CIE main line set was also locomotive-hauled so that, when we went to Dublin on the afternoon train, it was a UTA 2-6-0 to Dundalk and then a change to diesel. By now, passenger steam on CIE was confined to specials and cover for diesel failures, but there was still steam at Amiens Street shed and, of course, through workings from Belfast. However, 1961 saw the scrapping of T2 4-4-2T No 116 and 0-6-0 Nos 47 (SG3), 55 (AL), 145 (UG), 150 (A), 178 (SG) and 180 (SG2), leaving just 34 GNR steam locomotives south of the border.

A year later, in 1962, the new CIE black and tan livery was starting to appear on passenger stock and steam was even less in evidence. That autumn, the second and larger wave of GM diesels, B141-177 with twin cabs, had arrived so that, early in 1963, all regular steam on CIE ended, even for goods traffic. The last GNR steam locomotive to be used operationally by CIE was SG2 0-6-0 No 15, which shunted at North Wall on 30 March 1963. A programme of scrapping followed throughout 1963, and into 1964. As described elsewhere, only six GNR locomotives escaped, two for preservation and four for further service on the UTA. When I next came to Dublin, in the summer of 1963, we had a UTA 2-6-4T as far as Dundalk, where a UTA 2-6-0 was also in evidence. Many CIE engines sat in the scrap line, but not a puff of steam was to be seen south of Dundalk.

These had received their last major overhauls in 1958, 1955, 1956, 1956 and 1957, respectively. Not surprisingly, No 198 was in poor shape and was scrapped immediately. Nos 199 and 203 were transferred to the Broadstone, to work suburban trains to Bray, whilst 197 and 204 stayed at Amiens Street. By 1962, all four were in a poor state compared to the UTA examples.

Steam in the early 1960s

Most of my early journeys on the GNR were from Portadown to Newry, or to Fermanagh via Clones, and I got few runs to Dublin in the 1950s. However, I was fortunate that my father decided to take a series of summer holidays in Dublin from 1960 to 1964, making full use of his UTA free passes and privilege tickets to explore the whole CIE network at that time. This allowed me to observe these transition years at first hand. By August 1960, the month of the first of these holidays in Dublin, the CIE green was well in evidence but there was still plenty of GNR steam around Amiens Street. Indeed, at our guest house I found a fellow railway enthusiast, Martin Heasley (I think) who later sent me shots of Qs 4-4-0

GNR diesel traction

Railcars and carriages had the letters 'CN' added to their GNR numbers in the manner 'C601N'. In contrast to the steam locomotives, CIE was much quicker than the UTA at repainting the ex-GNR railcars and passenger stock. Indeed, BUT car No 908 never ran in GNR colours and was completed in CIE apple green in October 1958. By December, five carriages were already in CIE colours. AEC cars 601, 605 and 609 followed early in 1959 and, in June 1959, the MAK diesel emerged in green livery, renumbered K801 – an odd numbering. In terms of power it could have been C235, or even B115.

CIE inherited ten AEC railcars (600/1/4/5/8/9, 612/3/6/7) and ten BUT cars (704/6/8, 710/2/4/6, 904/6/8). At the preliminary stages of the carve-up, 702 and 902 were also to go to CIE (a 12:12 split of the 24 cars) but, because of the Derry Road traffic, for which the class was also intended, the Belfast men made a convincing case for a 14:10 split in favour of the UTA. CIE also got the last remaining railbus, No 2, and four articulated cars – C1, C2, E and G. Railcar C1 saw some employment on the truncated mail service to Clones and Cavan on the Irish North, until that ceased in 1959. Railbus No 2 and railcar C2 worked to Oldcastle, but again, that service closed in 1959. Railcar E saw no further use and was sold to the UTA, early in 1960, to provide spares for railcar D, which had gone north. Railcar F was still active on off-peak services to Howth for several years but, in 1963, it too was sold to the UTA.

The ten AEC cars remained active until the early 1970s. They were standard with the main CIE railcar fleet built in 1952-54, but disappeared before the CIE-built examples.

The BUT cars were less fortunate. They were regarded as non-standard by CIE, as there were only ten of them, compared to a total of 76 AEC cars. To make things worse, No 908 was destroyed when the CIE 'Enterprise' caught fire at Finaghy, on 28 January 1960, leaving only two of the 'big cars'. Nevertheless, the BUT cars worked the CIE 'Enterprise' until 1961, when it became a GM locomotive-hauled set.

In 1959, some BUT cars were transferred to the Westland Row-Wexford service, where they were, allegedly, trashed mercilessly. By the mid 1960s they were in a poor state mechanically, whereas the UTA ones were still working the 'Enterprise'. They lay out of use for several years before scrapping, though, in 1974, Nos 712 and 714 were renovated with the intention of running them on light services which could have single car operation. However, despite this work, I don't think they ran again in revenue earning service.

The Ulster Transport Authority

For those not familiar with the UTA, I should explain briefly that the UTA was a nationalised transport undertaking, set up in 1948 to operate the road services of the Northern Ireland Road Transport Board and the railway lines owned by the BCDR and LMS (NCC). It was really a forerunner of Translink. By October 1958, when the UTA took over the northern half of the GNR, most UTA railway services which remained open, had been dieselised, or were in process of dieselisation. The last BCDR steam locomotives had gone in 1956 and, on 1 October 1958, the UTA had only 41 ex-NCC steam engines and three diesel shunters. The core of the NCC fleet consisted of modern LMS types, namely eighteen WT class 2-6-4Ts ('Jeeps') and eleven W class 2-6-0s ('Moguls'). There were also eight surviving U2 class 4-4-0s (with boilers identical to the LMS 2P class), three V class 0-6-0s (boilers as on the Fowler 2-6-2Ts) and one 0-6-0T(ex-LMS 'Jinty' No 7553).

Integrating the GNR fleet

Like CIE, the UTA inherited 83 GNR steam locomotives. At one stroke, this trebled the size of the UTA steam locomotive fleet to 124 locomotives. Given that the principal passenger diagrams could be operated by AEC and BUT diesel trains, it was reckoned in 1958 that there was work for only about fifty steam engines on the former GNR lines. With new MPD railcars under construction at York Road, it would also be possible to transfer many of the more modern UTA engines to the Great Northern.

When the GNR stock was surveyed, it was decided to immediately scrap 4-4-0 Nos 46, 76, 107, 121, 125 and 157, 4-4-2T Nos 21 and 69, 0-6-0 Nos 108, 109, 119, 160 and 162 and 0-6-4T No 22. All these had a large red 'X' painted on them and were sold for scrap on 5 August 1959.

This left 69 GNR locomotives, of which 34 were taken into capital stock. All of these were of the more modern types, basically 4-4-0s of the S, S2, U and VS classes; 0-6-0s of the SG, SG2, SG3 and UG classes and the RT 0-6-4Ts. Conspicuously, the V class Compounds and the T1/T2 4-4-2Ts were not taken into capital stock.

In May 1959, mainly as a result of pressure from Harold Houston of York Road, it was decided to completely renumber all the carriage and railcar stock (including former NCC and BCDR vehicles) into a single integrated list. The ex-GNR locomotives regarded as capital stock, were integrated into the UTA list, occupying the numbers 23-25 (0-6-4Ts), 30-49 (0-6-0s) and 58-67 (4-4-0s). In addition, two ex-SLNCR 0-6-4Ts were purchased by the UTA, becoming Nos 26 and 27, and diesel 28 retained its old

Above: The three surviving RT 0-6-4Ts became UTA Nos 23-25 and continued to shunt at Maysfields, Belfast until 1961. Here No 23 drifts down towards Ballymacarret Junction with a train of empty tank wagons for Sydenham. This bit of line is now a very busy double-track section of NIR, but all the buildings have disappeared under the M3.

Kelland Collection 10

BCDR number yet again!

The ex-GNR men at Belfast, like the Topley brothers, did not see the need for any renumbering and would have preferred to keep the GNR numbers on engines and carriages alike. However, Mr Houston was not to be dissuaded and the renumbering went ahead. Much of it was done using spare GNR transfers, until such times as the engines were overhauled at York Road. Certainly, it made a lot of sense for the carriage stock. Up to then, numbers were all over the place and the system inaugurated by Mr Houston became the basis of present day NIR/Translink fleet numbers.

The remaining 35 ex-GNR locomotives had a small 'x' added to their existing GNR numbers, indicating that they were to be scrapped when their mileage had run out. They formed a kind of duplicate list, as some numbers replicated engines in the capital list. The engines in this list were: 4-4-0 Nos 42, 43, 50, 74, 83, 86, 87, 122, 127, 135 and 156; 4-4-2T Nos 2, 4, 5, 30, 64, 66, 142, 185, 186, 187 and 189; 0-6-0 Nos 9, 10, 11, 32, 39, 56, 100-103, 111, 151 and 165.

GNR locomotives under the UTA

I spent a couple of months in early 1959 at Musgrave Park Hospital, Balmoral, close to the main line out of Belfast. This gave me the chance to observe this interesting period at first hand. For most of that time, there was no visual indication that the GNR was no more. The locomotives were still in blue (or GNR black) and the carriages in mahogany scrumble. Diesel trains still had the lovely Oxford blue and cream scheme. However, in May 1959, the first carriage appeared in UTA Brunswick green. Unable to read a number from the ward, we young lads concluded that it was a UTA coach transferred. I have since discovered that it was, actually, brake third No 369, renumbered 470N.

Up until 1958, the Belfast-shedded VS 4-4-0s had been 206 and 209. In October 1958, of the two allocated to the UTA, No 208 was being run-in after overhaul and No 210 was in Dundalk Works. Until they emerged, the brunt of the main line work was borne by Compounds 83, 86 and 87. Nos 208 and 210 never looked right as UTA 58 and 59. The lovely number plates were removed and the transfers were

applied to the scars left on the cab sides and the front buffer beam. Three of the SG3 class were also in good shape – Nos 7 (UTA 31), 13 (32) and 40 (34) were just after overhaul and No 49 (36) was in the Works. After this engine left the Works, Dundalk did not repair any other engines for the UTA.

In contrast to CIE, the UTA did not overhaul any GNR locomotives at all in 1959, preferring to wait until the surplus of engines had worked down a bit. However, several locomotives were transferred from the NCC – W class 2-6-0 Nos 91, 95 and 97 and 2-6-4Ts 53 and 56. These transfers proved surprisingly popular on the GN section and the NCC engines soon began to take over the Dublin passenger turns from the VS 4-4-0s, particularly the 14.30 (later 14.15) Up and 8.15 Down, though the 12 noon was still often a VS rostered job.

In 1960, York Road began to outshop former GNR steam regularly. Early in the year, SG3 Nos 33, 35 and UG 48 appeared in UTA lined black. The straw and red lining on this livery was much more elaborate than on GNR black and looked really well when freshly applied (see page 157 lower). Unfortunately, standards of cleaning were not what they once were, so the fresh look didn't last long. Two more UGs, Nos 45 and 49 followed before the end of the year and, of course, there were more transfers of NCC 'Jeeps' and 'Moguls' to the Great Northern.

There was also a further cull of ex-GNR steam in 1960. This comprised 4-4-0 Nos 42x, 43x, 50x, 83x, 87x, 122x, 127x and 156x; 4-4-2T Nos 2x, 4x, 64x, 66x, 142x, 185x, 186x and 189x and 0-6-0 Nos 9x, 11x, 32x, 39x, 56x, 101x, 102x and 103x, reducing the ex-GNR stock to 45 locomotives. As mentioned in Chapter 8, the last PPs 4-4-0 was actually No 74x. It masqueraded as No 42x for three years because Newry shed had switched the numbers, in 1960, to avoid 74 being scrapped!

Up to 1961, all eleven blue 4-4-0s had retained their GNR livery but, in that year, Nos 62 *Lugnaquilla* and 63 *Carrantuohill* were overhauled and received the black livery, followed by No 60 *Slieve Donard* in the summer. More 0-6-0s were also put through York Road in 1961 – Nos 32, 36, 37,

38 and 40. The year 1961 also saw the demise of another ten GNR locomotives in the UTA fleet. These included 86x, the last UTA Compound, 0-6-0s 100x, 151x and 165x and 4-4-2T 30x (leaving only two of this type).

However, the other five were from the capital stock, showing that even these were not immune from the cutter's torch. SG3 No 30 was not a total surprise. This was the only UTA SG3 not to have received a new boiler in the 1950s. SG2 0-6-0 Nos 39 and 42 were, probably, worth overhauling but there were now enough 'Moguls' to handle much of the goods traffic. The scrapping of blue U class 4-4-0 Nos 64 and 65 was a disappointment, but they were over forty-five years old.

The Derry Road

The general pattern of steam operations on the UTA portion of the Great Northern should be explained. Firstly, all the freight traffic was steam hauled and was still very heavy in the early 1960s. Much of the traffic originated south of the border and was destined for Belfast or Londonderry. Portadown, where I lived, was used as a staging post for freight. Here, trains were remarshalled, wagons from the Derry Road being redirected to Belfast or Dublin-bound trains. Shunting went on all day or night and in those days, my waking hours (and usually my sleeping hours as well!), were punctuated by the sounds of steam at work.

Each night there were two heavy goods trains for Derry and one for Omagh. These met their opposing workings en-route and the Derry and Portadown crews swopped trains at Pomeroy. The two engines which were worked up to Derry each night stayed there until the following evening and then came back. During their stop-over at Derry, one put in some passenger turns and the other shunted at Strabane.

Similarly, the engine on the Omagh goods stayed all day in Omagh and shunted the Markets Branch thrice daily. Another engine was used for the pick-up goods from Portadown to Dungannon and covered the Coalisland goods-only branch. Thus, a minimum of seven engines were needed each day for Derry Road goods rosters. The preferred locomotives for these trains were the 'Big Ds', as the SG3

class was called. However, there were not enough of them to cover the rosters, so ex-NCC 2-6-0s were regularly employed. These were rough engines and hadn't the same power (they counted as GNR power class C) but, eventually, there were up to five of them on the GN at any one time – drawn from Nos 91, 93, 94, 97, 98, 99 and 104. 'Jeeps' were not used on these trains, at least not until late 1964. This was because the crews wanted maximum braking power on these long, largely un-fitted, trains over the steep banks on the Derry Road.

Main line steam

On the Portadown-Dundalk section the pattern was different. Here freight generally moved in daylight, as it was a double track route. The rostering arrangements involved a careful integration of passenger and freight diagrams so that the ex-NCC engines, particularly the efficient and free running 2-6-4Ts, were the favoured motive power. Thus the engines working express passenger trains from Belfast came off at Dundalk and might return on a Down goods. There were also a lot of special workings through to Dublin, especially in the summer and, in the winter, for international rugby specials. These were the preserve of the big VS class 4-4-0s, and of Compound No 86 up to 1961.

Goods trains from Portadown to Belfast, and in the reverse direction, were worked by anything that was available. Often passenger 4-4-0s, which had worked commuter trains, like the heavy 8.00 Down to Belfast, fitted in a goods run to Portadown and got back in time for the crowded 17.35 Up.

Each day, in the 1963-65 period, a Portadown engine (usually a UG) worked a goods to Newry and then stayed on

the branch all day, filling in with passenger turns to Goraghwood and Warrenpoint, time about with the local articulated railcar (104 or 105). However, in the early 1960s, Newry had its own allocation, usually two PPs and an 0-6-0. Nos 42x, 50x and 74x all worked there in their last days. Sometimes Newry also had one of the last Glover tanks, 5x or 187x, before they became unfit for anything but shunting.

Effectively, the old pattern of allocating engines to specific sheds was abandoned in the 1960s. All engines were based at Portadown or Adelaide. This meant that Newry, Omagh and Londonderry had no allocation as such, and all repairs were concentrated at Adelaide, where the sheer legs allowed all but the heaviest work to be carried out. Portadown was the favourite depot for 'disposing' of engines. Every locomotive visited the shed there at least once fortnightly, for boiler wash-out purposes and at weekends the shed was full. I spent many a happy Saturday here in my school days, sneaking down the path from West Street to the shed and enjoying the glow of Shedmaster Ted Willis' fire as we 'talked engines'.

Other steam turns

As far as passenger work was concerned, the diesel railcars covered most of the diagrams during the day. However, there were a number of regular steam passenger trains rostered, other than the main line ones. Most were local runs from Portadown or Lisburn to Belfast, but on Saturdays heavy patronage of some services on the Derry Road led to extra steam trains being diagrammed. Summer Sundays brought heavy excursion trains to Warrenpoint, on Carlingford Lough. These were nearly always worked by GNR 4-4-0s and were popular with enthusiasts. Gradually, the short local steam trains on the Derry Road were removed from the timetable and each year less steam was required.

Nevertheless, there was always seasonal traffic which required steam. In the summer, there was a constant procession of excursion trains from GNR stations like Dungannon, Portadown and Lurgan, to the seaside, mainly to Warrenpoint, Bangor and Portrush. The last two involved GNR engines working over 'foreign' metals and usually brought a U or an S class 4-4-0. Then there were football specials, especially if Portadown was drawn against a Belfast team like Linfield or Glentoran and, of course, the specials connected with those particularly Ulster occasions like 'the Twelfth' or the 'Relief of Derry'. This traffic is now history, but in those days it required the maintenance of about six eight-bogie trains of excursion stock to cover it. All in all, the GNR section of the UTA was the last bastion of regular Irish steam, at least up to February 1965. Whilst there was some steam on the NCC, it was scarcer and virtually all 2-6-4Ts. Only the GNR offered variety.

Diesel traction 1959-65

The UTA inherited railcars A, C3, D and F, as well as ten AEC cars and fourteen of the new BUT cars. This gave it sufficient diesel traction to cover the principal services on each route and over 90% of passenger trains were diesel, even in 1959.

As part of the general renumbering of 1959, railcars A, C3, D and F became 101-104 respectively. The AEC cars (603/2/7/6, 611/0/5/4/9/8 in that order) became 111-120. The twin cab BUT cars (701-3/5/7/9, 711/3/5) became 121-129, and the single cab BUT cars (901-3/5/7) Nos 131-135. At first, all cars retained GNR Oxford blue and cream, with the UTA roundel and numbers replacing the GNR insignia.

The UTA made better use of its ex-GNR railcars than CIE. The pioneer car of 1932, No 101, was based at Londonderry and proved useful on local services to Strabane and Omagh. In the summer of 1961, it was re-engined and received UTA green livery. The Belfast Transport Museum intended to acquire it but, in 1963, it was damaged in a shunting accident at Londonderry and the bodywork was badly damaged. It was then sold to the contractor lifting the Clonsilla Junction-Navan line for CIE in 1964, and he later used it on the Derry line, when lifting it in 1966-67. The car which saw least use was No 102. It was never repainted and was scrapped in December 1961 at Queen's Quay, having lain derelict at Adelaide for two years.

The bigger articulated cars were extensively used on the Warrenpoint branch, both 103 and 104 being based at Newry. The UTA also bought railcar E from CIE in January 1960, to be broken up as a source of spares for 103. Up to the Spring of 1961, 104 was the mainstay of the branch. Its roster included an afternoon trip from Newry to Portadown and back and I have a vivid memory of standing on Platform 4 watching it depart from Platform 2 for Newry, its distinctive Gardner roar forcing all conversation to be suspended.

For a few months in mid-1961 neither car was serviceable and steam took over. However, Queens' Quay repaired both cars, 103 appearing first in June 1961, after a patch up job. No 104 got a full repaint and thorough overhaul and returned to Newry in December 1961. In 1962, 103 ceased to run, after breaking a driving axle. It was never in green and was scrapped in September 1963. Meanwhile, the UTA had purchased railcar G from CIE in March 1962. After overhaul, it was repainted in UTA colours, as No 105, and went into service at Newry in July 1963.

The ex-GNR multiple-unit railcars were the mainstay of passenger services on the Great Northern section of the UTA after 1958. The service required an eight-car BUT set, using dining car 552, for the 'Enterprise'. Two six-car BUT sets, using buffet cars 551 and 553, were on the principal Derry Road expresses. The remaining BUT cars made up one or two four-car sets for Portadown locals. There were five three-car AEC sets. Two formed the backbone of the Belfast-Newry-Warrenpoint service and another made two round trips to Omagh. The fifth was used on Lisburn or Portadown locals, as available.

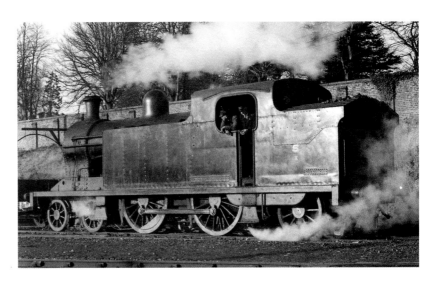

In addition, the UTA transferred its own AEC set (6-528-7) to the Great Northern in December 1959, for local services to Lisburn. The diesel fleet remained in GNR colours until 1960. In that year, following an accident to permanent way men, the front of all railcars was painted with a high visibility yellow and black wasp pattern (see opposite). In the early Autumn of 1960, car No 121 appeared in green and, within a year, most BUT cars had been repainted. The AEC cars followed in 1961-62. In 1962 the AEC cars were recabled so that six-car sets could operate. Around the same time, all ex-GNR cars were given roof level exhausts.

Developments with steam traction in 1962-64

By the time 1962 dawned, the UTA green carriage livery was beginning to dominate and, by that summer, only some excursion stock still sported GNR mahogany (or 'teak' as some mistakenly called it). U class 4-4-0 Nos 66 *Meath*, 67 *Louth* and 68 *Down* all visited York Road in the course of the year and lost their blue livery but, at least, they were alive and well. Although No 58 *Lagan* visited York Road in March, it was not repainted and no Compound or VS locomotive ever received UTA black. Incidentally, to get to York Road, No 58 had to traverse the lightly laid Knockmore Junction to Antrim branch and the Crumlin Viaduct, both prohibited to it in GNR days, due to its axle load!

Other locomotives to get the UTA treatment in 1962 were Nos 43, 44 and 47, in the spring, and 34 in November. There were now about eight ex-NCC 'Jeeps' on the Northern, as well as the 'Moguls', so there was plenty of variety. No locomotives at all were scrapped in 1962, and Nos 5x, 10x, 74x, 111x, 135x and 187x still soldiered on, mostly on shunting or ballast work, in the case of the tanks and 0-6-0s.

By 1963, some gaps were beginning to appear in the ranks. No 59 *Erne* was unfit for Dublin runs and No 61 *Galteemore*, the last blue S class on the UTA, was unfit for

much either. Old Nos 74x and 135x, the last representatives of the PPs and Qs classes, were scrapped in July, along with No 59, 0-6-0s Nos 41, 46 and 111x and all three RT 0-6-4Ts.

Whilst this reduced the ranks of ex-GNR locomotives to twenty-six and left only Nos 58 and 61 in blue livery, there was something to delight enthusiasts in June. CIE steam had ended that Spring and the UTA purchased four of the CIE locomotives – S class Nos 170, 171 and 174 and VS class No 207 – all still in blue livery. Their nameplates had been removed at Dundalk, before they came north, but someone at Adelaide made replica plates out of wood for *Boyne*.

None of the ex-CIE engines was renumbered and, for a time, something of the old GNR atmosphere returned. Nevertheless, with the publication of the Benson Report, recommending the end of rail freight and the closure of the Warrenpoint and Coalisland branches and the Derry Road, a 'Sword of Damocles' hung over the UTA and we sensed that the end of steam was nigh. Only four GNR engines went through the Works in 1963, Nos 35, 33, 48 and 49. Poor old No 48 emerged with a pink front buffer beam and no number – the transfers had run out!

In February 1964, I decided to start train photography in my own right, commencing at Portadown, with shots of Nos 33 and 38 on station pilot duty. Had I known where to look, I might just have got pictures of No 61, not to mention 10x, the last PG 0-6-0, and the last two 4-4-2Ts, 5x and 187x. All were scrapped the following month. However, like most enthusiasts, I made the best of what was there, even though my efforts would not merit publication! No GNR locomotives received a full shopping in 1964. York Road was busy renewing the fireboxes on the 2-6-4Ts. However, Nos 34, 36, 47, 170, 171 and 174 received minor attention.

The end of GNR steam, 1965-67

The end came in early 1965. The Warrenpoint branch closed in January and, after a stay of execution, the Derry Road closed on 14 February. For the death throes, several more NCC 2-6-4Ts had to be drafted in to keep services running. Eleven, in total, were on the GNR, though the only remaining 'Mogul' was No 97. Of the twenty-six ex-GNR

locomotives still on the books, several were out of traffic and, in May 1965, all were scrapped, except for the four purchased from CIE, and three 0-6-0s. Of these, Nos 48 and 49 were retained for the last season of the Bangor excursion traffic, and No 37 with a view to using it on the Derry line lifting train. Portadown shed closed in November 1965 and all remaining steam was concentrated at Adelaide.

In the summer of 1965, I was having another session of surgery at Musgrave Park Hospital and saw what little steam there was. Most specials were worked by 2-6-4Ts, but UG Nos 48 and 49 handled all the Bangor traffic. No 49 worked the last

special to Bangor on 28 July 1965, though both 48 and 49 were employed on a spate of ballast workings to the Bangor line in July and August, before the Belfast Central line was finally severed. This line remained closed until NIR days.

The Twelfth brought out five 2-6-4Ts and VS No 207. Thereafter, the main entertainment was the 9.00 to Dublin, a shoppers' special which ran most days and was nearly always hauled by No 207 *Boyne*, the last GNR three-cylinder VS class 4-4-0s. If there were two specials to Dublin, it was *Boyne* and a 2-6-4T. That July, I used to go out of the ward in my wheelchair, in the late evening, to see *Boyne* returning from Dublin, an unforgettable sight, soon to be gone forever. My notes record her as running on July 10th, 12th, 15th and 16th, at least.

The last train worked by *Boyne* was the inaugural RPSI railtour on 11 September, when it double-headed No 171 to Portadown.

At the end of 1965, Nos 170, 174 and 207 were scrapped, leaving only Nos 37, 48 and 49 at Adelaide to carry the banner for GNR steam. For a short time in 1966, V class 4-4-0 No 85 *Merlin* was stored at Adelaide, having arrived

from Dundalk August. Also there, was S class 4-4-0 No 171 *Slieve Gullion*, which passed to the RPSI on 1 January 1966. No 37 was reputedly steamed from time to time, but I never saw her anything but dead.

During 1966, Adelaide had about four 2-6-4Ts, as well as the 0-6-0s, the former being adequate for specials to Dublin and Portrush and occasional diesel failures. However, the GNR spirit was not entirely dead and the Adelaide men generally steamed a UG for station pilot duties at Great Victoria Street. In July 1966, UG No 48 was dispatched to York Road to shunt for a couple of weeks, during a phase of engine shortage, caused by MPD diesel failures. It also, reputedly, worked the 15.55 Larne perishable on 16 July.

No 49 worked to Ardee and Kingscourt, on 14 May, on another RPSI Special, getting a special clean-up for the occasion (see opposite). The last occasion that a GNR locomotive hauled a *service* train on the GNR, was on Thursday 29 September 1966 when, due to the failure of an AEC diesel set, No 49 was taken off station pilot duty to cover the 17.18 and 18.20 locals to Lisburn. In October 1966, a 2-6-4T worked the 'Last Steam to Dublin', after

Above: One of the last occasions that a GNR locomotive hauled a passenger train (other than in preservation) was this run by UG 0-6-0 No 49 (149) on an RPSI special up the Navan-Kingscourt line on 14 May 1966. No 49 is seen here at Nobber.

S C Nash

which Adelaide shed closed for ever. Most of it is now buried under the Adelaide Industrial Estate.

The NCC tanks returned to York Road for further service, and Nos 37 and 49 were stored for two years, in the open, at Grosvenor Road goods yard. No 49 was, apparently, steamed on 27 January 1967, in a week when she did 593 miles.

In July 1967, No 48 was sent round to York Road, for trial as a relief engine to the York Road pilot, 0-6-4T No 27 *Lough Erne*. It was steamed on 6 July, but was too far gone to be used and this was the last recorded steaming of a GNR engine, other than in preservation. With that, the penultimate chapter in the story of GNR steam came to an end. There was still, of course, the preservation chapter to be written!

Diesel traction after 1965

After the closure of the Warrenpoint branch, the Gardner railcars saw no further service. In December 1965, No 104 was purchased by the contractor who lifted the Derry Road in 1966-67, and was used to transport his workmen. After the closure of Adelaide, No 105 lay derelict at Grosvenor Road goods yard, alongside 0-6-0 Nos 37 and 49, and was cut up in 1968.

In June 1965, the UTA 'Enterprise' set was refurbished and repainted in blue and white, as part of a policy of introducing 'regional' liveries. The blue aped the GNR livery but was a much lighter shade of blue and the GNR cream was now white. This set did two round trips daily to Dublin, in contrast to the previous one. Over the next eighteen months, BUT cars 121-123, 127, 128, 131, 134 and AEC cars 111, 115, 117 and 118 appeared in this livery.

In early 1967, as part of the preparation for creating Northern Ireland Railways, the livery on all regions was standardised as white upper panels and red lower. Even at this stage, virtually all trains on the Belfast-Dundalk line were using former GNR diesel stock, the only exceptions being the CIE trains and a few UTA MPD railcars. In the winter, one CIE set and one UTA set handled all Belfast-Dublin traffic.

By the time NIR officially took over in April 1968, the railcars were in a variety of colours – UTA green, UTA blue and cream, and NIR red and white. Some AEC sets had all three liveries! However, by 1970 all sets were in the new NIR colours. The only car not repainted was 111, which remained cream and blue until scrapped.

Until 1974, NIR remained dependent on the aging ex-GNR cars to maintain its Belfast-Portadown service. Only the 'Enterprise' got new stock, in the shape of a brand new locomotive-hauled train using new Hunslet Bo-Bos 101-103 and BR-designed Mk 2 stock. By the time the AECs were scrapped in 1973, they were 23 years old. The BUTs were also worn out, having run up enormous mileages. The arrival of the NIR '80 class' diesel-electric trains in 1974 allowed their withdrawal as well. All were scrapped in 1975.

Thus, as late as 1974, almost a century after the company was formed, it was still possible to travel behind GNR motive power. This was a tribute to the durability of the company.

Chapter 12
GNR(I) Tenders

Up to now, little has been written about GNR tenders. The main sources of information on the subject are the Dundalk Tender Drawings book, which was compiled in 1938, and a typed description of GNR tender types. This was probably written by R N Clements, in consultation with H E Wilson, the last Mechanical Engineer of the GNR. It was based on official orders, the drawing book and Mr Wilson's own experience during his work on the GNR. This document, in turn, was used, in summary form, by R M Arnold on page 136 of his *The Golden Years of the GNR* Vol I (Belfast 1976).

In compiling Chapter 12, I have used R N Clements' description, and the drawing book, but have also studied Mr Clements' transcripts of company minute books and manufacturers' order books, as well as hundreds of photographs, to extend knowledge of the subject even further back, into the pre-1876 period.

Whilst to many readers, tenders may not be very interesting, a knowledge of the different types is very useful in helping to date photographs and I have commented on them in quite a few of the captions. Unfortunately, many drawings of early locomotives omit the tender, no doubt regarding the tender as little more than a four or six-wheeled truck, which is not really part of the locomotive! However, many early locomotives had no engine brakes whatsoever so, as well as carrying the coal (or coke) and water, tenders also often acted as the only braking system a steam locomotive had.

Early tenders were very small, with only 700-800 gallons capacity, and had four wheels. In the mid-1840s, 1000 gallon tenders with six wheels became the standard, gradually increasing in capacity to 1100, 1200 and, by 1870, 1500 gallons. Coal capacity rose from 1 ton in 1839 to 2 tons by 1870. If the small size of these tenders is surprising, bear in mind that, in the mid-nineteenth century, trains made lengthy stops at stations and there was ample time to take water and coal. As far as I can see, all tenders of the GNR constituent companies, and of the GNR itself up to 1882, had narrow tanks, with the springs placed above the running plate. Tenders to this design are sometimes referred to as 'breadcart tenders'. One inherent danger with narrow tenders, was the possibility of the fireman accidentally stepping back from the cab and falling through the gap between the narrow tender sides and the wider cab side sheets. However, on the GNR, this was prevented by a strategically placed grab rail (as seen opposite).

All early tenders had the same basic shape of tank, with the top of the sides, and rear, curved outwards to form a slight coping. On the GNR, this basic shape remained standard until about 1902 and, despite its universality, is often described as the 'old Beyer type of tender'.

A UR specification for Sharp 0-4-2 No 3 (dated 12 October 1859) includes a detailed description of the tender and specifies a 'horseshoe tank'. This was a tank running around three sides of the tender with the coal in the centre. The fact that this was *specifically* requested would imply that some earlier tenders were of the two box configuration – coal at the front and water at the rear.

The main variation in early tender design was in the shape of the frames. I presume this is because each manufacturer (Sharp, Beyer, Neilson, etc) had its own design of frame, so that the shape varied depending on who the frames were ordered from, or who manufactured the tender.

Dublin and Drogheda Railway

There is not a lot of evidence about D&DR tenders. As far as I can discover, the only four-wheeled tender was an 850 gallon example, built for Sharp 0-4-2 No 1. The other early Sharps had 1000 gallon six-wheelers with a wheelbase of 5'3"+ 5'3". Nothing is known about the Grendon tenders, except that they were thought to be 1200 gallon capacity (but note the comments in the INWR paragraph below).

There is no reference in the minutes, or the order books, to tenders for the Sharps and Fairbairns of 1854-55. It is certain that most, if not all, of the eight Beyers built in 1858-64 used second-hand Sharp tenders. We also know that the two Sharp singles of 1863-64 came with 1400 gallon tenders.

The tenders for 2-4-0 No 12 (1871) and 0-6-0 No 5 (1872) were built in Dublin and, although there is no direct evidence for this in the minute books, it is likely that new tenders were built in Dublin to replace the old 1000 gallon Sharp tenders on the earlier Beyers. Certainly, the tender in the photo of 2-2-2 No 13 (page 21) bears a works plate 'GNR Works 1879 Dublin' and it is highly likely that the GNR tenders built in 1877-81 were essentially a D&DR design.

One other type of tender associated with the D&DR can be seen on 0-6-0 No 21A, shown opposite. This tender has sandwich frames, but the distinctive feature is the way that the mountings for the springs are attached to the outside of the frame, below footplate level. Examples of this type but with plate frames also appear (see 2-2-2 No 16 on the rear cover, and B class 0-6-0 No 65 on page 53).

Dublin and Belfast Junction

The D&BJR had fifteen Sharp tenders and five Beyer Peacock. We know from the Sharp order books, that Nos 1-14 had 1000 gallon tenders with 3'6" wheels, but 0-4-2 No 15 of 1857 had a slightly larger 1100 gallon tender. These tenders were probably similar to the early D&DR ones.

The five Beyer tenders were, probably, much larger. The last two were definitely 1500 gallon and those of 1866-68 (see photo at the top of page 25) were probably the same or slightly smaller. As there is no mention in the minutes, of tenders being built *by* the D&BJR, we may assume that these twenty were the only ones owned by the company.

Above: Dublin and Drogheda type tender, with outside springs, as built in the late 1870s by the GNR. These were 1500 gallon tenders, with an 11'6" wheelbase.

Real Photographs 88003

Irish North Western

The INWR obtained locomotives from a wide variety of builders, and its tenders probably were equally varied. Very little mention of tenders is made in the minutes and the evidence from official orders is patchy. We can probably assume that the Grendon tenders were similar to those on the D&DR engines, in which case they were, probably, 1200 gallon. An unusual tender appears behind Grendon 0-6-0 No 59A in the photo on page 29, and this may be a Grendon tender.

The Sharp singles of 1852-54 had 1000 gallon tenders and the 0-4-2s of 1858 had 1200 gallon 'horseshoe' tank tenders, all six-wheeled. The Beyer singles of 1859-61 had Beyer 1400 gallon tenders, although the one supplied for the first Beyer single did not arrive until April 1860 – a year after the locomotive! – so No 11 must have borrowed a tender from an engine out of service.

There is absolutely no documentary evidence on the tenders supplied for the Neilson 0-4-2s of 1861-63 or the Dübs engines of 1866-67. The photograph of Neilson No 102, on page 31, shows a tender with a short wheelbase and very shallow framing, so this could be of Neilson or Dübs origin. The first two E class 0-6-0s, built by Dübs in 1871-72, had 1500 gallon tenders carrying 2 tons of coal.

The tenders for Dundalk-built 2-4-0 Nos 30 and 31 were built by the INWR but no specification is known. The photograph of No 30 (as GNR 43), on page 36, shows it with a GNR-built tender. However, it is highly likely that Nos 30 and 31 had tenders built at Dundalk to the Dübs design. There is no record of a tender for the third member of the E class though, since it replaced a Grendon single, a spare tender was theoretically available. Unfortunately, INWR six-monthly reports show no evidence of other tenders being built at Dundalk.

The L&ER used mainly tank locomotives and the only tender engines were the three 1846 Longridge ones, the two second-hand Sharps and the Jones 2-4-0s of 1855. No evidence on any of these has survived, though it is likely that the Sharps came with their original four-wheeled tenders of 1841.

Ulster Railway tenders

All nine UR broad gauge tenders were four-wheeled. The only other four-wheeled tenders were those supplied with the three Sharp 0-4-2s of 1866, which were 1200 gallons. The standard (Irish) gauge Sharp engines of the 1840s had six-wheel, 1000 gallon tenders with a wheelbase of 5'3"+ 5'3", as had the goods engines of 1853. 0-4-2 No 16 of 1857 had a 1100 gallon tender but, from 2-2-2 No 17 onwards, 1500 gallon tenders seem to have been the norm, at least for Sharp orders.

Judging by the detailed specification for No 3, the famous UR rear toolbox became a feature of tenders built from 1860 on. This toolbox fitted transversely on the rear of the tender, behind the tank, and had a hinged lid. The UR also painted the engine number high up on the rear of the tender and since this practice continued into early GNR days, tenders cannot have been exchanged too often. Nevertheless, the photographic evidence for locomotives which survived into the 1890s, suggests that there were latterly two basic types of UR tender.

Type 1 – A Beyer Peacock design with large elongated cut outs in the frames between the axles and a smaller cut out just behind the footplate. These had a rear toolbox. Some of this design were also manufactured by the UR and GNR (Northern Division) using a variety of frames. These tenders appear to have had an 11'6" wheelbase with 1500 gallons of water and 2 tons of coal and appear regularly on 0-6-0 and 0-4-2 types (see page 50).

Type 2 – A slightly smaller design with long axle horns and the frames deep only at the front end. These have no rear tool box and, judging by the photographs, were largely used on the 2-4-0 types (see pages 45 and 46). Since 13 tenders were built at the UR Belfast Workshops between 1872 and 1881, I suspect that some of them were of this type.

Newry and Armagh

The N&AR had five tender locomotives, about which we do know a little. The Stephenson 0-6-0s (GNR 83 and 84) had four-wheel, 1200 gallon, tenders with an 8'0" wheelbase. The Vulcan 0-4-2s (GNR 81 and 82) had Avonside tenders, built in 1872. Since No 82 was converted to tender type, probably back in 1865, there is evidence that it used a tender hired from Grendons in 1866 and later returned. The Sharp-built 0-4-2 of 1878 had a standard Sharp 11'6" wheelbase tender of 1500 gallon capacity.

Neither the NW&RR nor the BCR had tender locomotives, apart from the 0-4-2 just referred to, which was bought by the BCR in 1880.

GNR tenders 1875-1881

In the period 1875-81, 19 locomotives were built for the Southern and Irish North Western Divisions and 9 for the Northern Division. Judging by the prices paid, and the absence of any mention of tenders in the official orders, these locomotives were all delivered as engine only (with the exception of two Northern Division 0-6-0s in 1879), and tenders for them were constructed by the GNR in Dublin or the Northern Division at Belfast. All of these had been scrapped before the Tender Drawing Book was compiled in 1938, so we do not know the building dates, running numbers, or even, for certain, capacity.

However, from the photographic evidence, we can conclude that the Dublin-built tenders represented a perpetuation of D&DR practice. These were 1500 gallon tenders, on an 11'6" wheelbase, carrying 2 tons of coal and weighing 20 tons. The Northern Division, naturally, continued UR practice, so those constructed in Belfast may have included some of the UR type 1, with rear toolbox. Since frameplates were ordered from the Yorkshire Engine Co (1876), Beyer Peacock (1877) and Dübs (1878) there was scope for variation in final appearance. As mentioned above, two tenders were built by Beyer Peacock in 1879 for the last two C class 0-6-0s and these were of 1540 gallon capacity, the rest being 1500 gallons.

All tenders of this era, regardless of origin, were of the outside spring type and this probably includes the tenders originally built for the H class 2-4-0s of 1880-81. Although Mr Clements quotes the B class as having 1550 gallon and the G class 2000 gallon tenders, I am certain that this refers to the tenders running with them around 1900. On 4 August 1880, Curry was authorised to build three new tenders and, on 21 February 1882, Park was authorised to build five at Dundalk. Probably these represented, respectively, the last of the old type and the first of the new.

Park's standard tenders 1883-1896

As explained in Chapter 6, James Park, in 1882, introduced Doncaster Stirling-type tenders, with the springs below the running plate on the inside of the frames, and the tank built to the full width of the frames. There was no change, however, to the traditional shape of tank. These tenders were fitted with builder's plates which had works numbers or, to be more correct, works letters. These read "Great Northern Railway JJ Makers 1892 Dundalk" or similar (JJ identifying the individual tender).

The first series of tenders (1883-88) were identified by the letters A-Z. The second series bore AA-ZZ and were built in 1888-96. From then on, tender works plates carried a sequential works number followed by the tender class (eg 56B, 127D2). Since these numbers commenced at 53, we must conclude that 1-26 was taken as representing A-Z and 27-52 as representing AA-ZZ. This means that 53 tenders (A-Z, AA-ZZ, 53A) were built at Dundalk in 1883-96, to Park designs, plus four by Beyer Peacock. The Dundalk builder's plates were attached to the frame, just above the centre axle box. It was much later that tenders were given 'running numbers', carried on a separate plate.

In the Park era, four different capacities of tender were produced – 1550, 1700, 2000 and 2400 gallons. The 1550 gallon type had an 11'6" wheelbase, and differed from the others in not having adjustable springs. The others had a standard 12'0" wheelbase and adjustable springs. The 1550 and 1700 gallon sizes had 6'6" wide tanks (inside measurement) whilst the 2000, 2400, and later B type 2500 gallon tenders, had 6'8" tanks. They looked very similar externally, and the only way the four sizes can be distinguished in photographs is by looking at the position of the vertical handrail beside the cab.

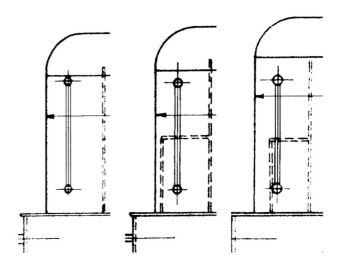

Fig 65: The position of the front handrails helps to distinguish the different types of Stirling tender. From left to right we have the 1550 gallon, 1700 gallon and 2000 gallon types.

Examples of each type survived until 1938, so we know the numbers and dates of some, but not all. Since only 51 new tender locomotives were constructed in this period (not counting the two A class 0-6-0s of 1882), but 57 tenders, then six tenders must have been built to replace earlier ones. Of the total of 57 tenders built, only five were 2000 gallon and four 2400 gallon, so the 1550 and 1700 gallon types must have had 48 examples between them. In 1938, there were only 3 x 1550 gallon and 12 x 1700 gallon surviving.

Left: H class 2-4-0 No 87 at Enniskillen on 12 September 1898. The tender is a 1700 gallon standard type with inside springs to Diagram 9, probably built in 1883-84.

Ken Nunn Collection H252

Below left: A 2400 gallon tender to diagram 6. This is tender No 'JJ' built at Dundalk in 1892 and used for the bogie single *Victoria*. The only difference between this and the 2000 gallon type was a 400 gallon well-tank between the frames.

J D FitzGerald collection

Below right: A B1 tender fitted with plated over coal rails and with staff collecting apparatus for the Derry road. In this view, the net has been lowered.

L J Watson (WG203)

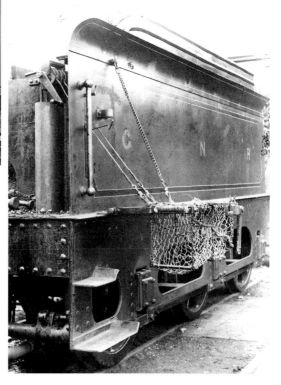

1550 gallon 1884 (diagram 10)

The diagram numbers referred to in this section are from the GNR tender diagram book of 1938. The 1550 gallon tender had an 11'6" wheelbase and was 19'6¼" overall length. It was basically a Stirling version of the old outside sprung tenders of the 1870s. In 1938 there were only three survivors, two dated 1890 and one 1894. Clearly, at one time this was a much more numerous type, with examples built in the 1880s. L J Watson regarded this as the standard type for G and J class passenger engines, and A, AL, B and D 0-6-0s. However, it is likely that the 1700 gallon type were used on the Js. Those still identified with plates in 1938 were EE (1890) and PP (1894)

1700 gallon diagram 9 (1883) and 8 (1891)

These were the earliest of the 'Stirling type', with a 12'0" wheelbase and a length of 20'6" over buffers. Five to Diagram 9 survived in 1938. Of these, three were dated 1883 and two 1884. Two of the 1883 ones were lettered 'C' and 'D', so the other was probably 'A' or 'B'. The 1884 ones had no letters in 1938. Probably, this was the standard passenger tender until 1895 and was used on the H, J, JS and P classes.

Diagram 8 was identical except it had a slightly shallower frame and different design of axle box keep. Seven survived in 1938 – two by Beyer Peacock in 1892, plus Dundalk built MM (1892), QQ, RR, SS, and TT (all 1894). From photographic evidence, LL (probably 1892) was also of this type.

A Type, 2000 gallon 1895 (diagram 7)

Two tenders to this design were built in 1895 (WW and XX) and three in 1896 (YY, ZZ and 53A). The numbering of the latter indicates that Clifford regarded this as the A type and it was probably intended as a new standard goods and light passenger type. They had the same frame as the 1700 gallon, 2400 gallon and 2500 gallon types. The respective tank heights were 3'3" (1700), 3'6½" (2000), 3'6½" with a well tank (2400), 3'8½" with a well tank (2500).

2400 gallon 1892 (diagram 6)

This type differed from the 2000 tender, only in having a well-tank below footplate level, which held 400 gallons. They were identical to the later B1 type, except that the tanks were

2" lower. Two (JJ and KK) were built in 1892, for use with the JS class bogie singles on the 'Limited Mails'. It is just possible that this pair were originally 2000 gallon (and therefore A type), but were converted later by adding well tanks. Two more were built by Beyer Peacock in 1896, for the first two PPs. Beyer Peacock tenders did not carry works plates. Although R N Clements' description lists the latter pair as built in 1894, as listed in the Diagram book, it has been altered in the Diagram book to *1896*, probably indicating that 1894 was an error.

B1 Type, 2500 gallon 1897 (diagram 5)
This was the most numerous type of GNR tender and a total of 52 were built at Dundalk between 1897 and 1909. They were the last type to have the awkward inside spring arrangement and their works numbers were 53B-103B and 1C. After the introduction of the B2 type, they became known as B1.

There are a number of mysteries surrounding the works numbers. Firstly, why was there a 53A and a 53B? Does this mean that, after numbering 53A, it was discovered that only 52 had been built up to then and 53B was designed to correct a mistake? Secondly, no tender carried the number 101B. However, one tender had no works number, so this, very likely, was 101B. For comments on 1C, see C type below.

Until 1902, no GNR tenders had copings other than the traditional 19th century flared out top on the side and rear sheets. From 1902, tenders had two coal rails, extending to the back of the coal space (page 82), this being applied, retrospectively, to earlier tenders. From 1908, shallow coping plates replaced coal rails and again stopped level with the back of the coal space (page 91). Engines already fitted with coal rails now had them plated in (page 189, lower).

B2 Type, 2500 gallon 1910 (diagram 4)
The B2 type tender was identical to B1 except for having the more modern arrangement of outside springs below footplate level (page 93). The GNR was, I think, the last railway in the British Isles to build tenders with inside springs. Three (104B2-106B2) were built at Dundalk in 1910 and four (107B2-110B2) in 1911. These had the same shallow copings, as described for type B1.

Despite the introduction of the more modern B3 (1911) and B4 (1913) types, the B2 type continued to be constructed at Dundalk, with eleven more examples built in 1916-26. These had the more modern high coping, introduced with the B4 class in 1913, and their works numbers were 111B (1916), 112B2, 113B2 (1920), 114B2, 115B2 (1921), 116B2, 117B2 (1923), 118B2, 119B2 (1924), 120B2 (1925) and 121B2 (1926). These were clearly intended to be replacement tenders, as new locomotives in this period were delivered with manufacturer's tenders. In the 1930s, this later batch of tenders were converted into the B3 type.

B3 Type, 2500 gallon 1911 (diagram 3)
The B3 was the same as the B2, except that the tank, instead of forming only the back and sides of the bunker, was extended forward to form a sloped shovelling plate rising to 18" high. This was more convenient for firemen than the older bunkers in the B1, B2 and earlier types, which were at floor level. Another change was that the low coping extended to the rear of the tender, a change soon extended to the B2 type. Seven tenders were built to this pattern in 1911, six by Nasmyth Wilson (Works Nos 433, 435-438, 448) and one by Beyer Peacock (page 96).

Four of the Nasmyth Wilson tenders were fitted with Drummond feed water heaters for running with the Phoenix superheater engines (see Chapter 7). It is possible that these replaced all or part of the well tanks. As mentioned above, eleven B2 tenders were later altered to the B3 type, making seven of the former and eighteen of the later. Once all tenders had the standard higher coping, it became impossible to distinguish B2 and B3 externally.

Running numbers for GNR tenders
There is no documentary evidence as to when the tender stock received fleet (or running) numbers. However, I agree with R N Clements' conjecture that the original numbers corresponded to the numbers of the engines they were paired with. By analysing the numbers, I have concluded that the fleet numbers were applied in 1912 and, probably, were a Glover innovation. They even include numbers of duplicate engines (eg 24D, 39D). Certainly, the numbers would make sense if related to the likely distribution of tenders that year. The B1 type were mainly on the P, PP, Q, QL, PG and LQG types. The B2 and B3 types were on a variety of passenger classes and the 1911 NQGs.

The only exception to this numbering is that several tenders had tank engine numbers. This can be simply explained. Since the highest tender number was 152, then the tenders for 153-165 must have been allocated numbers used by tank engines. Since GNR tenders were regularly moved from engine to engine, and a stock of spares maintained, it did not take long for tender numbers to bear no relationship whatsoever to the numbers of the engines with which they were paired.

B4 Type, 2500 gallon 1913 (diagram 2)
This type was introduced with the S and SG classes in 1913. The only change from type B3 was that they were fitted with a new design of high coping, but the coping was designed as an integral part of the tender rather than an add on. Although the overall dimensions were as before, the side of the tender was 5½" shorter than B1-B3, allowing room for a hand pillar running from footplate to coping, in place of the external grab-rail used before (page 112). This enables the enthusiast to distinguish them from the B2/B3 type.

Ten were built by Beyer Peacock in 1913 and thirteen more in 1915, for the S2, SG2 and U classes. In 1924,

Nasmyth Wilson built five more for the later batch of SG2s (Works Nos 1428-32).

C Type

The only clue to the absence of a C type is that one of the 1908 B1 tenders was numbered '1C'. It is possible that this tender was built as a prototype for a new tender type, using the old inside spring chassis. Perhaps, as Mr Clements suggests, it was built with a larger tank and then later altered to a standard B1. Mr Clements also associated this tender with the missing works number 101 but, as I said above, I am inclined to the view that tender 125 (fleet number) had no works plate and was very likely the missing 101, and thus probably built in 1909.

D Type

This was never built, but was designed in December 1911 for fitting to the proposed S class. It was to have been a 3500 gallon tender, but with a 13'6" wheelbase and 7'0" wide tanks instead of the standard 6'8". In contrast to the eventual D1 type, it would have retained a slight outward flare at the top of the sides. The plan for a 3500 gallon tender was dropped at this stage, possibly because it was believed that superheated engines would be easier on water, and that 2500 gallon tenders would suffice.

D1 Type, 3500 gallon 1920 (diagram 1)

The first 3500 gallon tenders were built by Beyer Peacock for the SG3 class 0-6-0s in 1920-21 (page 116). This type had a 13'0" wheelbase and an overall length of 21'11" including buffers. The D1 tender was more modern in appearance than the standard 2500 gallon types. They were slab-sided, though the side sheet had a double concave downwards curve at the cab end and a single one at the rear, basically the shape of the B4 without being flared out. The tank was 7'4" wide and 4'6" high, with the usual well tank. These tenders held 5 tons of coal and weighed 38½ tons in working order. Fifteen of this type were built, with running numbers 3-8,

10, 12, 14-17, 19, 21 and 22. Several of these tenders were later transferred to V class Compounds and, still later, had their side sheets extended upwards to form an inwardly curving coping. This increased the coal capacity, and the weight went up to 39½ tons. The altered tenders were Nos 3, 21 and 22.

Others were transferred to the Qs class 4-4-0s and to the S class, but these did not receive copings. In 1958, No 19 was running with V class 4-4-0 No 85 *Merlin*. No 7 later became a unique tender. It was attached to S2 4-4-0 No 190 and, in 1946-47 the downwards sweep at the rear was removed to increase coal capacity for use on the non-stop 'Enterprise' trials. Neither the D1 nor the D2 type was allowed across the Boyne Viaduct at Drogheda before 1932. The present tender of preserved S class 4-4-0 No 171 *Slieve Gullion* is No 12 of this type.

D2 Type, 3500 gallon 1928 (diagram 1)

There was really no difference between the D1 and the D2, except that the D2 type was built at Dundalk. The common notion that the flared top type were D2 is a fallacy. The first ten D2s were built at Dundalk in 1928-32, with works numbers 122-131, as part of a replacement programme for older tenders. The running numbers (not in

Above right: E type 2500 gallon tender, with roller bearings, as provided for the U and UG classes of 1948. This example is on U class No 201 *Meath* on 26 January 1948.

Duffner L609

Right: F type 4000 gallon, roller bearing tender, as running on No 207 *Boyne* in September 1959. Only five of this type were built, for the VS class of 1948. Compound No 85 *Merlin*.used one in CIE days.

D Anderson

the same order) were 1, 2, 9, 11, 13, 18, 20, 33, 36 and 39. Of this batch, Nos 33 and 39 went to the Compounds and, after 1935, received the high coping. In 1958, No 13 was the tender attached to the, now-preserved, No 171 *Slieve Gullion*.

A further five were built in 1937, for the UG 0-6-0s of that year. These too had the high coping. They had works numbers 132-136 and running numbers 23-27. In 1958, these five were running with engines Nos 135 (Qs), 112 (NQGs), 172 (S), 174 (S) and 125 (Qs), respectively.

D3 Type

This was never built. It was basically a variation on D2 with the frame 6'2" apart instead of 6'4". It exists only as an undated specification signed by G B Howden, perhaps in case the UG tenders were contracted out.

E Type, 2500 gallon 1948

Two new modern designs of tender were introduced in 1948, and would have been widely multiplied, had it not been for the demise of steam in the 1950s. In appearance, they resembled the Stanier LMS types, introduced in the 1930s, with very high sides which dropped down almost to tank level at the rear and had a short, but deep, down sweep at the front. They also had modern Hoffmann roller bearing axleboxes. Both held 6 tons of coal and all were built by Beyer Peacock. The E type were 22'0" long and had a 12'0" wheelbase. Ten were built in 1948 for the new U class 4-4-0s and UG class 0-6-0s of that year. Nos 37, 40-42 and 44 (running numbers) were on the UGs and Nos 45, 48, 73, 76 and 87 on the Us.

They largely remained attached to these engines, except that, by 1958, No 48 was a spare and UG No 148 was attached to a later example of the E type. A further seven

tenders of this type were delivered in 1955-56, though all were dated 1954. Two of these were built at Dundalk and the remainder by Beyer Peacock. The Dundalk-built examples (Nos 43, 46) lacked the usual cut outs in the frames, between the axles and, in 1958, were attached to U class No 198 and LQGs No 163, respectively.

The Beyer-built examples had the following numbers (engines to which attached in 1958 given in brackets): 32 (SG3 20), 34 (UG 148), 47 (LQGs 110), 158 (spare), 160 (spare). It is known that PPs No 46 ran with an E type tender for a time. The present tender fitted to preserved V class 4-4-0 No 85 *Merlin* is No 73 of this type (originally on No 203 *Armagh*), but now modified, to make it look like a D1 type with raised coping. It holds 3100 gallons of water.

F Type, 4000 gallon 1948

This was the final design of GNR tender and was broadly similar to the E type except for water capacity, an overall length of 23'6", and much greater height. This design looked for all the world like an LMS 'Black Five' tender. Five, Nos 28-31 and 35, were built by Beyer Peacock, for the new VS class 4-4-0s of 1948. But there were plans to build ten more for the SG2s proposed in 1952 (see Chapter 9). They were never in any other livery than sky blue.

There are only two instances of the F type being fitted to engines other than the VS. No 30 (or possibly 35) was used by CIE on V class 4-4-0 No 85 *Merlin* in the early 1960s. When *Merlin* was preserved, tender No 31 from No 207 was retained for it. This tender has run on 171 *Slieve Gullion*, as well as *Merlin*. However, it is now regarded as rather heavy and unstable, and the modified E type is preferred.

Chapter 13
Preservation

A total of four GNR steam locomotives have survived into preservation. For a small railway, like the GNR, this is quite good, especially when three of them are 4-4-0s. The first organisation involved in the preservation field was the Belfast Transport Museum, which had already acquired two GNR locomotives, before the formation of the Railway Preservation Society of Ireland in 1964.

The RPSI was formed primarily to save one of the S class 4-4-0s and maintain it in working order. This was achieved by the end of 1965. It was a time of difficult decisions. At that time, it would have been possible to save the last VS 4-4-0, No 207 *Boyne*, or a UG 0-6-0, but there were only resources to save one engine and the Transport Museum had already saved a three-cylinder Compound. There was also a possibility at the time, that Billy Butlin would purchase No 207 as a static exhibit for his holiday camp at Mosney, Co Dublin. Hopes were raised, only to be disappointed. Preserving a UG remained, theoretically, possible up to the scrapping of the last pair in 1968, but the RPSI already had a GS&WR 0-6-0 and had no funds for anything else.

The fourth engine owes its survival primarily to CIE, who kept No 131 when all the other GNR locomotives were cut up in 1963-65. This engine has had a more chequered history, as will be seen below.

JT class 2-4-2T No 93, 1895

The oldest GNR locomotive in preservation was the first of six JT class 2-4-2Ts (Nos 90-95), built at Dundalk between 1895 and 1902 (page 76). No 93 was completed in August 1895 (Works No 16). It was rebuilt with a new boiler in December 1917, and 16½"x 22" cylinders in 1921 (page 114). It has 5'7" driving wheels and was one of the first two of this class to be withdrawn in 1955. The GNRB presented it to the Belfast Transport Museum, then building up a collection. Oddly, one member of this class survived in service until 1963. The fact that it was a JT which went to the Museum, owed much to the compact size of the type, as the Museum had not much display space. If the GNRB had waited a year, a Ps5'6" 4-4-0 might have been donated instead.

Initially, No 93 was at the original premises of the Museum, the old rail motor shed at Queen's Quay. From 1962, it was displayed at the larger Witham Street Transport Museum, until the opening of the new Railway Gallery at the Ulster Folk and Transport Museum in Cultra in 1993, where the engine can now be seen. It is displayed in standard GNR black livery and is the only surviving engine of Park design (page 158)

Qs 4-4-0 No 131, 1901

This locomotive is the last survivor of a class of thirteen inside cylinder 4-4-0s built by Charles Clifford in 1899-1904, and rebuilt by George Glover in 1919-24. This example was built by Neilson Reid of Glasgow (later part of the North British Locomotive Co) in 1900 (Works No 5757) and delivered in February 1901 as No 131 *Uranus*. The class comprised Nos 120-125 and 130-136. No 131 lost its name in 1914 and was rebuilt at Dundalk, in November 1920, into its present superheated form. It has 6'7" driving wheels and 18½"x 26" cylinders.

In September 1958, No 131 was overhauled at Dundalk. It then passed to CIE in October 1958 and ran alongside No 132, until the end of CIE steam in January 1963 (page 176).

Although the bulk of GNR locomotives were cut up between 1963 and early 1965, No 131 was retained at Inchicore for several years, along with GS&WR 0-6-0 No 184 and D&SER 2-6-0 No 461. In 1968, it was repainted in GNR blue livery (which it had never carried in service) with the wheel rims painted white and the 'GN' on the tender positioned much too close to the crest (below).

Later, it was repainted in black, and displayed at Dundalk station from the late 1970s to 1984. It was paired with the

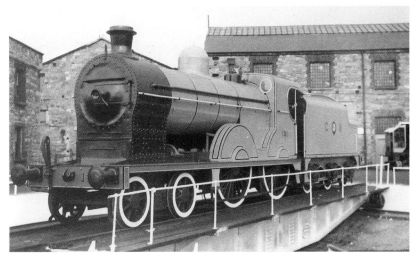

Above: Preserved Qs class 4-4-0 No 131 on display at Inchicore in 1968, wearing a highly unlikely interpretation of the GNR blue livery.   *C P Friel*

No 131 on display at Dundalk on 19 June 1979.

C P Friel, 5149

modern E type 2500 gallon tender, with which it ran in the period 1958-63.

In June 1984, the locomotive was acquired by the Great Southern Railway Preservation Society which took it, by rail, to Mallow, Co Cork and commenced restoration. The boiler was removed for restoration, but then the project ran into difficulties and was abandoned. It remains at Mallow, with its boiler removed. This is the forgotten member of the GNR 4-4-0 trio.

S class 4-4-0 No 171 *Slieve Gullion*, 1913

Slieve Gullion is the last representative of a class of five locomotives (Nos 170-174) built by Beyer Peacock in 1913 and renewed at Dundalk in 1938-39. No 171 (Works No 5629) was delivered in February 1913, to the design of Charles Clifford with modifications by George Glover (page 104). It was renewed at Dundalk in September 1938 (Works No 42) and passed to CIE in 1958. In September 1959, it received a final overhaul and repaint at Dundalk Works, before withdrawal by CIE in January 1963 (page 176). However, it was then purchased by the UTA in June 1963 (along with Nos 170 and 174 and VS No 207) and saw further service until the autumn of 1965, one of its last duties being on the inaugural railtour of the RPSI on 11 September 1965.

No 171 was placed in the care of the RPSI on 1 January 1966. *Slieve Gullion* first ran under RPSI ownership on 8 October 1966 on a trip to Larne Harbour. However, it was in poor shape and was laid aside for a year until its first overhaul, which was at Harland and Wolff's in 1968. In 1969 the locomotive was repainted in GNR blue livery and has been active on RPSI tours from then to the present, except for periods when it was receiving additional overhauls.

Slieve Gullion has 6'7" driving wheels and 19"x 26" cylinders. In active preservation it was initially paired to the large 4000 gallon F type tender held over for *Merlin*. This was because its own 3500 gallon tender was in poor shape, at the time. However, in 1973, this tender was restored and the engine now looks every inch an S class. *Slieve Gullion*

remained in blue livery right up to 1995, but is currently in GNR black livery arising from its use in a major film contract that year (page 158). Although not strictly authentic (the renewed engines were never in black), this livery gives some idea of what the locomotives were like in the early 1930s and some enthusiasts have enjoyed the change. Nevertheless, it is intended to restore the blue livery when *Slieve Gullion* has its next overhaul, due in 2001.

V class 4-4-0 No 85 *Merlin*, 1932

The largest of the preserved GNR 4-4-0s is *Merlin* which is the only active three-cylinder compound in the British Isles. *Merlin* was the last survivor of five locomotives (Nos 83-87), built by Beyer Peacock in 1932. It was delivered on 23 April 1932 (Works No 6733) and, in May 1950, was the last of the Compounds to be rebuilt with a Belpaire firebox. It has 6'7" driving wheels, one high pressure cylinder 17¼"x 26" and two low pressure cylinders 19"x 26". *Merlin* was overhauled in the autumn of 1958 and was the last Compound to remain in service, being withdrawn by CIE in 1963 (page 177).

At one point the UTA considered buying it, but selected VS No 207 in preference. In April 1964, No 85 was towed to Inchicore for scrapping but was then rescued by the Belfast Transport Museum, who purchased it for £600. In May 1965 it was moved to Dundalk and, in Belfast, the 4000 gallon tender from No 207 was saved for it, at the end of that year. In August 1966 it was moved to Belfast and stored at Adelaide shed, and I remember seeing it there before the shed closed in November 1966; my first sight of a Compound since 1961. After three years stored in Lisburn goods shed, *Merlin*, minus its tender, arrived at the Witham Street Museum, looking rather woebegone.

In 1977, at the instigation of the late Lord Dunleith who put much of his own money into the project, *Merlin* was leased to the RPSI and sent to Harland's for overhaul. This was a very protracted restoration and it was to be 24 December 1984 before the locomotive was steamed. During 1985, it ran a number of proving trips, as final jobs were attended to. Finally, in June 1986, the fully restored locomotive made its public debut.

During this first season, *Merlin* ran with the 3500 gallon tender. From 1987 to 1994, it had to use the big tender, if *Slieve Gullion* was in service. In 1994 a 1948 E type tender was procured from Iarnrod Éireann. This tender has been modified to look like a D1 tender with high coping.

At present, *Merlin* and *Slieve Gullion* continue to fly the flag for the GNR on mainline RPSI railtours. Long may it continue! Perhaps they may yet be joined by 131!

Two delightful full colour booklets, by Charles P Friel, titled *Merlin* and *Slieve Gullion* and telling the story of these two locomotives, have been published by Colourpoint Books at £2.99 each.

Appendix 1
GNR locomotives by type

2-2-2 tender locomotives

No	Name	Crank	Origin	Date	Works No	DW	Cyls	Renumbered	Rebuilt (by GNR)	Withdrawn
2	*Mars?*	Q	D&DR	1863	SS 1484	5'6"	15"x 20"	23 (1877), 23A (1888)	–	9/1894
7	*Venus*	T	D&DR	1847	Grendon	5'6"	13"x 18"	7A (1890)	–	1891
13	–	N	D&DR	1860	BP 185	6'0"	15"x 20"	13A (1895)	3/1876, 1881 (15½"x 20")	5/1896
14	–	N	D&DR	1859	BP 105	6'0"	15"x 20"	14A (1895)	1/1885 (15½"x 20")	5/1896
15	–	N	D&DR	1859	BP 106	6'0"	15"x 20"	15A (1898)	1880 (renewed, 16"x 20")	2/1902
16	–	N	D&DR	1861	BP 195	6'0"	15"x 20"	16A (1898)	1877, 11/1887 (15½"x 20")	11/1898
17	*Apollo*	U	D&DR	1854	SS 809	5'6"	15"x 20"	17A? (1885)	–	late 1886
18	*Diana?*	U	D&DR	1854	SS 810	5'6"	15"x 20"	18A? (1885)	–	late 1886
22	*Neptune??*	Q	D&DR	1863	SS 1473	6'0"	15"x 20"	22A? (1887?)	–	1888
(23)	–	–	DBJ 2	1848	SB 530	5'6"	15"x 20"	–	–	1876
24	–	–	DBJ 3	1848	SB 534	5'6"	15"x 20"	–	–	1877
25	–	–	DBJ 4	1848	SB 535	5'6"	15"x 20"	–	–	1879
26	–	–	DBJ 5	1852	SS 707	5'6"	15"x 20"	–	–	1879
27	–	–	DBJ 13	1854	SS 787	5'6"	15"x 20"	–	–	1879
43	–	T	INW 1	1848	Grendon	5'6"	14"x 18"	–	1877	1886–7
46	–	U	INW 4	1852	SS 706	5'6"	15"x 20"	–	–	1880–3
47	–	U	INW 5	1854	SS 785	5'6"	15"x 20"	–	–	1880–3
48	–	U	INW 6	1854	SS 786	5'6"	15"x 20"	–	3/1877	1885
55	–	N	INW 13	1861	BP 223	5'6"	15"x 20"	13(1895?), 13A (1902)	1878, 2/1890 (16"x 20")	1910
56	–	N	INW 14	1861	BP 224	5'6"	15"x 20"	14(1895), 14A (1902)	1883, 5/1892 (16"x 20")	6/1907
60	–	O	INW 18	1846	Longridge	5'6"	15"x 22"	60A (1890)	1877 (new boiler)	4/1892
(10)2	*Blackwater*	–	UR 2	1859	Fairbairn	5'6"	15"x 20"	–	–	renewed as 0-4-2 1881
(10)9	*Pluto*	M	UR 9	1864	UR	5'6"	15"x 20"	–	–	renewed as 0-4-2 1882
111	*Cerberus*	M	UR 11	1864	UR	5'6"	15"x 20"	111A (1899) renamed *North Star*	1884 (renewed G 16"x 22")	6/1901
120	*Ulidia*	–	UR 20	1861	SS ?1275	5'6"	15"x 20"			renewed as 2-4-0 6/1879
121	*Dalriada*	–	UR 21	1861	SS 1276	5'6"	15"x 20"			renewed as 2-4-0 6/1877
122	*Iveagh*	N?	UR 22	1861	BP 225	5'6"	15"x 20"	110 (1895), 110A (1899)	1879	2/1900
124	*Breffney*	G	UR 24	1862	Fairbairn	5'6"	15"x 20"	–	1878	1895
125	*Clanaboy*	G	UR 25	1862	Fairbairn	5'6"	15"x 20"	75 (1895), 75A (3/1898)	1879	12/1897

0-4-2 tender locomotives

No	Name	Crank	Origin	Date	Works No	DW	Cyls	Renumbered	Rebuilt (by GNR)	Withdrawn
1	*Nestor*	P	D&DR	1843	SB 239	5'2"	14½"x 20"	1A (1887)	–	8/1892
6	*Samson?*	P	D&DR	1844	SB 258	5'2"	14½"x 20"	2 (1877), 2A (1887)	–	10/1892
10	–	G	D&DR	1862	BP 257	5'0"	16"x 22"	10A (1904)	7/1884	8/1905
11	–	G	D&DR	1858	BP 75	5'0"	16"x 22"	–	1879, 1897	1/1903
20	*Vulcan*	G	D&DR	1858	BP 76	5'0"	16"x 22"	9 (1887), 9A (6/1911) 201 (10/1914)	1880, 4/1900	6/1915
31	–	S	DBJ 10	1854	SS 774	5'0"	16"x 22"	31A (1889)	1877 (16"x 24", B crank) 1889, 1898	6/1903
32	–	S	DBJ 11	1854	SS 775	5'0"	16"x 22"	–	–	1885–7
33	–	S	DBJ 12	1854	SS 776	5'0"	16"x 22"	–	–	6/1890
34	–	S	DBJ 15	1857	SS 1006	5'0"	16"x 22"	–	–	1880

No	Name	Crank	Origin	Date	Works No	DW	Cyls	Renumbered	Rebuilt (by GNR)	Withdrawn
35	–	B	DBJ 9	1853	SS 738	5'0"	16"x 22"	35A (6/1895)	6/1876	5/1900
36	–	B	DBJ 14	1857	SS 992	5'0"	16"x 22"	–	1879 (0-6-0, A crank)	5/1893
45	–	T	INW 3	1849	Grendon	4'4"	14"x 18"	–	–	1885
51	–	S	INW 9	1858	SS 1052	5'0"	16"x 22"	51A (1891–2)	1880	10/1895
52	–	S	INW 10	1858	SS 1053	5'0"	16"x 22"	–	–	early 1885
57	–	B	INW 15	1861	N 692	5'3"	16"x 24"	102 (1895), 102A (1901)	1882	3/1907
58	–	B	INW 16	1861	N 693	5'3"	16"x 24"	103 (1895), 103A (1901)	1883	6/1902
70	–	B	INW 28	1861	N 950	5'3"	16"x 24"	100 (1895), 100A (1900)	1881	2/1901
71	–	B	INW 29	1861	N 951	5'3"	16"x 24"	101 (1895), 101A (1901)	1883	3/1904
76	–	E	INW 34	1867	Dübs 124	5'3"	16"x 24"	44 (1888), 78 (1898), 78A (1899), 78 (9/1906), 78A (3/1908)	1888 (A crank)	1/1909
81	–	X	N&A 6	1864	Vulc 509	5'0½"	16"x 22"	81A (1886)	–	1887
82	–	X	N&A 7	1864	Vulc 510	5'0½"	16"x 22"	82A (1886)	1880–1	1/1896
102	Blackwater	K	(Fbn 2-2-2)	1881	GNR (ND)	4'6"	16"x 22"	102A (1894), 100A (1901)	–	3/1901
(10)3	Erne	B	UR 3	1860	SS 1156	4'6"	16"x 24"	–	renewed (as 0-6-0)	1877
(10)4	Owenreagh	B	UR 4	1861	SS 1274	4'6"	16"x 24"	–	renewed (below)	1880
104	Owenreagh	K	(above)	1880	GNR (ND)	4'6"	16"x 22"	104A (1895)	–	5/1899
105	Typhoon	K	UR 5	1874	UR	5'0"	16"x 22"	105A (1906)	3/1893	10/1911
106	Tornado	K	UR 6	1873	UR	5'0"	16"x 22"	106A (1906)	10/1889	8/1906
107	Cyclone	K	UR 7	1871	UR	5'0"	16"x 22"	107A (1906)	8/1888	5/1908
109	Pluto	K	(UR 2-2-2)	1882	GNR (ND)	4'6"	16"x 22"	109A (1899)	–	3/1907
(1)16	Bann	B	UR 16	1857	SS 975	4'6"	16"x 24"	–	renewed (as 0-6-0)	1877
130	Nore	K	UR 30	1866	SS 1649	5'0"	16"x 22"	–	1880	1894
131	Ovoca	K	UR 31	1866	SS 1651	5'0"	16"x 22"	131A (1901)	1882, 2/1897	8/1909
132	Foyle	K	UR 32	1866	SS 1652	5'0"	16"x 22"	132A (1901)	1879	4/1904
133	Shannon	F	UR 33	1866	BP 634	5'0"	17"x 24"	109 (1899), 109A (6/1911)	1882, 10/1901	1913
134	Liffey	F	UR 34	1866	BP 635	5'0"	17"x 24"	110(1899), 110A (4/1908)	12/1890	10/1911
135	Carntual	F	UR 35	1866	BP 636	5'0"	17"x 24"	111 (1899), 111A (4/1908)	6/1890	10/1909
136	Donard	F	UR 36	1866	BP 637	5'0"	17"x 24"	112 (1899), 112A (6/1911)	1883, 2/1902	11/1912
139	Tempest	K	UR 39	1874	UR	5'0"	16"x 22"	104 (1895), 104A (1896)	6/1893	3/1908
140	Sirocco	K	UR 40	1876	SS 2560	5'0"	16"x 22"	108 (1895)	10/1895	12/1907
141	Simoom	K	UR 41	1876	SS 2561	5'0"	16"x 22"	130 (1895), 78 (1901)	10/1893	8/1906

2-4-0 tender locomotives

No	Name	Crank	Origin	Date	Works No	DW	Cyls	Renumbered	Rebuilt (by GNR)	Withdrawn
4	Drogheda	?	D&D	1856	Grendon	5'6"	15"x 22"	22? (1887)	–	6?/1888
9	Saturn	R	D&D	1844	SB 273	5'6"	14½"x 20"	–	–	1885
12	Achilles	G	D&D	1871	BP 1042	6'0½"	16"x 22"	12A (6/1911)	8/1889, 1897	12/1911
19	Pluto	?	D&D	1855	Fairbairn	5'0"	16"x 22"	–	–	1887
30	–	?	DBJ 1	1848	SB 529	5'6"	15"x 20"	–	–	1885
53	–	L	INW 11	1859	BP 107	5'6"	15"x 20"	54 (1892), 22 (1895) 22A (1908)	1883, 5/1889 (G class)	1914
54	–	O	INW 12	1846	Longridge	4'9"	15"x 24"	–	1878 (15"x 22")	4/1890
59	–	O	INW 17	1846	Longridge	4'7"	15"x 24"	79 (1877)	–	1879
68	–	W	INW 26	1855	Jones	4'7"	15"x 20"	68A (1892)	1876	8/1894
69	–	W	INW 27	1855	Jones	4'7"	15"x 20"	69A (1892)	1879	7/1896
72	–	L	INW 30	1874	INW	6'0"	16"x 21"	43 (1895), 43A (6/1911) 202 (10/1914)	1898, 1/1901	1921
73	–	L	INW 31	1873	INW	5'6"	15"x 21"	–	–	8/1892
74	–	L	INW 32	1866	Dübs 122	6'0"	15"x 21"	124 (1895), 124A (1902)	1878, 1885	3/1906
75	–	L	INW 33	1866	Dübs 123	6'0"	15"x 21"	125 (1895), 125A (1902)	1884	6/1904
101	Lagan	H	UR 1	1876	UR	5'6"	16"x 22"	114 (1886), 114A (11/1904)	1897	1913

No	Name	Crank	Origin	Date	Works No	DW	Cyls	Renumbered	Rebuilt (by GNR)	Withdrawn
108	*Lucifer*	M	UR 8	1867	UR	5'6"	15"x 20"	108A (1893), 113 (1895)	1876, 1896 (16"x 22") 113A (11/1904)	2/1906
110	*Jupiter*	M	UR 10	1869	UR	5'6"	15"x 20"	122 (1895), 112A (1899)	1885	2/1906
112	*Vulcan*	M	UR 12	1867	UR	5'6"	15"x 20"	122 (1899), 122A (1903)	1885	8/1905
113	*Spitfire*	M	UR 13	1869	UR	5'6"	15"x 20"	–	1876	1888
(1)17	*Shamrock*	U	UR 17	1857	SS 989	5'6"	15"x 20"	117A (1885)	–	1886–7
(1)18	*Rose*	U	UR 18	1857	SS 1007	5'6"	15"x 20"	118A (1885)	–	1887
(1)19	*Thistle*	U	UR 19	1858	SS 1008	5'6"	15"x 20"	–	–	1886–7
120	*Ulidia*	H	UR 20	1879	GNR (ND)	5'6"	16"x 22"	120A (5/1904)	–	1/1906
121	*Dalriada*	H	UR 21	1877	GNR (ND)	5'6"	16"x 22"	121A (5/1904)	–	10/1914
123	*Tyrone*	H	UR 23	1874	UR	5'6"	16"x 22"	–	1885	7/1903
126	*Ulster*	H	UR 26	1863	BP 367	6'1"	16"x 22"	126A (5/1907)	1881, 5/1897	9/1909
127	*Munster*	H	UR 27	1863	BP 369	6'1"	16"x 22"	127A (5/1907)	1881, 2/1899	3/1911
128	*Leinster*	H	UR 28	1863	BP 368	6'1"	16"x 22"	128A (5/1907)	1883, 5/1898	1914
129	*Connaught*	H	UR 29	1863	BP 370	6'1"	16"x 22"	129A (6/1911)	1883, 6/1899	3/1912

<table>

G Class   5'7" 16"x 22"

No	Works No	Delivered	Rebuilt	Renumbered	Wdn
3	BP 1539	11/1875	11/1893	23 (1888), 23A 10/1908	12/1911
24	BP 1750	12/1877	7/1896	24A (3/1910)	1914
25	BP 1749	12/1877	12/1894	25A (6/1911)	12/1913
42	BP 1540	11/1875	12/1887	42A (6/1911)	3/1912
46	BP 2342	5/1883	4/1903 1915	48 (1898), 48A (7/1913) 48 (1914)	3/1921
47	BP 2343	5/1883	4/1903 1915	47A (7/1913), 47 (1914)	3/1921
59	BP 1752	12/1877	2/1897	50 (1885), 50A (6/1911)	12/1914
80	BP 1751	12/1877	2/1899 1915	49 (1885), 49A (7/1913) 49 (1914)	5/1921

H Class   6'0½" 16"x 22"

No	Works No	Delivered	Rebuilt	Renumbered	Wdn
37	BP 632	3/1866	6/1888	44 (1898), 44A 6/1911	9/1914
38	BP 633	3/1866	12/1886	45 (1898), 45A 3/1910 201 (6/1915)	1920
39	BP 835	7/1868	12/1885	46 (1898), 46A 3/1910	1911

(Nos 37–39 were ex–D&BJR Nos 18–20)

No	Works No	Delivered		Rebuilt	Wdn
84	BP 2103	11/1881		3/1890, 10/1902	11/1932
85	BP 2104	11/1881		5/1891, 1/1902	11/1932
86	BP 1968	7/1880		1900, 12/1900	11/1932
87	BP 1969	7/1880		4/1891, 6/1902	11/1932

</table>

4-2-2 tender locomotives

JS class   6'7" 16"x 22"

No	Name	Works No	Delivered	Wdn	No	Name	Works No	Delivered	Wdn
88	*Victoria*	BP 2519	2/1885	10/1904	89	*Albert*	BP 2520	2/1885	12/1904

4-4-0 tender locomotives

J class   5'7" 16"x 22" (names removed 1912-13)

No	Name	Works No	Delivered	Rebuilt	Renumbered	Wdn	No	Name	Works No	Delivered	Rebuilt	Renumbered	Wdn
17	–	BP 2517	3/1885	10/1906	–	7/1924	48	*Iris* (c1896)	BP 2656	4/1885	6/1907	16 (1898)	7/1924
18	–	BP 2518	3/1885	3/1906	–	7/1924	115	*Lily*	BP 3018	7/1889	5/1902	–	12/1924
19	–	BP 2818	5/1887	5/1903	–	9/1924	116	*Violet*	BP 3019	7/1889	5/1905	–	12/1924
20	–	BP 2819	5/1887	1/1904	–	1/1921	117	*Shamrock*	BP 2515	3/1885	7/1906	–	1921
21	–	BP 3017	7/1889	4/1904	–	12/1924	118	*Rose*	BP 2516	3/1885	5/1902	–	7/1921
45	*Pansy* (2/96)	BP 2655	4/1885	5/1905	15 (1898)	7/1924	119	*Thistle*	BP 2820	5/1887	12/1903	–	7/1921

Nos 118 and 119 were sold to the SLNCR in July 1921, becoming *Blacklion* and *Glencar* respectively.

P 6'6" class 6'7" 17"x 24" (names removed 1913-14)

No	Name	Works No	Delivered	4'6" boiler	Superheated	Renumbered	1958	Wdn
72	*Daffodil* (12/97)	BP 3664	3/1895	9/1914	1/1931	–	CIE	10/1959
73	*Primrose* (12/96)	BP 3665	3/1895	6/1915	10/1931	–	CIE	10/1959
82	*Daisy* (1/97)	BP 3455	2/1892	12/1913	3/1932	27 (12/1931)	CIE	10/1959
83	*Narcissus* (8/97)	BP 3456	2/1892	9/1914	1/1931	26 (12/1931)	–	1957

P 5'6" class 5'7" 17"x 24" (names removed 1912-13)

No	Name	Works No	Delivered	4'6" boiler	Superheated	Renumbered	1958	Wdn
51	*Hyacinth* (c1898)	BP 3501	10/1892	8/1907	12/1925	–	–	1950
52	*Snowdrop* (c1898)	BP 3502	10/1892	3/1906	12/1923	–	–	1950
53	–	BP 3503	11/1892	10/1907	5/1924	–	–	1950
54	–	BP 3666	2/1895	6/1916	4/1927	–	–	1950
88	*Victoria*	GNR 27	12/1904	as built	4/1923	–	–	1956
89	*Albert*	GNR 28	12/1904	as built	3/1925	–	–	1956
104	*Ovoca*	GNR 29	1906	as built	10/1924	–	–	1956
105	*Foyle*	GNR 30	1906	as built	9/1925	–	CIE	5/1960

PP class 6'7" 18"x 24" (Nos 75-7 18½"x 24") (names removed 1914)

No	Name	Works No	Delivered	4'6" boiler	PPs 4'3"	PPs 4'6"	1958		Wdn
12	*Ulster* *	BP 5468	1911	–	2/1930	4/1943	CIE		10/1959
25	*Liffey*	GNR 33	4/1911	–	6/1927	1/1932	–		1957
42	*Munster* *	BP 5469	1911	–	9/1929	6/1938	UTA 42x		3/1960
43	*Lagan*	GNR 34	2/1911	–	10/1928	2/1941	UTA 43x		3/1960
44	*Leinster*	BP 5467	1911	–	7/1928	5/1944	CIE		2/1960
45	*Sirocco*	BP 5327	12/1909	–	–	2/1928	–		1957
46	*Typhoon*	BP 5328	12/1909	–	1/1927	9/1945	UTA		8/1959
50	*Donard*	BP 5465	1911	–	8/1929	6/1939	UTA 50x		3/1960
70	*Precursor*	BP 3799	3/1896	12/1920	–	9/1930	–		1957
71	*Bundoran*	BP 3800	4/1896	9/1920	6/1930	3/1943	CIE		10/1959
74	*Rostrevor*	BP 3801	4/1896	9/1917	–	11/1930	UTA 74x	42x (3/1960)	7/1963
75	*Jupiter*	BP 3926	3/1898	7/1919	–	4/1931	CIE		10/1959
76	*Hercules*	BP 3927	3/1898	11/1919	–	3/1930	UTA		8/1959
77	*Achilles*	BP 3928	3/1898	4/1920	–	7/1931	–		1957
106	*Tornado*	BP 4736	2/1906	–	6/1928	9/1944	CIE		10/1960
107	*Cyclone*	BP 4737	2/1906	–	–	8/1929	UTA		8/1959
129	*Connaught*	BP 5466	1911	–	3/1929	–	–		1957

* built with Phoenix superheater

Q class 6'7" 18½"x 26" (names removed 1914)

No	Name	Works No	Delivered	Rebuilt	1958	Wdn	No	Name	Works No	Delivered	Rebuilt	1958	Wdn
120	*Venus*	BP 4565	5/1904	7/1923	–	1957	131	*Uranus*	NR 5757	2/1901	11/1920	CIE	10/1963
121	*Pluto*	BP 4566	5/1904	1/1924	UTA	10/1959					(preserved, not on display)		
122	*Vulcan*	NB 15766	8/1903	12/1924	UTA 122x	3/1960	132	*Mercury*	NR 5758	2/1901	8/1922	CIE	11/1963
123	*Lucifer*	NB 15767	9/1903	6/1923	CIE	10/1959	133	*Apollo*	NR 5557	9/1899	12/1919	–	1957
124	*Cerberus*	NR 6156	8/1902	4/1924	–	1957	134	*Adonis*	NR 5558	9/1899	12/1921	–	12/1951
125	*Daphne*	NR 6157	7/1902	8/1924	UTA	12/1959	135	*Cyclops*	NR 5559	9/1899	2/1922	UTA 135x	6/1963
130	*Saturn*	NR 5756	1/1901	7/1922	CIE	10/1959	136	*Minerva*	NR 5560	9/1899	6/1920	CIE	10/1959

QL class 6'7" 18½"x 26" (names removed 1915-20)

No	Name	Works No	Delivered	Rebuilt	1958	Wdn	No	Name	Works No	Delivered	Rebuilt	1958	Wdn
24	*Juno*	BP 5329	2/1910	3/1924	–	1957	127	*Erebus*	NB 17815	4/1907	2/1928	UTA 127x	3/1960
113	*Neptune*	NB 16190	10/1904	1922	(SV)		128	*Mars*	NB 17816	4/1907	10/1923	–	1957
				4/1924	–	1957	156	*Pandora*	NB 16510	11/1904	5/1925	UTA 156x	3/1960
114	*Theseus*	NB 16191	10/1904	1920	(SV)		157	*Orpheus*	NB 16511	11/1904	1919	(SV)	
				6/1923	–	1932					9/1922	UTA	12/1959
126	*Diana*	NB 17814	4/1907	1923	–	1957							

(SV) = Rebuilt initially with slide valves, but later with piston valves.

S and S2 classes 6'7" 19"x 26"

No	Name (as built)	Works No	Delivered	Rebuilt	Renewed	Name (1938-9)	1958	Sold to UTA	Wdn
170	*Errigal* (to 1929)	BP 5628	2/1913	7/1927	6/1939	*Errigal*	CIE	6/1963	12/1965
171	*Slieve Gullion* (to 1925)	BP 5629	2/1913	12/1926	9/1938	*Slieve Gullion*	CIE	6/1963	12/1965
						(Preserved by RPSI 1/1/1966)			
172	*Slieve Donard* (to 1923)	BP 5630	2/1913	6/1926	10/1938	*Slieve Donard*	UTA 60	–	5/1965
173	*Galtee More* (to 1924)	BP 5631	2/1913	8/1928	5/1938	*Galtee More*	UTA 61	–	3/1964
174	*Carrantuohill* (to 1923)	BP 5632	2/1913	4/1927	10/1939	*Carrantuohill*	CIE	6/1963	12/1965
190	–	BP 5901	2/1915	5/1929	7/1939	*Lugnaquilla*	UTA 62	–	5/1965
191	–	BP 5902	3/1915	3/1928	1/1939	*Croagh Patrick*	CIE	–	12/1960
192	–	BP 5903	3/1915	4/1930	6/1938	*Slievenamon*	UTA 63	–	5/1965

U class 5'9" 18"x24"

No	Name	Works No	Delivered	1958	Wdn	No	Name	Works No	Delivered	1958	Wdn
196	*Lough Gill* (3/1953)	BP 5904	4/1915	UTA 64	10/1961	201	*Meath*	BP 7244	1/1948	UTA 66	5/1965
197	*Lough Neagh* (4/1949)	BP 5905	4/1915	CIE	11/1962	202	*Louth*	BP 7245	1/1948	UTA 67	5/1965
198	*Lough Swilly* (1950)	BP 5906	4/1915	CIE	10/1959	203	*Armagh*	BP 7246	1/1948	CIE	11/1962
199	*Lough Derg* (5/1949)	BP 5908	4/1915	CIE	11/1962	204	*Antrim*	BP 7247	1/1948	CIE	1963
200	*Lough Melvin* (5/1950)	BP 5907	4/1915	UTA 65	10/1961	205	*Down*	BP 7248	1/1948	UTA 68	5/1965

V class 6'7" 17¼"/19"x 26" (3 cyl compounds)

No	Name	Works No	Delivered	Rebuilt	1958	Wdn	Remarks
83	*Eagle*	BP 6731	4/1932	7/1949	UTA 83x	3/1960	
84	*Falcon*	BP 6732	4/1932	9/1947	CIE	10/1959	Broken up 2/1961
85	*Merlin*	BP 6733	4/1932	5/1950	CIE	1963	Preserved by UFTM, operated by RPSI
86	*Peregrine*	BP 6734	4/1932	11/1948	UTA 86x	5/1961	
87	*Kestrel*	BP 6735	5/1932	12/1946	UTA 87x	3/1960	

VS class 6'7" 15¼"x 26" (3 cyl simples)

No	Name	Works No	Delivered	1958	Sold to UTA	Wdn	Remarks
206	*Liffey*	BP 6961	8/1948	CIE	–	2/1960	Broken up 2/1961
207	*Boyne*	BP 6962	9/1948	CIE	6/1963	12/1965	
208	*Lagan*	BP 6963	9/1948	UTA 58	–	5/1965	
209	*Foyle*	BP 6964	9/1948	CIE	–	2/1960	Broken up 2/1961
210	*Erne*	BP 6965	9/1948	CIE	–	7/1963	

0-6-0 tender locomotives (names removed 1912-13)

No	Name	Crank	Origin	Date	Works No	DW	Cyls	Renumbered	Rebuilt (by GNR)	Withdrawn
5	*Hercules*	A	D&DR	1872	BP1161	5'0"	17"x 24"	29 (1889), 29A (1895)	3/1889	6/1911
21	–	G	D&DR	1863	BP 430	5'0"	16"x 22"	32 (1889), 21A (1894)	3/1887	6/1908
40	–	D	DBJ 21	1872	BP 1159	5'1½"	17"x 24"	40A (1913), 40 (1914)	6/1889, 1/1913	1937
41	–	D	DBJ 22	1872	BP 1160	5'1½"	17"x 24"	41A (1913), 41 (1914)	10/1888, 9/1915	1934
44	–	E	INW (2)	1876	INWR	5'0"	17"x 24"	76 (1888), 37 (1898), 37A (3/1913), 37 (10/1913)	1903	6/1948
49	–	–	INW 7	1855	Grendon	5'0"	16"x 24"	49A (1885)?	1880 (16½")	3/1889?
50	–	–	INW 8	1856	Grendon	5'0"	16"x 24"	59 (1885), 59A (1894)	1879 (16½")	12/1903
77	–	E	INW 35	1871	Dübs 462	5'0"	17"x 24"	38 (1898), 38A (6/1911), 193 (10/1913)	1894, 1915	6/1948
78	–	E	INW 36	1872	Dübs 595	5'0"	17"x 24"	39 (1898), 39A (6/1911), 194 (10/1913)	1892, 1915	6/1948
83	–	?	N&A 1	1859	RS 1280	4'7½"	16"x 24"	83A (1882)	–	1886
84	–	?	N&A 4	1858	RS 1190	4'7½"	16"x 24"	84A (1881)?	–	1881
137	*Stromboli*	C	UR 37	1872	UR	5'0"	17"x 24"	137A (temporarily 1913)	1885, 7/1912	9/1939
138	*Vulcano*	C	UR 38	1872	UR	5'0"	17"x 24"	138A (temporarily 1913)	1885, 2/1913	6/1948

0-6-0 tender locomotives (names removed 1912-13)

C class 4'7" 17"x 24" (built for Northern Division)

No	Name	Works No	Delivered	No (1885)	Renumbered	Rebuilt 3'11½" blr	Wdn	Remarks
3	*Etna*	GNR ND	12/1877	103	139 (1895)	4/1895	1925	
14	*Vesuvius*	GNR ND	4/1876	114	144 (1886)	3/1894	1924	Cut down chimney in latter days
15	*Hecla*	GNR ND	6/1876	115	147 (1889)	6/1896	1924	
16	*Teneriffe*	GNR ND	6/1878	116	148 (1889)	4/1895	1925	
42	*Torrent*	BP 1870	7/1879	142	–	11/1899*	1925	* 4'2" boiler
43	*Avalanche*	BP 1871	8/1879	143	–	10/1898*	1925	* 4'2" boiler

B class 4'7" 16"x 24" (1877) 17"x 24" (1879-80)

No	Name	Works No	Delivered	Renumbered	17" cyls	Rebuilt	Wdn	Remarks
25	*Meath*	SS 2680	2/1877	6 (1877), 30 (1889)	4/1887	5/1896*	1925	* 3'11½" boiler on rebuilding
26	*Armagh*	SS 2924	1880	–	as built	8/1898	6/1932	(All others 4'2" boilers)
27	*Dublin*	SS 2842	9/1879	–	as built	9/1900	4/1930	
34	*Louth*	SS 2925	1880	–	as built	11/1897	11/1932	
62	*Tyrone*	SS 2677	2/1877	–	3/1887	3/1897	3/1930	
63	*Donegal*	SS 2678	2/1877	–	4/1887	6/1897	4/1930	
65	*Derry*	SS 2679	2/1877	–	6/1893	10/1898	3/1930	
66	*Monaghan*	SS 2844	9/1879	27 (1930), 149 (1932)	as built	8/1899	8/1938	Cut down chimney in latter days
67	*Fermanagh*	SS 2843	9/1879	–	as built	11/1900	3/1930	

A class 4'7" 17"x 24"

No	Name	Works No	Delivered	Renumbered	Rebuilt	1958	Wdn	Remarks
28	*Wexford*	BP 2904	6/1888	–	10/1909	–	1956	Cut down chimney (1937)
31	*Galway*	BP 3273	11/1890	–	8/1910	–	1927	To SLNCR 6/1928, *Glencar*, wdn 1949
33	*Belfast*	GNR 8	2/1891	–	2/1916	CIE	10/1959	Cut down chimney; cut up 11/1960
60	*Dundalk*	GNR 7	10/1890	–	6/1918	CIE	10/1959	Cut down chimney; cut up 11/1960
61	*Sligo*	BP 2394	11/1883	–	9/1905	–	1935	
64	*Down*	BP 2395	11/1883	67 (1930)	12/1910	–	9/1937	
79	*Cavan*	BP 2116	4/1882	69 (5/1937)	12/1905	–	3/1930	To SLNCR 3/1940, *Sligo*, wdn 1949
80	*Antrim*	BP 2784	10/1886	–	7/1909	–	1936	Cut down chimney (1925)
81	*Leitrim*	BP 2785	11/1886	–	4/1909	–	1936	Cut down chimney in latter days
82	*Kildare*	BP 2786	11/1886	68 (1892)	9/1908	–	6/1948	frames ex-149 3/1941
83	*Newry*	BP 2117	4/1882	69 (1892)	10/1913	–	1937	
145	*Carlow*	BP 2905	6/1888	–	6/1905	–	1937	
146	*Wicklow*	BP 2906	6/1888	–	6/1910	–	1937	
149	*Roscommon*	BP 3274	11/1890	–	7/1906	–	1931	To SLNCR 1932, *Sligo*, retd 3/1940 (scr 1941)
150	*Longford*	BP 3275	12/1890	–	12/1905	CIE	10/1961	Cut down chimney in latter days

AL class 4'7" 17"x 24" (Named until 1912-13)

No	Name	Works No	Delivered	Renumbered	Rebuilt	1958	Wdn	Remarks
29	*Enniskillen*	GNR 14	2/1895	–	11/1918	CIE	10/1959	Cut up 11/1960
32	*Drogheda*	GNR 13	11/1894	–	12/1916	UTA 32x	3/1960	
36	*Waterford*	BP 3583	12/1893	–	4/1918	–	1957	
55	*Portadown*	GNR 15	11/1895	–	8/1918	CIE	3/1961	Cut up 7/1961
56	*Omagh*	GNR 18	12/1896	–	12/1914	UTA 56x	3/1960	
57	*Cork*	BP 3797	12/1895	–	12/1916	CIE	10/1959	Cut up 10/1960
58	*Kerry*	BP 3798	1/1896	–	9/1917	CIE	10/1959	Cut up 11/1960
59	*Kilkenny*	BP 3584	1/1894	–	4/1915	CIE	10/1959	Cut up 9/1960
151	*Westmeath*	BP 3607	5/1894	141 (6/1895)	3/1918	–	1957	
152	*Limerick*	BP 3608	5/1894	140 (6/1895)	4/1919	–	1957	
153	*Clare*	BP 3609	5/1894	35 (6/1895)	9/1916	CIE	10/1959	Cut up 5/1960

PG class 4'7" 18½"x 24"

No	Name	Works No	Delivered	Renumbered	Rebuilt	1958	Wdn
10	*Bessbrook*	GNR 26	3/1904	–	12/1925	UTA 10x	3/1964
11	*Dromore*	GNR 25	9/1903	–	5/1924	UTA 11x	3/1960
78	*Strabane*	GNR 21	12/1899	151 (2/1902)	8/1921	UTA 151x	12/1961
100	*Clones*	GNR 22	6/1900	–	7/1924	UTA 100x	12/1961
101	*Balmoral*	NR 5753	2/1901	–	5/1927	UTA 101x	3/1960
102	*Belleek*	NR 5754	2/1901	–	5/1928	UTA 102x	3/1960
103	*Dunleer*	NR 5755	2/1901	–	4/1929	UTA 103x	3/1960

QG class 4'7" 18½"x 26"

No	Name	Works No	Delivered	Rebuilt	1958	Wdn	No	Name	Works No	Delivered	Rebuilt	1958	Wdn
152	*Lurgan*	NB 15890	9/1903	3/1926	CIE	1963	154	*Lambeg*	NB 16433	9/1904	2/1928	CIE	11/1962
153	*Scarva*	NB 15891	9/1903	8/1928	CIE	11/1962	155	*Navan*	NB 16434	9/1904	7/1926	CIE	11/1962

LQG class 4'7¼" 18½"x 26"

No	Name	Works No	Delivered	Rebuilt	1958	Wdn	No	Name	Works No	Delivered	Rebuilt	1958	Wdn
78	*Pettigo*	GNR 31	3/1908	6/1929	UTA	12/1959	159	*Cootehill*	NB 17083	3/1906	4/1929	CIE	1964
	(renumbered 119 in 1937)						160	*Culloville*	NB 17084	3/1906	11/1926	UTA	10/1959
108	*Pomeroy*	GNR 32	4/1908	6/1928	UTA	12/1959	161	*Adavoyle*	NB 18288	4/1908	12/1929	CIE	11/1962
110	*Laytown*	NB 18286	4/1908	12/1930	CIE	10/1959	162	*Ballyroney*	NB 18289	4/1908	10/1927	UTA	12/1959
111	*Malahide*	NB 18287	3/1908	6/1928	UTA 111x	7/1963	163	*Banbridge*	NB 18290	4/1908	9/1927	CIE	11/1962
158	*Ballybay*	NB 17082	3/1906	10/1921			164	*Fintona*	NB 18291	4/1908	7/1930	CIE	11/1962
				2/1927	CIE	1963							

NQG class 4'7" 18"x 26"

No	Name	Works No	Deliv	NQGs	LQGNs	1958	Wdn	No	Name	Works No	Deliv	NQGs	LQGNs	1958	Wdn
9	*Kells*	NW 929	1911	1930	1945	UTA 9x	3/1960	109	*Moira*	NW 930	1911	–	4/1930	UTA	12/1959
38	*Kesh* *	NW 932	1911	1931	–	CIE	2/1960	112	*Keady*	NW 931	1911	1931	–	CIE	11/1962
39	*Beragh* *	NW 933	1911	1931	3/1956	UTA 39x	3/1960			* built with Phoenix superheater						

NLQG class 4'7" 18½"x 26"

No	Name	Works No	Delivered	Rebuilt	1958	Wdn
165	*Newbliss*	NW 950	11/1911	9/1929	UTA 165x	12/1961

SG (175-79) and SG2 (15-19, 180-84) classes 5'1" 19"x 26"

No	Works No	Delivered	New boiler	1958	Wdn	No	Works No	Delivered	New boiler	1958	Wdn
15	NW 1428	12/1924	–	CIE	1963	178	BP 5634	4/1913	1949	CIE	3/1961
16	NW 1429	1/1925	1948	UTA 38	5/1965	179	BP 5635	4/1913	1944	CIE	1963
17	NW 1430	1/1925	–	UTA 39	12/1961	180	BP 5896	3/1915	1942	CIE	3/1961
18	NW 1431	12/1924	1951	UTA 40	5/1965	181	BP 5897	3/1915	1942	CIE	1963
19	NW 1432	1/1925	–	CIE	10/1959	182	BP 5898	3/1915	1938	UTA 41	6/1963
175	BP 5636	4/1913	1948	UTA 43	5/1965	183	BP 5899	4/1915	1925	UTA 42	5/1961
176	BP 5637	4/1913	1941	UTA 44	5/1965	184	BP 5900	5/1915	1941	CIE	11/1963
177	BP 5633	4/1913	1952	CIE	11/1962		(Nos 177-79 were Nos 47-49 until 10/1913)				

SG3 class 5'1" 19½"x 26"

No	Works No	Delivered	New boiler	1958	Wdn	No	Works No	Delivered	New boiler	1958	Wdn
6	BP 6040	11/1920	–	UTA 30	5/1961	49	BP 6048	1/1921	1948	UTA 36	5/1965
7	BP 6041	12/1920	1948	UTA 31	5/1965	96	BP 6049	1/1921	–	CIE	11/1962
8	BP 6042	12/1920	1953	CIE	1963	97	BP 6050	2/1921	1948	UTA 37	12/1965*
13	BP 6043	12/1920	1948	UTA 32	5/1965	117	BP 6053	3/1921	1932	CIE	1963
14	BP 6044	12/1920	1949	CIE	11/1962	118	BP 6054	5/1921	–	CIE	10/1959
20	BP 6045	12/1920	1952	UTA 33	5/1965	201	BP 6051	2/1921	1953	UTA 34	5/1965
47	BP 6046	12/1920	1953	CIE	3/1961	202	BP 6052	3/1921	1953	UTA 35	5/1965
48	BP 6047	12/1920	–	CIE	11/1962		(Nos 201, 202 were renumbered 40, 41 in 1/1948)				

*UTA No 37 was not cut up until 1969.

UG class 0-6-0 5'1" 18"x 24"

No	Works No	Delivered	1958	Wdn	Cut up	No	Works No	Delivered	1958	Wdn	Cut up
78	GNR 35	3/1937	UTA 45	5/1965		145	BP 7249	1/1948	CIE	3/1961	9/1961
79	GNR 36	4/1937	UTA 46	7/1963		146	BP 7250	1/1948	UTA 48	6/1967	1968
80	GNR 37	6/1937	CIE	1963		147	BP 7251	1/1948	CIE	10/1960	10/1961
81	GNR 38	8/1937	CIE	10/1960	2/1961	148	BP 7252	2/1948	CIE	1963	
82	GNR 39	10/1937	UTA 47	5/1965		149	BP 7253	2/1948	UTA 49	1/1967	1968

Early GNR tank locomotives

No	Type	Crank	Origin	Date	Works No	DW	Cyls	Renumbered	Remarks	Withdrawn
2A	0-4-2T	?	N&A 2	c1852	Hawthorn	4'6"	13"x 18"	–	named *Newry*	1884
8	2-2-2ST	?	D&DR	1862	N 855	5'0"	12"x 18"	–	–	1885-7
28	2-2-2WT	R	DBJ 16	1858	SS 1081	5'0"	12"x 18"	–	–	1885-7
29	2-2-2WT	R	DBJ 17	1858	SS 1082	5'0"	12"x 18"	29A (1889)	–	1889
61	0-6-0ST	V	INW 19	1859	MW 4	3'3"	11"x 17"	61A (1883), 91 (1885)	Ex-*Rutland*	8/1892
62	2-2-0WT	–	INW 20	1852	KTH 288	5'2"	10"x 16"	–	–	1876
63	2-2-0WT	–	INW 21	1852	KTH 289	5'2"	10"x 16"	–	–	1877
64	0-6-0ST	V	INW 22	1860	MW 18	3'3"	11"x 17"	64A (1883), 92 (1885)	Ex-*Malvern*	10/1891
66	2-2-0WT	–	INW 24	1852	RS 818	5'2"	11"x 18"	–	–	1879
67	2-2-0WT	–	INW 25	1852	RS 819	5'2"	11"x 18"	–	–	1879
85	2-4-0T	–	N&A 5	?1862	JJ? SS?	5'0"	15"x 22"	85A (1881)	–	12/1894
90	2-4-0T	O	NWR 5?	1882	BP 2142	5'0"	14"x 20"	90A (1895)	named *Warrenpoint*	6/1898
93	0-6-0ST	?	BCR 1	1868	BH 59	3'6"	14"x 20"	–	–	9/1892
94	0-6-0ST	?	BCR 2	1874	BH 356	3'6"	14"x 20"	–	–	1895?
95	2-4-0T	O	BCR 3	1878	BP 1707	5'0"	14"x 20"	–	–	6/1898
96	4-4-0T	P	BCR 4	1880	BP 1935	5'0"	15"x 20"	96A (1906), 195 (1915)	Rebuilt: 1887 (16"), 1904	1950
100	2-2-2T	?	NWR 1	?1851	Grendon	5'0"	11"x 16"	100A (6/1887), 100 (1888)	named *Rostrevor*	8/1896

Post-1885 tank locomotives

BT class 4-4-0T 4'7" 15"x 18" (Nos 1, 97-99 14"x 18")

No	Works No	Delivered	Renumbered	Rebuilt	Wdn	Remarks
1	GNR 1	6/1887	119 (9/1921)	5/1909, 4/1920 (0-6-0T)	12/1935	No 100 until 1888
2	GNR 2	12/1887	–	1/1909	3/1921	used as a stationary boiler after withdrawal
3	GNR 3	7/1888	–	12/1914	3/1921	
4	GNR 4	11/1888	–	7/1912	5/1921	
5	GNR 5	6/1889	–	11/1911	1921	used as a stationary boiler until 1931
6	GNR 6	12/1889	–	12/1910	12/1920	
7	GNR 9	6/1891	–	–	12/1920	
8	GNR 10	6/1892	–	–	1/1921	
91	GNR 11	8/1893	13 (3/1920)	–	1/1921	
92	GNR 12	11/1893	14 (3/1920)	–	8/1921	
97	BP 2623	10/1885	–	9/1906	5/1921	named *Lisburn* (c 1895-8)
98	BP 2624	10/1885	98A (1/1905)	–	2/1910	not broken up until after 1921
99	BP 2625	10/1885	99A (1/1905), 96 (9/1906)	8/1906	5/1921	named *Windsor* (c 1906)

JT class 2-4-2T 5'7" 16"x 22" (Nos 13-14 17"x 22") Names removed c1912-3

No	Name	Works No	Delivered	Renumbered	16½" cyls	Reboilered	1958	Wdn	Remarks
13	*Tulip*	GNR 23	1/1902	91 (3/1920)	1924	7/1925	CIE	1963	
14	*Viola*	GNR 24	8/1902	92 (3/1920)	1930	–	–	1956	
90	*Aster*	GNR 19	1/1898	–	1918	12/1922	–	1957	
93	*Sutton*	GNR 16	8/1895	–	1921	12/1917	–	7/1955	preserved at Cultra
94	*Howth*	GNR 17	2/1896	–	1921	4/1919	–	1956	
95	*Crocus*	GNR 20	7/1898	–	1919	1/1923	–	1955	

T1 class 4-4-2T 5'9" 18"x 24"

No	Works No	Delivered	Superheated	1958	Wdn	No	Works No	Delivered	Superheated	1958	Wdn
185	BP 5737	12/1913	3/1924	UTA 185x	3/1960	188	BP 5740	12/1913	6/1927	CIE	10/1959
186	BP 5738	12/1913	1923	UTA 186x	3/1960	189	BP 5741	12/1913	11/1926	UTA 189x	3/1960
187	BP 5739	12/1913	4/1926	UTA 187x	4/1964						

T2 class 4-4-2T 5'9" 18"x 24"

No	Works No	Delivered	1958	Wdn	Cut up	No	Works No	Delivered	1958	Wdn	Cut up
1	BP 6035	8/1921	CIE	10/1959	11/1960	65	BP 6633	1/1930	CIE	11/1960	
2	BP 6036	8/1921	UTA 2x	3/1960		66	BP 6634	1/1930	UTA 66x	3/1960	
3	BP 6037	8/1921	CIE	1963		115	NW 1425	9/1924	CIE	10/1959	10/1960
4	BP 6038	8/1921	UTA 4x	3/1960		116	NW 1426	9/1924	CIE	10/1961	
5	BP 6039	8/1921	UTA 5x	3/1964		139	NW 1427	9/1924	CIE	10/1959	5/1960
21	NW 1423	8/1924	UTA	8/1959		142	NW 1435	9/1924	UTA 142x	3/1960	
30	NW 1424	8/1924	UTA 30x	12/1961		143	NW 1436	9/1924	CIE	1963	
62	BP 6630	12/1929	CIE	11/1960	6/1961	144	NW 1437	9/1924	CIE	10/1959	2/1961
63	BP 6631	12/1929	CIE	11/1959	10/1960	147	NW 1438	9/1924	CIE	11/1960	3/1961
64	BP 6632	1/1930	UTA 64x	3/1960		148	NW 1439	10/1924	UTA	8/1959	

QGT and QGT2 class 0-6-2T 4'7" 18½"x 26"

No	Works No	Delivered	Superheated	1958	Wdn	No	Works No	Delivered	Last used	Wdn
98	RS 3137	1/1905	9/1932	–	1957	168	RS 3454	11/1911	1946	9/1957
99	RS 3138	1/1905	12/1935	CIE	11/1960	169	RS 3455	11/1911	1953	9/1957

RT class 0-6-4T 4'3" 17"x 24"

No	Works No	Delivered	1958	Last used	Wdn	No	Works No	Delivered	1958	Last used	Wdn
22	BP 5093	9/1908	UTA		8/1959	166	BP 5531	11/1911	UTA 24		7/1963
23	BP 5094	8/1908	UTA 23	1961	7/1963	167	BP 5531	11/1911	UTA 25	1961	7/1963

Miscellaneous shunting tanks

No	Type	Origin	Built	Works No	DW	Cyls	Acquired	Remarks	Wdn
31	0-6-0T	–	3/1928	HL 3690	3'4"	14"x 20"	new	Crane tank, Dundalk Works shunter	1965
203	0-4-0ST	CK&AR	11/1904	HE 859	2'8½"	10¾"x 15"	6/1913	Formerly *Kells*, new firebox 1914	11/1930
204	0-6-0T	CK&AR	5/1889	HE 482	3'4"	15"x 20"	6/1913	Rebuilt 1904, formerly *Mullingar*	1930

Steam railmotors

No	Type	Built	Works No	DW	Cyls	Remarks	Wdn	Engine scrapped
1	0-4-0T	5/1905	NB 16607	3'7½"	12"x 16"	Altered to J^3 coach No 201	1913	1914
2	0-4-0T	5/1905	NB 16608	3'7½"	12"x 16"	Altered to J^3 coach No 202	1913	1914
3	0-4-0T	5/1905	NB 16609	3'7½"	12"x 16"	Altered to J^3 coach No 203	1913	1914
4	0-4-0T	6/1906	MW 1684	3'9"	12"x 16"	Altered to J^2 coach No 204	1913	1916
5	0-4-0T	6/1906	MW 1685	3'9"	12"x 16"	Altered to J^2 coach No 205	1913	1913
6	0-4-0T	7/1906	MW 1686	3'9"	12"x 16"	Altered to J^2 coach No 206	1913	1914
7	0-4-0T	7/1906	MW 1687	3'9"	12"x 16"	Altered to J^1 coach No 207	1913	1913

Abbreviations

BCR	Belfast Central Railway	HL	Hawthorn Leslie	NWR	Newry Warrenpoint and Rostrevor Railway
BH	Black Hawthorn	INW	Irish North Western Railway		
blr	boiler	KTH	Kitson Thompson & Hewitson	RS	Robert Stephenson
BP	Beyer Peacock	MW	Manning Wardle	SB	Sharp Brothers
Cyls	cylinders	N	Neilson	SS	Sharp Stewart
DBJ	Dublin & Belfast Junction Railway	N&A	Newry and Armagh Railway	UR	Ulster Railway
D&DR	Dublin & Drogheda Railway	NB	North British Locomotive Co	Vulc	Vulcan Foundry
DW	driving wheel	ND	Northern Division	Wdn	Withdrawn
Fbn	Fairbairn	NR	Neilson Reid		
HE	Hunslet Engine Co	NW	Nasmyth Wilson		

Appendix 2

Principal dimensions of steam locomotives

Class	Type	DW	Cyls	Boiler	Fbx	HS	BP	TE	Weight	Wheelbase	Remarks
A	0-6-0	4'7"	17"x 24"	4'2"x 10'0"	4'7"	1097.1	165	17,686	34t 6c	7'3"+ 7'3"	final condition
AL	0-6-0	4'7"	17"x 24"	4'6"x 10'2"	5'0"	1197	175	18,758	38t 11c	7'6"+ 7'6"	final condition
B	0-6-0	4'7"	17"x 24"	4'2"x 10'0"	4'7"	1097.1	160	17,073	33t 18c	7'3"+ 7'3"	final condition
BP	4-4-0T	5'0"	16"x 20"	4'2"x 9'9"	4'11"	1074.5	165	11,968	42t 6c	4'0"+ 7'3"+ 7'6"	final condition
BT	4-4-0T	4'7½"	15"x 18"	3'7"x 8'10¼"	3'10"	594.5	160	9924	31t 10c	5'3"+ 5'10½"+ 6'6"	as rebuilt
BT	0-6-0T	4'7"	15"x 18"	3'7"x 8'10¼"	3'10"	594.5	160	10,014	30t 6c	6'9½"+ 6'6"	after 1921
C	0-6-0	5'0"	17"x 24"	4'2"x 10'3"	4'11"	1126	175	17,196	34t 2c	7'2"+ 7'10"	final condition
C	0-6-0	4'7"	17"x 24"	3'11½"x 11'0"	4'4"	1070.5	140	15,007	33t 0c	7'2"+ 7'10"	Nos 142,143 had 4'2" blr
D	0-6-0	5'1¾"	17"x 24"	4'2"x 10'0"	5'5"	1110.3	175	16,708	36t 8c	7'3"+ 8'3"	final condition
E	0-6-0	5'0"	17"x 24"	4'2"x 10'5"	4'11"	1142.3	175	17,196	37t 0c	7'3"+ 7'9"	No 37 was 34T 16c
F	0-4-2	5'0"	17"x 24"	4'2"x 10'10"	4'7"	1178.8	160	25,385	35t 3c	7'9"+ 6'11"	Nos 109, 112
G	2-4-0	5'7"	16½"x 22"	4'2"x 9'9"	4'4"	1069.1	160	12,158	32t 10c	6'11"+ 7'1"	final condition
H	2-4-0	6'0½"	17"x 22"	4'2"x 10'3"	4'7"	1031.5	175	13,045	33t 10c	7'0"+ 8'0"	final condition
J	4-4-0	5'7"	17"x 22"	4'2"x 9'9"	4'4"	1069.1	165	13,309	35t 15c	5'3"+ 6'4½"+ 7'1"	final condition
JS	4-2-2	6'7"	16"x 22"	3'11⅝"x 9'11⅝"	4'4"	970	140	8,484	34t 0c	5'3"+ 6'8½"+ 7'0"	as built
JT	2-4-2T	5'7"	16½"x 22"	4'2"x 9'9"	4'4"	1068.8	175	13,298	46t 2c	7'0"+ 7'1"+ 6'5"	final condition
K	0-4-2	5'1"	16"x 22"	3'11½"x 10'3"	4'4"	1004.5	140	10.987	c30t 0c	7'2"+ 6'10"	final condition
P5'6"	4-4-0	5'7"	17"x 24"	4'1"x 10'3"	4'11"	1135	140	12,319	38t 15c	5'3"+ 6'10½"+ 8'0"	1892 version
P6'6"	4-4-0	6'7"	17"x 24"	4'1"x 10'3"	4'11"	1135	140	10,448	39t 6c	5'3"+ 6'10½"+ 8'0"	1892 version
PP	4-4-0	6'7"	18"x 24"	4'2"x 10'2"	5'5"	1128.5	160	13,387	41t 12c	5'3"+ 6'10½"+ 8'3"	1896 version
PG	0-6-0	4'7"	18½"x 24"	4'6"x 10'2"	5'5"	1262	175	22,215	39t 10c	7'6"+ 8'1"	as built
Q	4-4-0	6'7"	18½"x 26"	4'6"x 11'0"	5'10"	1357.4	175	16,755	46t 0c	5'9"+ 7'6½"+ 8'8"	
QG	0-6-0	4'7"	18½"x 26"	4'6"x 11'0"	5'10"	1357.4	175	24,066	41t 10c	7'10"+ 8'10"	
QL	4-4-0	6'7"	18½"x 26"	4'9"x 11'0"	6'5"	1531.2	175	16,755	49t 10c	5'9"+ 7'6½"+ 9'3"	
LQG	0-6-0	4'7¼"	18½"x 26"	4'9"x 11'0"	5'10"	1396.5	175	23,957	45t 3c	7'10"+ 8'10"	
NQG	0-6-0	4'7"	18"x 26"	4'6"x 11'0"	5'10"	1332	175	22,783	45t 16c	7'10"+ 8'10"	Nos 38, 39 160 lbs, 47T
NLQG	0-6-0	4'7"	18½"x 26"	4'9"x 11'0"	6'7"	1429.8	175	24,066	48t 6c	7'10"+ 8'10"	
QGT	0-6-2T	4'7"	18½"x 26"	4'6"x 10'2"	5'10"	1266	175	24,066	55t 6c	7'6"+ 8'6"+ 6'0"	
QGT2	0-6-2T	4'7¼"	18½"x 26"	4'6"x 10'2"	6'2"	1257	175	24,080	60t 0c	7'6"+ 8'10"+ 6'0"	
RT	0-6-4T	4'3"	17"x 24"	4'2"x 10'2"	5'0"	1086.5	175	20,230	56t 8c	7'0"+ 6'6"+ 5'0"+ 5'3"	
T	4-4-2T	5'9"	18"x 24"	4'3"x 10'2"	5'5"	1076	175	16,763	65t 2c	5'3"+ 6'10½"+ 8'3"+ 8'0"	
Crane	0-6-0T	3'4"	14"x 20"	3'4⅛"x 8'1"	4'5"	637	190	15,827	45t 0c	5'0"+ 5'0"	BP later 200 lbs

Superheated classes

Class	Type	DW	Cyls	Boiler	Fbx	HS	BP	TE	Weight	Wheelbase	
Ps 5'6"	4-4-0	5'7"	18"x 24"	4'6"x 10'2"	5'0"	1103	175	17,264	42t 2c	5'3"+ 6'10½"+ 8'0"	
Ps 6'6"	4-4-0	6'7"	18"x 24"	4'6"x 10'2"	5'0"	1103	175	14,641	44t 8c	5'3"+ 6'10½"+ 8'0"	
PPs 4'3"	4-4-0	6'7"	18"x 24"	4'3"x 10'2"	5'5"	1032	175	14,641	42t 12c	5'3"+ 6'10½"+ 8'3"	
PPs 4'6"	4-4-0	6'7"	18"x 24"	4'6"x 10'2"	5'5"	1111.2	175	14,641	45t 0c	5'3"+ 6'10½"+ 8'3"	
PGs	0-6-0	4'7"	17½"x 24"	4'6"x 10'2"	5'5"	1116	175	19,879	39t 14c	7'6"+ 8'1"	
Qs	4-4-0	6'7"	18½"x 26"	4'6"x 11'0"	5'10"	1285	175	16,755	49t 4c	5'9"+ 7'6½"+ 8'8"	HS later 1229 sq
QGs	0-6-0	4'7¼"	17¾"x 26"	4'6"x 11'0"	5'10"	1257	175	22054	42t 16c	7'10"+ 8'10"	HS later 1218.5
QLs	4-4-0	6'7"	18½"x 26"	4'9"x 11'0"	6'5"	1395	175	16,755	49t 19c	5'9"+ 7'6½"+ 9'3"	
LQGs	0-6-0	4'7¼"	19"x 26"	4'9"x 11'0"	5'10"	1431.8	175	25,270	48t 15c	7'10"+ 8'10"	HS later 1385.8
NQGs	0-6-0	4'7¼"	19"x 26"	4'6"x 11'0"	5'10"	1243.5	175	25,270	47t 12c	7'10"+ 8'10"	HS later 1207.5
LQGNs	0-6-0	4'7¼"	19"x 26"	4'9"x 11'0"	5'10"	1395.8	175	25,270	49t 10c	7'10"+ 8'10"	
QGTs	0-6-2T	4'7"	18½"x 26"	4'6"x 10'2"	5'10"	1121	200	27,520	55t 6c	7'6"+ 8'6"+ 6'0"	BP later 175 lbs
S/S2	4-4-0	6'7"	19"x 26"	4'6"x 11'0"	6'7"	1239.5	175	17,673	53t 6c	6'0"+ 7'6½"+ 9'6"	Final condition
SG/SG2	0-6-0	5'1"	19"x 26"	4'6"x 11'0"	6'7"	1354	175	22,887	48t 19c	8'1"+ 8'10"	
SG3	0-6-0	5'1"	19½"x 26"	5'0"x 11'0"	6'7"	1599.8	175	24,107	52t 10c	8'1"+ 8'10"	
T1	4-4-2T	5'9"	18"x 24"	4'3"x 10'2"	5'5"	1036	175	16,763	65t 4c	5'3"+ 6'10½"+ 8'3"+ 8'0"	
T2	4-4-2T	5'9"	18"x 24"	4'3"x 10'2"	5'5"	1056	175	16,763	65t 15c	5'3"+ 6'10½"+ 8'3"+ 8'0"	
U	4-4-0	5'9"	18"x 24"	4'3"x 10'2"	5'5"	1056	175	16,763	44t 6c	5'3"+ 6'10½"+ 8'3"	
UG	0-6-0	5'1"	18"x 24"	4'3"x 10'2"	5'5"	1022	175	18,962	45t 12c	7'3"+ 8'4½"	
V	4-4-0	6'7"	17¼"x 26"(1)								
			19"x 26"(2)	5'1¼"x10'10¾"	7'6"	1531	250	25,245	65t 1c	6'6"+ 7'7"+ 10'8"	
VS	4-4-0	6'7"	15¼"x 26"(3)	5'1¼"x10'10¾"	7'6"	1531	220	21,469	66t 6c	6'6"+ 7'7"+ 10'8"	

Appendix 3
Diesel railcars, railbuses and locomotives

Early diesel railcars

No	Built	1958	Wdn	Remarks	No	Built	1958	Wdn	Remarks
A	7/1932	UTA 101	5/1964		D	5/1936	UTA 103	9/1963	
B	1932	–	10/1946	Conv to coach No 500	E	6/1936	CIE	10/1961	Sold to UTA for spares
C1	11/1934	CIE	9/1961		F	3/1938	UTA 104	11/1965	Sold to a contractor
C2	6/1935	CIE	9/1961		G	4/1938	CIE	10/1961	Sold to UTA (105)
C3	6/1935	UTA 102	12/1961						Last used 1965, Scr 1968

Railbuses

No	Conv	Renumbered	1958	Wdn	Remarks	No	Conv	Renumbered	1958	Wdn	Remarks
D	9/1934	D1 (1936)	–	1939	Sold to SLNCR	F3	1944	2 (1947)	CIE	c1961	
E	10/1934	E2 (1936),				3	1935		–	1955	Orig DNGR No 1, bought 1947
		1 (1947)	UTA	1963	Civil Eng 8178, 1956	4	7/1935		CIE	c1961	Orig DNGR No 2, bought 1947
					Now preserved UFTM						
F	1/1935	F3 (1938)	–	4/1944	Accident damage						

AEC diesel railcars

No	Built	1958	Wdn	Remarks	No	Built	1958	Wdn	Remarks
600	6/1950	CIE	1975	Conv to push-pull use	610	11/1950	UTA 116	7/1973	Sold to CIE
601	6/1950	CIE	1975		611	11/1950	UTA 115	6/1973	
602	7/1950	UTA 112	6/1973		612	12/1950	CIE	1975	
603	7/1950	UTA 111	6/1973		613	12/1950	CIE	1975	
604	8/1950	CIE	1975		614	12/1950	UTA 118	6/1973	Destroyed by fire 9/1952
605	8/1950	CIE	1975						Replaced Autumn 1953
606	9/1950	UTA 113	6/1973	Sold to CIE	615	12/1950	UTA 117	6/1973	
607	9/1950	UTA 114	7/1973	Became parcel van 621	616	1/1951	CIE	1975	
608	10/1950	CIE	1975		617	1/1951	CIE	1975	
609	10/1950	CIE	1975		618	4/1951	UTA 120	6/1973	Became parcel van 622
					619	4/1951	UTA 119	6/1973	

BUT diesel railcars

No	Built	1958	Wdn	Remarks	No	Built	1958	Wdn	Remarks
701	6/1957	UTA 121	1975	Conv to hauled coach	713	3/1958	UTA 128	1975	
702	6/1957	UTA 122	1975	Conv to hauled coach	714	3/1958	CIE	1976	refurbished 1974
703	6/1957	UTA 123	1975	Conv to hauled coach	715	5/1958	UTA 129	6/1973	Destroyed by fire 5/1960
704	6/1957	CIE	1975						Rebuilt 1962
705	7/1957	UTA 124	1975	Conv to hauled coach	716	5/1958	CIE	1975	
706	7/1957	CIE	1975		901	7/1958	UTA 131	1975	
707	9/1957	UTA 125	1975	Conv to hauled coach	902	7/1958	UTA 132	1975	
708	9/1957	CIE	1975		903	8/1958	UTA 133	3/1972	bomb damage
709	10/1957	UTA 126	1975	Conv to hauled coach	904	7/1958	CIE	1975	
710	10/1957	CIE	1975		905	9/1958	UTA 134	1975	
711	1/1958	UTA 127	1975	Conv to hauled coach	906	9/1958	CIE	1975	
712	1/1958	CIE	1976	refurbished 1974	907	10/1958	UTA 135	1975	
					908	10/1958	CIE	1/1960	Fire damage, scr 5/1969

Diesel locomotives

No	Works No	Delivered	1958	Wdn	Remarks
800	800028	12/1954	CIE K801	1977	Sold to Galway Scrap Metal Co for use as a power plant. Still extant.
28	H&W	1957	UTA 28	1969	500 hp Harland & Wolff diesel, built 1937. Hired to GNRB to shunt at Belfast. 1A-A1, DW 3'7", 48¾ tons. Originally on BCDR Ardgass branch.

Bibliography

Books

C J Bowen Cooke, **British locomotives** (Whittaker 1894)

Anon, **The locomotive of today** (LPC 1904)

E L Ahrons, **The British steam railway locomotive Vol I 1825-1925** (LPC 1927)

R W Kidner, **The railcar 1847-1939**, (Oakwood Press 1939)

Kevin Murray, **The Great Northern Railway (Ireland), past, present & future** (GNR 1944)

E L Ahrons, **Locomotive & train working in the latter part of the nineteenth century, Vol 6** (Heffer 1954)

E M Patterson, **The Great Northern Railway of Ireland** (Oakwood press 1962)

L H Liddle, **Steam finale** (IRRS London Area 1964)

J W Lowe, **British steam locomotive builders** (TEE Publishing 1975)

R L Hills and D Patrick, **Beyer Peacock – Locomotive builders to the world** (TPC 1982)

O S Nock, **Irish steam** (David & Charles 1982)

O S Nock, **British steam locomotives of the 20th century** (PSL 1983)

C P Friel, **Merlin** (Colourpoint 1995)

C P Friel, **Slieve Gullion** (Colourpoint 1995)

J D FitzGerald, **The Derry Road** (Colourpoint 1995)

J D FitzGerald, **The Warrenpoint Branch** (Colourpoint 1996)

C P Friel & N Johnston, **Fermanagh's railways** (Colourpoint 1998)

Articles

R N Clements, *GNR Locomotive Development* (**Journal of the IRRS** No 24, 1959)

John Poole, *Dundalk and the GNR in 1906* (**Journal of the IRRS** No 24, 1959)

R N Clements, *The S class locomotives of GNR* (**Journal of the IRRS** No 34, 1964)

R N Clements, *QL and 321* (**Journal of the IRRS** No 38, 1965)

R N Clements, *Beyer engines in Ireland* (**Journal of the IRRS** No 42, 1967)

R N Clements, *The GNR Q class* (**Journal of the IRRS** No 46, 1968)

R N Clements, *Grendon locomotives* (**Journal of the IRRS** No 49, 1969)

D Murray, *The GNR V and VS* (**Journal of the IRRS** No 56, 1971)

R N Clements, *The GNR-GS&WR locomotive exchange of 1911* (**Journal of the IRRS** No 71, 1976)

L H Liddle, *The GNR – the last 20 years* (**Journal of the IRRS** No 71, 1976)

F Graham, *The Glover 4-4-2 tanks* (**Five Foot Three** No 4 1968)

F Graham, *The S class* (**Five Foot Three** No 5 1968)

F Graham, *The Banbridge line* (**Five Foot Three** No 5 1968)

F Graham & A Donaldson, *The P & PP classes of the GNR* (**Five Foot Three** No 7 1969)

C P Friel, *High summer on the Bundoran line* (**Five Foot Three** No 7 1969)

C Natzio, *Dundalk swansong* (**Five Foot Three** No 11 1971)

B McGirr, *A driver remembers* (**Five Foot Three** No 14 1973)

D Grimshaw, *The Belfast Central Railway* (**Five Foot Three** No 20, 1976)

P Mallon, *The Great Northern 4-6-0* (**Five Foot Three** No 25, 1981)

Dr R A Reid, *It all began at Pettigo Part 1* (**Five Foot Three** No 26, 1981)

Dr R A Reid, *It all began at Pettigo Part 2* (**Five Foot Three** No 27, 1982)

C P Friel, *Irish royal train – 1903* (**Five Foot Three** No 30, 1985)

I Pryce, *It's not so simple* (**Five Foot Three** No 31, 1985)

J A Cassells, *Steam finale: The Great Northern (Ireland)* (**Railway World** October 1985)

IRRS – Irish Railway Record Society

Five Foot Three – Society magazine of the Railway Preservation Society of Ireland

Index

*(Numbers in **heavy type** indicate photographs or drawings)*

Locomotive engineers and designers

Locomotive manufacturers

Preserved locomotives